State of Recovery

Bloomsbury Academic

An imprint of Bloomsbury Publishing Plc

50 Bedford Square	1385 Broadway
London	New York
WC1B 3DP	NY 10018
UK	USA

www.bloomsbury.com

Bloomsbury is a registered trade mark of Bloomsbury Publishing Plc

First published 2013
Paperback edition first published 2014

British Library Cataloguing-in-Publication Data
A catalogue record for this book is available from the British Library.

ISBN: HB:	978-1-4411-2364-0
PB:	978-1-6289-2325-4
ePDF:	978-1-4411-7788-9
ePub:	978-1-4411-0324-6

Library of Congress Cataloging-in-Publication Data
Zellen, Barry Scott, 1963–
State of recovery : the quest to restore American security after 9/11 / Barry Scott Zellen.
p. cm. Includes bibliographical references and index.
ISBN 978-1-4411-2364-0 (hardcover : alk. paper) 1. National security–United States.
2. National security–Technological innovations–United States.
3. Terrorism–United States–Psychological aspects. I. Title.
UA23.Z37 2013
355'.0330973–dc23
2012035409

Typeset by Newgen Imaging Systems Pvt Ltd, Chennai, India

State of Recovery

The Quest to Restore
American Security after 9/11

Barry Scott Zellen

B L O O M S B U R Y
LONDON · NEW DELHI · NEW YORK · SYDNEY

Contents

Foreword

Innovation Leads the Way:
From "Long War" to Longer Peace

When mass terror came to America's shores over a decade ago, it came at a widely unexpected time for America. The digital revolution was in full force, connecting America in new ways and at an unprecedented pace, with both wired and wireless networks proliferating across the American heartland, unlocking a tremendous surge in innovation, transformation, and creativity. It was thus no surprise then that technology would play a huge role in the coming struggle, and America's technological prowess and unmatched capacity for innovation would, as it had during the Cold War, provide us with what technology professionals call our "competitive edge" in the long and complicated war that followed.

It was thus with much anticipation that I first read Barry Scott Zellen's newest book *State of Recovery*, a chronicle of the often unsung but nonetheless vital role played by thousands of America's technology and policy professionals in the effort to restore American security after 9/11.

Zellen once again delivers right on the mark, providing us with a fascinating glimpse at what he rightly describes as *our* generation's equivalent of the "greatest" generation's Manhattan Project that would, through unprecedented (and to most, unfathomable) gains in scientific knowledge early in the twentieth century, usher America forth into the nuclear age. While less secretive than that infamous project, and perhaps more tactical in nature—it involved a host of technical and policy innovations as both government and private industry came together to address the threat of international terrorism—the massive recovery effort that restored both security and hope to a wounded America would involve millions of Americans, all united in their effort to reestablish homeland security, and protect America from future 9/11s. The story is a fascinating one, with a huge cast of characters large and small—and it is well told by Zellen.

Zellen is a prolific author whose works cover the Cold War, the post–Cold War period, and the post-9/11 era, and *State of Recovery* is his tenth book to date. He is also a theorist of world order and founder of a new school of international relations theory known as "constructive realism," which challenges the dominant theory during the Cold War period called "neorealism" or "structural realism" as developed by Kenneth Waltz. In contrast to Waltz's over-emphasis of systems and structures and the restraint they presumably automatically impose on international behavior, Zellen argues persuasively that the individual has been—and remains—the most essential "level of analysis" of them all, and is thus the key driver of international behavior, resulting in a more volatile, and passionate, unfolding of historical events. This is because of the undiminished (if not always acknowledged) role in world history of the *individual's* creativity and passion for change.

Zellen is also a journalist and editor specializing in strategy and national security, and he draws upon these skills here to tell this story in a manner that is refreshingly free of jargon and overly academic language; this ensures his newest work is accessible not just to theorists and experts but the layperson as well—a welcome departure for Zellen whose recent works have tended to be high theory. *State of Recovery* requires both the instincts and clarity of a journalist to capture the mood that followed 9/11 when hope suddenly gave way to fear—and to chronicle how technology emerged as one of the few bright lights that would not only restore hope across America but security as well. The critical role that technology has played in the long struggle against terrorism is a fascinating story to behold, one that continues to evolve under the present administration. Indeed, technology remains an important element of not only our struggle *against* terror, but in helping to foster democracy and civil society around the world as we build a new foundation for peace.

As the United States ambassador and permanent representative to the United Nations Education, Social and Cultural Organization (UNESCO), I work every day with some of the America's most creative and innovative minds, in fields as diverse as the arts, scientific research, and information technology, among others. From its inception, UNESCO has worked hand-in-hand with civil society to effect change and promote peace. UNESCO helps legitimize and strengthen global civil society by engaging scientists, teachers, architects, and engineers in UNESCO planning and its field work. Indeed, the US mission to UNESCO includes a National Committee made up of over 100 members of civil society, representing groups such the US Chamber of Commerce, the National Marine Sanctuary Foundation, the Institute for International Education, the Library of Congress, and NGOs to help guide us on critical issues. They are our panel of experts from some of the most influential institutions around the world, and serve as a resource and an essential "ear to the ground."

A key area where UNESCO has been active is science. "Science diplomacy" may sound odd to some, but it is a highly effective way to promote cooperation and technological advancements worldwide. Our nation's top scientists and engineers have a forum through UNESCO that helps them forge connections with colleagues around the world in support of projects to improve access to clean water for billions of people, monitor and predict changes in the world's oceans and waterways, and protect countries by developing better, faster tsunami warning and mitigation systems. The teamwork on this level never ceases to amaze me.

UNESCO is also directly involved in building scientific knowledge and fostering innovation capacity around the world, especially in developing countries. For example, UNESCO is currently assisting the Iraq government in drafting and implementing a science and technology policy, and has recently launched a program with Nature Publishing Group to create free, high-quality, online education resources in the life and physical sciences for secondary and university level students around the world. Or, consider one of UNESCO's newest public-private partnerships—with Apple's iTunes University. It is only fitting that UNESCO and Apple came together, as both institutions share a deep and abiding commitment to and belief in the values of both education and innovation, even if they approach it from different perspectives: UNESCO focuses on helping countries adopt the effective policies and practices to educate their populations, while Apple, as a private sector institution, works to advance teaching and learning through innovative improvements in technology. Especially in this day and age, as our world becomes ever more globalized and interconnected, we think there is great value in bringing together and sharing the expertise of both the public and private sectors to foster innovation and learning, and making education more accessible by adapting it to the changing world. This particular partnership does just that, making the research and learning that UNESCO has helped develop accessible to a much wider audience. At the same time, it will help Apple continue to develop and expand its amazing tool—iTunes University—by linking it to UNESCO, a respected United Nations agency recognized around the world for its work in education, science, culture, and communication.

UNESCO is perhaps the most visible, nonpartisan forum and partner for us to reinforce our commitment not only to multilateral diplomacy but also other very tangible, salient issues such as scientific research and development, and freedom of inquiry and expression—cornerstones of innovation. I'm very proud of the role the United States plays in helping make that happen, and delighted by the dynamic work taking place at UNESCO intersecting technology and education.

As the long war against terror continues to transform into an even *longer* peace, technology will continue to play an important role, as will scientific diplomacy. That is why I believe it's so vitally important that the United States remain committed to UNESCO—an organization founded on the very principles that Americans hold dear—defending and promoting human rights. Our leadership in a body of over 190 members means we are able to leverage a modest budget of $70 million a year—or 22 percent of UNESCO's operating budget—to help further these goals. Member-states often turn to UNESCO, and to us, for help formulating key building blocks of peaceful societies, such as education, culture, open media, and science. It's thus in the national interest to see that UNESCO develops and promotes guidelines and policies based on shared democratic ideals, as these become points of reference for societies around the world.

Don't just take my word for it; listen to the voice of the private sector: the amazing story that is unfolding includes the many companies knocking at UNESCO's door to team up on projects in education, science, and technology. Companies like Apple, Nokia, Cisco, Intel, Procter and Gamble, and Microsoft, just to name a few, see the value of working with UNESCO as part of their global engagement strategy and already have projects underway. An important part of my role at UNESCO is to help make these private-public sector partnership connections and support them—which brings new energy and ideas to education, science, and culture. The many American researchers and students we are helping to connect with their peers around the world are planting many seeds for better, more collaborative research, development, and understanding that will in turn take root, and help to build a better world for all of us.

The world is changing, and so is diplomacy. All of us—governments, NGOs, private sector companies, teachers, researchers, technologists, scientists, and journalists—must continue to work together and listen to each other more than ever to get the job done. This is twenty-first-century diplomacy in action—and I am both privileged and proud to be a part of it.

And so it is with this spirit of hope in the continuing role technology will play in the coming years, as the *long war* continues to evolve into a *longer peace*, that I am so very pleased to introduce this new and important work by Barry Scott Zellen on how technology helped not only restore security to the American homeland—but to also restore hope in the hearts of Americans and thereby reinvigorate the American spirit, part of a process that continues today and will continue as we journey forth into the future, as we look to science and technology and innovation as not only important tools for a time of war but also essential seeds from which a lasting peace can grow.

Ambassador David T. Killion
US Permanent Representative to UNESCO
Paris, France

Abbreviations

ABL	airborne laser
APHIS	Animal and Plant Health Inspection Service
AQAP	Al Qaeda in the Arabian Peninsula
AQI	Al Qaeda in Iraq
ATA	American Trucking Association
AWS	Arrow Weapon System
BATF	Bureau of Alcohol, Tobacco, and Firearms
BCBP	Bureau of Customs and Border Protection
BDS	Biological Detection System
BICE	Bureau of Immigration and Customs Enforcement
BMDS	Ballistic Missile Defense System
CBP	Customs and Border Protection
CBW	chemical-biological warfare
CDC	Center for Disease Control
CDSS	cockpit door surveillance system
CMRL	Counter-Multiple Rocket Launch
CSI	Container Security Initiative
DARPA	Defense Advanced Research Projects Agency
DEW Line	Distant Early Warning Line
DHHS	Department of Health and Human Services
DHS	Department of Homeland Security
DMZ	Demilitarized Zone
DPRK	Democratic People's Republic of Korea
EPA	Environmental Protection Agency
EUROPOL	European Police Office
EWORS	Early Warning Outbreak Recognition System
FAA	Federal Aviation Administration
FBI	Federal Bureau of Investigation
FDA	Food and Drug Administration
FEMA	Federal Emergency Management Agency
GOARN	Global Outbreak Alert and Response Network
GWOT	Global War on Terror
HSAS	Homeland Security Advisory System
ICAO	International Civil Aviation Organization
IDF	Israeli Defense Force
IED	improvised explosive device
INS	Immigration and Naturalization Service

IOC	International Olympic Committee
JNLWD	Joint Non-Lethal Weapons Directorate
LRAD	Long Range Acoustic Device
MAD	Mutual Assured Destruction
MARAD	Maritime Administration
MDA	Missile Defense Agency
MUAV	Maritime Unmanned Aerial Vehicle
NBIS	National Biosurveillance Integration System
NEDSS	National Electronic Disease Surveillance System
NLW	Non-Lethal Weapon
NSA	National Security Agency
NSC	National Security Council
NTAS	National Terrorism Advisory System
OAS	Organization of American States
OEF	Operation Enduring Freedom
OIF	Operation Iraqi Freedom
PIN	personal identification number
PKI	public-key infrastructure
PSI	Proliferation Security Initiative
QATT	Qualified Anti-Terrorism Technology
QDR	Quadrennial Review
QRF	Quick Reaction Force
RFID	Radio-frequency Identification
RTR	Real Time Radiography
RTV	Rapid Terrain Visualization
SAR	Synthetic Aperture Radar
SARS	Severe Acute Respiratory Syndrome
SBI	Secure Border Initiative
SBR	Space Based Radar
SOF	Special Operations Forces
SOX	Sarbanes-Oxley
TATP	Triacetone Triperoxide
THAAD	Terminal High Altitude Area Defense
TIA	Total Information Awareness
TSA	Transportation Security Administration
UAV	Unmanned Aerial Vehicle
USPIS	US Postal Inspection Service
VBIED	vehicle-borne improvised explosive device
VLAD	vehicle lightweight arresting device
WHO	World Health Organization
WHTI	Western Hemisphere Travel Initiative
WMD	Weapons of Mass Destruction
WTC	World Trade Center

Introduction

State of Recovery presents an examination of the race, in the days, weeks, months, and years that followed the mass-terror attacks on American soil on September 11, 2001, to restore a sense of security across the vast American heartland, so long perceived to be immune from the scale of violence and chaos witnessed in the many hotspots of world conflict during and after the Cold War era. New, and pervasive, feelings of insecurity gripped the land after the Twin Towers fell, and the seemingly impenetrable walls of the fortress-like Pentagon lay smoldering after being breached. New, transformative homeland security policies would be quickly announced, and generously funded, to restore the shattered calm—and new technologies would be rapidly advanced from the drawing boards to production in order to enable the new security mindset to be achieved. New mobile and digital technologies played a central and unprecedented role in the way the events of 9/11 were observed, recorded, and understood, presenting a preview of the underlying technological landscape of the coming Global War on Terror (GWOT); they would soon play an important role in the race to secure America after 9/11, as a veritable Manhattan project of innovation and product development was unleashed to restore America's security.

I was among several thousand technology writers, analysts, and industry professionals from all over the world who were in San Diego for the Cellular Telephone and Internet Association's (CTIA) Wireless IT 2001 convention on the morning of September 11, 2001, ready to spend the week immersed in the latest innovations on mobile telecom, wireless data, and the continuing miniaturization and acceleration of microprocessing capabilities at the root of the wireless revolution transforming American business, culture, and society. But then those unspeakably—and until September 11, unimaginably—cruel acts of terror struck New York and Washington, DC, thousands of miles away.

As things turned out, this was the only conference in America not canceled as a result of the carnage and our communal heartbreak, leaving us stranded, miles from home, to make sense of the day's horror. We watched in real time as history was violently reawakened from its decade-long slumber since the Berlin Wall had fallen twelve years earlier, when events of equal suddenness transformed our awareness of how much the world had changed, and how beneath the surface and behind those boundaries etched on maps lay an evolving, transforming, dynamic reality. History had not ended; we had only allowed ourselves to surrender to the illusion that it had concluded, and a new era of perpetual peace was upon us. Or was it? For the many Balkanizing fringes of the old Communist world, the new era was anything but peaceful. But compared to the apocalyptic terror that was only a push of the button away during the generation that grew up during the Cold War, these conflicts were modest, and though savage in their ferocity they seemed limited in their geographic breadth.

But when the events of 9/11 took place, many of us realized in a split second that the long, simmering feud between East and West had been replaced by a new festering wound in the international body politic, between North and South, and between secular modernity and theocratic neomedievalism. It was a lot to process, as we watched in real time as the Twin Towers collapsed upon themselves—a metaphor for our new age. In the cavernous San Diego Convention Center, with large-screen TVs wheeled out to display for us the events that were unfolding, surreally, across the country, we turned to our colleagues for support, to talk, to cry, to share our feelings about those terrible events of that day, and how this era of innovation could be brought to a sudden end by such neomedieval barbarity. The CTIA organizers, recognizing that thousands of people were now in San Diego and unable to return to their homes and families, made the decision not to cancel its conference.

At first, some attendees were surprised, others angry at what seemed an insensitive decision—how could there be "business as usual" on such a day as this? But as the week continued, we all realized that having our community of friends, peers, and colleagues together made it somehow easier to make sense of September 11th's seeming senselessness, especially since our community was a community of innovators, and all the gadgets and gizmos on display for the pre-9/11 conference planned in peacetime would surely play an important role in the coming showdown between past and future, between modernity and neomedievalism. And so with America's airspace closed until further notice, many of us had no other place to go. One group chartered a bus for the long road journey back to the Pacific Northwest, and others boarded Amtrak trains and rented cars for their long, slow journeys home—but hundreds of us stayed put, until the crisis had passed, the airports had reopened, and some sense of normalcy had returned.

All week long, the San Diego Convention Center, stretching many blocks in length, felt so empty, though many exhibitors were there—more often providing a listening ear and hug than a product demonstration. Some trade show booths were fully stocked with brochures, sample products, and the usual conference give-aways, but many company reps remained stranded far away, unable to man their booths, leaving the conference floor feeling much like a ghost town, a reminder of what might have been. It was a very different kind of convention, for a very different kind of week, one when our nation journeyed from peace to war. Instead of wanting to talk about technology for technology's sake, we wanted to talk about our feelings, our fears and anger, our sympathy for the thousands of families who experienced tragic losses, and the role technology could play in the coming struggle. How could our technological edge serve our nation as we headed to war? How might it bring justice to Osama bin Laden and his henchmen who had plotted to attack our homeland, to bring down our proudest symbols of commerce and freedom?

The president and CEO of CTIA, Tom Wheeler, began the conference with a moment of silence to remember the victims—and a pledge that we would not, as an industry and as a country, be defeated by the forces of darkness and terror. With our thoughts on the victims in New York and Washington, we stumbled through the convention; as the week unfolded, we learned how the technology that had brought us all together—wireless telephony and mobile computing—had provided our nation, and world, with a unique and intimate perspective on the tragic events of September 11. It transported us right onboard those doomed flights, where we were privy to the farewell messages to loved ones by those brave passengers, whose very calmness, remarkable lack of panic, and heroism in the face of imminent death helped us to heal—and whose eloquent farewell messages helped bring us and their loved ones a sense of closure and left us with a new catchphrase for the coming battles: "Let's roll."

Because of the ubiquity of wireless technology, particularly cellular mobile and air phones, we were provided with this unique and intimate perspective on that day's tragic events. On United Airlines Flight 93, wireless technology helped to inspire heroic action, bringing news to those passengers of the World Trade Center attacks, and informing them of the peril that they faced—motivating them to action and quite possibly saving the White House, or Capitol Building, from destruction. Were it not for their decisive and bold action to retake their aircraft—and to ensure it did not complete its cruel mission—America may well have lost one more symbol of its freedom, and many thousands more innocent civilians may have died.

During the ongoing search and rescue efforts, cell phone records helped to identify who was in the vicinity of the World Trade Center, identifying some of those whose voices were suddenly silenced, and others who, by a quirk of fortune, were not. Stories emanated from the rubble of survivors calling loved ones who were as far away as Israel; and those, less fortunate, who called to say goodbye, trapped above the fiery remains of those crashed planes, unable to descend to safety. A startled President Bush was reported to have asked the traveling press corps aboard Air Force One to turn off their cell phones, afraid that the terrorists would turn our wireless networks against us as they had our aircraft—cutting off what he feared could be a beacon, leading terror directly to the airborne presidential jet.

Networks and the plethora of digital devices that connect to them thus provided us with much more than a window to that day's infamous events. It provided such a close and intimate connection that it enabled us to become very much more than observers, helping us to shape the outcome of events and lessen their ferocity. It enabled so many deeply moving messages of farewell and love, and helped surviving loved ones with closure and to find meaning instead of meaninglessness in this tragedy. That events were influenced by the knowledge of the other attacks, delivered by cellular and satellite phones to airborne passengers—allowing them to transform in a moment of boldness from victims to heroes, from hostages to freedom fighters—suggests something more powerful: an ability to thwart, and even defeat, terrorists, thanks to the ubiquitous nature of this new technology.

It is truly amazing and intriguing how a technology like this has changed our world so quickly, making the world a truly "flatter" place as Thomas Friedman has so eloquently described it. We now can observe and hear things that we never could before, and the potential of these global networks to help restore order to this new, asymmetrical, and dangerous world is only now being discovered. Ever mobile, we can remain in touch with those we love—even, it seems, from the heavens above. Solitude, I believe, has become a thing of the past, and as a result, we are more closely connected than ever before, but with the loss of our solitary condition, we have not sacrificed solace. We now inhabit a world of both talkers and listeners, engaged in a dialogue that knows no limits—in this cacophony, we have the disembodied voices of both good evil. As in the primeval state of nature itself, there remains much debate and a good deal of enduring ambiguity on whether the new world of networks is a world of continuous netwar of man against man—fought not only on the ground, or out at sea, or in the skies above, but also in this new cyber realm where network effects are only just now being understood, where swarms can instantly form to strike and just as instantly go their separate ways—or one of netpeace, where our ideals and values can not only take root but fertilize once hostile lands, making the world yet flatter and more integrated, as fewer and fewer members of the world community inhabit the far-flung "gap" and more and more join the "leviathan," as argued by Thomas Barnett, and imagined by his mentor, the late vice admiral Arthur Cebrowski, who believed in his heart that the new networked world would favor American values, and could be harnessed to help enhance American security through ingenuity, innovation, and military transformation.

True, there is still evil in the world, and in spite of technological change, fanatical and violent people can still cause harm to countless thousands, even on occasion leveraging our own technology against us as demonstrated on 9/11. But technology itself, while no silver bullet for the risks and dangers that we face, has made the world smaller, allowing us to grieve together and heal together—and during that week's most poignant moments, bid our heroes and our loved ones farewell. Now, from the morning of 9/12 and henceforth, we can also fight together, united not only in spirit, and in cause, but by the very networks and technologies that brought the terror of 9/11 into our homes and hearts. In the years that followed, as we recovered from the shock and awe delivered unto us on 9/11 and restored the security of our homeland, we went forth on the offensive in a war against the very roots of terror, at home and abroad—a war in which the very same technology that gave us such an unique and open window into the unfolding of history in real time on 9/11 would provide us with a new set of tools with which to wage and, ultimately, win the continuing struggle.

Looking back upon the decade that followed the 9/11 attacks, *State of Recovery* examines the numerous efforts by technologists and homeland security policy makers dedicated to restoring security and ameliorating the insecurity felt after the attacks more than a decade ago. Since 9/11, the world's most technologically advanced countries have been waging a long war of attrition against a global, Islamist non-state movement straight out of the mediaeval era that lacked its own strategic-military industrial capacity, but which has demonstrated an ingenious capacity to adapt the innovations of its opponent to its own advantage. While the GWOT was at one level an asymmetrical clash between modernism and primitivism, it was also the first global *netwar* and the first truly global struggle of the digital era—with both sides actively engaged in conflict in the digital and cyber domains. In the chapters ahead, I will examine the many new technologies that were harnessed in this struggle, as America's innovators took part in what we can think of as this generation's "Manhattan Project," a nationwide—indeed, a worldwide—effort by the most advanced industrialized nations to erect a great, new firewall of sorts, applying their knowledge of new, and expanding, communications networks, and the proliferation of miniaturizing and increasingly mobile microprocessors, to what we long called the Global War on Terror, or in some circles the Long War. This volume discusses these efforts.

Part I of this book, "Technology, to the Rescue," examines the vital role played by new technologies to help secure America after 9/11, and how the rapid pace of innovation in information technology has created a rich tool kit for America to apply to the many challenges of the post-9/11 era. The rise in technology spending, and efforts to leverage new technologies like biometric sensors and new tools for information security, early in the GWOT, are discussed.

Part II, "Securing Our Borders," examines efforts to strengthen American border security, lessons learned from the pressing border security challenges faced by allied nations such as Israel and Singapore, and from America's own wartime experiences along insecure frontiers adjacent to hostile nations such as the Korean and Vietnamese DMZs. A wide range of border security technology and policy solutions is discussed, for both America's land and sea borders—from new fencing systems to aerial surveillance solutions to methods to secure pipelines. Part III, "Protecting the Populace," recounts how, after 9/11, imaginations ran wild with new and dangerous scenarios of the risks of mass terror, including nuclear terrorism, bioterrorism, and other methods of mass-terror attack. As well, the increasing frequency and lethality of conventional truck and car bombs or vehicle-borne improvised explosive devices (IEDs) are examined, as are the vulnerabilities of numerous venues such as sports stadiums, public transit systems, courthouses, Olympic Games, and the long porous land and sea borders of the US homeland.

Part IV, "Ensuring Our Survival: Thinking about the Unthinkable after 9/11," looks to America's efforts to bring the fight to the enemy and ensure that future engagements with the opponent take place far from America's shores, including the articulation early in the war on terror of a new doctrine to prevent and preempt the acquisition of weapons of mass destruction (WMD) by America's opponents. The "Axis of Evil" construct that united the three primary "rogue" states America felt to be the most menacing is examined, finding the axis to be an inadequate construct primarily because its members were largely disconnected from one another, both diplomatically and strategically (and in the case of Iran and Iraq, were actual blood enemies). Attacking Iraq therefore did not weaken the axis, but in fact motivated its two remaining "members" to redouble their efforts to develop a nuclear weapons as well as an intercontinental ballistic missile capability. Amidst this menacing strategic landscape, America's continuing effort to erect a ballistic missile shield, and thus fulfill the cherished dream of President Ronald Reagan to innovate a solution that would protect America's homeland from strategic nuclear attack, is considered.

Just as President George H.W. Bush once described the "thousand points of lights" dotting the vast American heartland, echoing what President Reagan described as a beacon of light and of hope to the world, thousands of America's best and brightest minds, scattered across a vast and in so many ways ingenious nation, would hit the books as the sun rose anew on September 12, 2001—imagining new and innovative solutions to help America recover its lost sense of security, and to eventually achieve victory in what has now become its longest and in many ways most challenging war.

Part I

Technology to the Rescue

1

Moore's Law and the Evolution of Security Technology

The contrast couldn't be more extreme. First, there were the go-go days of the late 1990s technology boom—when America fell in love with digital technology, and investors fell in love with digital technology companies—and the entire nation appeared excited about the seemingly limitless potential that digital innovation promised to bring. Then, in a fiery instant, came the wakeup call of 9/11—when a pan-Islamist movement aiming to restore a mediaeval theocracy upon Southwest Asia struck at America's heartland, downing the Twin Towers, a symbol of America's economic leadership, while delivering a solid, but not a knockout blow, against the sprawling Pentagon complex, headquarters of the US Department of Defense (DoD).

The ensuing David and Goliath struggle pitted the most advanced, technological society on earth, and also one of the most open—America—against one of the least technologically developed nations on earth, governed by a theocratic tyranny—Afghanistan, which was hosting Al Qaeda. So it's no surprise that America, in its GWOT, turned to its newest technological know-how to bolster its border security—and help to prevent the next 9/11 from happening. As a result, one byproduct of the 9/11 attacks was an unprecedented surge in government investment in new technologies for homeland security, and a massive intra-governmental reorganization giving birth to the Department of Homeland Security (DHS) on January 24, 2003—described by DHS as "the largest federal reorganization in more than 50 years."[1]

Technology and security after 9/11

As reported by Charles J. Murray in the *EE Times* in January 2005, "as the United States struggled to adjust to its dark new reality following the terror attacks of September 2001, one of the first phenomena to rise from the rubble was a booming security-technology market that today remains in runaway expansion mode."[2] Indeed, he wrote that "development activity in a raft of security technologies—from biometric sensors and scanning software to electromagnetic systems for detecting virtually any kind of concealed weapon—took off so quickly in the wake of the attacks that even the most determined industry watchers underestimated the sector's growth."[3] With the

2003 creation of the DHS came a new and unprecedented concentration of funding for securing America in a single administrative entity, creating the expectation among IT vendors—eager to kick-start their ailing stock prices and revitalize investor sentiment in the wake of the great "Tech Wreck" when the internet bubble collapsed—of an unprecedented federally funded feeding frenzy.

But not everyone was happy with the early days, when DHS' bark was stronger than its bite. As reported in the first edition of Homeland Security Tech Watch on October 1, 2003: "President Bush signed the first regular Appropriations Act for the Department of Homeland Security (DHS) granting budget authority in 2004 for $29.4 billion—a 1.8% increase ($535.8 million) over the fiscal year 2003 budget."[4] And only "days later, frustrated IT executives—anxious to finally size the addressable homeland security market for their particular products and services—heard the same recitation of high-level budget numbers from top DHS officials."[5] Homeland Security Tech Watch noted that "across town on Capitol Hill, a poorly attended congressional hearing on the DHS Enterprise Architecture (the IT Roadmap) gave clues as to why: the Appropriations Act contains very little detail on technology spending because DHS' Enterprise Architecture to guide investment decisions had not yet been drawn up when the bills were written."[6]

Hence early frustrations were the result of the newness of the endeavor and the complexity of the challenge. As Homeland Security Tech Watch explained, while "it seems like an eternity for waiting vendors, it was only a few short months ago that the most complex government reorganization in US history began—merging 22 agencies into one. Merger integration doesn't happen overnight."[7] In so short a time, it adds, "pay scales still haven't been set nor procurement policies issued, much less business processes re-engineered or decisions made about needed technologies."[8] But at the same time, "there were signs of progress in the testimony on the DHS Enterprise Architecture," and "a plan now exists, though still somewhat conceptual, to begin the transition from the current state to the target," and while tech vendors were cautioned not to "expect the floodgate on spending to open wide," they were encouraged to "look for the trickle to gradually become a steady stream."[9]

And while "early estimates indicate that Congress appropriated roughly $3 billion for technology—10% of the total DHS budget," this was "down from the President's original request of $3.8 billion."[10] Homeland Security Tech Watch noted that "appropriations for technology did not increase over last year's budget which was approximately $3 billion, as well," and that Congress actually "decreased funding from the President's request for many of the major technology projects that have the most immediate impact on fighting terrorism—such as the US Visitor and Immigrant Status Indicator Technology (US VISIT) and security screening equipment," and "most technology project funding was down roughly 25% to 30% from the President's request"—as Congress began "exercising increased oversight and greater scrutiny on major technology projects," driven by its perception of a slow start for several major projects that "appeared to get off to a slow start because they were held up by the DHS reorganization and initial efforts at building an Enterprise Architecture."[11]

But it did not take long for DHS spending on technology to ramp up. DHS announced, on February 3, 2003, that its FY2004 budget would fund efforts to prevent "terrorist attacks within the United States" while "reducing America's vulnerability to terrorism," and "minimizing the damage and recovering from attacks that do occur."[12] As such, DHS was empowered to "move forward with a sustained and cohesive strategy in key areas such as improving security at the nation's borders"; "decreasing the vulnerabilities of the nation's critical infrastructure"; and "advancing research in science and technology aimed at countering terrorist attacks."[13] And, as reported by *Government Security* magazine in July 2003, DHS "moved to implement an act" that was drafted by Congress in 2002, "granting many companies protection from lawsuits if they invest in developing and deploying qualified anti-terrorism techniques."

The "Support Anti-Terrorism by Fostering Effective Technologies Act of 2002," better known as the SAFETY Act, was designed to "motivate further investment in anti-terrorism technologies" by empowering DHS to "determine if a company's anti-terrorism technology is considered qualified."[14] Under the new law, the undersecretary for Science and Technology was made "responsible for review and approval of applications for Designation and Certification of Qualified Anti-Terrorism Technologies (QATTs) under the SAFETY Act," as part of Washington's effort to "encourage the development and deployment of anti-terrorism technologies that will substantially enhance the protection of the nation," and to "ensure that the threat of liability does not deter potential sellers from developing and commercializing technologies that could significantly reduce the risk of, or mitigate the effect of, acts of terrorism."[15]

For its second full year of operations, the FY2004 budget request for DHS totaled $36.2 billion—reflecting a 7.4% increase in funding over FY2003, and a 64% increase over FY2002." In the FY2004 budget, $803 was requested "for the Department to use American ingenuity and develop new partnerships with the private sector to research, develop and deploy homeland security technologies that will make America safer—an eight-fold increase over 2002."[16] Additionally, the Science and Technology Directorate's Advanced Research Project Agency was tasked to "direct $350 million in new funding to address gaps in high-priority operational areas like protecting critical infrastructure and our borders."[17] And, $18.1 billion was requested "for the Border and Transportation Security Directorate to meet the strategic goals of improving border security and transportation security—while at the same time facilitating the unimpeded and reliable flow of commerce and people across our borders and through our airports, seaports, highways and railways."[18] An additional $100 million was requested for the comprehensive Entry-Exit system, designed to "enable the Department to track the entry and exit of visitors to the United States,"[19] bringing the total to $480 million.

A year later, the FY2005 budget requested "total new resources for FY2005 of $40.2 billion" for "an increase of 10% above the comparable FY2004 resource level," which "substantially increases funding for DHS from 2003—the year that the Department was created—and continues the dramatic growth for agencies that are now a part of DHS."[20] The FY2005 budget request included "$411 million in new funding to maintain and enhance border security activities," and "$340 million in 2005—an increase of $12 million over the FY2004 funding—to continue expansion of the US VISIT system."[21] As well, the FY2005 budget request included $50 million "for the next generation of screening devices for our nation's ports of entry," plus "$64.2 million to enhance land-based detection and monitoring of movement between the ports," $28 million to "increase the flight hours of P-3 aircraft and $12.5 million for long range radar operations."[22]

Technology spending on the rise

By 2005, DHS spending on technology had finally achieved the scale frothily anticipated by IT executives during those frustrating, early post-9/11 days when DHS was just ramping up. In the June 2004 edition of the National Defense Magazine, Harold Kennedy wrote that an "array of emerging technologies is the key to defending the United States from its enemies," and "developing those technologies is the mission of the S&T division," short for Science and Technology, of DHS.[23] According to Kennedy, Charles E. McQueary, the undersecretary of homeland security for science and technology, led the S&T division of DHS since its inception in 2003, and as its budget grew "by $126.5 million—nearly 14 percent—to a requested $1.03 billion in 2005," it allowed S&T to accomplish "a great deal in a short amount of time," though McQueary noted "much more remains to be done."[24]

Indeed, as reported by Dibya Sarkar on *Federal Computer Week*'s website, FCW.com, President Bush's proposed FY2006 budget for DHS "underlines a heavy reliance on information technology for better border and port security uses" and "improved screening and credentialing of individuals."[25] The FY2006 budget proposed for DHS totaled $41.1 billion, up 6.6% from FY2005, and its "IT portion would rise nearly 25%—to $5.96 billion from $4.78 billion in fiscal 2005."[26] Sarkar cited DHS acting Secretary Admiral James Loy, who said that "technology holds enormous potential to meet many of our most pressing security needs and we must bring these resources to bear in our fight against terrorism."[27] That's why the FY budget called for the Office of the Chief Information Officer to "get a $28.43 million increase, from the current $275.27 million to $303.7 million—which includes ongoing maintenance and operations and department-wide technology projects."[28] In the coming year, DHS planned to "consolidate various screening and identification activities to form the Office of Screening Coordination and Operations (SCO) within the Border and Transportation Security Directorate," using over $840 million "to consolidate and integrate these."[29] As well, the S&T Directorate planned to "consolidate its research and development activities under one authority to better leverage funding" with a proposed R&D budget of $127.5 million.[30] The US-VISIT program would get a $50 million increase, taking it to $390 million, and an additional $174 million "to complete the installation of the High Speed Operational Connectivity to passenger and baggage screening checkpoints to improve management of screening system performance."[31]

While the budget for new technology kept pace with expectations, channeling resources into innovative new programs and technology solutions, it remained to be seen whether money itself could solve the problem facing America as it struggled to secure its borders. A closer look at biometrics technology illustrates some of the hopes and challenges inherent in America's use of technology to win the war on terror.

Biometrics to the rescue?

Back in 2001, Murray recalled, that the Washington, DC–based International Biometrics Industry Association predicted that sales of biometric hardware and software would hit $2 billion annually within ten years, while the Boulder, CO–based Acuity Market Intelligence has predicted that "the biometrics core-technology market would hit $4.6 billion by 2012, up from $644 million this year," and that the "end-customer identification system solutions"—many using biometrics—"would reach a staggering $27 billion in the same time frame."[32]

As reported by Susan M. Menke on the *Government Computer News* website, GCN.com, in November 2001, the use of biometrics "is expanding so fast within the Homeland Security Department" that Assistant Secretary Stewart Verdery Jr., who oversaw the DHS' Border and Transportation Security Directorate, said the department now had over 60 "stovepiped or loosely coordinated biometric projects". He believed the department must next "develop a vision for collecting, analyzing, storing and exchanging the data under common standards, unified processes and a single identity."[33] Verdery noted DHS had "five biometric pilots under way or about to begin for the Transportation Security Administration's Registered Traveler program, the Transportation Worker ID Credential and other efforts," and "when the five pilots are done," DHS planned to "make them interoperable as a real system of systems."[34] Menke wrote that "various airports are testing fingerprint authentication of travelers, others use iris scans and some are switching," such as Reagan Washington National Airport, which was switching "from prints to iris scans."[35] Verdery added that DHS was "extremely proud of deploying biometrics without affecting travel in a negative way" and to date "10 million foreign visitors have been checked at 129 ports of entry, with 1,200 hits against terrorist and criminal watch lists."[36] He believed the department's efforts "greatly reduced the number of travelers selected for extra screening."[37]

The vision thing

But unfortunately, as *EE Times'* Murray observed, some industry experts believed "all that activity hasn't yet translated into an effective vision for enhancing public safety."[38] Indeed, to some critics, the technology—while promising—had not yet matured to the point where it could be practically deployed as part of America's border security system. That's why, Murray observed, a "multitude of applications that had been considered fertile ground for authentication systems have yet to embrace them."[39] Indeed, while "some frequent-flyer programs use biometric authentication," Murray observed that such systems "are not yet applied to air travelers at large." Additionally, "the notion of a national IC card system, widely discussed shortly after 9/11, hasn't made much headway."[40]

However, for more limited access security deployments, biometrics were finding a place. Hence, Murray observed, "a plethora of sensors are finding use at airports in employee identification cards that allow access to such safety-critical areas as tarmacs and baggage handling."[41] Yet while believers in biometrics think this emerging technology "helps plug the security holes left by simple photo IDs, particularly when such photos aren't updated on a regular basis," Murray cautioned that some experts "warn that such cards are not a panacea"—as even the nefarious 9/11 hijackers "carried legitimate identification and driver's licenses."[42]

The magic of Moore's Law

With funding for new security technologies on the rise, half the battle is solved. But the other half of the battle is achieving the necessary capability for biometrics to enhance border security without slowing, or stopping, the flow of people across our borders. As with all silicon-based technologies, where the underlying computing power determines what's ultimately possible, biometrics will benefit from the inexorable advance in computing power promised by Moore's Law. According to Murray, "Moore's Law is helping drive down processor-based sensor pricing," which was fast making biometrics more affordable, and more powerful, as it scaled out, with prices dropping from upwards of $50 per scanner to as low as $5—and with even lower prices inevitable. Murray added that in "developments that could help the system-level vision jell, developers of silicon fingerprint sensors have cut prices, and accelerated the devices' scan times."[43]

An April 19, 2005 article in *CNET's* News.com titled "New Life for Moore's Law" recalled that "Intel co-founder Gordon Moore's early observation about the rate of progress in the electronics industry—specifically, that the number of transistors on a microchip double every one to two years" has enabled chip makers and computer vendors "to steadily boost the performance of their products while simultaneously dropping the price—a rare confluence that has allowed digital technology to seep into virtually every segment of the world economy."[44] And on March 30, 2005, Michael Seese—an information security consultant and freelance writer based in Cleveland, Ohio—wrote: "the oft-cited 'Moore's Law' would seem to support the hypothesis that computing power will advance sufficiently in the coming decade."[45]

He recalled how back in 1965, "Intel co-founder Gordon Moore noted that the number of transistors per square inch on an integrated circuit had doubled every year since its inception."[46] Seese added: "Moore predicted that this trend would continue for the foreseeable future." While "in subsequent years, the pace slowed down a bit," Moore was prescient in that "data density has doubled approximately every 18 months—and this is the current definition of Moore's Law."[47] Seese commented that "most experts, including Moore himself, expect Moore's Law to hold for at least another two decades," and "according to one study, the physical limitations could be reached by 2017."[48] Moore's Law might continue even past that date. After 40 years of predictive success, Moore's Law has survived several naysayers' predictions that it would soon become obsolete: "in 1978, IBM scientists predicted Moore's Law had only 10 years left," and "when they got to 1988, they said it would end in 10 years again."[49] Even Gordon Moore "thought it would end at 250-nanometer manufacturing, a landmark the industry passed in 1997."[50]

Not yet ready for prime time

Glen Fest, in the August 2005 edition of BankTechNews.com, reported that "despite biometrics' growing impact and hype in the public sector, biometric-based payment systems could remain on the back burner of financial services companies for awhile," as "standards issues, technical difficulties and low-tech hurdles—like a finger cut or a cough-ravaged voice—can play havoc with biometrics systems—raising the bar further for wide adoption of biometric options."[51]

He cited a TowerGroup report on challenges for biometrics in bank card systems that noted "fingerprint technology at best has achieved a 99 percent success rate against 'false non-matches,'" but "with tens of millions of payment transactions done daily, hundreds of thousands of improperly denied transactions—or in TowerGroup's terms, 'insults'—would take place through the ubiquitous use of fingerprint-reading verifications, which are currently the most used and most cost-effective biometric option domestically."[52] That's why "rollouts for consumer use of biometrics in financial services have been limited," much as they have in the equally security-conscious post 9/11 public sector."[53]

In his article in the July 30, 2005, edition of IT journal TheInquirer.net, Charlie Demerjian reported from the Defcon 2005 conference, where "the first talk of the day was called 'Attacking Biometric Access Control Systems,'" where a hacker named Zamboni described "the nine places to attack a biometric control system," and shared "a little on how to do it."[54] As Demerjian explained, "the grand scheme of it all is that there are several places to attack, the sensor, the feature extractor, the storage computer and the comparison unit."[55] As well, he noted, "you can also attack communication between these points, be they traces on a circuit board or a network link." One method to hack biometrics "is to fake the data," such as putting "a gummy bear finger in the sensor with a legitimate fingerprint on it."[56] One may "also tap the data coming off the sensor to the extractor—in many cases this is sent in the clear over a TCP/IP link to a remote machine," and one may "capture this data, and replay it when you want to get in."[57] Because "most devices do not add a timestamp, sequence number, or have any authentication, much less encryption, it just trusts the sensor,"[58] creating a gaping vulnerability that can be exploited.

According to an April 5, 2005, article in *The Register,* biometrics security flaws have entered the popular imagination, with Hollywood tapping into some emerging public worries.[59] As such, "the rise of biometric security is a boon not only to those who need to ensure the safe-keeping of an object, but also to Hollywood."[60] That's because "the more prevalent its use, the more movies and TV shows can feature people running around with someone else's eye or finger and have it not seem so outlandish."[61] This took place in an episode this past spring in the hit TV show *Alias,* where art imitated life. As *The Register* recounted, in real life, Malaysian authorities have reported that a "man was hijacked in his Mercedes S-class," and "the car thieves forced the victim to place his finger on the security panel to restart the car, and he was tossed in the back seat."[62] But "after they no longer needed the owner, they realized they *did* need his index finger," so "they chopped it off with a machete and left him naked on the side of a road."[63]

But efforts to enhance the security of biometrics continued to be made, and standards developed, across the industry. As BankTechNews.com's Fest noted in 2005, "one step toward standardization took place two years ago when the American National Standards Institute adopted a biometrics framework for the financial services industry"—and "more standards are coming into place in the public sector—where government investment in the technology, primarily through homeland security, has propelled more activity from standardization bodies and solutions on the horizon. The federal government plans to issue biometrics data into the next generation of passports."[64] As with many technologies, Fest believes that "cost may be the driver that has to justify the biometrics investment,"[65] but with Moore's Law advancing the power of biometrics and driving down the cost, the technology will inevitably commoditize, benefiting from its growing scale.

The biometrics of tomorrow

A hint of what lay around the corner was discussed on Geek.com, where Christopher R. Anderson wrote on August 12, 2004, that biometrics, "loosely defined in I.T. as technologies for analyzing characteristics of the human body for authentication, is no longer just in science fiction movies—it is at grocery stores, airports, hotels, and national monuments . . . and you should expect to see it more and more often in the next 10 years."[66] Indeed, he noted a new biometrics systems is in place at the Statue of Liberty, which started "using fingerprints to allow customers to rent, close, and reopen lockers." And while this use of biometrics is "nothing mind blowing," Anderson thinks "it represents a shift of biometrics into the general public."[67] He added that "similar systems have been in use at airports, train stations, and amusement parks all over the US and in Europe," and "as the trend continues to grows, the public will be forced to gain a level of trust and comfort with them."[68] Anderson finds that biometrics was also now "in use in other aspects of life," noting that one "luxury hotel in Boston is using retina scans to let guests into its upscale suites," and that even the Piggly Wiggly grocery store chain based in the southern United States "has pay-by-fingerprint systems in four stores, with plans to install them in 116 other locations."[69]

But not everyone was comfortable with biometrics, with privacy rights advocates fearful of their inherent intrusiveness. But as Tom McLaughlin noted in the View section of *Wired* magazine in February 2003, "law enforcement has been using biometric identification for over a hundred years—it's called fingerprinting, and the existing database is very robust," having served the authorities well. And while "scanning devices can increase efficiency" as Moore's Law boosts their underlying processing power, he commented that "the quality of the engineering is crucial," and explained that "'liveness detection'—a way to spot facsimiles or copies that can spoof the system—was still being perfected. And in the end, the intrusiveness of ID scans was bound to make some people feel less secure," especially as the technology matures to the point of being ready for mass deployments.[70]

With so many concerns about biometrics, the fact that its core technology was fast maturing, its price dropping, and its processing capability getting faster and more powerful did not necessarily mean the public was ready to accept its ubiquity. Nor did it mean that the technology was ready for mass deployments, particularly on a global basis. That's why efforts by the US federal government to promote the adoption of biometrics passports kept getting delayed. As noted in a press statement issued by White House deputy spokesman Adam Ereli on August 10, 2004, "the requirement for Visa Waiver travelers to have biometrics included in passports was mandated in the Enhanced Border Security and Visa Entry Reform Act of 2002."[71] This law "requires countries participating in the US Visa Waiver Program to issue machine-readable passports and incorporate biometric identifiers that comply with international standards," and "citizens of 27 countries, mostly in Europe, would not be required to obtain US visas if they have a passport with a chip."[72] The Visa Waiver countries included Andorra, Australia, Austria, Belgium, Brunei, Denmark, Finland, France, Germany, Iceland, Ireland, Italy, Japan, Liechtenstein, Luxembourg, Monaco, the Netherlands, New Zealand, Norway, Portugal, San Marino, Singapore, Slovenia, Spain, Sweden, Switzerland, and the United Kingdom.

However, privacy groups opposed the inclusion of biometrics data in passports. As reported by *BBC News* on March 30, 2004, "civil rights campaigners have voiced concerns over plans to implement a global biometric identity system for air travelers," and the American Civil Liberties Union had become "increasingly concerned that the biometric travel document initiative is part and parcel of a larger surveillance infrastructure monitoring the movements of individuals globally."[73]

On top of such privacy concerns, the US tourism industry worried about a possible travel slowdown, and concerns among some Visa Waiver countries as to whether they could meet the original deadline led the White House to agree to a one-year delay, from October 26, 2004 to October 26, 2005—the "deadline by which new passports issued must be biometrically enabled."[74] BBC noted that "this extension was necessary to avoid potential disruption of international travel and provide the international community adequate time to develop viable programs for producing a more secure, biometrically enabled passport."[75] The Associated Press reported on June 15, 2005, that the Visa Waiver countries had "failed to meet an October 2004 deadline requiring biometric passports, and many were expected to miss the Oct. 26 deadline as well."[76] But the new, "scaled-back standards" were expected to "address concerns raised by France, Italy and other European Union nations that complained they could not have the technology ready in time."[77]

With more time, participating nations would become better able to prepare for the brave new world of biometrics passports, and at the same time help prepare their citizenry for this new era. And as Moore's Law has long promised, with the passage of time, we can expect all silicon-based products to become ever more powerful and ever cheaper, biometrics included. These factors would contribute toward the eventual uptake of biometrics, in passports and beyond—although privacy concerns would fade more slowly as "Big Brother" stood poised to grow yet bigger.

Notes

1 Department of Homeland Security, "DHS: Fact Sheet: Leadership and Management Strategies for Homeland Security Merger," February 11, 2004, www.dhs.gov/xnews/releases/press_release_0345.shtm.
2 Charles J. Murray, "Security Techs Go Begging for a Clear Safety Strategy," *EE Times*, January 31, 2005.
3 Ibid.
4 *Homeland Security Tech Watch*, Volume 1, Issue 1, October 1, 2003.
5 Ibid.
6 Ibid.
7 Ibid.
8 Ibid.
9 Ibid.
10 Ibid.
11 Ibid.
12 DHS Press Release, "Homeland Security Budget Released: Protecting the Homeland: Fiscal Year 2004 Budget," February 3, 2003. Online at: www.dhs.gov/xnews/releases/press_release_0078.shtm.
13 Ibid.
14 See Program Assessment: SAFETY ACT. Online at: www.whitehouse.gov/omb/expectmore/summary/10003630.2006.html.
15 Ibid.
16 DHS Press Release, "Fiscal Year 2004 Budget Fact Sheet," Department of Homeland Security, March 2, 2003, www.dhs.gov/xnews/releases/press_release_0077.shtm.
17 Ibid.
18 Ibid.
19 Ibid.
20 DHS Press Release, "Department of Homeland Security Announces FY2005 Budget in Brief," February 2, 2004, www.dhs.gov/xnews/releases/press_release_0341.shtm
21 Ibid.
22 Ibid.
23 Harold Kennedy, "DHS Technology Budget to Exceed $1B in 2005," *National Defense Magazine*, June 2004.
24 Ibid.
25 Dibya Sarkar, "Tech Saturates DHS budget," *Federal Computer Week* (FCW.com), February 7, 2005.
26 Ibid.
27 Ibid.
28 Ibid.
29 DHS Press Release, "Fact Sheet: U.S. Department of Homeland Security FY 2006," Department of Homeland Security, February 7, 2005, www.dhs.gov/xnews/releases/press_release_0613.shtm.
30 Ibid.
31 Ibid.
32 Murray, "Security Techs Go Begging."

33 Susan M. Menke, "DHS Short of Technology to Manage Its Biometric Pilots," *Government Computer News* website (GCN.com), November 15, 2004.

34 Ibid.

35 Ibid.

36 Ibid.

37 Ibid.

38 Ibid.

39 Ibid.

40 Ibid.

41 Ibid.

42 Ibid.

43 Ibid.

44 "New life for Moore's Law," CNET News.com, April 19, 2005.

45 Michael Seese, "Business Contingency Planning in the Future: The Office-Less Office," MichaelSeese.com, March 30, 2005.

46 Menke, "DHS Short of Technology."

47 Ibid.

48 Ibid.

49 "New life for Moore's Law."

50 Ibid.

51 Glen Fest, "Cards: Biometrics Stalled Amid the Hype: Shortfalls in Fingerprint Technology Are Curbing Widespread Adoption of New Card Projects. However, a Handful of Small Projects Are Moving Forward, Thanks to the Technology's Buzz," BankTechNews.com, August 2005.

52 Ibid.

53 Ibid.

54 Charlie Demerjian, "How to Hack Biometrics: Not as Hard as You Might Think," TheInquirer.net, July 30, 2005.

55 Ibid.

56 Ibid.

57 Ibid.

58 Ibid.

59 "The Dangers of Biometric Security," *The Register*, April 5, 2005.

60 Ibid.

61 Ibid.

62 Ibid.

63 Ibid.

64 Fest, "Cards."

65 Ibid.

66 Christopher R. Anderson, "Biometrics Becoming Mainstream," Geek.com, August 12, 2004.

67 Ibid.

68 Ibid.

69 Ibid.

70 Tom McLaughlin, "View," *Wired*, February 2003.

71 Adam Ereli, Deputy Spokesman, US Department of State, "Press Statement: Extension of Requirement for Biometric Passport Issuance by Visa Waiver Program Countries," August 10, 2004.

72 Ibid.
73 *BBC News*, "Concern over Biometric Passports," March 30, 2004.
74 Ereli, "Press Statement."
75 *BBC News*, "Concern over Biometric Passports," March 30, 2004.
76 Associated Press, "U.S. Confirms Delay in Biometrics Passports," June 15, 2005.
77 Ibid.

2

Information Security in a World of Cyber Insecurity

In this post-9/11 world of endless terror alerts, wars of preemption, and a rising tide of cyber-attacks, it was no wonder that IT professionals, whether in the private or public sector, have been increasingly worried about security. Once the realm of fantasy and science fiction, cyber warfare was now part of our new reality, and it caught the attention of IT vendors and managers the world over. IT pros feared there might be something coming that would prove more damaging than Code Red, Nimda, or the Slammer worm—and Code Red and Nimda cost enterprises as much as $3 billion.

In the spring of 2003, the world faced a brand new self-replicating computer virus that quickly attacked millions of corporate networks—the Fizzer worm. It spread rapidly over the web, via e-mail as well as via the KaZaa file-sharing network, after first appearing in Asia on May 8, 2003. It spread so rapidly that it was classified a "Level One" threat by F-Secure, a computer security company based in Helsinki, Finland. Infected e-mails arrive with innocuous subject lines such as: "I thought this was interesting . . ." and "so, how are you?" "Fizzer worm has a built-in IRC backdoor, a DoS (Denial of Service) attack tool, a data stealing Trojan, a HTTP server and some more components," warned an advisory from F-secure. According to F-Secure, "the worm has the functionality to kill tasks of certain anti-virus programs"—not unlike the real world's AIDS virus that attacks the human immune system.[1]

In days, the Fizzer virus quickly became one of the most widespread viruses in the world—a reminder that the dangers that lurk in cyberspace now present a clear and present danger to our corporate and national security.

Where fiction and reality collide

Cyber-attacks are no longer the stuff of fiction. Sadly, they have become a part of daily life in the world of IT. Indeed, the real challenges of information systems (IS) are beginning to resemble the vision put forth by thriller writer Tom Clancy, famous for his espionage novels, including his Net Force series. Net Force takes place in what was imagined by Clancy at the start of the century to be the net-centric future, set in the year 2010—our current era—when "computers are the new superpowers" and "those who control them, control the world."[2] In Clancy's fictional world, "to enforce the Net Laws, Congress creates the ultimate computer security agency within the FBI: Net Force."[3]

The scenarios imagined by Clancy no longer sound far-fetched. Indeed, two scenarios portrayed in *Net Force: Hidden Agendas* are as follows:

- "Instructions on how to make a bomb . . . a list of every US spy in the Euro-Asian theater . . . Someone with access to classified information is posting it on the Internet—and it's costing lives."
- "Meanwhile, a virus is unleashed that throws the federal financial systems into chaos. And the Net Force operatives must hunt the wily hacker through the twists and turns of cyberspace—down a path that leads them dangerously close to home . . ."

When the time came to select keynote speakers for Gartner's 2003 IT Security Summit in Washington, DC, the IT analyst firm decided to pick both novelist Clancy, whose imagined world of cyber-terror increasingly resembles our post-9/11 world, as well as US admiral Stansfield Turner, the former director of Central Intelligence, whose job was once to confront America's most worrisome foes. Combining fiction and reality at the keynote podium was just one sign of the changing times. As well, Gartner decided to combine its Enterprise IT Security Conference and the SECTOR 5 Summit on cyber-terrorism and critical-infrastructure protection, since the world of cyber-terrorism and the world of enterprise IT security are now one and the same.

On June 2, 2003, Clancy was featured in a discussion along with Gartner analysts, providing his unique perspectives and intelligence on the pressing concerns about national security and the intersection of technology with the expanding scope of threats facing the United States. According to Gartner, this is the first such forum at which Clancy has ever accepted an invitation to speak. Two days later, Turner shared his perspectives on national and homeland security, modern warfare, terrorism, and information gathering. "During the past year, safeguarding information assets and protecting the integrity of the systems and computing infrastructures that are vital to business and society have become more challenging and crucial," observed Victor Wheatman, vice president and research area director for Gartner. Gartner's three-day summit will explore critical issues, best practices, and case studies through panel discussions with top experts from the private and public sectors. Also included will be breakout sessions tailored to the critical infrastructure sectors such as transportation; energy, utilities and water; banking and financial services; telecommunications and information services; and vital health, safety, and emergency services.

The rising tide of cyber warfare

In 2003, still early in the war on terror, AFCOM—which started off in 1981 as the Association For Computer Operations Management but nowadays serving the needs of enterprise datacenter managers—completed a survey of 257 senior data center managers, finding that cyber-security remains a top issue for 71.2% of the organizations surveyed. AFCOM's Data Center Institute, its internal think tank dedicated to making life easier for data center managers, has found that IS has been catapulted to the top of the agenda at the nation's largest data centers. Nearly one in three organizations experienced a cyber-attack last year, a quarter of which were successful. And while two-third of organizations surveyed allocate 3–8% of their IT budgets to IS, 1 in 6 allocates 9–20% of its IT budget to security needs.

Even with homeland security dominating federal spending, manufacturing organizations continued to spend more on IS than government agencies. Security expenditures were rising, even in this era of depressed IT spending. Almost half of the surveyed organizations, or 47.9%, hiked their security budgets 5–15%, whereas 34% of the respondents say their IS budgets stayed the same. Most respondents (63%) say their organizations are going to spend $100,000–250,000 on IS this year, while 36.9% plan to allocate between $250,000 and $1 million.

Virus attacks and unauthorized access were now the main security concerns to the enterprise data center: over 98% of respondents told AFCOM their organizations now deploy antivirus solutions and firewalls, while 89.1% use card-key access, 75.9% maintain VPNs, 58.8% install intrusion detection devices, and 5.1% deploy biometrics solutions.

Enhancing security, ignoring hype

Yet, just as IS worries began to rise to the top of IT's agenda, Gartner observed a backlash against the security hype. While IT security remains a top initiative for most companies, many enterprises are trying to maneuver through a lot of hype to find products that suit their real needs. "Investing in an over-hyped technology too early can result in a complete waste of enterprises' security funds. Enterprises should focus on their assessment of business needs and threats to prioritize security needs," noted Gartner's Wheatman. Enterprise IT is now navigating through what Gartner said are "minefields of over-promoted products, or products so advanced, the need is not readily apparent."[4] To make this somewhat easier, Gartner has identified the top 11 security issues facing IT. They include: web services security; wireless LAN security; identity management and provisioning; the role of security platforms and intrusion prevention systems; the correlation of events for reporting/monitoring/managing consoles; the next Cod Red/Nimda; instant messaging (IM) security; homeland security (industry specific); tactical security to infrastructure security; protecting intellectual property; and transaction trustworthiness/auditability.[5]

To help its customers navigate these turbulent IS waters, on May 6, 2003, Gartner introduced its new IT Security Directors Membership Program to provide market analysis, decision support tools, onsite workshops, newsletters, bulletins, and access to analysts via a web portal designed to address the growing issues and concerns of IT security directors, bringing together expertise from across Gartner in an integrated package tailored specifically to the needs of IT security directors. "In today's risk-intensive security environment, the consequences of less-than-perfect IT security are more serious than ever before," observed Eileen McPartland, senior vice president, Gartner Research and Advisory Services.[6] "Surveys show that security is a critical concern for businesses, and the outlook for IT security is complex and growing more challenging. In this difficult environment, more than ever, security directors need a combination of resources centered on sound, actionable advice."[7]

As the worldwide war on terrorism continues, both the terrorists as well as those who fight them are finding that the internet has become a theater of war unto itself. Operation Iraqi Freedom demonstrated how C4ISR—Command, Control, Communications, Computers, Intelligence, Surveillance and Reconnaissance—has become a critical element of America's warfighting strategy, ushering forth the age of net-centric warfare, not long ago a concept found only in science fiction and Clancy-esque thrillers. In today's world, our commanders are waging an ongoing battle against terrorists who are as at home on the internet as the most agile of hackers—forcing all IT professionals to take extra caution, and think extra hard, about protecting cyberspace and enhancing the security of our networks and the critical data they contain.

The battle against identity theft heats up

Little more than five years after 9/11, on December 16, 2006, a new and worrisome threshold would be crossed sending shivers down the spines of many a security expert: That's when the 100 *millionth* data record was exposed due to security breaches since the Privacy Rights Clearinghouse began tracking such privacy violations in February 2005. According to that privacy rights organization, since then nearly half a million more files had been compromised, bringing the total to 100,453,858. A closer look at the long list compiled by Privacy Rights Clearinghouse is truly ominous—revealing the depth and breadth of the problem of identity theft for organizations large and small, public and private.

Keith D. Carr, the president and CEO of Tallahassee, Florida–based Identity Theft Solutions Corporation, pointed out to me that "according to the Federal Bureau of Investigation, identity theft is the fastest growing crime in America." He explained that "identity theft, also known as identity fraud, occurs when someone wrongfully uses your personal identification to obtain credit, loans, and services, establish accounts, and in some instances, commit crimes using the victim's name."[8] He added that "typically, the impersonator steals hundreds, thousands, or in some cases even hundreds of thousands of dollars in the victim's name without the victim knowing for months or even years."

When added up, Carr calculated that "the costs associated with identity theft are huge. It is estimated that the current nationwide cost is $2.5 billion and is projected to grow by 30% per year reaching $8 billion by the year 2005." Carr explained that thieves have increasingly recognized "how easy it is to use personally identifying information to commit crimes to acquire goods and services or commit crimes in another person's name," as today's cyber-savvy thieves "understand that it is easier for them to obtain your personal information and establish new accounts or access current accounts." From the calculus of crime and punishment, Carr pointed out that "ID Theft is low risk with huge rewards to criminals without them having to commit a physical crime against a person," and that "no one is totally protected from identity theft," as "it is an equal opportunity crime that affects consumers whether they are rich or poor, black or white, from the city, suburbs or the country, or have a high school degree or PhD."

While media attention on the problem of identity theft has increased as the numbers of victims has risen, Carr noted that identity theft is "not necessarily a new problem," but that it's "become more of an issue in the last several years, largely due to an increase in access to information and dramatic changes in the way that information is used to purchase goods and services" such as "e-commerce/online purchases, increase in credit offers—i.e., instant credit, higher use of credit cards by consumers, etc." Carr has found that identity thieves have been "going after large systems and industries such as data brokers, national banks, credit card processing/systems companies, HMOs, hospitals, universities, etc., to get access to thousands of identities, rather than just going through your trash or sending consumers fake or bogus e-mails luring them to give up their personal information."

One case of identity theft recalled by Carr, which helped bring the issue to national prominence, involved ChoicePoint—the leading provider of identification and credential verification services for businesses and government. On February 15, 2005, it admitted that bogus accounts had been established by identity thieves to steal the personal data of some 163,000 people. Then, just ten days later, Bank of America announced it had lost a backup tape with data from 1.2 million accounts. Carr also noted the case of the Department of Veterans Affairs (VA), which in May 2006 experienced "the loss of personal data on an estimated 26.5 million US military veterans, and up to 2.2 million current service members and an unknown number of spouses" when a laptop and storage device were stolen by two teens from a VA employee's home, including their names, social security numbers (SSNs), dates of birth (DoBs), and in many cases phone numbers and addresses. Carr observed that in December 2006 "some 800,000 people associated with UCLA have been notified that their names and certain personal information were in a database that was compromised by a hacker."

Carr called on the government to "set the standard for privacy and security laws and penalties" and to "enhance its current capabilities to monitor and police potential points of vulnerability." Carr believes "government needs to increase privacy and security measures as it relates to the handling and processing of personal information of citizens and its own employees," and that "in addition, new laws need to be developed that place stiffer penalties on companies that do not have proper safeguards in the workplace to prevent unauthorized access to personally identifying information." Carr adds that "government also needs to monitor how agencies are adhering to current privacy and security laws, rate agencies accordingly, and place fines and corrective actions as needed." In addition to not using anyone's SSN as a client or employee identification number," Carr advises agencies to "protect/encrypt information transferred electronically—including laptops, establish privacy and information security policies and procedures, and conduct regular staff training and surprise check ups."

But government can only provide part of the solution. Carr said it's up to consumers to "consider the following low tech identity protection tips recommended by the Identity Theft Solutions Corporation," such as: checking your credit report; putting passwords on all of your credit card and bank accounts; cross-cut shredding and/or tearing up documents with personal/financial information; using caution when shopping online; being careful of e-mail requests for personal information, especially when they come from companies that should already have such data, and checking for errors or omissions, sloppiness, and telling giveaways, such as poor grammar, that are a hallmark of "phishing" scams; using computer/internet security measures such as firewalls; always protecting your personal information and never providing your SSN, DoB, or personal identification number (PIN), passwords and security codes unless you ask why it is necessary for them to have this information and how that information will be safeguarded; playing it safe in internet cafes, and not using them for bill paying or other tasks that could reveal personal information.

But solving the identify theft problem will require more than changes in individual behavior; a comprehensive solution will require buy-in from the many organizations, corporations, and government agencies that handle our personal information. To understand the scale of identify theft at the enterprise level, and to learn about enterprise solutions to the problem, I spoke with Richard Blackham, the CTO of FastPass Corp, a provider of self-service identity and access management solutions for medium- to enterprise-sized companies and organizations across all industries and sectors, headquartered in Lyngby, Denmark. Blackham explained that "identity theft affects the enterprise in ways we are still only just discovering"—and as illustrated by the continuing losses of PCs and backup storage drives chock full of personal data, Blackham believes that "bad working culture" is "mostly to blame."[9] He observed that "information workers in many organizations still share IDs and passwords, so audit trails on access attempts and access to discrete workloads are forever compromised." He added: "Recently I heard of an organization in London where up to 20 people are still using the same shared ID and password. This is unforgivable behavior."

Blackham believes there's "nothing new about" identity theft, and explained "it's a legacy that's hard to get rid of but remains a growing problem because IT Managers don't want to admit to ownership of a problem that falls right smack dab in the risk management category," and that "consistent de-provisioning practices that have never existed in most organizations and most notoriously prevalent in the public sector means there are old IDs sitting out on legacy systems left in the stewardship of colleagues that want but do not need access to systems they are not entitled to. This is a problem of unknown proportion." And, Blackham added, "the scale of the challenge is in the time it will take to get around all organizations [that] are in need of cleansing their directories: The longer the problem exists for organizations the higher the risk of abuse." This adds up to a "risk management problem that IT Managers won't own up to for fear of uncovering the 'time bomb' and losing their jobs." And during "all the time this exists, there is no accountability for the security of information security in any organization—and I don't just mean external security breaches attack from outside or a lost laptop. This is endemic within the organization—and so just imagine what the public sector looks like, with users having multiple identities and many that they should have no entitlement to." As Blackham calculated, "accessing data beyond the entitlement of the user can lead to untold damage," and "when corporate directories are compromised and sold, then a lot of personal information goes with that kind of abuse—and all manner of discomfort is caused to potentially millions of people."

The government has helped encourage organizations to improve their accountability, and protect the security of their information. Blackham observed that "this is precisely what SOX is all about," referring to the Sarbanes-Oxley Act of 2002, also known as Sarbox—the US federal law passed in response to a slew of corporate and accounting scandals including those affecting Enron, Tyco International, Peregrine Systems, and WorldCom. As Blackham noted, the IT Governance Institute suggests that for SOX compliance to be achieved, controls must now be put in place to "provide reasonable assurance that any problems and/or incidents are properly responded to, recorded, resolved or investigated for proper resolution." And, Blackham believes, "now that SOX has pushed accountability into the c-Suite, we will hear a lot more about controls being implemented."

As Blackham explained, "it's for IT to implement with the relevant controls and the relevant identity and access management software packages, but it is the sponsorship of the c-Suite and executive management that will ultimately garner support in the organization." Blackham further observed that "no-one wants to go to prison for activities in their enterprise they knew nothing about," and he believes "the promotion of team effort will be the best weapon against the criminal element. All organizations should be unified in this pursuit for their own well-being and so they can sleep nights."

Notes

1   See F-Secure website, www.f-secure.com/v-descs/fizzer.shtml.
2   See the Tom Clancy FAQ page, www.clancyfaq.com/Hold%20Originals/Netforce.htm.
3   Ibid.
4   Gartner, "Gartner Says Previously Over-Hyped Security Initiatives Are Resulting in More Cautious Implementation in 2003; Analysts at Gartner Symposium/ITxpo 2003 Discuss Top Security Issues," March 25, 2003, www.gartner.com/press_releases/pr25mar2003a.html.
5   Ibid.
6   Ibid.
7   Ibid.
8   Barry Zellen, "Combating Identity Theft: Rise in Cyber-Crime Demands a Coordinated Response by Consumers, Corporations, and Government Agencies," SecurityInnovator.com, January 16, 2007, http://securityinnovator.com/index.php?articleID=9586&sectionID=25. Subsequent quotations from Keith D. Carr are from this same article.
9   Ibid. Subsequent quotations from Richard Blackham are also from this article.

3

Document Fraud: From Criminal to Terrorist Enterprise

By any stretch of the imagination, the economic cost to the US economy from document fraud is huge. The Association of Certified Fraud Examiners (ACFE) estimates that over $650 billion was lost in 2006 to American businesses from fraud, with two-third of that caused by counterfeiting and doc fraud.[1] That's more than the $532.8 billion US defense budget for 2007, or the $626.1 billion outlay for US social security in 2007. And in this age of heightened insecurity and global terrorism, the *noneconomic* costs, such as the increased risk of a terror attack on the US homeland that could result from travel document fraud, are equally daunting.

According to Dayton, Ohio–based Standard Register, a document management and security company, doc fraud "continues to grow as advancements in technology make it easier to commit. Commercial checks, birth certificates, identification cards, licenses, motor vehicle titles, prescriptions, college transcripts, tickets and passes for events—any document of value is at risk."[2] Dan Thaxton, Standard Register's senior manager of Document Security Solutions, observed there's been a "terrific growth rate" in the economic toll resulting from occupational fraud, as it climbed from around $400B in 1996 to over $650B a decade a later.[3] This amount is so large, he added, that "it gets lost by the sheer scope," and this is "an annual cost." With some 300 million Americans, he noted it works out to be "about $2,200 for every man, woman and child in the US—that's just huge."

Creating fraudulent documents is easier than ever—and much easier to do than a generation ago, when counterfeiting was the domain of craftsman in the basement working with plates and printing presses, as illustrated in the 2002 Hollywood film and 1980 best-selling autobiography *Catch Me If You Can*, about master fraudster-turned-security consultant Frank Abagnale. As Abagnale explained on his company's website, "punishment for fraud and recovery of stolen funds are so rare, prevention is the only viable course of action."[4]

Like many digital age conundrums, technology has been integral to both the problem *of* and solution *to* doc fraud. As Thaxton explained: "Technology helps to create the problem of document fraud. The 'baddies' are not lazy, they are mercilessly efficient and they continuously adapt technology to improve their handiwork until they create something victims will accept. Still, technology offers help in the form of unique capabilities that continually complicate and challenge criminal attacks." The range of technologies available to prevent doc fraud include "applied technologies," such as color-shifting ink, thermochromic inks that change color when warmed, fluorescing inks that glow under a UV black light, converting inks that convert an invisible infrared (IR) or UV laser beam to visible light, and a variety of 'taggants'—those small, covert components that are integrated into the document's material or applied to its surface that make it so hard to copy. Thaxton noted that "most of the new technologies are emerging in the taggant space."

There are also a variety of design technologies—such as the void pantagraphs that use interference patterns that when copied reveal messages in the printing; microprinting; substrate technologies such as watermarks, security threads, color and fluorescing fibers; embedded chips ranging from RFID locator chips to chips storing biometric data points ranging from iris scans to fingerprints; and even embedded DNA molecules—complex and unique chains of atoms that provide a unique microscopic signature to official documents, which resemble "manufactured molecular structures that can act almost like a bar code." Thaxton joked that when people say to him, "'You work for a paper company, how boring!', I'm thinking, I am on the bleeding edge, the hypothetical edge of physics, chemistry," as "things being discovered today will probably be applied to security technology within six months or a year."

While doc fraud in general takes a huge toll on the US economy, the specific challenge of *travel* document fraud has been on the minds of many, making headlines coast to coast, especially in border states dependent upon a steady flow of goods and travelers across the Canadian and Mexican borders—as officials at the US DHS and in the 50 state governments lock horns over how to simultaneously secure the border while fostering a free flow of tourism and trade dollars. Even the American citizen is feeling conflicted, feeling at once a desire to make America more secure from terrorist attack, while at the same time not wanting to spend the extra time or money for a more secure ID.

The federal response to the border security challenge has included the Real ID program, described by DHS as "a nationwide effort intended to prevent terrorism, reduce fraud, and improve the reliability and accuracy of identification documents that state governments issue."[5] As Thaxton explained: "With Real ID, they're saying we have to have viable identity credential"; all 50 states should start to "use a common design in a common format with some common security details, so a cop in any of these 50 jurisdictions will know what they are looking at is real." The genesis of Real ID dates to the 9/11 Commission, which was set up in 2002 and issued its final report in 2004, advocating that Washington "set standards for the issuance of . . . sources of identification, such as driver's licenses," which led Congress to pass the Real ID Act of 2005, which came into effect in May 2008, aiming to achieve full compliance within five years.[6]

Even more pressing, under the terms of the Western Hemisphere Travel Initiative (WHTI) of 2004, on January 31, 2008, US travelers would be required to show proof of citizenship when returning to America by land or sea, such as a passport or birth certificate, along with a valid state ID to prove their identity. With many citizens balking at the high cost of a passport, which is now $110 plus a $25 execution fee for first time applicants, $80 for a child, and a $60 surcharge for expedited service, a movement emerged to develop enhanced licenses that can serve dually as proof of identity as well as of citizenship, and which were expected to cost just $10 or $15 more than a traditional license. In March 2007, DHS signed a Memorandum of Agreement (MoA) with the state of Washington to launch a pilot program to enhance the security of state driver's licenses to "potentially serve as an acceptable alternative document for crossing the United States' land and sea borders."[7]

Washington abuts the Canadian province of British Columbia, which would be hosting the 2010 Olympics. According to the website of the Washington Department of Licensing (DoL), the state is "creating enhanced driver licenses and identification cards that can be used as travel documents at US land and sea border crossing stations. To preserve travel, trade, and cultural ties with British Columbia, Governor Chris Gregoire is proposing an alternative to recent federal legislation requiring people traveling into the US to present a valid passport as proof of identity."[8] Its enhanced licenses "will have a special icon on the front that indicates the holder is a US citizen," and "on the back, the license will have text that can be scanned by border agents. The license also will have a radio frequency identification chip (RFID) required by the federal government to facilitate rapid identification checks at border crossings."[9] DoL is working with Digimarc, a secure ID provider based in Beaverton, Oregon, to develop its enhanced license.

Andy Mallinger, senior director of project management at Digimarc, told me that Washington will be "the first state in the nation to issue enhanced driver license" that will "verify the applicant's identity," so the user may be able to cross the border with it as proof of citizenship.[10] Added Mallinger: "We're going to be producing that." As Mallinger described it, there will be a "more intensive applicant verification/ authentication process including an interview" in addition to "behind the scenes checks" to authenticate the applicant"—all steps that "standard driver licenses won't necessarily go through." Washington's enhanced license program was set to be "live in January," and Digimarc "will be producing cards for them at this time." These enhanced licenses will feature "functionality beyond the traditional license," as the driver license is "taking on additional responsibilities. Way back when, it was truly a license just to drive, but today it is really an identity document," so the driver license now "has a much broader use." With enhanced licenses, Mallinger explained, "the federal government sees an opportunity to provide a lower cost option for border crossings" than using passports.

As for what makes the enhanced license more secure, Mallinger explained there is a four-part lifecycle that includes: secure enrollment; secure production; secure credential; and post-issuance inspection. "I think it is important to look at this as an ecosystem, a workflow that involves both the capture of the demographic, the information about the person, the authorization of the person, and the creation of the document"—followed by "the inspection process to validate the document," since one "could put a really high-end security feature on the card, but if nothing's out there to authenticate it, it's not doing much good."

Mallinger explained: "When we talk about the security of the credentials themselves, we get into all the options of how the card is designed"—which includes the specific overt and covert security features of the ID card, as well as the types of plastic, number of layers, and laminates that go into it. "There are a lot of things you might see, and a number you can't see." Just as "you can't do just one thing to secure the home, you must look at the whole, and how they all overlap and intersect and interact with each other. We call it link-and-layered security," which involves not only the materials but also "protecting the supply chain of those materials, which are not available to the casual counterfeiter, so producing an illegal copy outside of our factory would be very, very difficult." For instance, an enhanced license might have a "color image and ghost image, which is the same picture, but smaller and somewhere else on the card, and which overlaps with another piece of security feature. The design element, the personalization of the data, etc.—each item is matched together to make sure it is very hard to duplicate the card."

Today's driver's licenses will more often than not be made of plastics and laminates that will not only resist tampering, but will reflect efforts at tampering, to "make it easy for someone to spot," so if someone tries "to change something, break into the card, or remove the top layer, it becomes evident by the tearing, or the distortion of data on there." Compare that to "twenty years ago, when you used to be able to cut your picture out and put your brother's in, and it was hard for anyone to tell. That's much more difficult now on a well designed card."

Mallinger explained that "with the capabilities of things like Photoshop, printers and price-points," counterfeiters are moving "along the sophistication curve rapidly— that's why we need to continue to be innovative to bring new features that make them valid, and make cards more and more difficult to counterfeit." And while there is a line separating the "basement counterfeiter and the really sophisticated criminals and terrorists, there are a lot of tools available." To counter their efforts, Mallinger explained, "a lot of elements that go into designing these cards" range all the way from the low to the high tech. "It's a very wide and broad continuum."

Mallinger pointed out that there has been "a lot of innovation, it's always changing—it needs to," as "people who might be trying to cheat the system have become more sophisticated." And to counter the threat they pose, "preventive systems have to keep their lead." That's why, Mallinger explained, there are "constantly new security features we are always looking at."

Closing terrorism's revolving door

Before terrorists strike, they must first gain entry to their target countries, and reside there until zero hour; this nearly always involves some form of doc fraud to succeed. To prevent future attacks, it is thus essential to shut terrorists' revolving door. Doc fraud has long been part and parcel of terrorist efforts to enter and reside in their target countries and has been described by many, from the authors of the *9/11 Commission Report* to the infamous warrior and defense columnist Oliver North, as America's *backdoor to terror.*[11] But a backdoor suggests a hidden portal where a stealthful entry can transpire, like an illicit lover enroute to a forbidden union. Terrorists have become so adept at coming to and staying in America for protracted pre-attack periods, misusing common travel and entry documents with such frequency and confidence, that a better description would be *revolving door* to terror.

To gain insight on the pervasiveness of this threat, I spoke with Susan Ginsburg, director of the Mobility and Security Program at the Washington-based Migration Policy Institute (MPI), and member of the DHS Quadrennial Review (QDR) Advisory Committee, whose task it is to draft America's doctrine for protecting the homeland. Ginsburg has been exploring these issues for many years, serving on the Secure Borders and Open Doors Advisory Committee established by Secretary of State Condoleezza Rice and Homeland Security Secretary Michael Chertoff, and as senior counsel and team leader on the 9/11 Commission where she was responsible for research on the entry of the 9/11 hijackers, terrorist travel, and border controls. Her research shows that "terrorist groups make decisions about who will participate in operations based on the ability to gain access to the country where the attack is to occur."[12]

Ginsburg noted the work of Jean-Louise Bruguiere, a top French terrorism investigator, who has observed that "for these groups passports are as important as weapons." As Ginsburg put it, doc fraud is a "pervasive reality in global travel channels. The United Nations has recognized the importance of border controls and the Security Council has mandated that countries maintain secure travel documents and borders (UNSC 1373)." In the United States, she adds, "document fraud of some kind has been a factor in all the plots" of terror, and that "the four main ways in which Al Qaeda altered passports during the 9/11 period were substituting photos, adding false cachets and visa, removing visas and bleaching stamps, and counterfeiting passports and substituting pages."

Indeed, as the 9/11 attackers implemented their nefarious plans, she explained that "every hijacker submitted a visa application falsely stating that he was not seeking to enter the United States to engage in terrorism. They were inadmissible at ports of entry for the same reason." She added that "at least two hijackers and possibly as many as seven of the hijackers presented passports manipulated in a fraudulent manner to consular officers," and further, "at least two hijackers and as many as 11 presented passports similarly manipulated at ports of entry. Two of the Saudi hijackers may have obtained passports with the help of a family member who worked at the passport office. One hijacker attended flight school without properly adjusting his immigration status, another did not attend school after entering on a student visa, two hijackers overstayed the terms of their admission. One hijacker failed to present a proper vocational school visa upon entry." All said, she calculates that "the 19 hijackers used 384 aliases, including different spellings of their names and noms de guerre in traveling through various countries."

The interconnection of doc fraud to terror dates further back, as "Ramzi Yousef, mastermind of the 1993 World Trade Center bombing, and Ahmad Ajaj a confederate, were able to direct aspects of attack despite being in prison for using an altered passport, traveled under aliases using fraudulent documents," Ginsburg observed. "The two of them were found to possess five passports as well as numerous documents supporting their aliases; a Saudi passport showing signs of alteration, an Iraqi passport bought from a Pakistani official, a photo-substituted Swedish passport, a photo-substituted British passport, a Jordanian passport, identification cards, bank records, education records and medical records." Six years later, "following a familiar terrorist pattern, in 1999 Ahmed Ressam and his associates used fraudulent passports and immigration fraud to travel."

Doc fraud has been a perennial tool of terrorists for gaining entry to, and extending their stay, in their target countries. Janice L. Kephart, director of National Security Policy at the Washington-based Center for Immigration Studies (CIS), told me that "lost and stolen passports, either assuming another identity, or photo-substituting an identity into a passport" are a prime means for gaining entry to a target country.[13] "However, this is increasingly harder to do now that passports are being checked for every person making entry through much more robust data-checking." MPI's Ginsburg noted that "passports, visas, and supporting documents, including breeder documents, are the three types of documents subject to misuse." She added that "the patterns of misuse vary around the world, from country to country, based on the vulnerabilities." She pointed out that "all terrorists acquire visas and/or enter the United States based on fraud," and that they "provide false information about their intentions on their visa applications, rendering those applications fraudulent. This is visa fraud by deceit. Thus, there is no such thing as a 'clean' or 'legal' entry for a terrorist. A terrorist who obtains a student or religious worker visa from a consulate is presenting a visa based on fraud if the individual is in fact a terrorist."

Ginsburg adds that a terrorist "might present a genuine passport obtained under an alias name; present an imposter passport, that is, present a genuine passport belonging to someone else who resembles the traveler enough to pass through the US land border which does not have biometric readers; or present a counterfeit pre-RFID chip passport under an alias name from a visa free travel country." Additionally, she noted visa foils "may be stolen and inserted into counterfeit passports," and that "there are quite well developed counterintelligence operations by illicit market document providers surrounding consulates, assisting applicants in lying their way through interviews and building convincing files of supporting documents. Consulates in some parts of the world believe that the fraud rate is extremely high, up to 90 percent." As well, "visa applicants may put false stamps—very easy to counterfeit—in their passport to indicate a trustworthy travel pattern," and compounding the problem is "corruption or complicity in passport offices and at border points."

Once inside the country, the doc fraud continues. According to Dr Ronald Mortensen, author of "Illegal, But Not Undocumented: Identity Theft, Document Fraud, and Illegal Employment," and a retired career US Foreign Service Officer who now works with the CIS: "Once an individual is in the United States, he can easily obtain fraudulent social security cards, green cards, birth certificates, drivers licenses, etc., in almost any major city through a widespread network of fraudulent document dealers who cater primarily to the millions of illegal aliens who need these documents in order to obtain jobs."[14] He told me that the "cost is minimal in most cases. Given the tolerance of state and local elected officials, law enforcement officials, etc., for illegal alien identity theft, it would be easy for terrorists to obtain documents through these same networks."

Moreover, as MPI's Ginsburg noted: "To stay in the country, the individual might overstay any visa and not be caught, because there is no system for tracking and apprehending visa overstays. To acquire a driver's license—which permits opening a bank account and other administrative necessities—the terrorist need only present various forms of seemingly valid ID and have an address in most states. Birth certificates are very insecure documents in the United States, entirely unregulated by federal security standards. Blanks may fairly easily be stolen and copies easily obtained."

While this nexus between doc fraud and terror has been both persistent and pervasive, numerous solutions to reduce the threat now exist. Ginsburg noted that "many new countermeasures are in place and they have made terrorist travel significantly more difficult." She adds that the "most basic is a much expanded terrorist identities list accessible to visa and port authorities," while "perhaps the most advanced program is real-time information sharing about lost and stolen passports among Australia, New Zealand, the United States and the UK through a distributed network using a broker. INTERPOL maintains a lost and stolen passport database increasingly accessible to border authorities."

Other vulnerabilities from the pre-9/11 world have been redressed through policy changes in the more security-conscious, post-9/11 world. For instance, Ginsburg noted that "using ten fingerprints in visas that are verified at ports of entry (US VISIT) has detected and deterred fraud. The United States now has a student tracking system that alerts authorities when a student is not complying. Countries through the International Civil Aviation Organization (ICAO) have raised standards for passport design and western countries are assisting developing countries in incorporating these and other mobility security standards bilaterally and through international organizations such as the United Nations' Counter Terrorism Executive Directorate and the International Organization for Migration, and regional organizations like the OSCE and ASEAN. The United States provides many countries with computers and software to mount watchlists at border ports of entry."

CIS' Mortensen believes greater use of the US E-Verify program could also help close this revolving door, noting it's "a free, federal government program that determines employment eligibility," designed to prevent SSN fraud by undocumented workers, which could also make it harder for terrorists to remain hidden beneath the radar in America: "Once an employer has registered and completed the tutorial, s/he enters the identifying data of all new hires and in most cases a response is received within seconds," Mortensen added. He noted: "Congress could mandate its use by all employers in all 50 states but the US chamber of commerce and advocates for illegal aliens strongly oppose this." Mortensen adds that "massive identity theft by illegal aliens provides perfect cover for foreign nations using false identities because they do not stand out. The failure of US political and law enforcement leaders to address this serious problem which impacts literally millions of American citizens makes the use of false documents and fake identities a relatively easy and safe practice for illegal aliens, terrorists, pedophiles, sexual predators, etc."

State of Recovery

Greater awareness of and attention to the problem can go a long way toward reducing the risk. To help close the revolving door of terrorists, Ginsburg believes that "we first have to recognize the problem—that securing human mobility is one of the arenas of counterterrorism. Second, it has to be recognized that all levers of national power are important to addressing the establishment of the rule of law in global mobility channels—intelligence, law enforcement, immigration enforcement, regulatory reforms, new international institutions and agreements. Secure travel documents and identity management are one important pillar of that effort." She adds that "some of the important tasks associated with dealing with this are to gain international agreement on and implementation of travel document design and issuance standards, settling on information sharing methods and standards, building border and mobility management capacity in developing countries, and cooperating internationally on apprehending document producers." One silver lining, Ginsburg pointed out, is that "at the same time that terrorist travel represents a challenge to security officials in countries terrorists may be targeting, it also represents a vulnerability for them, because they must surface and encounter government officials. How to take advantage of this fact needs to be carefully considered, in the same way officials have focused on financial and communications flows."

Notes

1 "AICPA and ACFE Join Forces to Prevent Fraud," *Journal of Accountancy*, January 2007, www.journalofaccountancy.com/Issues/2007/Jan/AICPAandACFEJoinForces.htm.
2 Standard Register, "Secure Documents," www.standardregister.com/business/secure-documents.asp.
3 Barry Zellen, "Document Fraud and Technology, a Double-Edged Sword," SecurityInnovator.com, January 15, 2008, http://securityinnovator.com/index.php?articleID=14174&sectionID=25. Subsequent quotations from Dan Thaxton are from this article.
4 Abagnale and Associates, www.abagnale.com/index2.asp.
5 Biometrics.gov, www.biometrics.gov/ReferenceRoom/FederalPrograms.aspx.
6 Department of Homeland Security, "Dollars and Sense," *Homeland Security Leadership Journal Archive*, June 20, 2008.
7 Office of the Governor of Washington State, "Department of Homeland Security and the State of Washington Team Up to Advance Western Hemisphere Travel Initiative," March 23, 2007,www.governor.wa.gov/news/news-view.asp?pressRelease=526&newsType=1.
8 Washington State Department of Licensing, "Enhanced Driver Licenses and ID Cards: Border Crossing FAQ," www.dol.wa.gov/about/. . ./priorities/borderCrossingFaq.pdf.
9 Ibid.
10 Zellen, "Document Fraud and Technology." Subsequent quotations from Andy Mallinger are from this article.
11 See Oliver North, "Back Door to Terror," Townhall.com, October 20, 2006, http://townhall.com/columnists/OliverNorth/2006/10/20/back_door_to_terror.

12 Barry Zellen, "Decreasing Doc Fraud," SecurityInnovator.com, October 30, 2009, http://securityinnovator.com/index.php?articleID=15846&sectionID=27. Subsequent quotations from Susan Ginsburg are from this article.
13 Ibid. Subsequent quotations from Janice L. Kephart are from this article.
14 Ibid. Subsequent quotations from Ronald Mortensen are from this article.

4

Business Continuity in Dangerous Times

The twenty-first century has presented business and government leaders with a series of epic disasters, both natural and man-made, from the 9/11 mass-terror attacks to Superstorm Sandy. Increasingly, government and industry are working together to prepare for the next calamity, and to ensure continued business continuity after disaster next strikes. Since the start of the twenty-first century, a series of catastrophic events—both natural and man-made—has forced decision-makers at the helm of both public and private sector organizations to more carefully consider the potential impact of disasters on the continuity of business operations. Consider Hurricane Katrina, which flooded the city of New Orleans when it made landfall on August 29, 2005—killing over 1,300 people, displacing some 770,000 people, destroying or severely damaging some 300,000 homes, battering offshore energy infrastructure, and ultimately costing an estimated $96 billion. Katrina proved once and for all that *it can happen here*.

Widely held views of a bungled government response to the tragedy forced the US federal government to take a close look at what went wrong. President Bush ordered a comprehensive review of the federal government's response to Hurricane Katrina, to help us become "better prepared for any challenge of nature or act of evil men that could threaten our people." The end-result of this review was the February 23, 2006, submission of a report titled *The Federal Response to Hurricane Katrina: Lessons Learned*.[1] In its preface, Frances Fragos Townsend, assistant to the president for Homeland Security and Counterterrorism wrote that "Hurricane Katrina was a deadly reminder that we can and must do better, and we will," and that "No matter how prepared we think we are, we must work every day to improve."[2] At the start of Chapter 1, the report explained that "our obligation is to work to prevent the acts of evil men; reduce America's vulnerability to both the acts of terrorists and the wrath of nature; and prepare ourselves to respond to and recover from the man-made and natural catastrophes that do occur."[3]

One September 23, 2004—a full year before Katrina's fury flooded New Orleans and decimated the US Gulf Coast—the US DHS, in partnership with the Advertising Council and a variety of business organizations, launched its Ready Business initiative focusing on business preparedness, to "help owners and managers of small to medium-sized businesses prepare their employees, operations and assets in the event of an emergency."[4] Though Katrina was still a year away, the wrath of nature as well as man was on the mind of then–DHS secretary Tom Ridge, who explained that "the terrorist attacks of 9/11 and more recently hurricanes Charley, Frances and Ivan showed that disastrous events can paralyze business operations."[5] Developing an emergency preparedness plan, he added, would make "our nation and our economy more secure."

While having an emergency preparedness plan "can greatly improve the likelihood that a company will survive and recover from all emergencies, natural disasters or terrorist attacks," DHS noted in its media release announcing the Ready Business launch that "too few businesses are taking the necessary steps to prepare."[6] The Ready Business website explained while "business continuity and crisis management can be complex issues depending on the particular industry, size and scope of your business," DHS believes that "putting a plan in motion will improve the likelihood that your company will survive and recover."[7]

Marc Johnson, a principal at Cupertino, California–based Symantec Global Services, the services arm of IT security solutions vendor Symantec, Corp., explained to me that events like "Hurricane Katrina and the Northeast regional power outage of 2003 are classic cases that illustrate the problem of business continuity: Too often, organizations believe that it will never happen to them and when it does, they will not be too adversely affected."[8] Johnson noted that "these cases have also enlightened the fact that a piece of paper indicating that an organization has a business continuity plan—as required by Sarbanes-Oxley, Graham-Leach-Bliley, and other regulatory acts—is not enough. Actual well documented and exercised plans—with real resumption tasks—are the safeguard that key stakeholders and their organization require."

In the wake of a string of large-scale disasters, Johnson noted that "we learned that planning for events of this magnitude are by no means out of scope." But we also "learned that even the most well laid plans have faults, especially if they are not exercised on a regular basis. We learned that organizations cannot perform a business impact analysis, design an appropriate strategy to mitigate the risks, implement technology, and document business continuity plans once: The only constant in business is change; thus, business continuity must be a program that constantly improves upon itself."

Harprit Singh, CEO of Philadelphia, Pennsylvania–based Intellicomm, a unified communications service firm, explained to me at the "principle challenge of business continuity is lack of adequate planning by businesses and other institutions," and that "having a business continuity plan requires a significant amount of planning, identification of workflows and business processes most impacted due to disruption, and having a contingency plan in place to address them."[9] Singh observed that "the lack of adequate communications facilities during the 9/11 tragedy and Hurricane Katrina in New Orleans" illustrates the scale of the business continuity challenge: "In both cases, the traditional telecommunications facilities were severely destroyed and unavailable thereby creating a mess in managing rescue and recovery efforts." But not all business continuity problems are caused by large-scale disasters like 9/11 or Katrina.

As Singh explained: "Such large scale disasters usually get all the attention and are typically the driving force behind business continuity planning. However, companies face similar situations every once in a while even when unrelated to major disasters on company premises. For example, do companies have an alternate way to manage their incoming phone calls if the local carrier has a fiber cut, power disruption or fire?

Most would answer No. Having a contingency plan for larger natural disasters affords companies the luxury of invoking them in unanticipated or unforeseen business disruptions," regardless of their scale.

Singh believes business continuity can best be addressed "by distilling business continuity to smaller, manageable challenges that can be addressed with limited resources with the intent of building a holistic approach over time." He has found that "too many companies want to address everything but don't have the resources available, thereby abandoning even smaller implementations." Singh observed that "larger companies tend to have plans in place for relocating their people and processes in case of disasters" while "small to mid-size businesses find that task largely daunting and expensive." But, he pointed out, "not all aspects of a business continuity plan are expensive if carefully researched and evaluated"—so that "small to mid-size companies can start planning in smaller increments with an eventual goal of a more comprehensive plan."

Beyond data protection

Singh noted that current trends in business continuity "are still largely confined to business continuity plans in terms of data protection and management," and while "telecommunication business continuity planning is an extremely important aspect of any contingency plan—but surprisingly, it gets very little attention, even though a command and control structure collapses when there is no communication." He has found that "the telecommunications business continuity issues still remain largely ignored and unaddressed—whether by telecom carriers, vendors or business owners." Singh believes businesses "should establish external backup systems, phone numbers, fax numbers, voicemail or announcement lines as alternate sources of communication for employees as well as customers should the primary phone systems be unusable. Even a voice message left by a customer and employee is far more useful in a disaster recovery situation than no communication with them at all." Indeed, Singh explained "it does no good if you have another location for people and processes if there is no communication between various parties." He added that "it is critical that customers know you are still in business and plan to keep them posted about the progress of recovery."

In addition to ensuring continuity of business communications, Jim Gildea, vice president of marketing at Cupertino, California–based Grisoft, a software company specializing in computer-virus solutions, told me that the issue of network continuity is also important to consider within the context of business continuity. He observed that "by and large business continuity is defined by the ability of organizations to quickly recover from major interruptions, either technological, man-made or acts of God."[10] He added that "typically this has been held within the realm of data backup, secure offsite archiving and geographically dispersed redundant data centers." But more recently he's found that "organizations are now regarding business continuity as the ability to avoid an interruption to their businesses by hardening their defenses against hackers, viruses and malicious code."

Unpredictable nature

One of the greatest challenges for business continuity is the unpredictable nature of disasters, whether natural or man-made. When and where the next disaster will strike is impossible to know; but not being prepared when it does can spell doom for any business and its stakeholders. Sunil Cherian, director of product management for Array Networks, a provider of secure VPN remote access solutions, explained to me that "the fundamental premise is that disasters/disruptions are unpredictable," and one thing large-scale disasters like Hurricane Katrina and the 9/11 attacks taught us is that "we can't predict disasters."[11] Cherian added: "We don't have solutions for all disasters, but we can be better prepared to deal with the aftermath of such a disaster, when it happens. Organizations that are better prepared face less loss and are up on their feet quicker." He pointed out that "if you are a small business, one disaster will kill you"—whereas "if you are a large business, you are probably hurt—but you can likely afford the loss of a limb or two."

Cherian believes that "we need to take our collective heads out of the sand, and start thinking about 'what if' scenarios and how to address it. Organizationally, it starts with education and awareness that it is indeed a problem." He added that organizations "need to identify the critical elements and start costing the damage associated with not being able to do a specific function . . . Depending on the prioritization, and the criticality, you can spend significantly more to get complete online redundant data centers, or spend less, but take a little bit of downtime by taking an offline approach to data recovery or restore." Cherian defined "a true solution to business continuity" as one that "needs to address the productivity issue, needs to address the issue of a large number of typically wired users who now become remote users, needs to address the issue of having backup data and applications that can be brought online and accessed without taking too long. It needs to address processes and communication mechanisms used in the event of a disaster or disruption."

Cherian pointed out that "technology is available today to provide multiple data centers, to provide data backup and recovery, and to provide scalable remote access," and that "leading edge organizations are putting in plans to have scalable remote access, data backup/recovery, redundant data centers, emergency communication mechanisms, etc."

A time for leadership

Ensuring business continuity requires leadership both within the organization and without. As Grisoft's Gildea explained, "responsibility for a comprehensive business continuity best practices must be driven from the executive level, validated and executed by the IT organization, and adopted as practice company-wide." Cherian agrees, explaining that "business continuity is about the survival of the company. It needs executive leadership." Singh concurs, noting business continuity "certainly requires the executive leadership's involvement as the champion and chief visionary of any business continuity plan." IT departments are an important part of the solution, but cannot solve the problem on their own. As Cherian explained: "IT is a significant component of it, but processes, procedures and planning are just as important." Singh noted: "IT and other departments can help implement a business continuity plan, but it needs to be initiated at the top." And, as Johnson explained: "IT is only one business unit within an organization and subsequently cannot bear the burden alone."

Addressing the challenge of business continuity internally may prove difficult for some companies, especially smaller ones. Fortunately, there are external vendors willing to share their expertise. Singh explained that "depending on the level and sophistication of a business continuity plan, it may be prudent to involve external specialists as companies can leverage the collected experience, wisdom, and resources of an external vendor specializing in it." As Cherian noted, "vendors can help with pieces of the solution—but what you spend, how much you spend and where depends on your business and a keen understanding of the elements that make up your business and the problems that need to be addressed." Symantec's Johnson has found that "many organizations need external specialists to assist in the building of consensus. Left as an internal initiative only, many organizations fail to see the business objectively and effectively question the priorities associated with the risks and threats. It is often thought to be too monstrous a task when an organization tries to tackle it alone. Specialists are practical educators that provide expertise from many industries and organizations as well as practical experience. This helps businesses get to recovery quicker through that practical experience and objective perspective."

In addition to executive leadership, government has an important role to play in encouraging business to prepare for the worst. Johnson observed that "government has taken distinct action in the form of regulatory requirements such as BASEL II, Sarbanes-Oxley, and other domestic acts." He reflected: "Are these perfect in purpose and execution? No. Are these regulations detailed enough to explain what to do and not do? No. Is it the government's responsibility to protect the business? No." He commented that "unfortunately, the existing regulations are quite vague and open to wide interpretation," and he believes that "the government should help companies meet their business continuity challenges by being more specific in the requirements that organizations must meet for compliance with regulations meant to protect stakeholders."

Cherian believes "government needs to raise awareness about the need for business continuity," and that "it can probably help by approving financial/tax incentives for organizations to be prepared for business continuity" and "perhaps encourage insurance companies to offer programs similar to earthquake insurance—but more general, disaster insurance policies." Singh believes government needs to do more, and that so far, it "has done very little in terms of helping companies meet their business continuity challenges." While "there is usually an up tick in discussion right after a disaster happens," this "quickly fades away without any concrete plans." Singh believes that "at the very least, governments can establish a set of best practices and educate companies, especially small to mid-size companies with limited resources, in addressing the business continuity challenge."

However, Grisoft's Gildea takes a contrarian view on the role of government in business continuity. He believes "legislation and regulation are not the answer to technological business interruptions." He recalled how "the CAN-SPAM Act, for instance, has not reduced the amount of unsolicited email users receive," and that "in fact, research has shown spam levels have risen 33% in 2006. Furthermore, industry focused regulations, such as Sarbanes-Oxley, have put such an administrative burden on companies that it has actually decreased productivity."

Gildea believes the best approach is through self-help: "Organizations must take it upon themselves to protect themselves from technological threats as they evolve. To that end, a thoughtful, documented best-practices policy must be crafted taking into considerations all aspects of activity within the organization. Relying on governmental legislation and regulation will not address these threats because they evolve too quickly."

Notes

1 Frances Fragos Townsend, *The Federal Response to Hurricane Katrina: Lessons Learned*, archived at http://georgewbush-whitehouse.archives.gov/reports/katrina-lessons-learned/index.html.
2 Frances Fragos Townsend, "Letter to the President from Frances Fragos Townsend," *The Federal Response to Hurricane Katrina.*
3 Frances Fragos Townsend, "Chapter One: Katrina in Perspectuve," *The Federal Response to Hurricane Katrina.*
4 DHS Press Release, "Homeland Security and Business Organizations Launch Ready Business," Department of Homeland Security, September 23, 2004, www.ready.gov/america/about/pressreleases/release_040923.html.
5 Ibid.
6 Ibid.
7 DHS, "Overview," Ready.gov, www.ready.gov/business/overview/index.html.
8 Barry Zellen, "After Katrina: Confronting the Business Continuity Challenge," SecurityInnovator.com, February 2, 2007, http://securityinnovator.com/index.php?articleID=9871&sectionID=238. Subsequent quotations from Marc Johnson are from this article.
9 Ibid. Subsequent quotations from Harpit Singh are from this article.
10 Ibid. Subsequent quotations from Jim Gildea are from this article.
11 Ibid. Subsequent quotations from Sunil Cherian are from this article.

Part II

Securing Our Borders

5

Border Security and the War on Terror

After the Twin Towers fell, America—and much of the world—began to grapple with the issue of how to erect both physical and metaphorical walls to stop future acts of terror. And ever since that surreal day of horror on 9/11, America has been waging a GWOT—recognizing that one of the frontline battlegrounds in this war would be at home. Looking north and south at virtually undefended borders, porous and easily infiltrated, much attention has gone into addressing America's new border security challenge.

On January 25, 2002, President Bush, in a speech in Maine, said: "You know, none of us ever dreamt that we'd have a two-front war to fight: one overseas and one at home. But we do. That's reality. And as a result, we must respond, and continue to respond, and stay on alert, and help defend America. The biggest chore I have, my biggest job, is to make sure our homeland is secure."[1] That is why, Bush explained, he asked for $38 billion in funds for homeland security—including $11 billion "for controlling of our borders. It is so important for our nation to work with our friends to the north, Canada, and our friend to the south, Mexico, on border initiatives—that one doesn't tie up commerce but, on the other hand, prevents illegal drugs, terrorists, arms from flowing across our border . . . We're analyzing every aspect of the border and making sure that the effort is seamless, the communication is real, that the enforcement is strong."[2]

The United States has a 7,500-mile land and air border shared with Canada and Mexico, and an exclusive economic zone encompassing 3.4 million square miles. Each year, over 500 million people are admitted into the United States, of which 330 million are noncitizens. Over land, 11.2 million trucks and 2.2 million rail cars cross into the United States, while 7,500 foreign-flag ships make 51,000 port calls in the United States each year. The White House's Action Plan for Creating a Secure and Smart Border described the "Smart Border of the Future" as a border management system that "keeps pace with expanding trade while protecting the United States and its territories from the threats of terrorist attack, illegal immigration, illegal drugs, and other contraband. The border of the future must integrate actions abroad to screen goods and people prior to their arrival in sovereign US territory, and inspections at the border and measures within the United States to ensure compliance with entry and import permits. Federal border control agencies must have seamless information-sharing systems that allow for coordinated communication among themselves, and also the broader law enforcement and intelligence gathering communities."[3] The plan calls on "the use of advanced technology to track the movement of cargo and the entry and exit of individuals is essential to the task of managing the movement of hundreds of millions of individuals, conveyances, and vehicles."[4] Among the $11 billion in border security initiatives in the 2003 budget, $380 million was for the Immigration and Naturalization Service (INS) to construct a state of the art Entry-Exit visa system, and a $619 million increase in the inspection budget of the Customs Services, to $2.3 billion. The Customs Service also aimed to complete the hiring of approximately 800 new inspectors and agents to carry out additional security activities along US borders and seaports.

The northern front

The previous December, Homeland Security Director Tom Ridge, and John Manley, then–minister of Foreign Affairs in Canada, who would a month later be appointed deputy prime minister responsible for security measures after 9/11, signed the Smart Border Declaration with a 30-point action plan designed to help speed and secure the flow of people and goods between the United States and Canada. The Smart Border Declaration recognizes that "our current and future prosperity and security depend on a border that operates efficiently and effectively under all circumstances."[5] The pillars of the Smart Border were defined as maintaining the secure flow of people, the secure flow of goods, a secure infrastructure, and coordination in enforcing these objectives.

Negotiations proceeded throughout the winter. Manley told the *Ottawa Citizen* in March that Canada and the United States were close to agreement on controversial portions of the 30-point Smart Border program and that he expected the complete package to be ready by the G8 summit in Alberta in June. "There are no more red light issues," Manley said, adding: "There are still some yellows. We've moved a few of those to green so everything is essentially on schedule or ahead of schedule."[6] On June 28, 2002, White House Homeland Security Advisor Tom Ridge and John Manley, now serving as Canadian deputy prime minister, released a joint report on ongoing efforts to implement the Smart Border Declaration and 30-point Action Plan launched in December 2001. The report was issued during a meeting between Manley and Ridge in Niagara Falls, Ontario, to discuss bilateral security issues. Highlights of the progress report include increased cooperation to intercept high-risk travelers before they arrive in either country; the initialing of a "safe third" text that will promote the orderly handling of asylum applications and reduce misuse of both asylum systems; the deployment of a border-wide "fast lane" program called NEXUS to speed the flow of pre-screened, low-risk travelers and launching a NEXUS-Air pilot project; progress on a new joint program, Free and Secure Trade (FAST), to securely and efficiently move commercial shipments across the border; a binational steering group to reduce risks to shared critical infrastructure; increased speed for sharing information and intelligence, including the creation of 14 Integrated Border Enforcement Teams over the next 18 months; and conducting joint counterterrorism training exercises, including a major exercise scheduled for May 2003. "The Smart Border is the border for the future," Ridge declared, adding that US-Canadian cooperation in implementing these public security initiatives efforts "is a model for the world."[7] The United States planned to deploy 700 soldiers along the Canadian border and to add six helicopters to its border surveillance activities. A similar Smart Border effort was concurrently underway with Mexico.

The southern front

Along the US-Mexico border, border security has been a high priority for many years—in response to the ongoing US and Canadian antidrug wars as well as Washington's efforts to reduce illegal immigration. Dr Jason Ackleson, of the Department of Government at New Mexico State University, in an article called "Border Security in the Wake of 9/11" published in San Diego's *La Prensa* on December 20, 2001, observed: "Since the mid-1990s, the US Border Patrol has increasingly been involved in security efforts, especially along the southern boundary. Modeling their frontier-wide efforts on 'Operation Hold the Line'—a restrictive, 'line-watch' strategy imposed along the US-Mexico boundary in El Paso, Texas in 1993—the Immigration and Naturalization Service (INS) began intensive surveillance designed to deter unauthorized migrant crossings. These initiatives utilized high-technology, such as electronic monitoring devices, and deployed agents to monitor the border in new ways."[8]

Ackleson observed that from 1993 to 2000, "the Border Patrol more than doubled from 4,000 to 9,000 agents while the overall INS budget increased from $1.5 billion to over $5 billion. Much of this growth was authorized by the 1996 Illegal Immigration Reform and Immigrant Responsibility Act. Embedded in this act was an often unnoticed provision called Section 110, which required, within a two year period, the registration of all entrants into the United States through the establishment of a high-tech, 'secure' entry and exit system at border crossings, especially those on the northern frontier."[9] Ackleson added: "Geographically, the immigration debate has shifted from the nation's southern border with Mexico to the more porous northern border with Canada, a nation which some perceive has a liberal refugee and immigration policy and is seen as a conduit for terrorist movements."[10]

Technology and the war on terror

Throughout the 1990s, research and testing of new technology solutions for border security, driven both by efforts to stem the flow of illegal immigrants into the United States along its southern border, and by ongoing efforts to reduce the illegal drug trade across the same frontier, continued. The National Institute of Justice, the research and development agency of the US Department of Justice, has an Office of Science and Technology—and one of its programs was operating the National Law Enforcement and Corrections Technology Center (NLECTC), which includes a national technology center, five regional centers, and two special offices that provide technology assistance, information, and support to the law enforcement, corrections, and criminal justice communities.

These tech centers coordinate research in various border security technologies including perimeter surveillance and intrusion detection capabilities, thermal imaging and other specialized surveillance tools, communications interoperability between agencies, and vehicle stopping technology. The Rocky Mountain Region's technology emphasis was Command, Control, and Communications, including dispatch, force management, radio and data communications, GPS/GIS tracking, and other related areas. The Western Region provided a focus on forensic analysis and imaging technologies. The Northeast Region's emphasis was on concealed weapons detection, speech processing, and timeline analysis. The Border Research Technology Center had the responsibility for technologies that provide increased capabilities in border surveillance, security, and identification. It worked closely with the US Customs Service and the US Border Patrol, falling under the administrative oversight of the Western Region Technology Center.

In addition, the Counterdrug Technology Assessment Center (CTAC), established within the Office of National Drug Control Policy (ONDCP) in 1990, was the central counterdrug technology research and development organization of the US government. It sponsored research in a variety of border security areas including: wide-area surveillance, physical security design, thermal imaging, drug-tunnel detection, counterdrug air and ground surveillance coordination, unmanned aerial vehicles and low-noise profile surveillance aircraft, mobile and stationary aerostat communication and optical sensor platforms, covert ultra-wideband communication systems, high-frequency surface wave radar and small boat detection, and third-generation mid-wave infrared sensors.

While the war on drugs met with recurring criticism for its ineffective results in reducing drug trafficking to, and drug consumption in, the United States, it did help to concentrate attention and resources on addressing security issues along the southern US border, contributing to a more secure environment and a technology resource base well-suited for the current war on terror.

Since 9/11, technologists have quickly emerged with a variety of new solutions, many based on border security solutions crafted during the war on drugs, and many new solutions that include biometric authentication tools that can, when coupled with more tradition border security technologies such as remote video surveillance, thermal imaging, and infrared sensors, monitor and track the movements of known terrorists by matching their biometric signatures. But these new-fangled technologies—while impressive—are at best one component in a complex system of perimeter security that includes both the old, and the new.

Biometrics on the border

Biometrics technology has been present along the US/Canada border for many years. Dr Judith A. Markowitz, founder and CEO, J. Markowitz, Consultants, told last year's SpeechTek 2001 conference how "biometrics is used to authenticate travelers' identities at borders," noting that the US/Canada border in Montana has become "the first fully automated port of entry in the world."[11] While this use of biometrics is designed more to facilitate ease of entry for local residents across the border, and not for counterterrorism, its potential for the latter has been recognized in both technology and policy circles.

Bill Spence, in a white paper published by Recognition Systems, Inc., called *Biometrics in Physical Access Control: Issues, Status and Trends*, wrote: "Biometrics identify people by a unique human characteristic: the size and shape of a hand, a fingerprint, the voice, or certain aspects of the eye, for example. No longer are these devices found only in James Bond movies and Star Trek reruns . . . Early installations were expensive and therefore limited to very high security applications such as nuclear facilities. In recent years, inexpensive microprocessors and advanced imaging electronics have greatly reduced the cost of biometric devices, while increasing their accuracy."[12]

The increased accuracy, decreased cost, and maturation of biometrics have caught the attention of Washington. Bruce Mehlman, assistant secretary for Technology Policy in the US Department of Commerce, told the Biometrics Consortium Conference in February 2002: "For many years, we have looked to biometrics as a promising, emerging technology. That calculus has now changed. At this conference over the past three days we have learned that biometrics are no longer emerging—they're here. And September 11th taught us that biometrics are more than promising—they will be essential to our future security. . . From airports to nuclear power plants, from cyber security to building access technologies, biometrics will play a vital role in protecting our citizens and our way of life."[13] The precise role of biometrics along our borders is yet to be determined, but as time goes by—and more solutions come of age—they will increasingly contribute to our border security. And when combined with new, remote surveillance technologies, the porousness and vulnerability of our borders will be greatly mitigated.

Physical barriers and perimeter defenses

Without physical barriers to complement what the "eyes" (video surveillance, infrared motion detectors, radar systems, vibration detectors, and taut-wire sensors) can see and what the "brain" (biometrics, computerized command and control, communications interoperability) can analyze, our borders will remain vulnerable.

A Delta Scientific white paper, *For Governments Today, Security Starts with the Perimeter*, states: "Whether a courthouse, military base, parliament building, school or mass transit authority yard, the starting point for any security plan, especially since September 11, begins at the boundary line perimeter and its access points, not at the buildings themselves. When one restricts movement at the perimeter, one is most likely to deter the opportunistic intruder who creates the preponderance of problems for security professionals. Camera surveillance as well as automatic gates and barriers are the keystones of any state-of-the-art perimeter security plan."[14]

In the wake of the 1995 Oklahoma City bombing, the United States has deployed perimeter protection and physical barriers to more than 160 US embassies and consulates, 110 domestic federal buildings, and 85 percent of all US nuclear power plants. It is clear that America has the ingenuity and a diverse array of technology companies innovating solutions that can be adapted for our long and—along the northern frontier—open borders. But integrating these ingredients in a successful manner, with layers of complementary detection and defense, will require much learning. America's experiences bolstering border security along its southern border during the 1990s will provide much insight for this integration process—but not since the war of 1812 brought America and Britain to war along the Canadian border has America faced an armed and dangerous military threat from across its border. And, in the time since 9/11, the United States has yet to experience any known terrorist infiltration from across its borders, though it has rounded up several domestic terror cells (or wannabe cells) and a few lone-wolf troublemakers.

Notes

1 Office of the Press Secretary, Department of Homeland Security, "President Increases Budget for Border Security," January 25, 2002, www.dhs.gov/xnews/speeches/ speech_0063.shtm.

2 Ibid.

3 Office of the Press Secretary, Department of Homeland Security, "Securing America's Borders Fact Sheet: Border Security," January 25, 2002, www.dhs.gov/xnews/releases/ press_release_0052.shtm.

4 Ibid.

5 Ibid.

6 Mike Trickey, "Canada, U.S. Close to Reaching Border Deal: 'No More Red Light Issues,' Manley says," *The Ottawa Citizen*, March 9, 2002, http://ericsquire.com/articles/ oc030902.htm.

7 "U.S., Canadian Officials Laud Border Security Efforts," June 28, 2002, http://ottawa. usembassy.gov/content/textonly.asp?section=can_usa&subsection1=borderissues&doc ument=borderissues_security_062802.

8 Jason Ackleson, "Border Security in the Wake of 9/11," *La Prensa*, December 20, 2001.

9 Ibid.

10 Ibid.

11 Barry Zellen, "Technology, Strategy and Innovation: Border Security and the War on Terror," SecurityInnovator.com, September 5, 2002, www.securityinnovator.com/index. php?articleID=515&sectionID=25.

12 Bill Spence, "Recognition Systems White Paper: Biometrics in Physical Access Control: Issues, Status, and Trends," November 24, 2002, http://enterpriseinnovator.com/index. php?articleID=687&sectionID=25.

13 Bruce Mehlman, Assistant Secretary for Technology Policy, US Department of Commerce, "Putting Biometrics to Work for America: Remarks to the Biometrics Consortium Conference on February 14, 2002, in Crystal City, Virginia,"

SecurityInnovator.com, November 24, 2002, http://securityinnovator.com/index.php?articleID=694&sectionID=25.
14 Delta Scientific White Paper, "For Governments Today, Security Starts with the Perimeter," November 24, 2002, http://nextinnovator.com/index.php?articleID=803&sectionID=31.

6

Counterterrorism Mentors:
Allied Insights and Lessons

Lessons from the Holy Land: Israeli insights on secure borders

America's closest Middle East ally, Israel, has been fighting terror from across its borders since its birth in 1948. Much can be learned from its experiences fighting terrorism, most notably the suicidal "martyrdom operations" that have claimed hundreds of lives before its West Bank security fence stopped the bloodshed. The Israelis, long accustomed to terrorism, have approached the problem creatively, juggling an ever-changing mix of political, military, and technology solutions. As Israel's Ministry of Defense website observed in 2002: "Even today, as civilians have become the daily target of various terrorist groups, over 80 percent of all planned attacks are aborted through sophisticated early warning technologies and intelligence capabilities."[1] Israel was at the time constructing a new security fence along the boundary between Israel proper and the West Bank, where most of its recent terror had originated, as well as in Jerusalem. Israel had twice before—in 1994 and 2001—considered such a Manhattan Project–scaled initiative to enhance its security along the entire West Bank, but the high price of the project (up to $2 million per mile) and the politics of disengagement prevented it from going forward. After 18 months of terrorism and over 500 lives lost, that calculus had changed. Now, neither its high price tag nor Israel's political aversion to marking a boundary between Israel proper and the West Bank stand in the way. The new security fence would thus wind its way along the entire West Bank, replacing what has been described by AP journalist Yoav Appel as a "hodgepodge" of barriers and fences constructed during its last surge in terror, but which were easily by-passed.[2] Israel's defense minister, Binyamin Ben-Eliezer, observed that the new security fence was not meant to define an international border, or erect a permanent wall between the Palestinian and Israeli people. Rather, "it has one and only one clear aim—to defend the lives of Israeli citizens."[3]

Yarden Vatikay, the spokesman for Defense Minister Ben-Eliezer, told me the strategic objective for the new security fence along the West Bank was simply "to stop the infiltration of the suicide bombers, and by extension, explosives and other arms, from the West Bank and Jerusalem to Israel proper. It's very simple!"[4] Vatikay said that "altogether, the fence will be more than 350 kilometers long." Only the first portion of the fence has been authorized by Israel's Cabinet to date, and that will be 115 km long, or around 70 miles, running along "the main areas of the infiltration," from Salem Junction in northern Israel to just northeast of Tel Aviv. Work has also begun on a shorter security fence to protect Jerusalem, with two segments: one 7 km long, and the other 9 km. The idea of deploying a security fence to mitigate and prevent terrorism is not a new one in Israel. The Gaza Strip is already encircled by a security fence, and has been for a couple of years, according to Vatikay, who observed there "has been almost zero infiltration, due to the fact that the Gaza Strip is surrounded by fence."

As for the technology used to enhance Israel's security fence's functionality, Vatikay said that "all kinds of detectors and means to give us early warnings are used. For us, the goal is to prevent the infiltration, we don't want the terrorists to reach the fence, we want them to be stopped by us in advance and therefore you need all kinds of obstacles in the area before the fence, and you need all sorts of means as I said to detect them. And if they reach the fence, this would be the last line."

At the Israeli Pavilion at Eurosatory 2002, held during June 17–21, Israel's border security system was on display for the first time. A statement on the defense ministry's website explained: "We believe that [border] security tasks cannot be achieved using a single piece of equipment or sensor, but rather a full string of sensors and equipment integrated together to form a comprehensive system. The heart of this system is a central command, control and operation system that coordinate and route information and activities."[5] Rachel Naidek Ashkenazi, a spokesperson for Israel's Ministry of Defense, told me the Ministry of Defense prefers to call the security fence a "Buffer Zone," as its concept of security is to provide layers of early detection and defense, including but not limited to the physical fence structure itself.[6]

The Israeli Defense Force's (IDF) border security concept incorporates the following activities: Detection and warning, surveillance and tracking of suspected targets, establishment of operational intelligence and support of information received from other sources, improvement of reaction time and capabilities of reaction forces, prevention of infiltration, creating a deterrent, and supporting routine operational activities. The components required to achieve this concept were developed by a variety of vendors in Israel's defense industry, in accordance with IDF needs and technical specifications. The resulting border security system consists of the following elements: passive sensors deployed at tactical points for early warning; observation aerostats including day and night surveillance capabilities; observation towers including day/night and radar surveillance system; hovering observation and surveillance provided by interface to an unattended aerial vehicle (UAV; mobile observation systems including day/night and radar surveillance system; electronic fence for intrusion detection and warning; and a command and control system for integrating all system elements and enabled to create a situation display in real time for the different levels.

Ashkenazi told me that the decision had not yet been made about which new technology components would be integrated into the West Bank security fence—but she noted that among its many elements, thermo-imaging, electro-optics, and UAV systems were being considered. "As far as technology means are concerned, the operational requirement will be defined by the IDF. At this point of time, nothing has been decided yet," she said. Vatikay added: "We are still in the early stage to determine which kinds of devices exactly will be used, what sort of monitoring devices will be there," noting that as with Israel's earlier fences, the West Bank security fence will deploy a variety of technologies from Israel's security industry.

But every bit as important as technology, Vatikay explained, is the human factor: vigilance and troop support. "The Gaza fence is not standing on its own—we have a lot of forces supporting and acting on two sides of the fence. We have, as they say, all the means we need to detect terrorists, and they understand this—[that is why] they are not even exactly trying [from Gaza]. They are trying from the West Bank, which is of course open—there is no fence, there is nothing. So they are concentrating on infiltrating from the West Bank into Israel proper."

Israel's security fence captured headlines in news media around the world— suggesting that the fence offers up a profound new metaphor for separating warring parties. Associated Press journalist Yoav Appel wrote an article in July 2002 called "The Great Wall of Israel."[7] Ross Dunn, in Australia's *The Age*, posted an article on June 12, 2002, with the title, "Israel Starts Work on Its Berlin Wall."[8] And a Slate.com editorial published on May 8, 2002, by Warren Bass, director of the Terrorism Program at the Council on Foreign Relations and editor of its Terrorism: Questions and Answers website, has the title "Hitting the Wall: Why a West Bank Fence Won't Protect Israel."[9] Journalists, everywhere it seems, had jumped on the Wall metaphor.

While headlines screamed "Great Wall," "Berlin Wall," and so forth, Vatikay stated emphatically: "There is no wall!" He added: "It is a fence, like every other fence, with passageways, with everything. What is it, a wall? A Chinese Wall? Come on, really— there is nothing to that, it is not a wall." According to Vatikay, sealing off the West Bank "wasn't thinkable earlier because a year, a year and a half ago, we did not stand in a situation where, let's say, [there are] sometimes around five to six attempts to infiltrate Israel each day and explode themselves in buses and discos and restaurants and at parties, etc . . . We were in a different situation, we thought there is still a chance to sort things out and stop the terror by using political means. But right now, after a year and a half of massive terror and mainly suicide bombers, we have no other choice. There is no other alternative." But Vatikay believes the fence may come down some day, "when Arafat decides to stop the terror, and when the Palestinians address Israel in order to reach an agreement. Then, we would be happy to do everything in coexistence because we believe our existence here with the Palestinians should be in coexistence. But this is so far away, as we see with the Palestinian terror policy."

As the frequency—and ferocity—of terrorist attacks originating in the West Bank accelerated to intolerable levels prior to the fence's construction, the political will to "disengage" physically from the West Bank finally crystallized. As Vatikay observed: "When you have 560 Israelis murdered in a year and a half, of course there is a lot of public demand to do your utmost to provide security." The case for disengagement was argued by former prime minister Ehud Barak, in a widely read *New York Times* op-ed. Barak argued that "Israel must embark on unilateral disengagement from the Palestinians and establish a system of security fences. Israel's very future depends on this. Only such a border could secure a solid Jewish majority inside Israel for generations to come, and in so doing secure Israel as a democracy and its identity as a Jewish state." Barak explained that "the immediate and long-term result of installing the security fence, with sensors and military forces along it, would be a dramatic reduction in suicide attacks inside Israel. Around the Gaza Strip there is a fence, and there are practically no suicide attacks originating from Gaza." The logic of disengagement as a tool to fight terror in the absence of an immediate political solution quickly permeated Israeli society—and within weeks of Barak's articulation of his vision of disengagement, actual fence construction had begun along the West Bank and in Jerusalem.

As America began to grapple with its own security challenges since 9/11, and worked to create a "Secure and Smart" border, it began considering various technologies and systems to bolster its security along its 7,500 borders with its neighbors, which like the West Bank's open, rolling border is mostly not fenced off. Fortunately for America, its neighbors have in recent generations been more friendly, so it does not face the same frequency or intensity of terrorist infiltration. But as it learned when US customs agents arrested a would-be Al Qaeda bomber on the eve of the Y2K Millennium celebration at a US/Canadian border crossing in Washington state with a trunk full of bomb-making components, its long and open border—particularly along the northern frontier, where the war on drugs had less impact—is vulnerable to terrorist infiltration, too. America could thus learn from Israel's experience and determination in the face of persistent terror, and its half a century of experience creating a layered border security system that integrates traditional security fences with state-of-the-art surveillance and early detection systems, backed up by old-fashioned vigilance. As Vatikay said: "Although I think that the threats we face are different—but of course, if America wants any advice or help, they know our address!"

Lessons from the "scariest place on earth": For over a half century, technology has tamed the Korean DMZ

It's not the first time that technology has stood sentinel before such a grave threat. Just as the Israelis have long applied technology in the defense of their border security, the South Koreans, in conjunction with their war-time allies the United States, have relied upon technology to secure the demilitarized zone (DMZ) separating North and South Korea, a border zone once described by former US president Bill Clinton as "the scariest place on earth."[10] And during a visit to the DMZ in January 1998, former defense secretary William S. Cohen said the DMZ was "perhaps the hottest flash point in the world." Well, with Pyongyang now a nuclear power and on its way to deploying an intercontinental missile capability, it's hotter than ever.

In October 2002, Pyongyang—smarting from its inclusion in the "Axis of Evil," and increasingly worried about the new US doctrine of preemption as the US conflict with Iraq escalated—admitted to an illegal nuclear weapons development program in the hopes of deterring a US preemptive strike. The North Korean declaration of a nuclear weapons capability triggered an international crisis, and suddenly the DMZ was hotter than ever. In his February 24, 2003, *Time Magazine* article, "Kim's War Machine," Donald Macintyre wrote that earlier this year, "North Korea has taken yet another step toward building multiple atomic weapons," reactivating its Yongbyon nuclear reprocessing facility, suggesting that Kim Jong Il "appears to have concluded that his country can't win a war without the ultimate weapon," and that "he needs an equalizer like the Bomb because his military almost certainly lacks the capacity to win a prolonged ground conflict involving conventional forces—the most likely scenario should a conflict erupt across the DMZ between North and South Korea."[11]

Indeed, on June 9, North Korea explicitly linked—for the first time—its quest for nuclear arms to the idea it could save money and help revive its struggling economy. An editorial from North Korea's official news agency said nuclear weapons would enable Pyongyang to reduce its standing army of more than one million troops, and to redirect the funds to badly needed economic development. North Korea believes it needs nuclear weapons to deter a possible US attack, particularly in the wake of a US-led war against Iraq over the issue of WMD. The United States has asked North Korea to reduce its massive deployment of conventional forces near the inter-Korean border—but North Korea has emphasized the importance it sees in using military force to stave off a possible US attack in the wake of the war against Iraq. Pyongyang keeps two-third of its 1.1 million-strong military near the border. "If the US keeps threatening the DPRK [Democratic People's Republic of Korea] with nukes instead of abandoning its hostile policy toward Pyongyang, the DPRK will have no option but to build up a nuclear deterrent force," the official media said.[12]

Eye-to-eye across the DMZ

The DMZ is considered by military experts to be the world's most heavily fortified border. Along both sides of the DMZ—some two to three miles deep, and 151 miles long—nearly two million soldiers face off, trapped in a twilight zone leftover from the Cold War, a no-man's land that is neither peace nor war. Dotted with watchtowers, razor wire, land mines, tank-traps, and heavy weapons systems, the DMZ is less a national boundary, and certainly not intended to be a permanent border, and though it has stood for half a century, it is in fact little more than a temporary armistice line. Beneath the DMZ are thought to be dozens of tunnels dug by the North Koreans as surprise invasion routes for battalions of tanks, several of which have been discovered by the South in years past. But others remain hidden, and North Korean DMZ penetrations continue as they have for decades.

North Koreans have penetrated the DMZ along many routes—most simply walk into South Korea, through the largely mountainous DMZ, where, in this age of advanced surveillance technology, it can still be difficult to spot a handful of people at night. The DMZ's alpine cliffs and forests as well as lowland brush still provide hiding places, and hidden tunnels still remain. Infiltration by sea is also popular, as the North Korean Navy possesses a fleet of subs, mini-subs, gunboats, and merchant ships capable of ferrying agents onto South Korean shores; infiltration by air continues, by helicopters masquerading as belonging to the United States or the Republic of Korea (ROK), or by aircraft.

The ROK Army (ROKA) provides most of the front line military forces south of the DMZ, as well as the 1,024 DMZ Civil Police authorized by the Armistice agreement to man 114 guard posts along the southern side. A small number of American soldiers perform DMZ duties inside the zone, assigned to the United Nations Command (UNC)

Security Force-Joint Security Area (JSA), which supports the Military Armistice Commission (MAC) either as security guards or in administrative, communications, and logistics missions. (The UNCMAC Secretariat is the staff agency responsible for ensuring that UNC units comply with the 1953 truce, making sure UNC and component forces do not violate the truce, and investigating and reporting to MAC all the details relating to violations by either side.)

No ordinary border

Though the last large-scale battle waged along this frontline was a full half century ago, the two Koreas remain technically in a state of war, and dozens of border incidents, claiming hundreds of lives, have reminded both sides that this is no ordinary border. Indeed, over 50 military incidents along DMZ and the coast since 1953 have left 677 dead, including 62 Americans.

The ROK faces the immediate threat of a heavily armed, million-man plus North Korean military force, the majority of which is forward deployed in fortifications near the DMZ. On the southern side are some 560,000 South Korean troops and some 37,000 Americans. Over the past two decades, the DPRK has increasingly deployed its combat forces forward, so that the majority of North Korea's active duty combat forces are arrayed behind the DMZ in a menacing attack position, and in 1999, it forward deployed additional artillery systems to hardened sites along the DMZ. Military readiness of key elements of the force, including artillery, Special Operations Forces (SOF), and mechanized units, has been improved through ambitious training cycles. The DPRK continues to augment its forward corps with large numbers of long-range artillery and multiple-rocket launchers, and to develop weapons of mass destruction and their associated delivery systems, including rapidly improving ballistic missile capabilities and its recently verified nuclear weapons program, declared in 2006 and demonstrated later that year with what appeared to be a partial detonation, and more persuasively communicated in 2009 with an undeniably successful detonation.

Yet while the DMZ remains a powder keg unlike any other on earth, a flashpoint capable of triggering total warfare, it is oddly enough becoming a popular tourist zone, providing hundreds of thousands of visitors with a glimpse of one of the few remnants of the Cold War that once divided much of the world. In a 1989 article in *VFW* magazine titled "DMZ: Dangerous and Unpredictable," Richard K. Kolb described the DMZ as "a barren collar stretched around the neck of a dragon to keep its two heads from biting each other," and that the "soldiers charged with keeping that dragon at bay are in an unenviable position."[13] He cited William Hollinger, who described the DMZ in *The Fence-Walker* as "a landscape of nightmare, this wasteland of a demilitarized zone: artillery craters, barbed wire, minefields, graveyards, the skeletons of villages and the remains of rice paddies. The earth has been shelled, mined, overgrown, booby-trapped, burned and abandoned to grow wild yet another time."[14] And ironically—because the DMZ has been immune from the sort of development and land use experienced to its south and north—it has evolved into a sanctuary for endangered species driven to, or near, extinction outside the zone. According to DMZForum.org, "while economic development has ravaged much of the land elsewhere in the two Koreas, the border area has become the peninsula's most important animal refuge," with "rare birds and animals, including endangered cranes, egrets and bears, and perhaps even leopards and tigers" that "coexist with soldiers and minefields on terrain that ranges from rugged, forested hills to wetlands and rice paddies."[15]

A tense no-man's land

The DMZ has witnessed frequent, though minor, military clashes since the 1953 armistice—and the DMZ is more like a tense no-man's land rather than a secure buffer zone. The risk of surprise attack from across the DMZ is a constant threat to military and political stability on the Korean peninsula. If the North crosses the DMZ in force, the United States remains bound by its 1954 treaty, blessed by the UN, to defend South Korea; the US troop presence, often described as a "tripwire" linked directly to the frontline defense of South Korea, is really a mobile reserve force meant for rear action to help push back an invading North Korean army.

Indeed, as if to remind the nation and the world of this, in early June 2003, US Defense Secretary Donald Rumsfeld announced US troops would pull back from the DMZ, where they were stationed for the last half century—out of the line of fire of North Korean artillery, and into a better defensive position south of Seoul. And though the troop shift wasn't scheduled until 2004, the United States expected North Korea will perceive the US move as a hostile act, one indicative of a US step closer to war. As reported in the *Wall Street Journal*: "North Korea has long assumed that in advance of a war, the US would pull its troops away from the demilitarized zone that separates North and South to avoid a withering hail of North Korean artillery shells and rockets."[16] From the safety of their new position, the US troops can "drive north, supported by air power from South Korea, Guam and Japan."[17] The United States has the capability for high-speed sealift of troops stationed in Japan, and thousands of marines stationed in Okinawa can be ferried across the Sea of Japan to reinforce South Korea in less then 48 hours using high-speed transport ships.

Quantity versus quality

North Korea's armed might along the northern edge of the DMZ is numerically superior to that of the ROK, and as reported in the *Seattle Times*, "the North's edge is more than matched by US and South weaponry support and technology."[18] Indeed, the ROK Navy enjoyed a decisive victory in a sea skirmish near Yonpyong in June 1999, demonstrating that ROK naval weapon systems and combat capability are superior to those of North Korea. If Pyongyang does attack first, "the casualties could exceed one million, largely because of its chemical arsenals," and though the United States and South Korea "would almost certainly win any war on the Korean peninsula," the price of that victory would "be appalling."[19] In the event of a North Korean first strike, "South

Korean defenses could be pulverized for several hours by as many as 500,000 artillery rounds per hour from North Korean positions just 30 miles from Seoul. North Korea's 500 to 600 Scud missiles, many carrying chemical weapons, could pound targets across South Korea, and longer-range missiles could hit civilian and US military targets as far away as Japan and possibly even America's West Coast."[20] But in spite of the devastation the North could unleash on South Korea, neighboring Japan, and the western United States, "there's a wide consensus that combined US and South Korean forces would eventually win. North Korea doesn't have the fuel, spare parts or air power to win a sustained war against forces as imposing as the United States and South Korea" and "North Korea's tanks and aircraft are obsolete."[21] Thousands of well-armed, well-trained US and ROK troops guard the border, "precision missiles are already targeting North Korean positions, land mines and razor wire are blocking the invasion route across the North–South border, South Korean ships are patrolling coastal waters and U-2 spy planes are keeping close watch on North Korea's military."

Defensive layers and defensive topology

Anticipated North Korean attack routes are heavily defended by hardened ROK defenses densely packed along the DMZ. The ROK has a series of defensive lines that cross the peninsula, designed to withstand an attack until counterattack forces are assembled. The Korea Barrier System (KBS) is an in-depth, integrated series of obstacles, including minefields, concertina wire, and dragon's teeth arrayed in three concentric defense lines called the Forward Edge of Battle Areas (or FEBAs) in the South. However, on the northern side of the DMZ there are no such defensive fortifications.

With 151 miles of border zone stretching between the two Koreas, half blocked by mountains, the topography of the DMZ is not exactly conducive for rapid offensive thrusts, and this gives ROK defensive forces a measurable advantage. Logical attack routes and preventive bridge and road demolition can help to funnel an attacking force in a narrow "kill zone" targeted by ROK defensive weaponry in hardened bunkers. But this defensive advantage is less evident in winter, which opens up more attack routes. So as powerful as the North Korean military machine is, just a fraction of its firepower can be brought to bear against the ROK, whose longer-range and more accurate weapons systems, protected by strong defensive positions, can pack a greater punch. So while both Koreas have a menacing amount of artillery arrayed along the DMZ, the ROK's defensive forces have a topological advantage.

Mines

One element of the DMZ that has come under political fire, particularly since the Ottawa Treaty banning land mines came into existence, is the use of antipersonnel mines within the DMZ. When the US and ROK armed forces erected a barrier system separating North and South Korea, it included an estimated two million antipersonnel land mines in the DMZ, and a million more land mines in the six-mile wide Military Control Zone south of the DMZ. It is now the only such static emplacement of land mines used in defense of US forces, as a similar landmine barrier system protecting the US base in Guantánamo Bay, Cuba, was dismantled in 1998, and considered essential to the ROK and US military for completing defensive preparations in the event of war.

Artillery

The North Koreans have two different 240-mm rocket launchers—the 12-round M-1985 and 22-round M-1991. Hundreds of these multiple rocket launchers (MRLs) are deployed along the DMZ, posing a significant military (and psychological) threat to Seoul and surrounding communities, where the majority of South Koreans live. In addition to its 240-mm MRLs, North Korea has also deployed 170-mm self-propelled guns in hardened underground bunkers near the DMZ, which are difficult to target—and capable of raining 10,000 artillery rounds on the nation's capital. In 1996, Combined Forces Command (CFC) in Korea recognized the urgency of this threat, and the US Joint Precision Strike Demonstration (JPSD) program has been working on a solution.

The Precision/Rapid Counter-Multiple Rocket Launch (CMRL) Advanced Concept Technology Demonstration (ACTD) developed and demonstrated a new adverse weather, day/night, end-to-end, sensor-to-shooter, precision deep strike capability, capable of neutralizing the threat posed by the 240-mm MRLs and 170-mm Self-Propelled (SP) Guns deployed just north of the DMZ in North Korea. In addition, Theater Precision Strike Operations (TPSO) will develop an enhanced joint and combined, sensor-to-shooter, C4I system that incorporates intelligence, surveillance, and reconnaissance (ISR); rapid targeting and shared Common Operating Picture (COP), all linked through command, control, communication, and computer systems to responsive weapons delivery systems. In addition, a Rapid Terrain Visualization (RTV) ACTD is developing the capability of rapidly producing high-resolution digital terrain products for US early entry combat forces. In February 1999, Raytheon was awarded a five-year, $95 million follow-on contract by the US Army Topographic Engineering Center to support execution of the JPSD program.

Aerial surveillance

Circling high and low above the DMZ is an armada of aerial surveillance platforms, ranging from Korea-based U2 high-altitude surveillance aircraft, persistent sea- and ground-launched UAVs—an increasingly important element in the aerial component of DMZ surveillance, and Japan-based USAF RC-135 Rivet Joint surveillance planes, RC-7 Airborne Reconnaissance Low aircraft, and propeller-driven Navy EP-3 Aries II reconnaissance planes—all watching closely over the battlefield below, frozen in time since 1953. (The OV-1 Mohawk, which entered production in 1959, flew 24/7 above the DMZ from 1964 through 1996, providing early warning on enemy activity using a variety of sensors, including still and infrared photography and side-looking airborne radar. It was returned when the RC-7 came along.)

EP-3 spy planes are propeller-driven Navy reconnaissance planes based in Japan, and used to conduct electronic warfare and reconnaissance throughout East Asia. Capable of over 12 hours of continuous flight, and with a range of about 3,000 nautical miles, the EP-3 is equipped with electronic surveillance equipment for SIGINT collection to reveal the location, and intention, of enemy forces and report on threatening activity. The RC-7 was developed a decade ago to provide counterinsurgency and counternarcotics surveillance for US Southern Command, has been used to support peacekeeping operations in Bosnia, and is currently deployed in South Korea to provide surveillance along the DMZ. According to John Pike, director of GlobalSecurity.org, the RC-7 has a number of different sensors on them including high-powered radar, communications intercept capabilities to monitor radios, and telescopic video, as well as lowlight and nocturnal infrared surveillance capabilities. The RC-135 is equipped with multiple electronic receivers. It has large circular windows in the fuselage for the photography of foreign ballistic-missile tests at long range, and has multiple infrared telescopes.

Four North Korean fighter jets intercepted a US Air Force plane over the Sea of Japan on March 2, 2003. Two North Korean MiG-29 fighters and two other North Korean aircraft believed to be MiG-23s engaged an American RC-135S "Rivet Joint" reconnaissance aircraft on a routine mission 150 miles off the coast of North Korea. The *New York Times* has characterized it as an attempt to force the US jet to land in North Korea and take its crew hostage. Defense officials say the incident is the first such direct hostile act by North Korea since MiG-17 fighters from that country shot down a US Navy EC-121 reconnaissance plane over the Sea of Japan in April 1969, killing all 31 persons aboard, and 15 months earlier, North Korean sailors boarded and captured USS Pueblo off the coast of North Korea.

The North Koreans claim US RC-135 flights have "intruded into North Korean airspace above the country's east coast almost every day since February 21," and that the United States conducted more than 220 spy flights over its territory in March, a 40-flight increase from February. In response, the United States deployed 24 B1 and B52 bombers to Guam to deter an escalation by Pyongyang. North Korea said 220 further cases of aerial espionage were committed against it in April, by RC-135s, RC-12s, RC-7s, U2s, and EP-3s.

The ROK later accused the DPRK of violating its airspace with a MiG-19. *Xinhua News* reported that a North Korean MiG-19 crossed the North Limit Line (the de-facto border between North and South) and was met by six ROK Air Force F-5E fighters. The MiG-19 returned to DPRK airspace right away, but it was the first aerial incursion by the DPRK since 1983.

Earlier that year, on January 27, 2003, an American U2 reconnaissance jet, part of the 5th Reconnaissance Squadron based at South Korea's Osan Air Base, crash-landed about six miles from the base on its way back from a mission over the DMZ. Ideal for intelligence gathering, it flies above 20,000 meters—well beyond the range of North Korean anti-aircraft range—and provides continuous night and day surveillance. Pilots assigned to the 5th Reconnaissance Squadron have flown more than 7,000 sorties in U2s on the peninsula since 1976.

The missile threat

North Korea continues to enhance its ballistic missile capabilities and—in conjunction with its nuclear weapons program—is increasingly becoming a strategic threat not just to the ROK but to neighboring Japan as well as the continental United States. As reported in the February 28, 2003, edition of *Yomiuri Shimbun*, Pyongyang had "tested a rocket booster in January at a Taepodong ballistic missile launch site."[22] Japan and the United States announced a joint "plan to improve their monitoring of the facility by deploying electronic surveillance aircraft and other surveillance devices," including space-based platforms, as US satellite intelligence showed the launch facility to be heavily camouflaged and equipped with a fiber-optic network, making it difficult for "conventional information-gathering methods, such as intercepts of North Korea's radio transmissions, to detect signs of a missile launch."[23]

In response, Japan launched its first two reconnaissance satellites in March, primarily to keep an eye on North Korea—and generating strong North Korean criticism. Pyongyang said Japan's launch of the spy satellites "seriously violated the spirit of the [DPRK–Japan Pyongyang Declaration] that calls on both sides to refrain from threatening each other and sparked a new arms race in Northeast Asia."[24] *Voice of America* reported that Pyongyang "has alarmed Tokyo over the past several years, and especially in the last six months, with a series of acts that Tokyo views as highly provocative. They include restarting banned nuclear facilities and withdrawing from the nuclear Non-Proliferation Treaty."[25] And when North Korea launched an intermediate-range missile over Japan in 1998, it caught Tokyo and Washington by surprise, demonstrating "Pyongyang had the ability to reach Japan with missile-based weapons" and prompting Japan "to move forward with a program to develop its own surveillance capabilities, instead of having to rely on US intelligence data."[26]

On August 31, 1998, North Korea surprised much of the world when it test-fired its intermediate-range Taepodong I, which flew over Japan and landed in the Pacific Ocean. Japan believes that North Korea had been continuing its missile development program by conducting missile engine tests once or twice a year since autumn 1999, but it has not launched any further missiles. A Taepodong I missile has a range of 1,500 kilometers. The longer-range Taepodong II is believed to combine a new rocket engine as its first stage, and a short-range Rodong missile as its second-stage booster—putting the western United States at risk.

Improved C4I

According to a 2000 Report to Congress, *Military Situation on the Korean Peninsula*, the United States and the ROK have "adopted a security strategy that emphasizes deterrence and defense," requiring "the combined defense team to maintain constant awareness of the DPRK's intentions, respond to acts of North Korean provocation, and should deterrence fail, demonstrate resolve by deploying key US augmentation forces to support ROK forces. The cornerstone of deterrence is the unity of and strength of the ROK and US alliance."[27] In pursuit of these objectives, the report noted that "planners are faced with a significant adverse geographical fact: the capital city of Seoul, the military, political, economic, and cultural core of the ROK, lies only 40 kilometers from the DMZ and is highly vulnerable to a North Korean ground or artillery attack. Reflecting this defense imperative, the combined ROK/US forces are forward deployed to defend the capital and prevent large-scale peacetime infiltration by the DPRK."[28]

To strengthen the alliance and improve joint military capabilities, the United States and the ROK routinely engage in bilateral mutual security consultations and continuously seek improvements to its warfighting capability through its combined exercise program, close contact with wartime component commands, and capability enhancements through the appropriate national military command and service component channels. The combined forces also work to enhance interoperability, effective command and control systems, critical equipment acquisition, and logistical sustainability, which are key areas of effort to improve the combined combat force capability.

The ROK has long-realized the need for advanced technology to tip the strategic balance in its favor, and the profound need to deploy that technology along the DMZ for early detection and surveillance of North Korean intentions. The ROK Defense Improvement Plan (DIP) was initiated in 1976 to modernize and improve the combat effectiveness of South Korea's armed forces, and in recent years, the ROK has focused on securing its tactical early warning systems. Its navy has an advanced submarine program as well an expanding maritime surveillance program including naval air force ASW/maritime surveillance aircraft outfitted in 2000 with Inverse Synthetic Aperture Radar to increase its maritime patrol capabilities and P-3C aircraft to enhance the ROK Navy's maritime surveillance capability. Recent C3I improvements include using the US Navy's Global Command & Control System—Maritime (GCCS-M) and UHF SATCOM as its communications backbone as well as a new wide area network intelligence fusion and dissemination system connecting the fleet commanders and ROK Navy Headquarters, and the Korean Naval Tactical Data System.

For the last few years, South Korea has been bolstering its tactical data systems, and shifting to an automated command and control system to increase its capability for effective command and control. The ROK's communications systems were originally designed without combined interoperability in mind, and to compensate, it is working to improve its secure telephone and data encryption, interoperability of command post systems, and electronic interface of automated intelligence systems. Annual combined theater-level exercises with both ROK and US troops are conducted in a joint and combined environment to further improve cooperation, coordination, communication, and interoperability.

The WATCHCON system

According to GlobalSecurity.org, the ROK's "reconnaissance posture for strategic and tactical warning of attack" is called the Watch Condition—or WATCHCON—system.

It has four stages: WATCHCON 4 (normal peacetime position), WATCHCON 3 (important indications of threat), WATCHCON 2 (vital indications of threat), and WATCHCON 1 (wartime situation).[29] The WATCHCON level is raised by agreement of ROK and US military intelligence authorities, and around 180 notable North Korean military movements are on the "Indication and Warning Lists," and regularly monitored, depending on the WATCHCON level. In "normal" times—as much as normalcy is possible on the Korean Peninsula—South Korea maintains a WATCHCON 3 status.

Biochem sensors

One futuristic sensor recently deployed in the ROK for testing is called the Early Warning Outbreak Recognition System (EWORS), a software-driven surveillance tool that monitors, and analyzes, the signs and symptoms of patients reporting to medical treatment facilities with suspected infectious diseases. EWORS was developed at the US Naval Medical Research Unit No. 2 (NAMRU-2) in collaboration with the Indonesian Ministry of Health, and has been used in the public health sectors of Indonesia, Cambodia, Vietnam, and Laos. EWORS provides the added advantage of early detection of possible bioterror hazards by immediately recognizing patterns of syndromic case clustering.

Until recently, EWORS had not been applied in a military operational setting. However, in 2001, NAMRU-2 and the ROKA began working on an initiative to install EWORS technology in a pilot program at two field medical units and at the ROKA headquarters in Daejon. Early recognition is the intent of the ROKA, and while EWORS is not intended to replace conventional surveillance activities, it provides a targeted strategy that accommodates the timely and reliable requirements associated with early warning. In September 2002, NAMRU-2 personnel visited the ROK to make final revisions to the EWORS software, train Korean personnel in EWORS use, and test the newly installed pilot network, and in October 2002, EWORS was inaugurated for daily disease surveillance. EWORS operates with a host server that coordinates and receives data from field sites. In ROK, the host unit is the medical headquarters located in Daejon, and the two field sites selected for the pilot project are the 3rd and 6th Division medical units of the 3rd ROKA. The field sites are both in the northern section of the country, within ten miles of the DMZ, and the soldiers served by these medical units include infantry and artillery personnel deployed up to the border of the DMZ.

Sensor wars

On March 25, 2003, the American Forces Press Service reported that the face of future conflict will be an "escalating sensor war," as war becomes automated, and offensive threats such as that posed by North Korea become neutralized by automated, computerized weapons systems that create a seamless and lightning fast sensor-to-shooter network. Gerry J. Gilmore wrote: "Military commanders of the future will employ high-tech sensing equipment to detect the strength and positions of enemy forces, including those attempting to hide from prying electronic eyes."[30]

For instance, earth-orbiting satellites provide considerable sensor capability for US military planners today, so "America's enemies have invested heavily in finding ways to foil potential surveillance," by hiding or moving military assets, or employing deception techniques as the North Koreans have mastered.[31] "Consequently, the U.S. military's investment in sensor-related technology is going up."[32] As "potential enemies develop their abilities 'to sense and to strike,'" America will have to adapt in order to maintain its edge in the forthcoming "sensor wars."[33]

DoD's UAV roadmap

A fixture of the emerging, "netcentric" battlefield that is quickly becoming a reality—as 2003's "Shock and Awe" campaign of precision strikes against Baghdad demonstrated—is the uber-platform known as the UAV. As the *Air Force Print News* reported on March 28, 2003, the US DoD has unveiled its UAV Roadmap in Congressional testimony on March 26, which seeks to "ensure UAV programs proceed in a coordinated and efficient manner in order to move capability into the hands of the warfighter as soon as possible."[34] Operation Enduring Freedom provided "just a glimpse of the contributions UAVs can make on the battlefield of the future."[35] The Predator was one of the first ADCT demonstrators that "transitioned to a service and was successfully integrated into their force structure," and more than ten UAV systems in development were used for support operations in Operation Iraqi Freedom.[36] The Air Force's Predator, Global Hawk and Force Protection Surveillance System, provided warfighters with "a very broad capability," hinting at the transformation that pervasive surveillance coupled with sensor-to-shooter weapons systems will bring to the battlefield of the future— giving the United States and its allies an enhanced capability to adapt to new and emerging military threats.[37]

In an earlier *Air Force Print News* article, it was reported that the "Air Force's deputy chief of staff for air and space operations is cautiously optimistic about the growing role of unmanned aerial vehicles and remotely piloted vehicles in future conflicts," as "technology and miniaturization can now begin to give us things we haven't been able to do before."[38] Lt. Gen. Ronald E. Keys observed that UAVs let the Air Force "look at things adversaries don't want me to see," and to "stay in the area for a long time."[39] Keys added: "We'll have the ability to go into denied areas, and people won't know we're there looking at things they don't know we're looking at."[40] In short, DoD's UAV Roadmap seems to lead directly to the DMZ, where overhead, pervasive surveillance is increasingly necessary.

DMZ as electronic metaphor

The DMZ is so menacing, so worrisome, and so ominous a realm that it has become a metaphor in the electronic, digital world of computer science. According to TechTarget. com, the term "DMZ" stands for a computer host or small network inserted as a "neutral zone" between a company's private network and the outside public network. It prevents outside users from getting direct access to a server that has company data.[41] The term comes specifically from the geographic buffer zone set up between North Korea and South. While a DMZ may typically include a company's web pages, so these could be served to the outside world, it provides no direct access to any business-critical company data. Thus, if a hacker penetrates the DMZ, the worst case is that a company's web pages might be corrupted but no other company information would be exposed. Cisco, the leading maker of routers, is one company that sells products designed for setting up a DMZ.

Rethinking electronic barriers

With the emerging landscape of sensor warfare, and the emerging pervasive, ubiquitous overhead sensor platform provided by UAVs, the United States and the ROK will increasingly be able to identify and in many cases neutralize emerging threats from the other side of the DMZ. With technological change, the DMZ may manage to evolve beyond its half-century status as a high-risk, hard-to-monitor, sometimes frightening, no-man's land—and into a lasting, defensible, and secure international border. According to a 1985 Marine Corps Command and Staff College report, *Defeating Insurgency on the Border*, this was the dream, back in 1957, when the French constructed the then–state-of-the-art "Morice Line" along Algeria's 200-mile frontier with Tunisia, an elaborate barrier from the Mediterranean Sea to the Sahara Desert— featuring 8-foot high electric fences flanked by 45-meter minefields, barbed wire, and a footpath patrolled day and night by boots on the ground.[42] If the fence was penetrated, it triggered an instant reaction from 105-mm howitzers, and attacks by mobile strike forces combining helicopters, tanks, and airborne infantry.

Successfully designed to isolate Tunisian-based guerrilla from the civil strife in Algeria, this sort of electronic barrier was never envisioned as a viable strategic barrier against a mightily armed foe. Indeed, the United States had trouble adapting the concept to Vietnam, where it faced a far less menacing foe than along the DMZ in Korea. Even the US Army's 1967 Field Manual 31–16, *Counter Guerrilla Operations*, a "bible" for military operations in Vietnam, mentioned border operations only briefly, as did the 1985 report, *Defeating Insurgency on the Border*: "While certain definite portions of an international land border or shoreline may be placed under effective surveillance and control led by use of static security posts, reserve forces, ground and aerial observers, electronic listening posts, and patrols, the continuous surveillance and control of an extensive land border or shoreline is extremely difficult."[43] A "McNamara Line" was only partly constructed in Vietnam, primarily an electronic barrier using detection sensors and a barbed-wire fence—but it was never extended across the entire Vietnamese DMZ, and guerrillas easily bypassed it by going through Laos, and the use of border barriers was dropped from the lexicon of US counterinsurgency strategy.

But in Korea, an electronic barrier has managed to evolve to offset the many problems imposed by geography and topology, and with new pervasive aerial sensors and sensor-to-shooter weapons systems, even the mighty North Korean foe—with its growing armory of ballistic missiles and WMD—seems to be trapped on its side of the DMZ. Creating this high-tech barrier took a long time, and required half a century of trial and error. As Dr Peter Hayes, executive director of the Berkeley, California–based The Nautilus Institute, explained: "The DMZ in Korea was really the place that the electronic barrier in Vietnam that never happened actually happened."[44]

According to Seymour Deitchman, a private consultant on national security, who served as director of Overseas Defense Research at the Advanced Research Projects Agency (ARPA) where he was responsible for planning and executing ARPA's R&D program on counterinsurgency and related technical matters in support of US military operations in Southeast Asia and some operations in the Middle East, a 1960s effort to adapt seismic sensors—designed originally for use along the Ho Chi Minh Trail—failed, but the South Koreans found a great workaround. Deitchman knew General "Tick" Bonesteel, "who was US/UN commander in Korea at the time, and in conversation one day, we agreed that I would try to get him some of the seismic sensors we had been using against the Ho Chi Minh trails in the Vietnam War, for trial. This was done, and they were implanted along part of the fence along the DMZ. Unfortunately, the sensors had been obtained hastily for Vietnam, through the ARPA Agile program I was running at the time, and they hadn't been tested for cold weather (the usual rebellion against 'MilSpecs'—they were going to be used in the tropics, why waste the time and money, etc., etc.). When the Korean winter set in, the sensors froze in the ground and that was the end of that experiment."[45]

Deitchman added, "the problem I was trying to help solve was North Koreans sneaking up at night and trying to cut holes in the fence. I was told, when I received the sad news about our sensors, that the South Korean Army, not having our bent toward advanced technology, had simply tied large numbers of tin cans closely together on parts of the fence that were prone to attempted infiltration, and the acoustic signal was enough to alert the guards and to scare the infiltrators off." As the expression goes, you've come a long way, baby!

Lessons from the lion city: Singapore takes the lead on nformation awareness, risk assessment, and horizon scanning

Despite the end of the Cold War rivalry and the mitigation of its nuclear arms race that threatened, in the words of famed journalist Jonathan Schell, the very "fate of the Earth," today's post–Cold War world (and in particular, the post-9/11 world) has evolved into an unexpectedly risky place full of hidden dangers and strategic surprises. With a seemingly unforeseeable—or at least *unforeseen*—and unexpectedly swift lethality, external strategic shocks can still strike from beyond the horizon. Today's primary danger lies not in the ballistic overkill of mutual assured destruction (MAD) as held much of the world hostage during the Cold War, but instead in the world's increasing complexity and interconnectedness. And yet today's new, swiftly striking dangers looming just beyond the horizon of our strategic awareness curiously enough provide their very own antidote: with enough compute power and a willingness to break down the traditional "silos" and "stovepipes" that prevent the free flow of information from reaching the key decision-maker in time, analysts could—in theory—push back the horizon of strategic awareness, enabling earlier detection of strategic threats.

While we may never be able to predict the future with crystal-ball clarity, we could—by fostering greater collaboration among the gatekeepers of our strategic intelligence, and integrating classified pools of data with the vast reservoir of open source data—widen the footprint of what's knowable and seeable, so we'll get earlier warning of emerging threats to our national existence. As explained by Ambassador Barry Desker, dean of the S. Rajaratnam School of International Studies at Singapore's Nanyang Technological University in his opening remarks to the International Risk Assessment and Horizon Scanning Symposium held in Singapore on March 19–20, 2007: "Today, the current threat environment is marked by complexity and uncertainty. Thanks to what the journalist Tom Friedman calls the 'democratizations' of finance, information and technology, many nations are becoming increasingly vulnerable to a range of asymmetric threats such as transnational terrorism, financial shocks, pandemics and supply chain fragility."[46]

The spirit of TIA

The United States recognized this in those fiery moments of strategic shock following the 9/11 attacks, and sought to remedy the solution with the briefly lived Total Information Awareness (TIA) program, and its Information Awareness Office (IAO), conceived by the Defense Advanced Research Projects Agency (DARPA). According to the online encyclopedia *Wikipedia*, the IAO was established in January 2002 "to bring together several DARPA projects focused on applying information technology to counter transnational threats to national security."[47] IAO's research "was conducted along five major investigative paths: secure collaboration problem solving; structured discovery; link and group understanding; context aware visualization; and decision making with corporate memory." Its mission was defined to "imagine, develop, apply, integrate, demonstrate and transition information technologies, components and prototype, closed-loop, information systems that will counter asymmetric threats by achieving total information awareness."[48]

A backlash by the American public, fearful of the potential erosion of civil liberties, led the US Congress to defund the TIA program less than two years after it was established. As *Wikipedia* explained: "Following public criticism that the development and deployment of these technologies could potentially lead to a mass surveillance system, the IAO was defunded by Congress in 2003, although several of the projects run under IAO have continued under different funding. Notwithstanding the defunding of TIA and the closing of the IAO, several TIA projects continued to be funded under the classified annexes to the Defense and the Intelligence appropriation bills in 2003 and subsequently," "an unknown number of TIA's functions have been merged under the codename 'Topsail.'"[49] According to an October 3, 2003, commentary on the website of the Electronic Frontier Foundation ("Total/Terrorism Information Awareness (TIA): Is It Truly Dead?"), "the provision that de-funds TIA does not apply to 'the program hereby authorized for processing, analysis, and collaboration tools for counterterrorism foreign intelligence . . . for which funds are expressly provided in the National Foreign Intelligence Program for counterterrorism foreign intelligence purposes.'"[50] Thus DARPA "may continue to research and develop 'processing, analysis, and collaboration tools,' so long as they are not used within the United States."[51] EFF further pointed out that "while Congress eliminated funding for the Office of Information Awareness, it also expressly allowed several former TIA programs to continue," but without either the close public scrutiny or controversy that had accompanied TIA.[52]

Ironically, the very mission of TIA was echoed by the recommendations of the bipartisan *9/11 Commission Report* issued in July 2004, a year after the TIA project was mothballed. Indeed, TIA had been created to address the very information issues that the *9/11 Commission Report* concluded were responsible for America's failure to predict the 9/11 attacks, and which—with the proper processes and information systems in place—could have been prevented. According to the *9/11 Commission Report*: "The US government has access to a vast amount of information. But it has a weak system for processing and using what it has. The system of 'need to know' should be replaced by a system of 'need to share.'"[53] Accordingly, the *9/11 Commission Report* recommended that "the President should lead a government-wide effort to bring the major national security institutions into the information revolution, turning a mainframe system into a decentralized network," adding that "the obstacles are not technological. Official after official has urged us to call attention to problems with the unglamorous 'back office' side of government operations."[54] The report further explained that "no agency can solve the problems on its own—to build the network requires an effort that transcends old divides, solving common legal and policy issues in ways that can help officials know what they can and cannot do. Again, in tackling information issues, America needs unity of effort."[55]

Singapore shows the way forward

About 9,660 miles from Washington, where the internecine politics inside the Beltway are but a distant curiosity, the government of Singapore recognized the strategic importance of developing the very same type of collaborative information systems envisioned by the authors of the *9/11 Commission Report* and by DARPA in the days and weeks following the 9/11 attacks. Indeed, on July 20, 2004—just two days before the 9/11 Commission released the public version of its report—the government of Singapore introduced its new *Strategic Framework for National Security*.

According to the website of Singapore's National Security Coordination Centre (NSCC): "Even before 9/11, Singapore had been concerned with the issue of terrorism," and "as early as 1999, the National Security Secretariat—the precursor to the National Security Coordination Centre—a unit designed to strengthen coordination among Singapore's existing security agencies, had been set up to forge and strengthen inter-agency links through the strategic convergence of these organizations and other relevant government ministries, directing efforts against the emerging threats of non-conventional warfare and transnational terrorism."[56] The 9/11 attacks "reinforced the urgency and importance of dealing with terrorism and, where necessary, we had put in place several ad hoc coordinating arrangements to protect Singapore"—but Singapore realized it "cannot depend on such ad hoc arrangements in the long run," which must instead "be replaced by robust institutional structures."[57] Singapore recognized that "as transnational terrorism had transformed the national security landscape, we could no longer deal with it in the traditional stove pipe manner" and "to cope with the new security challenges, we needed to deal with current security threats on a 'whole-of-government' basis instead of dividing the tasks into watertight compartments to be dealt with by separate ministries, as was done in the past."[58]

The Strategic Framework for National Security

On July 20, 2004, Singapore's deputy prime minister (DPM), Dr Tony Tan, "laid out the case for a new strategic framework on national security in parliament. The *Strategic Framework for National Security* aimed to address the issues and close the gaps which we had identified and put in place the machinery to enable the Government to systemically deal with the security issues confronting our nation. When DPM Tan stepped down on 31 Aug 05, the NSCC came under DPM Professor Shunmugam Jayakumar, who was concurrently appointed Coordinating Minister for National Security."[59] Among the three core groups within the NSCC are the Policy Group, the Strategic Planning Group, and the Risk Assessment and Horizon Scanning Group; it's the third group, known as RAHS, that is tasked with the mission of transforming the culture of data analysis from stovepipes to collaboration, and integrating new information systems and analytical methods to see beyond the horizon, increasing the predictive power and early warning capabilities of Singapore's traditionally stovepiped government agencies.

As Ambassador Desker explained: "Given the kind of multidimensional challenges that states face today, leaders and decisions makers require actionable knowledge to operate effectively in a complex international environment. They must be prepared to meet a range of conventional and asymmetric threats." He noted that "frankly, this task will not be easy," and recalled that "one of the most recurrent aspects of human history is the persistence of strategic surprises such as Pearl Harbor, 9/11 and the SARS crisis." He believes the "roots of these intelligence failures are almost always the lack of information sharing amongst government agencies, or what is commonly referred to as 'stove-piping' or 'silos' as well as rigid mindsets within societies that can only parochially perceive information from one fixed frame of cognitive lenses." In our complex and connected world, he has found "one thing is clear: the traditional responses and mechanisms of national intelligence and security agencies are not enough." Hence the development of RAHS, which "as envisioned in the Singapore context, encompasses a unique combination of cutting edge concepts, methodologies and technological solutions, and aims to provide policy makers with anticipatory knowledge of the nature of potential upcoming issues so that risks may be minimized and opportunities maximized." Desker explained how "by detecting 'faint' signals; networking and linking the various governmental and private agencies; and fostering shared and informed analysis based on methodological diversity, it is envisaged that RAHS will empower people with greater foresight to minimize the possibility of strategic surprises."

RAHS 1.0: Fostering anticipation and collaboration

DPM Jayakumar, who serves as coordinating minister for National Security and Minister for Law, told attendees of the first International RAHS Symposium in Singapore that while "governments are not endowed with any special gift of foresight" and "while we cannot predict the future, we can develop more intelligent systems and robust processes towards monitoring new strategic trends and developments in order to anticipate a diversity of possible outcomes."[60] He noted that "this is not meant to accurately predict discrete events at a particular time and place in the future, but the capability to anticipate general trends and emerging patterns that may take hold in the future." Hence the strategic function of RAHS, which "is a process that would help uncover elements in the environment not obvious from the start, which could be missed by dependence on one particular approach or a reliance on just one strategic planning tool."

To illustrate both the problem and the solution, DPM Jayakumar recalled how during the 2003 SARS crisis, "Singapore started to receive reports of patients with viral pneumonia in March 2003," but while there had been "weak signals like open source reports in February which were already pointing to a mysterious lung virus in southern China that had stricken 305 people and killed five," the dots remained unconnected, largely because "there was no apparent context or pattern against which analysts could make inferences." He believes that the RAHS system will "help draw the disparate pieces of information together to alert analysts to potential crisis situations."

When telling the story of RAHS, Peter Ho, the head of the Singapore Civil Service and a permanent secretary for National Security and Intelligence Coordination, described several sources of inspiration for the RAHS program—and high among these is America's TIA program. Ho recalled the first time he was briefed on TIA: "I was impressed with the sheer audacity of the concept: that by connecting a vast number of databases, that we could find the proverbial needle in the haystack."[61] Ho was impressed by the many technologies being examined by the TIA program, which "demonstrated what technology could help us achieve." Ho believes that it's "unfortunate the US government shut down the TIA project," as "it had great potential." He added that "in some ways, RAHS is a modest, a very modest, version of TIA."

RAHS is not a panacea for mitigating risks presented by presently unknown strategic surprises looming over the horizon. But, as DPM Jayakumar explained, "as the RAHS program breaks new ground, our understanding of what works best in our particular context will improve," and "as such, RAHS is a long-term commitment as well as an R&D enterprise that will evolve over time." Already, he added, Singapore is "beginning to see the benefits of RAHS in other strategic areas," as "RAHS hinges critically on a collaborative approach linking ministries and agencies across Government. It already has, and will continue to show promise in connecting silos, challenging mindsets, and developing a 'need-to-share' instinct in contrast to the 'need-to-know' mindset, where departments safeguard information within agency silos." Mirroring the recommendations of the *9/11 Commission Report*, DPM Jayakumar showed how Singapore is taking the lead: "In this way, RAHS has provided a strategic opportunity to change mindsets at various levels of government and embrace a '"Whole-of-Government"' approach to horizon scanning. For us, the value of RAHS is clear. It has the potential to be a strategic planning process, to facilitate agency collaboration, and to put in place a whole-of-government framework to think about a complex and uncertain future."

RAHS 2.0

In a May 2012 interview on the continuing evolution of RAHS, Ping Soon Kok, director of Singapore's National Security Co-Ordination Secretariat (NSCS), recalled that when the program began back in 2005 it was part of the NSCS effort to "augment foresight work by canvassing a range of sources for weak signals of potential future shocks" and thereby "complement the traditional scenario analysis of driving forces."[62] With the "involvement of the Arlington Institute, Cognitive Edge, DSO National Laboratories and the Defence Science and Technology Agency (DSTA), the RAHS 1.0 system was incepted in July 2005 *to develop a suite of software tools* to support risk assessment and horizon scanning."

Just over two years later, in October 2007, the RAHS Experimentation Centre (REC) "was set up with DSTA to continue the development of the RAHS system. Along with REC, the Horizon Scanning Centre (HSC) was set up to identify capabilities for further development of the RAHS system based on operational needs and *workflows built around processes supported by software tools*." And, he added, "beyond the RAHS system, the HSC launched a daily, open-source information service 'SKAN' that puts together 7–8 articles focusing on emerging issues or trends across 14 national security domains. This is complemented by a monthly series 'VANGUARD' that provides analysis of emerging issues and trends in greater detail." He further noted: "To deliver on the vision of being a leading centre of expertise in strategic anticipation for national security, and the mission of enhancing policymaking capabilities through engaging analyses, robust processes and leading-edge systems, the RAHS Programme was formalised into the RAHS Programme Office (RPO) in January 2012, with three constituent centres of expertise: the RAHS Think Centre (RTC), the RAHS Solutions Centre (RSC) and the RAHS Experimentation Centre (REC)."

Kok reflected on how over these past seven years, "RPO has made significant progress and contributed to the build up of strategic anticipation capabilities within government" and that the "RAHS system has allowed the programme to be extended to local universities and research institutes as well as foreign agencies where pilot projects, experiments and case studies have been carried out." He added that "RAHS training has also been conducted in areas such as environmental scanning and the use of the RAHS system to augment the efforts of analysts. Released in January 2012, the latest version of the RAHS system—RAHS 2.0, provides new tools to support the work of analysts in areas such as system dynamics and Bayesian network modelling." In addition to this, Kok pointed out that "the Emerging Strategic Issues (ESI) project was conducted together with the Global Business Network (GBN) in 2009 to collect, cluster and rank ideas to generate 50 ESIs so as to better understand possible futures with far-reaching and consequential outcomes for Singapore." And, to "improve our futures thinking across agencies and across national boundaries, and develop understanding and mastery of methods," Kok added, "the inaugural International Risk Assessment and Horizon Scanning symposium (IRAHSS) was held in 2007. Four symposiums have since been organised in the series, and the fifth one is scheduled for July 2013," providing "a unique opportunity not only for Singapore to share developments in our RAHS Programme, but an excellent networking opportunity for participants to initiate collaboration projects. More importantly, IRAHSS has provided a means to promote the importance of developing a forward-looking and anticipatory mindset to manage the increasingly complex environment we live in."

Looking ahead to the future, Kok explained that the RPO "aims to excite policymakers with insights to emerging risks and opportunities with national security implications" and notes that "RTC's latest information product 'SKOOP', aims to provide alternative analysis and viewpoints on policy relevant issues in the national security domains, and serves to complement existing RTC information products such as SKAN and Vanguard, along with other analytical pieces." Second, the RPO aims to "enable policy practitioners with competence in strategic anticipation and explore new concepts. RSC will train agencies on its revised training curriculum involving RAHS processes and tools such as environmental scanning and foresight to strategy–a process which allows organisations to see what challenges and opportunities are on the horizon, and how they can maximise their advantage given these challenges and opportunities. RSC will also engage agencies on relevant case studies to address problems at hand through the use of developed RAHS methodologies, supported by the RAHS 2.0 system." And last, the RPO aims to "experiment with emerging processes and technologies to explore the technology frontier by engaging users in experiments to enhance policy making capabilities for users of the RAHS 2.0 system and the larger RAHS environment."

As Kok described, by "bringing stakeholders together to work collaboratively on specific issues with possible national security implications, agencies are able to tap on each other's capabilities and work towards a common goal"; he added that RAHS 2.0 "can support the analyst with some of the more tedious aspects of research work in areas such as conducting research, deploying and analysing surveys, and building models to pick up weak signals to better anticipate patterns on common issues of interest." But, he noted, "the technology system cannot replace the analyst or the ability to ask the right questions. As such, agencies will need to invest their time and energies during the course of such engagements for the analysis to be meaningful." As Kok further noted: "Given that today's counterterrorism efforts have a larger geographical impact, have diverse natures and transcend national boundaries, allied nations could think of the RAHS system as a means to develop a common language and to build up strategic anticipation capability, and promote a central awareness of research efforts carried out by various actors from government, civil society and the private sector, for example. Such collaborative efforts could help to foster greater synergies across nation states to develop a set of best practices to address the complex challenges that a fast changing international environmental could give rise to." Kok added: "Aside from such formalised engagements, RTC's range of information products such as SKAN, Vanguard and SKOOP could be a useful starting point for agencies that would like to have access to timely and insightful analyses on emerging and cross-cutting issues with possible national security implications, so as to develop a broader understanding in the field."

Moreover, in order to "facilitate the conditions for an active discourse on how one can anticipate the future and, on a more practical level, put in place the countermeasures to effectively respond to shocks and discontinuities, RPO has taken a broad-based approach to risk assessment and horizon scanning by working with like-minded organisations in operational, conceptual and technological areas over the years," and it "has developed a Foresight to Strategy cycle where different combinations of methods and tools may be applied at different stages, depending on the nature of the issue to be addressed." Kok explained that "methods and tools such as systems thinking and morphological analysis may be used by agencies to address problems at various levels to explore, analyse and monitor risks and opportunities, and develop more targeted scenarios and strategies to address emerging issues and their possible long-tail effects." In RPO's Foresight to Strategy cycle, he added, "environmental scanning is one of six components," all of which have their own "respective set of methods and tools." The other five components, he noted, are *defining focus*, *sense-making*, *developing possible futures*, *designing strategies*, and *monitoring*. Kok explained that the Foresight to Strategy cycle "is neither linear nor prescriptive. Methods, data and tools speak to each other as a function of the analysis at hand and are at the discretion of those applying the capabilities." That gives RAHS the flexibility to contribute not only to prediction, disruption or interdiction of terrorist attacks, but also to the challenge of deterring terror. "Hence," Kok explained, "if the objective of using the RAHS system is to develop strategies to deter terrorist aggression, then a tailored approach of *developing possible futures* to isolate critical scenarios that may play out in the future and *designing strategies* to overcome the adversities associated with these scenarios, clearly demonstrates how the Foresight to Strategy cycle may be used in various ways as part of a broader strategy within government to enhance overall strategic advantage and resilience to such threats and vulnerabilities."

Notes

1 Barry Zellen, "Technology, Strategy and Innovation: Border Security and the War on Terror," SecurityInnovator.com, September 5, 2002, http://securityinnovator.com/index.php?articleID=515&sectionID=25.

2 Yoav Appel, "Israelis Begin Work on West Bank Fence," Associated Press, June 17, 2002, http://lubbockonline.com/stories/061702/wor_0617020061.shtml.

3 Ibid.

4 Zellen, "Technology, Strategy and Innovation Subsequent quotations from Vatikay are from this article.

5 See www.mod.gov.il/.

6 Zellen, "Technology, Strategy and Innovation." Subsequent quotations from Ashkenazi are from this article.

7 Yoav Appel, "The Great Wall of Israel," Associated Press, November 24, 2002, www.securityinnovator.com/index.php?articleID=767&sectionID=27.

8 Ross Dunn, "Israel Starts Work on Its Berlin Wall," *The Age*, June 12, 2002.

9 Warren Bass, "Hitting the Wall: Why a West Bank Fence Won't Protect Israel," May 8, 2002, www.cfr.org/publication/4592/hitting_the_wall.html.

10 Janet Newenham, "The Scariest Place on Earth," *Journalist on the Run*, October 3, 2010, http://janetnewenham.wordpress.com/2010/10/03/the-scariest-place-on-earth/.

11 Donald Macintyre, "Kim's War Machine," *Time Magazine*, February 24, 2003.

12 KCNA statement on DPRK's nuclear deterrant force, June 10, 2003. Online at: www.globalsecurity.org/wmd/library/news/dprk/2003/06/dprk-030610-kcna05.htm.

13 Richard K. Kolb, "DMZ: Dangerous and Unpredictable," *VFW Magazine*, October 1989, www.koreanwar-educator.org/topics/dmz/p_dmz_dangerous_unpredictable.htm.

14 Ibid.

15 As cited by Barry Zellen, "Technology Tames the 'Scariest Place on Earth,'" SecurityInnovator.com, June 7, 2003, www.securityinnovator.com/index.php?articleID=6352&sectionID=29.

16 Ibid.

17 Ibid.

18 Paul Wiseman, "The Korean War II: Analysts Assess Both Sides in Hypothetical Conflict," *Seattle Times*, March 4, 2003, as reposted on www.globalsecurity.org/org/news/2003/030304-korean-war01.htm.

19 Ibid.

20 Ibid.

21 Ibid.

22 Yomiuri Shimbun, "Pyongyang 'Tested Rocket Booster in Jan,'" *Yomiuri Shimbun*, February 28, 2003, reposted at www.freerepublic.com/focus/f-news/853526/posts.

23 Ibid.
24 KCNA, "KCNA Refutes Japan's Sophism about Its Spy Satellites," *KCNA*, April 7, 2003, www.kcna.co.jp/item/2003/200304/news04/08.htm.
25 Voice of America, "N. Korea Issues Warning after Japanese Spy Satellite Launch," *Voice of America*, March 28, 2003, www.voanews.com/english/news/a-13-a-2003–03–28–10-N-66845682.html?refresh=1s.
26 Amy Bickers, "Japan Launches 1st Spy Satellites to Monitor North Korea," *Voice of America*, March 28, 2003.
27 Department of Defense, 2000 Report to Congress: Military Situation on the Korean Peninsula, September 12, 2000. Online at: www.defenselink.mil/news/Sep2000/korea09122000.html.
28 Ibid.
29 OPLAN 5027 Major Theater War—West, Phase 2-ROK Defense: www.globalsecurity.org/military/ops/oplan-5027–2.htm.
30 Gerry J. Gilmore, "Escalating 'Sensor War' Is the Face of Future Conflict," American Forces Press Service, March 25, 2003, www.defense.gov/news/newsarticle.aspx?id=29229.
31 Ibid.
32 Ibid.
33 Ibid.
34 "UAV Roadmap Helps the 21st Century Warfighter," April 3, 2003, *Air Force Print News*, as reposted on Spacewar.com: www.spacewar.com/reports/UAV_Roadmap_Helps_The_21st_Century_Warfighter.html.
35 Ibid.
36 Ibid.
37 Ibid.
38 Scott Elliott, "UAVs May Play Increasing Operational Role," *Air Force Print News*, March 3, 2003, as reposted at www.globalsecurity.org/intell/library/news/2003/intell-030303-afpn01.htm.
39 Ibid.
40 Ibid.
41 See http://searchsecurity.techtarget.com/sDefinition/0,,sid14_gci213891,00.html.
42 CSC 1985, *Defeating Insurgency on the Border*, www.globalsecurity.org/military/library/report/1985/HJR.htm.
43 Ibid.
44 Barry Zellen, "Technology Tames." Subsequent quotations from Hayes are from this article.
45 Ibid. Subsequent quotations from Deitchman are from this article.
46 Barry Zellen, "Mitigating the Dangers of Strategic Surprise: Singapore Rises to the Occasion with RAHS," SecurityInnovator.com, April 2, 2007, http://securityinnovator.com/index.php?articleID=11114&sectionID=25. Subsequent quotations from Desker are from this article.
47 See http://en.wikipedia.org/wiki/Information_Awareness_Office.
48 Ibid.
49 Ibid.
50 Electronic Frontier Foundation, "Total/Terrorism Information Awareness (TIA): Is It Truly Dead?" http://w2.eff.org/Privacy/TIA/20031003_comments.php.
51 Ibid.

52 Ibid.
53 "Unity of Effort: Sharing Information," *9/11 Commission Report,* Executive Summary, http://govinfo.library.unt.edu/911/report/911Report_Exec.htm.
54 Ibid.
55 Ibid.
56 Zellen, "Mitigating the Dangers."
57 Ibid.
58 Ibid.
59 Ibid.
60 Zellen, "Mitigating the Dangers." Subsequent quotations from Jayakumar are from this article.
61 Ibid. Subsequent quotations from Ho are from this article.
62 Barry Zellen, "RAHS 2.0: An Interview with Ping Soon Kok, Singapore's NSCS Director," Security Innovator.com, May 28, 2012, http://securityinnovator.com/index.php?articleID=26500&sectionID=27. Subsequent quotations from Kok are from this article.

Enhanced Border Surveillance for the Post-9/11 World

Since 9/11 shook the foundations of the Western world—and introduced us to the specter of mass-casualty terrorism by non-state actors—nation-states have been compelled to enhance their border surveillance with a mix of new and conventional surveillance technologies, enabling them to see further and clearer than ever before. Indeed, there is an emerging doctrine of digital warfare at the US DoD, which has evolved from Defense Secretary Donald H. Rumsfeld commitment to the "transformation" of the US military into a leaner, more technology-driven fighting force where IT replaces muscle. A central part of this emerging doctrine is the increased role of surveillance technologies, as tools developed to secure borders leapfrog to the battlefield, transforming the way wars are fought.

Looking beyond one's borders is an ancient strategic imperative—traditionally achieved through sentry towers, perimeter fences, and reconnaissance patrols of frontier regions. With the advent of long-range electro-optical imaging systems, and aerial and space-based surveillance platforms during and after World War II, border surveillance profoundly extended its reach. During the long Cold War, America's primary strategic threat came from "over the top," across the vast icy polar sea where Soviet bomber forces, and later land- and sea-based ICBMs, posed a potent threat to the American heartland. The primary means of early warning and detection came from high-altitude aerial surveillance platforms, orbiting space-based surveillance platforms, and a string of ground-based radar sites along the periphery of the Soviet Union, as well as along North America's northern coast—where the Distant Early Warning Line (DEW Line), a NORAD operated, continental over-the-horizon radar system, passively scanned the skies to provide early detection of a strategic bomber or missile attack.

Each DEW Line site was staffed during the long Cold War years by teams of isolated radar operators, who dutifully monitored their displays 24/7, in an effort to reduce the probability—and frequency—of false alarms and thus prevent an erroneous counterstrike. Though the DEW Line was modernized in the early 1990s, and renamed the North Warning System during the North American Air Defense Modernization (NAADM) program, and is now fully automated and centrally controlled, the primary post-9/11 threat to American security is no longer from strategic bombers or ballistic missiles. But in the coming years, as North Korea expands the reach of its ballistic missiles and China modernizes its nuclear forces, an external ballistic missile threat may once again resurface as North America's greatest threat.

Today, the salient threat appears to be from smaller, isolated attacks by terrorist groups and rogue states wielding unconventional weapons such as "dirty" radiological bombs, chemical and biological weapons, and "improvised WMD" such as the commandeered commercial jumbo jets used on 9/11. To provide as much early warning and detection as possible, America is literally looking both "high and low," deploying ground- and sea-based surveillance systems as well as aerial and space-based systems that include both the popular UAVs as well as orbiting satellite reconnaissance systems. On these platforms—all the way from the ground up to the skies above—can be found all manner of sensors, capable of providing a wide variety of imaging solutions, each telling us a little more about the external threat environment and—hopefully—providing a more complete and accurate picture of the world beyond our borders.

Izhar Dekel, president of Magal Security Systems Limited, explained to me that his company's goal is "to provide a total solution—including sensors, software, hardware, and a control unit" to ensure complete perimeter security.[1] And as Eli Yitzhaki, vice president of Business Development for UAV, Security and Tactical Systems, at Haifa, Israel-based Elbit Systems Ltd has observed: "At the end of the day, you want to make sure the security of a country or site or event has enough layers to protect it."[2]

Short- and medium-range surveillance

A standard border security system may include several platforms, providing short-range, medium-range, and long-range surveillance. Perimeter fences deploy a variety of electronic surveillance technologies for intrusion detection and warning. Being ground-based, the strengths of these ground-based systems are primarily short range, up to around 500 meters. Observation towers extend surveillance many tens of kilometers further from a border installation, provide a platform for ground-based, medium-range surveillance. Mobile surface observation platforms, including land vehicles as well as maritime vessels, patrol frontier regions and coastal waters, extending the reach of medium-range surveillance sensors through their mobility. And observation aerostats, generally tethered balloons, allow for extended observation over wider areas, extending the reach of surveillance sensors beyond what can be seen from an observation tower. Dekel said that short-range surveillance and perimeter detection systems are deployed to protect borders as well as sensitive infrastructure installations—Magal has developed systems to secure fiber-optic network junctions in India, and airports, defense, and government installations in five countries around the world.

Short- and medium-range platforms integrate a wide variety of sensors—including such systems as taut-wire perimeter detection, vibration intrusion detection, electromagnetic intrusion detection, electrostatic field disturbance, electro-optical observation, and even microwave field disturbance detectors. As well, for high-resolution imaging, motion detection, temperature-differentiation, and night vision, there are a variety of electro-optical (EO) imaging sensors available including optical video detection systems, using arrays of commercially available CCTV cameras well-suited for daytime surveillance; infrared video (IR) detection systems that can measure changes in thermal energy and provide night surveillance; and laser illumination systems that can illuminate targets, and enable higher-resolution imaging when combined with other EO sensors. Additional optical components include computer-operated pan/tilt/zoom cameras, visible or near-infrared illuminators for night vision with conventional cameras; and image-intensifiers for long-range night vision with conventional cameras.

Laser illuminated viewing and ranging can enhance long-range surveillance over wide-perimeter areas, and can identify threats over ten miles away. Unlike radar, laser illumination does not use microwaves, so the reflected signal is easily displayed as a digital video image. Kevin Fairbairn, CEO of Intevac Inc., a developer of laser-illumination surveillance systems, said this technology will enable next-generation surveillance systems to generate real-time, high-resolution imagery for threat identification at much longer ranges than currently possible.

Haim Rousso, a co-managing director of Rehovot, Israel–based El-Op Electro-Optics Industries Ltd, explained to me that layers of the above-mentioned surveillance platforms can be integrated to enhance border security.[3] He said that surveillance sensors are deployed on ground systems, attached to towers and fences; on ground vehicles and on ships; on stationary aerostats and on automated UAVs—also known as RPVs or remotely piloted vehicles, which can provide pervasive surveillance of wide areas, and on satellites.

Rousso added that as you go from short-range, ground-based surveillance platforms to aerial and space-based platforms, you face a trade-off with optical scanning sensors. "The trade-off is that long-range usually means lower resolution, and higher resolution usually means shorter-range." As well, different sensor technologies bring additional trade-offs. For instance, Rousso pointed out: "With electro-optical products you have some limitations of atmospheric conditions, which can't penetrate very dense smoke or clouds or all that, but in most cases it is still a very reliable solution," providing high-resolution images in comparison to radar and thermal imaging solutions. However, "infrared imaging can give you two advantages: night vision—which is needed in most cases IR is used; as well, its thermal characteristics allow you to measure temperature variation as well as to do night-surveillance. It is a good solution if you want for example, to detect people—even if camouflaged and hiding behind various obstacles. They are easy to detect using temperature effects. That is why IR systems are so popular for border surveillance."

Rousso explained that "a combination of lasers with other imaging systems" can provide "an excellent solution if you want very high resolution images and identification of your target. The combination of laser and other imaging systems gives you many advantages. You illuminate a target with the laser, and see with the CCD camera, and can get a very good sensitivity and a very good resolution, quite a unique solution."

Long-range border surveillance

Enhancing the above-mentioned short- and medium-ranged observation platforms, there are several long-range platforms briefly mentioned above that operate from the skies above. Pervasive Aerial Surveillance Platforms, using UAVs, can provide long-range pervasive surveillance, essentially hovering over a wide-area for an extended period. A well-known UAV is the Predator drone, which has become an increasingly popular tool for offensive operations in remote areas of Afghanistan, Pakistan, and Yemen, and has been embraced by President Obama and his administration for its precision-strike capabilities against Islamic militants with an unprecedented minimum of collateral damage in the ongoing war on terror.[4] UAVs can taxi, take-off, and fly autonomously, and can change navigation plans during flight—all the while sending a stream of observation data to a distant control center. High-Altitude Mobile Observation Platforms provide long-range mobile surveillance from the sky above—on planes, helicopters, and satellites. Their high-altitude enables wide-area surveillance. These long-range platforms employ a similar mix of EO sensors enabling optical and thermal imaging, as well as radar—enabling all-weather surveillance, as seen during the sandstorms in the opening days of Operation Iraqi Freedom when satellite and aerial surveillance platforms allowed for all-weather targeting of Iraqi positions.

Just as low-flying UAVs providing pervasive surveillance can provide greater resolution than a higher-altitude surveillance aircraft, low-orbiting satellite platforms can observe an area only during their transit time overhead—and higher-altitude geostationary satellites, hovering over a surveillance platform in high-earth orbit, have reduced imaging resolution. The tradeoff is thus between observation range and the resolution of the surveillance image. As Rousso explained, "the narrower the angle, the longer the range." With a high-altitude platform, maximizing observational detail requires narrowing the angle of view. "If you're seeking to get a 60 degree field-of-view, it is very difficult to get a long range. If you have a small angle, just one or two degrees, you can get better ranges."

Higher resolution images are harder to get with long-range surveillance. Rousso observed: "If you go to space, you have a larger lens, a larger telescope" than you can deploy on a UAV, for instance, "but you can still not see small detail, maybe a resolution of one meter but not better than that. You can see a car from space but it is very, very difficult to see a person from space, even with high resolution satellites today. But if you take a sensor on a tower—and you look 20 km, 40 km, 50 km you can still see people walking, even objects which are smaller than that!" Similarly, Rousso explained, "you get advantages if you are on airplane—you can cover very large areas in a very short time. But if you put it on a car, you get better performance—but then to cover 100 kilometers takes you more time, unless you use many vehicles, scanning or controlling along the line—it's always a tradeoff, of course—it is also a trade off, as in life."

Space Based Radar

In development for the next generation of satellite surveillance is the Space Based Radar (SBR) system. Dan Caterinicchia, in his March 19, 2003, article in *Federal Computer Week* ("Space-Based Radar Vendors Picked"), reported that the US Air Force has selected three vendors to develop and demonstrate a prototype radar payload for the SBR system to enable the US military to conduct surveillance and reconnaissance missions in dangerous areas at any time, and to further bridge the gap between the defense and intelligence communities.[5] Harris Corp., Northrop Grumman Corp., and Raytheon Co. were each awarded three-year contracts on February 21, 2003, for the SBR system. The SBR concept includes onboard processing technology and a large electronically scanned array that will enable each spacecraft to collect and process large amounts of data and imagery in near real time, Caterinicchia reported. Personnel on the ground then will use the data for tracking mobile targets.

Platform stabilization and integration

As you climb up what can be thought of as a "platform ladder" from the ground to the sky, a new challenge emerges: that of stabilizing the platform. As Rousso put it: "On most of these platforms you need stabilization technology. You have to stabilize your sensors if you want to get high resolution images. You can't just put a camera on a ship or airplane or RPV—you have to have very high stabilization, otherwise you lose detail."

On a sentry tower or perimeter fence, "you don't feel any change or movement, any vibration," Rousso said. But it gets harder as you increase your mobility as well as your altitude. "You can have an excellent camera, but if you vibrate or move it you lose all sorts of information—that is very crucial!" Using gyros and proprietary control technologies, vendors provide stabilization systems that can extend border surveillance from the earth to the sky—and make it possible to gather usable imaging from ocean vessels, helicopters, aircraft, and orbiting satellites.

All of the above-mentioned surveillance platforms can be integrated into a multi-tier surveillance system. To tie all of the data together, the system requires some form of processing, through a security management or a command and control system that can process data streaming in from the array of sensors. Smaller security systems can make do with a desktop security management system—composed of software loaded onto a PC connected to a communication board, but a larger system will require a bona fide control center that monitors, analyzes, and responds to the signals relayed to it from the sensors across a wide-area network, using signal analysis algorithms to process and assess the data on a central server—graphically presenting that data on display screens. As Rousso said: "To protect an area—a border, or a site—there's not just a need to have sensors, you need to have systems—you need to see how you connect all your different sensors." It's "not just a connection of this sensor and that sensor, there is still a system level design needed to complete the task."

The stream of data coming in from surveillance sensors can be hard to interpret. One solution is to use image processing, which Rousso said is "a very useful tool to improve capabilities of varying imaging systems," and "and in a way that is very fast." Additionally, image processing can aggregate images gathered from multiple sensors and generate a panoramic, 360-degree image.

A newer technology now emerging is called hyper-spectral imaging (or multi-spectral imaging), which scans and analyzes the spectral signature for different color characteristics. "There are objects that have a characteristic color signature," Rousso explained, "and if you just look at them when they are part of all the spectra, you will not be able to detect them. But if you just look at that color, it will be very significant." Rousso added: "This is a very, very powerful tool," and predicted that "this is going to be very useful in the future, especially from airborne platforms."

To manage all the sensor data, Rousso said there are two approaches that are common: data fusion and sensor fusion. Data fusion "takes data from radar, acoustic, thermal, and EO imaging" to a "central management software system" that analyzes the data and presents it so "you make your decision." For instance, this enables you to "fuse radar and EO images—with EO you get a good image of the scenario, with radar you get a bad image but you get excellent information about movement, about changes—so if you put them together, you get a nice image with an emphasis on the things that are changing." There is also "sensor fusion," which enables you to "take the data and fuse them together and compare the images to see the advantages of each of them." By merging the data from different sensors, you get "the benefits of IR and other sensors on the same image, and you get better performance." In most ground stations, you find different displays for the various sensors, Rousso said. "One for visible, one for IR, one for radar," which can be "difficult to watch"; but "once you put it on the same display, you get a lot of advantages."

Automated versus manned surveillance systems

Today, there are both manned and automated surveillance systems, but manned systems are much more common and continue to be popular. Manned systems do provide some benefits, particularly when it comes to reducing false alarms, just as they have done since the 1950s on the DEW Line—but manned systems require a recurring human resource cost for the ongoing surveillance effort, and during times of war place the operators in harm's way. However, Rousso said improvements are being made in automated systems, adding: "No doubt the trend is to be more and more autonomous," leading to further improvements in "your probability of detection and increasing your false alarm probability."

Surveillance beyond borders

Historically, border surveillance was conducted from frontier observation posts— sentry towers, perimeter fences, stationary aerostats tethered behind a border installation. But with advancing technology, border surveillance began to climb up the "platform ladder"—from the ground all the way up to the sky above, with each higher rung on that ladder providing wider and more pervasive surveillance.

After 9/11, the ongoing war on terror and the newly articulated military doctrine of strategic preemption asserted a proactive need for "extended surveillance" utilizing advanced technologies on all available platforms, both domestically and globally. Deploying new sensors along an increasingly fortified border is just the beginning. Operation Iraqi Freedom, waged by America to preempt—and, in theory, reduce future threats of—WMD proliferation, is contributing to the "mobilization" of traditional border surveillance technologies, extending them well beyond the frontier. As a result, border surveillance is becoming more active and less passive; more pro-active and less reactive; more tactically offensive than defensive.

This transformation in border surveillance has blurred the traditional boundary between frontier surveillance and battlefield reconnaissance, and the post-9/11 strategic environment is very much a world where the battlefield is everywhere, and the frontline and the homeland are both primary fronts in the war on terror. Indeed, after the Twin Towers fell on 9/11, NATO deployed AWAC radar aircraft to patrol America's skies after it became painfully obvious that America's border surveillance systems were inadequate to provide dynamic, continental early warning in a multi-threat, wartime environment. Consequently, we are witnessing a rapid integration of border surveillance and battlefield reconnaissance technologies with repercussions that will echo long after Operation Iraqi Freedom.

UAVs and pervasive surveillance

During the early battles of Operation Enduring Freedom, surveillance tools and weapons of war began to merge as surveillance technologies—designed to bring a measure of quiet and early warning to the frontier—developed teeth, turning state-of-the-art observation platforms into lethal weapons. Witness the UAV—which began life decades ago as an RPV designed to carry imaging sensors over a border region for wide-area, long-range surveillance. Considered by some to be little more than a toy plane, the UAV's full military significance as an offensive weapons platform did not begin to emerge until Operation Enduring Freedom in Afghanistan.

Predators armed with Hellfire missiles were first used by the CIA in Afghanistan, where they were credited with airstrikes against senior Al Qaeda members including Mohammed Atef, the terror network's military chief. A Predator strike in Yemen in November 2002 killed another top Al Qaeda operative, and the military used Predators frequently to patrol the no-fly zone over southern Iraq before the current war, and continue to provide "persistent surveillance" over Iraq. In the opening days of Operation Iraqi Freedom, a Predator was used to destroy an Iraqi anti-aircraft gun outside of Amarah on the Tigris River. The Global Hawk is another UAV that has been providing high resolution intelligence and surveillance imagery to the Air Force and joint battlefield commanders. And the US Navy uses the Neptune Maritime Unmanned Aerial Vehicle (MUAV), which can be launched either from small surface vessels or from land, and was designed for use where developed runways are unavailable, and can be recovered on land or on water.

Yitzhaki explained that UAVs can provide surveillance over "a larger area and can give a solution day or night, with high resolution—and if you need to go lower, because of clouds or angles, they can do so instantly." In Israel, he said, "we fly over UAVs here all the time," particularly if there is a need to confirm an intelligence report or respond to an alarm along a border outpost, or to provide wider-area surveillance before sending forces into harm's way "to make sure there is not somebody waiting for them. This is the perfect and the most cost effective solution I know."

Another component in America's military aerial surveillance system is the E-8C Joint Surveillance Target Attack Radar System, known as Joint STARS, a military version of a Boeing 707 jet that has been modified with the latest radar and imaging sensors suspended in a giant pod beneath the aircraft that can direct airstrikes against enemy targets, and provide battlefield reconnaissance of a much wider area and from a higher altitude than the elfin UAV.

Toward netcentric warfare

Byron Acohido, in his March 23, 2003, article in *USA Today* ("Warfare Enters the Digital Age"), reported on the emergence of "netcentric warfare" since the last Gulf War.[6] Now, the US military has a clearer and more continuous picture of the battlefield than ever before—helping to realize the concept of "netcentric warfare," which has been emerging ever since the 1991 Gulf War, linking sensors, communication devices, and weapons systems in a seamless digital network.

Acohido observed that netcentric warfare has been made possible during Operation Iraqi Freedom by the integration of data streamed from sensors on space-based and aerial surveillance platforms with sophisticated signal and image processing at the command and control center in Qatar—integrating imaging data from surveillance satellites, U-2 spy planes, and Global Hawk UAVs that detect radar and telephone emissions identifying the locations of enemy anti-aircraft systems, government buildings, and military facilities. AWACS aircraft circle 30,000 feet above the battlefield, scanning the sky for enemy aircraft and missiles. Joint STARS scan the ground below for moving vehicles, and Predator UAVs circle the battlefield at 15,000 feet ahead of US troops, ready to aim their video cameras on targets that Joint STARS planes identify. All together, this multilayered system of aerial surveillance—of manned and unmanned aircraft, as well as space-based satellites—send a stream of data from their sensor pods to the coalition's command and control center in Qatar, providing command staff a more complete picture of the battlefield than ever before experienced.

Since the opening volleys of Operation Iraqi Freedom, when a decapitation strike by precision munitions and satellite-guided cruise missiles sought to assassinate the senior Iraqi leadership, the role of C4ISR has been a critical element of coalition warfighting.

Meanwhile, back on the home front, a variety of new, short-range surveillance technologies are emerging—and many are being quickly deployed along America's borders and ports of entry to bolster the country's homeland security capabilities. Such technologies include the following. Biometrics scanners—including facial identification systems, thumb- and fingerprint scanners, iris scanners, and voice identification and authentication systems; nanocrystals and other chip-based sensors, such as those being developed at the University at Albany's Public Protection Technology Application Center, which hosts a nanotech research center that works with local high-tech companies to develop small chemical, biological, and surveillance sensors for enhanced border surveillance, intruder detection, and bio/chem weapons detection. Machine intelligence and automated surveillance—engineers at the nonprofit, San Antonio, Texas–based Southwest Research Institute have been working to integrate real-time image processing and machine perception with traditional video surveillance methods, to provide faster and more accurate analysis of surveillance from multiple video cameras. Using algorithms that incorporate temporal processing and model-based analysis, their system recognizes normal and abnormal motions and can be deployed for perimeter security as well as for under-vehicle surveillance—such as required at airports and defense facilities.

These solutions were just a few of the emerging technologies designed to bolster our surveillance capabilities, so that we could achieve the goal of extended surveillance and better meet the challenges of the post-9/11 world. Like the Manhattan Project a generation ago, the best and the brightest from academia, the military, and industry are applying their skills and their imagination—in thousands of research labs and technology centers all over the world—to this global effort to extend our surveillance capabilities further than ever before, innovating new sensors, platforms, and management systems.

Notes

1 Barry Zellen, "Enhanced Border Surveillance for the Post 9/11 World," SecurityInnovator.com, April 2, 2003, http://securityinnovator.com/index.php?articleID=1646&sectionID=31. Subsequent quotations from Dekel are from this article.
2 Ibid. Subsequent quotations from Yitzhaki are from this article.
3 Ibid. Subsequent quotations from Rousso are from this article.
4 Jo Becker and Scott Shane, "Secret 'Kill List' Proves a Test of Obama's Principles and Will," *New York Times*, May 29, 2012, www.nytimes.com/2012/05/29/world/obamas-leadership-in-war-on-al-qaeda.html.
5 Dan Caterinicchia, "Space-Based Radar Vendors Picked," *Federal Computer Week*, March 19, 2003.
6 Byron Acohido, "Warfare Enters the Digital Age," *USA Today*, March 23, 2003.

8

Less Lethal Border Security Solutions: Midway between "Shout" and "Shoot"

Long a popular tool for civilian law enforcement and riot control, nonlethal weapons (NLWs) are increasingly being used by border enforcement and military professionals who find themselves engaged in protracted counter-smuggling, counterinsurgency, and other messy post-conflict missions, where the use of deadly force can often clash with the political and diplomatic dimensions of their missions. Case in point: the September 16, 2007, incident involving Blackwater International that resulted in the shooting deaths of 17 Iraqi civilians and the injury of 24 others while protecting a US State Department convoy. A less lethal solution can help reduce diplomatic tensions as America's warfighters struggle to pacify insurgencies that threaten to topple our new democratic allies from Afghanistan to Iraq, where leaders face rising domestic discontent with each new civilian casualty.

To help American forces develop and diversify its nonlethal arsenal, in July 1996 the US DoD issued a policy directive on NLWs, establishing DoD policies and responsibilities for the development and deployment of NLWs, and designating the commandant of the United States Marine Corps (USMC) as the executive agent for DoD's Non-Lethal Weapons Program. The Joint Non-Lethal Weapons Directorate (JNLWD), based in Quantico, Virginia, was created to take charge of DoD's identification, evaluation, and development of NLWs, working with each of the armed services. Its motto is "Pax Custimus, Vita Custimus," which in Latin means "Safeguarding Peace, Safeguarding Life."

NLW technology and the post–Cold War era

The military utility of NLWs became increasingly clear during the chaotic days of the early post–Cold War era, when the word "Balkanization" described the crumbling international order, and ethnic cleansing and interethnic violence dominated the international security landscape. Before the Cold War's end, NLWs in the military arsenal were more traditional tools, like concertina wire, tear gas canisters, water cannons, and rubber bullets.

But during the 1990s, a new crop of technologies entered the nonlethal arsenal. During the withdrawal of UN forces from Somalia in Operation United Shield in 1995, this new generation of NLW technology was deployed operationally for the first time, including such tools as sticky foam guns, anti-traction lubricants, and beanbag ammunition. NLWs were also deployed in Kosovo, and have found repeated use during Operation Iraqi Freedom and Operation Enduring Freedom, providing American forces with an alternative to deadly force on the asymmetrical battlefields of the war on terror, such as Vehicle Lightweight Arresting Devices (VLADs), and Long Range Acoustic Devices (LRADs), which have been deployed at checkpoints to help protect soldiers from approaching vehicles, providing a less lethal substitute for deadly force. Flash-bang grenades were deployed during the battle of Fallujah, providing a less lethal alternative to fragmentation munitions, reducing collateral civilian deaths.

In its 2003 *Assessment of Non-Lethal Weapons Science and Technology*, the Naval Studies Board (NSB) recommended that the JNLWD "focus its resources on stimulating and exploring new ideas, and on strengthening the DOD's ability to characterize the effects and effectiveness" of NLWs.[1] It also recommended that the JNLWD narrow its mission space to "speed transformation of NLWs from specialty status to that of fully integrated warfighting options through strong advocacy and to increase confidence in non-lethal weapons options by expanding DoD's understanding of the effects of NLWs on human and materiel."[2] According to 2006 USMC Concepts + Programs report, *The U.S. Marine Corps: Creating Stability in an Unstable World*, "NLWs provide the warfighter and senior leadership with additional options for responding to irregular challenges," and "given the desire of our enemies to strike in the United States, non-lethal weapon capabilities for National Guard, Reserves and active forces in homeland defense and civil support operations will be critical in site security, maritime interdiction, area denial and consequence management operations."[3]

Between shout and shoot

I spoke with Capt. Teresa Ovalle, Strategic Communications Officer at the JNLWD, who noted there "has been an increase in non-lethal weapons available to our warfighters. Technology, availability, and requirements are all factors in the development and fielding of non-lethal weapons."[4] Ovalle explained that "NLWs are designed and employed to achieve military objectives while minimizing human casualties or damage to property and equipment," and that they're "used as part of the continuum of the escalation of force. They give the commander on the ground another opportunity to potentially de-escalate a situation. NLWs are often the difference between 'shoot' and 'shout.'" She added that NLWs "are applicable to the entire range of military operations, from humanitarian efforts to the Global War on Terrorism," and as such "they offer the warfighter an option to something other than lethal means, which can potentially de-escalate a situation."

According to Ovalle, "the types of missions supported by non-lethal weapons include: checkpoint security, facility or infrastructure security, entry control points, humanitarian aid distribution security, maritime or port security, crowd or mob dispersal," and "as research, development, testing, and evaluation continue to evolve, the Department of Defense is examining their future use in support of a variety of missions, such as temporarily disabling combatants, crowd or mob dispersal, disabling or disrupting logistics operations, perimeter security, checkpoints, and rendering enemy assets inoperable with little to no collateral damage. Non-lethal weapons do not replace the need for lethal force but enhance the capability of U.S. forces to accomplish mission objectives."

Ovalle pointed out that NLWs offer "both high- and low-tech solutions to warfighter requirements," and both these high- and low-tech capabilities "offer the commander on the ground another option in the escalation of force." She noted there are a "wide range of NLW technologies. Blunt impact munitions are an example of kinetic technology. Electro-muscular incapacitation and Active Denial technologies are examples of other cutting edge NLW technologies." The latter technology, which directs a millimeter-wave energy beam at crowds causing a burning sensation known as the "goodbye effect," has been developed by Raytheon, and was publicly demonstrated at Quantico on October 25. While well along in development, and sought by Marines to facilitate a less lethal approach to their pacification efforts in Iraq, the "pain ray" is yet to be deployed in the field.

Having a nonlethal option can make operating in a post-conflict environment go easier, Ovalle explained, since "through those efforts, local government and populace gain confidence of the warfighter's ability to minimize casualties and collateral damage." She explained that "non-lethal weapons can potentially play an important role in military operations across the spectrum of conflict from low intensity conflict through major theater operations," and "can protect US forces by providing troops with non-lethal counter-personnel and counter-materiel capabilities to engage targets at extended ranges and help to protect non-combatants in the escalation of force."

Ovalle noted that "various field reports have validated the successful employment of NLWs," and recounted several examples. In southeastern Kosovo in April 2000, the US Army's Task Force Falcon was the first American unit to use NLWs in a tactical situation, and the military policemen serving as peacekeepers used stinger rounds, sponge grenades, and foam batons—all 40-mm rounds fired from M203 grenade launchers—to move a crowd in defense of a landing zone. In April 2003, at the Rasheed Military Base in Iraq, civilians were looting the quartermaster's building inside the perimeter, and using a public address system, spotlights, nonlethal weapons, and riot batons in conjunction with lethal weapons, US military personnel were able to clear approximately one thousand people from the area within 10 minutes. Shortly after the capture of Baghdad in April 2003, US Army MPs and Marine Corps units conducted searches for Baath Party members. Trained in the use of the NLCS (Non-Lethal Capabilities Sets), the units used these capabilities to suppress urban crowds that attempted to interfere with the operations, and NLCS were also provided to Quick Reaction Forces (QRFs) to use in the relief of small units that have been surrounded by hostile crowds. In 2004, during Operation Secure Tomorrow in Haiti, the Vehicle Lightweight Arresting Device (VLAD) was used successfully to stop vehicles during nighttime curfew hours in Haiti, and was also successfully used in Iraq and Afghanistan.

Additionally, the Individual Serviceman Non-Lethal System (ISNLS) was used as a perimeter security weapon around several operating bases in support of Operation Enduring Freedom (OEF) and Operation Iraqi Freedom (OIF) to keep civilians from breaching base perimeters, prevent theft of the fencing around the perimeters and marking and tagging individuals for later apprehension." In February 2006, the US Army procured nonlethal Optical Distractors to support OIF missions. NLWs are also being utilized by the US Coast Guard (USCG), which is using the Running Gear Entanglement System (RGES) to intercept drug smugglers and illegal migrant boats in or near the coastal waters of the United States, and which in its migrant and drug operations is using both OC Aerosol and Pepperball Systems to enforce order and compliance during volatile close quarters encounters.

Civilian use of NLWs sparks controversy

NLWs have gained notoriety in recent years, particularly after Youtube sensation and rambunctious University of Florida student Andrew Meyer was "tased" (as the newly popular verb goes) by university police while trying to question former US presidential candidate and current Massachusetts senator John Kerry at a campus event in 2007. While being jolted by the Taser, he screamed out his now infamous words: "Don't tase me, bro. Don't tase me," followed by, "I didn't do anything. Ow, ow, ow, ow, ow!" Within 24 hours, online video footage of Meyer being tased had been viewed over 400,000 times, and Meyer became an instant cyber-celebrity.[5]

Meyer's *ow* heard around the world has sparked a wide debate on the use of NLWs, and how to balance the compelling benefits of a nonlethal solution so appreciated by law enforcement officials, with the associated risks described by groups like Amnesty International, which has become "concerned that Tasers continue to be used as a routine force tool and not as a weapon of last resort."[6] Taser, an electro-shock weapon, and other NLW vendors have come under scrutiny before. Amnesty International has tallied the mounting death toll, finding 156 Taser-related fatalities in the United States from 2001 to 2006, and a total of 245 deaths worldwide.

But while Amnesty emphasizes the risks and dangers of NLWs, evidence suggests their life-saving potential might offset these unintended collateral fatalities. Indeed, in the 2005 report from the Potomac Institute for Policy Studies, titled "Efficacy and Safety of Electrical Stun Devices," authors Dennis K. McBride and Natalie B. Tedder argue that "based on the available evidence, and on accepted criteria for defining product risk vs. efficacy, we believe that when stun technology is appropriately applied, it is relatively safe and clearly effective."[7] They calculate that "the odds are, at worst, one in one thousand that a stun device would contribute to—and this does not imply 'cause'—death," adding the odds might be considerably better and that "the probability of death after stun device administration to the body is from one in a thousand to one in one hundred thousand."[8] They point out that "the point of non-lethal technologies is that they are employed with an intent not to kill, but to incapacitate temporarily," and that the evidence suggests they do so successfully.[9]

A safer alternative to deadly force

Steve Tuttle, the vice president of communications at Taser International, explained to me that "Taser International's products protect life," and that Taser "provides advanced Electronic Control Devices (ECDs) for use in the law enforcement, medical, military, corrections, professional security, and personal protection markets" that "use proprietary technology to incapacitate dangerous, combative, or high-risk subjects who pose a risk to law enforcement officers, innocent citizens, or themselves in a manner that is generally recognized as a safer alternative to other uses of force."[10] Its products include the Advanced Taser M26, which was introduced in December 1999, and the Taser X26, which came out in 2001.

Tuttle explained that "these systems deploy two small probes up to 35 feet away that attach to clothing or skin," and "upon contact the two probes deliver a low current electrical current to cause instant incapacitation for 5-second cycles allowing a window of opportunity for the suspect to be safely cuffed while incapacitated." The Taser jolts its target with high voltage (up to 50,000 volts) but a very low current, just 2.1 milliamps. To date, Tuttle said, "over 11,500 law enforcement, correctional, private security, and military agencies deploy Taser systems to protect life every day," and "these hundred of thousands deployments range from suicidal, dangerous, combative, resisting suspects, or to protect someone who presents a danger to them self."

With regard to the Meyer incident, Tuttle said while "the recent use in Senator Kerry's speech incident is still an ongoing investigation," that the Taser X26 "was not used in the probe deployment mode." He noted that the expression "tased," made so famous by Meyer, is "actually an inaccurate description," as "the mode in this case was an extremely quick 'drive-stun' application and probably was applied twice for less than a 1/4-second in duration." He also noted "Taser" is a registered trademark and, much like Kleenex and Xerox, is a proper noun—and not a common noun in spite of its popular, and growing, usage.

Despite the controversy and criticisms by groups like Amnesty International that emphasize the Taser's misuse, Tuttle pointed out that "the Taser is the most accountable and transparent use of force with its built-in dataport microchip system" that "records the exact time, date, and duration of its applications that can be downloaded to a computer." Further, he noted "the Taser Cam accessory provides an audio/visual recording of the Taser system's deployments and provides a recording of the suspect's behavior." All said, Tuttle believes "it is the safer alternative to hands on force, kicks, pepper sprays, batons, bean bag rounds, and K-9s."

While the number of lives saved by using NLWs likely greatly exceeds those lost, each new death sparks closer scrutiny, and greater controversy, over the increasing role of NLWs in domestic law enforcement. Indeed, on October 14, 2007, Robert Dziekański, who was in the process of immigrating to Canada, died after being tased by police at the Vancouver, BC, airport in Canada—Canada's sixteenth Taser death; his death prompted numerous investigations including the Braidwood Commission Inquiry by the province of British Columbia, and sparked a nationwide debate over Taser use. The RCMP formally apologized to Dziekański's mother on April 1, 2010, and provided a cash settlement to her in lieu of dropping multiple lawsuits for her son's wrongful death. As NLWs find increased use by domestic law enforcement officials, it is inevitable that collateral injuries and deaths will also rise, and with it the controversy over their use, and potential misuse, by law enforcement officials.

A death in Boston

Before Andrew Meyer gained instant fame being publicly tased, the most notorious case of an NLW causing death was that of Victoria Snelgrove—a young college student at Boston's Emerson College who died after Boston police fired a FN 303, a blunt trauma/ pepper spray weapon manufactured by Fabrique Nationale de Herstal, into a riotous crowd following the historic Boston Red Sox American League pennant victory over the New York Yankees in October 2004. A projectile fired into the crowd from the FN 303 struck directly in her eye, fragmenting and penetrating into her brain. While her death was accidental, the city of Boston eventually agreed to a $5-million settlement with her family, and its police force no longer uses the weapon.

According to the September 12, 2005, report from the Suffolk County District Attorney's Office, *Investigative Findings in the Oct. 21, 2004 Fatal Police Shooting of Victoria Snelgrove*: "The officers operated under the mistaken but good faith belief that the FN 303, the weapon that fired the projectile that killed Victoria Snelgrove and inflicted non-fatal injuries on others in the crowd, was a reasonable, non-lethal weapon for the situation they were in. They also believed, again mistakenly, that they were using the FN 303 properly. They held those mistaken beliefs because they had not been adequately trained by the Boston Police Department in the weapon—including when it was proper to use it, and the fact that each specific weapon had to be properly sighted to ensure the most accurate trajectory of the projectile."[11] The report noted "two other factors also contributed to the officers' mistaken belief that the FN 303 was being used properly: The first is the gun's marketing as a non-penetrating, less-than-lethal weapon; the second is the fact that the officers were not aware that the gun had caused penetrating injuries to other people on the night in question."[12]

In an interview, Bucky Mills, director of sales of FNH USA, explained to me that "FNH does not dictate to the operators of their less-lethal devices when or how to use the less-lethal devices in certain situations," adding that "FNH believes that the deploying agencies are responsible for establishing policies and producers on when, where and how to utilize the FN 303 less-lethal devices."[13]

According to the FNH USA website, the FN 303 Less Lethal System has been designed specifically "for situations requiring less lethal response" and is "completely dedicated to reducing lethality," and "the basis of the FN 303 concept lies in its unique projectiles" that "utilize a fin-stabilized polystyrene body and a non-toxic bismuth forward payload to provide more accuracy and greater effective range than other less lethal systems."[14] While its primary effect is trauma, "which directly neutralizes the aggressor," secondary effects "can be delivered via a chemical payload depending on mission requirements."[15] Mills explained that "the FN 303 launcher utilizes compressed air to deliver a .68 caliber frangible impact projectile. The primary effect of the projectile is trauma, which directly neutralizes the aggressor." He noted the FN 303 launcher has been used by both domestic law enforcement and the US military, and that it has been deployed since 2002, and that there have been countless situations where it has proven effective, "too many successful less-lethal incidents to mention in this short space."

While this tragic use of the FN 303 generated much controversy in Boston in 2004, the weapon remains popular in both military and law enforcement circles for its ability to minimize deaths and serious injuries, and its dedicated use of nonlethal projectiles. As Kirk Hessler, a North Franklin, Pennsylvania police officer with 31 years experience who serves as an instructor and curriculum developer at the Non-Lethal Weapons Certificate Program at Penn State's Center for Community and Public Safety—one of the first ever programs dedicated to training and certification of NLW use for law enforcement and military professionals that opened its doors in 2004— recalled: "I fired the FN 303," and found it to be "an excellent weapon—accurate, good standoff distance," enabling the user to stand 50 meters away and still hit their target effectively. But after the incident, and subsequent investigation and civil suit by the victim's family, the Boston City Police stopped using the FN 303. Hessler noted that as a result, the department "got back to where they were before—using batons, OC spray, maybe beanbag rounds or something—I'd rather be hit by the FN 303 than a beanbag round."

FN 303s on the border

On October 2, the US Border Patrol announced that the FN 303 will be deployed along the border with Mexico as its "newest less lethal tool available for Border Patrol agents to use to protect themselves and the public against growing violence on the border." David V. Aguilar, the national chief of the US Border Patrol, explained that the FN 303 is "a less lethal device that equips the agent with an added option to address a confrontation and potentially diffuse it at a lower level of lethality than through the use of his or her firearm."[16] He noted agents are "trained, equipped, and prepared to take appropriate actions when confronted with assaultive actions. Split second decisions must be made by our officers in responding to threats and the means by which to engage the threats that they face in protecting our nation's borders."[17] He added that "criminal organizations and criminals that operate along our nation's borders with Mexico and Canada are aggressively and increasingly reluctant to abandon portions of the border where, in some cases, they have operated with impunity in the past," and believes "this 'entrenchment mentality' along with a willingness to engage our officers has resulted in an escalation in violence and assaults against Border Patrol agents."[18]

Despite saving lives, NLWs come under fire

Less lethal weapons—also known as less-than-lethal weapons and in military circles, nonlethal weapons—have gained notoriety over the years despite their intent to reduce fatalities, with several categories coming into disfavor and ultimately disuse after community backlashes against their employment. This happened to the seemingly ubiquitous water cannon after its widespread use putting down nonviolent protests during the Civil Rights movement in the 1960s; and to the side-handled baton after the infamous Rodney King beating in 1991. More recently, after a fatal accidental shooting by Boston City Policy in October 2004 using a FN 303 pepper pellet gun designed for nonlethal riot control, several US cities—including Boston—have stopped using this otherwise effective and well-regarded less lethal solution.

The Taser, the *uber* electro-shock weapon that's become increasingly popular with law enforcement professionals since coming to the market in 1999, has faced several waves of public scrutiny over the years, and again sparked controversy after Andrew Meyer became a global YouTube sensation when tased by university police while being videotaped. According to Amnesty's September 27, 2007, briefing to the Chief Medical Panel supporting a US Justice Department inquiry into deaths in custody following electro-muscular disruption since 2001—of which, by Amnesty's count, there have been 291 in North America to date, only 25 of whom were armed, and none with firearms—the "degree of tolerable risk involving Tasers, as with all weapons and restraint devices, must be weighed against the threat posed. It is self-evident that Tasers are less injurious than firearms where officers are confronted with a serious threat that could escalate to deadly force. However, the vast majority of people who have died after being struck by Tasers have been unarmed men who did not pose a threat of death or serious injury when they were electro-shocked. In many cases they appear not to have posed a significant threat at all."[19] Amnesty has called "on all governments and law enforcement agencies to either cease using Tasers and similar devices pending the results of thorough, independent studies, or limit their use to situations where officers would otherwise be justified in resorting to deadly force."[20]

But their life-saving potential continues to make them a popular weapon of choice among law enforcement and military professionals, and over 11,000 US law enforcement agencies now use the Taser or similar less lethal devices.

With such polarized views on the matter, it is understandable why the community-relations dimension of a weapons category designed to avoid fatalities—an objective one might logically expect all sides to embrace—has become so controversial. The lifesaving potential of less lethal weapons has boosted their popularity among law enforcement and military professionals, contributing to a rise in their deployments and employments; inevitably, the laws of large numbers kicks in, and over time, the number of controversial incidents inevitably rises. As Hessler explained to me, the "CNN effect" ensures each controversial incident is viewed by a large audience, overshadowing the much more frequent uses of less lethal weapons without incident, and leaving no lasting injuries or deaths.[21] Hessler explained that "the driving concept with less lethal weapons is safe and effective deployment or employments." The controversy with less lethal weapons is thus not with the intent—it's with use perceived by the community as inappropriate.

As Hessler noted: "You kind of have to marry up your need to control whatever it is that's going on, and stop the activity, and your ability to live with the effect that you produced—the trauma, or whatever. We have to be able to police the situation afterwards," and if "the public doesn't see the use as being appropriate, then you get into problems." This is precisely what happened with the tasing of Andrew Meyer, resulting in a vociferous response by the university community. But a single or even occasional incident like that can overshadow a long and successful track record of safe and responsible usage. As Hessler explained: "All they focus on is one employment when there might have been 200,000 other employments where nothing happened. A lot depends on the judgment of the operator of the less lethal technology." He added: "People really have to believe that your use of a particular weapon is logical and appropriate before they'll buy into it." To ensure community support, Hessler said, police officers "have to police themselves, make sure they are making good decisions on what weapon they use and in what circumstance—and make sure they don't abuse them, because when they abuse them, they're going to lose them. It's the community that sits on the juries, that pays their wages and funds their operations—you need to be heads-up on that, make sure they take proper training of their cadre and the public and why they're using them and how they should be used—and get the public to think about what's the alternative."

While the Taser has been in the news a lot, and is illustrative of the dilemma faced by police departments and military organizations that deploy and employ less lethal weapons, it's just one system of many available to law enforcement and military professionals. According to Robert J. Bunker, the editor of *Nonlethal Weapons: Terms and References* published by the US Air Force Institute for National Security Studies, less lethal weapons can be categorized into the following taxonomy: acoustics, opticals, antilethals, antiplant agents, barriers, batons, biotechnicals, electricals, electromagnetics, entanglers, holograms, markers, obscurants, projectiles, reactants, and riot control agents. The number of less lethal solutions can be dizzying, and it's growing all the time.[22]

As Hessler recalled: "When I first became a police officer, all we had was batons and mace," but "then they came out with OC spray (Oleoresin Capsicum), then beanbag rounds were out there." But now, in addition to Tasers and Taser-like weapons, there are frangible, nonlethal kinetic rounds like pepper spray balls, optical weapons, and odorants to augment more traditional tools like CS (2-chlorobenzalmalononitrile) and CN (chloroacetophenone) tear gases. Overall, nonlethal technology has "come along," noted Hessler. "It's relatively new in the scheme of things," especially when compared to "batons, kinetic rounds," which "are pretty much caveman technologies" by comparison. One traditional less lethal solution that dates back decades is the water cannon, an integral part of riot trucks still in use in Europe, Asia, and the Pacific. While popular overseas, they are seldom used any more in the United States despite—or perhaps because of—their effectiveness. The decline of American employment of water cannons illustrates the powerful influence exerted by the community when defining appropriate components of a nonlethal arsenal: As Hessler explained, in Europe "riot trucks are used big time, but since the '60s here, they're kind of frowned upon." Hessler noted "they're an effective less lethal weapon," but "with the Civil Rights movement"—during which "film was shot with rioters being hosed down"—water cannons were "used excessively against them, and now they're not used in the US." He attributed this to the CNN effect experienced by "people watching over and over again on the TV news people being hosed down with fire hoses—they probably didn't see it as logical or appropriate, so its gone," even though there's "no law against using them."

A similar fate befell the side-handled baton, which was infamously used against Rodney King during his televised beating in March 1991 by Los Angeles police officers using the Monadnock PR-24, an otherwise effective less lethal weapon. As Hessler recalled: "At one time, they were the best thing since sliced bread," but "after the videos of Rodney King getting beaten with the side-handled batons, they've really fallen into disuse, and people have gone to the straight batons now, although the PR-24 is a more effective baton." As Hessler explained: "Once again, it's just the reception of the public—and those are the people that are going to be sitting on the civil juries and the criminal juries."

The Taser now sits at a similar crossroads, with its fate ultimately to be determined by the community, as its will is articulated through jury verdicts, public opinion polls, and the evolution of public policy. Hessler suggested that when considering its fate, "people should just ask what the alternative was"—and "as long as the officers aren't misusing it, like to torture somebody, as long as they're being properly trained in deployment and employment, and learn to live with the effects," then it stands a good chance of surviving. As Hessler reflected: "I think the public is beginning to catch on—accepting the use of the Taser," and while they "don't want them used on little kids, or on the very elderly, something like that," there is nonetheless "a lot of room in between there" where their use is "logical, appropriate, and effective." Taser's 3Q-07 earnings release on October 24, 2011, reinforce Hessler's observations, noting "six more product liability suits were dismissed during the quarter representing a total of fifty-eight (58) wrongful death or injury suits that have been dismissed or judgment entered in favor of the Company since 2004," and that "overall we have seen a reduction in the rate of new litigation in 2007."

While each controversial tasing generates headlines, furthering the controversy, Hessler explained there may be a "lot more going on in the situation than you're going to get in the 30 second clip you see in the news," and "sometimes the media twists stuff trying to make a story where there isn't a story." When people view a news clip of a tasing, they're "not involved in rolling around on the floor with somebody," so "when they see three or four officers, they think you should be able to control anybody—but in reality, you could get hurt that way, in reality not everyone can be easily controlled—if you have a weapon that can prevent you from being hurt and won't leave any lasting effect on the subject, it's a win-win for everybody," as it "stops the escalation of the force, gets the situation under control—everyone is safe."

To help less lethal weapons make their case, police forces must ratchet up their communication effort, and engage the community, addressing its concerns and explaining the benefits of less lethal solutions. As Hessler noted: "I think they have to do some educational and training programs with the public," as "these departments that are going to use the weapon have to explain to the public how it's used, when it's used, then they have to police themselves to make sure they are deployed properly. When you abuse something, its taken away from you," as proven again and again throughout history. Programs like the Non-Lethal Weapons Certificate program offered by Penn State's Center for Community and Public Safety can play an important part in educating law enforcement and military professionals in the appropriate use of less lethal weapons. The program is "free to anybody in our military—anybody, from grunts just coming out of boot camp to majors, colonels—it runs the gamut of anywhere in between in the services branches." As for domestic law enforcement, Hessler noted that the program is "just getting the word out there," but since its inception in 2004, students have ranged "from patrol officers all the way up to commanders," and several hundred police officers have completed the program to date. On the military side, "well over a thousand" have gone through the program. One can take the course from the university, or view it on DVD, wherever you are, from Baghdad to Boston. "We get requests for them all the time," and it's "used all over the world."

Notes

1 Committee for an Assessment of Non-Lethal Weapons Science and Technology, Naval Studies Board, Division of Engineering and Physical Sciences, National Research Council, "An Assessment of Non-Lethal Weapons Science and Technology," National Academies Press, 2003, www.nap.edu/openbook.php?record_id=10538&page=R1.
2 Ibid.
3 USMC Concepts + Programs, *The U.S. Marine Corps: Creating Stability in an Unstable World*, 2006, www.usmc.mil/unit/pandr/Documents/Concepts/2006/PDF/Chapter%20 1/2006%20Chap1%20pg%20x-19.pdf.
4 Barry Zellen, "Less Lethal Solutions I: As War on Terror Continues, Non-Lethal Weapons Find a Growing Battlefield Role," SecurityInnovator.com, October 21, 2007, http://securityinnovator.com/index.php?articleID=13341&sectionID=31. Subsequent quotations from Ovalle are from this article.
5 You may view various YouTube videos of the Meyer tasing at: www.youtube.com/ results?search_query=Andrew+Meyer+taser&aq=f.
6 See "Amnesty International's Continuing Concerns about Taser Use," www.amnestyusa. org/document.php?id=ENGAMR510302006&lang=e.
7 Dennis K. McBride and Natalie B. Tedder, "Efficacy and Safety of Electrical Stun Devices," Potomac Institute for Policy Studies, March 29, 2005, www. securitymanagement.com/library/stungun0605.pdf.
8 Ibid.
9 Ibid.
10 Zellen, "Less Lethal Solutions I." Subsequent quotations from Tuttle are from this article.
11 Suffolk County District Attorney's Office, *Investigative Findings in the Oct. 21, 2004 Fatal Police Shooting of Victoria Snelgrove*, September 12, 2005. See Press Release at www.mass.gov/dasuffolk/docs/091205.html.
12 Ibid.
13 Zellen, "Less Lethal Solutions I." Subsequent quotations from Mills are from this article.
14 See "The Next Generation of Less Lethal Response," http://fnhusa1.com/PDF/ FNH08lesslethal.pdf.

15 Ibid.
16 CBP Press Release, "CBP Border Patrol Employs New Tool to Defuse Border Violence," CBP.gov, October 15, 2007, www.cbp.gov/xp/cgov/newsroom/news_releases/ archives/2007_news_releases/102007/10152007.xml.
17 Ibid.
18 Ibid.
19 See "Amnesty International's Concerns about Taser Use: Statement to the U.S. Justice Department Inquiry into Deaths in Custody," www.amnestyusa.org/document. php?id=engamr511512007.
20 Ibid.
21 Zellen, "Less Lethal Solutions III: Despite Saving Lives, NLWs Come Under Fire as 'CNN Effect' Kicks in," SecurityInnovator.com, November 2, 2007, http:// securityinnovator.com/index.php?articleID=13448&sectionID=31. Subsequent quotations from Hessler are from this article.
22 Robert J. Bunker, ed., "Nonlethal Weapons: Terms and References," INSS Occasional Paper 15, USAF Institute for National Security Studies, USAF Academy, www.usafa. edu/df/inss/OCP/ocp15.pdf.

9

Securing the Maritime Front: Protecting America's Seaports

The 9/11 terror attacks radically redefined America's perception of the world beyond its borders and the dangers it faces at home. Ever since, America has reinvigorated its efforts to secure not only its long land frontiers with Mexico and Canada, but also its hundreds of seaports that are scattered along its thousands of miles of coastline. Once, America felt secure and isolated from the world, protected by the vast Atlantic and Pacific oceans off both its shores. But now, America feels uniquely exposed to the world's dangers, with long, porous borders and seaports that appear, in hindsight, remarkably unprotected. And which now are proving exceedingly difficult to secure and defend from the new array of threats in the post-9/11 world, ranging from nuclear and radiological attack to bio/chemical attack.

With an increasingly globalizing world economy crying out for more open markets, more international trade and commerce, America's economic vitality demands on more and more openness. Yet America's post-9/11 security requirements requires greater vigilance, greater scrutiny of the commerce that sustains America's, and most of the world's, economy. How do we juggle the competing requirements of security and economic vitality in this new world? The answer comes down to two words: vigilance and innovation. In the months since 9/11, was a veritable Manhattan Project of innovation going on, from university campuses to the research and development labs at technology companies all across America, as technologists sought to innovate their way through this crisis of historical significance, and find a way to harness new technologies and government programs to bolster America's border security, so that its ports could remain open and functioning, enabling the international commerce upon which it depends to continue even as new threats and dangers emerged.

Homeland Secretary Tom Ridge addressed America's new security challenges at the Port of Newark, New Jersey, on June 12, 2003, where he announced a new series of programs to bolster America's port security. In his speech, Ridge announced that America's security would be cobbled together by an ambitious series of interconnecting programs that include "smart borders to protect our shores and waterways, tough international container standards, highly trained screeners at our airports, intensive measures to protect our physical and cyber infrastructures, an early warning network of sensors to detect a biological attack, [and] resources to prepare our public health systems in the event of an attack."[1] He added that over \$4 billion has been distributed to America's first responders "to help them train and ready for any threat, whether a force of nature or a force of evil."[2]

Ridge observed that "from the sea-faring borders of our homeland, to the innermost quarters of our heartland, we're doing everything possible, using every means possible, to ensure that the facilitation of trade moves ever forward—with no disruption and no danger to our economy, our people and our way of life."[3] Balancing the need for security with the need for commerce is proving to be a big challenge, but Ridge and his department continue to plug away at their seemingly impossible mission to secure America's immense, and largely unprotected, borders.

The Container Security Initiative

In his speech, Ridge announced a series of new port security initiatives and investments "designed to strengthen port protections through increased international cooperation, new technology and the necessary funding needed to meet these new security enhancements, at strategic ports located around the world."[4] In particular, he announced the Container Security Initiative (CSI), Operation Safe Commerce, the Maritime Transportation Security Act, and new Port Security Grants "to provide added layers of security that build on a comprehensive port security."[5] Ridge added that "these layers—greater information sharing with our international partners, increased levels of inspection, state-of-the-art technology and added intelligence on the crews, cargo and vessels long before they reach our shores—are allowing us to screen and board 100 percent of high-risk vessels coming into our ports."[6]

Ridge noted that phase 2 of the CSI had just begun, a measure spearheaded by DHS Bureau of Customs and Border Protection with four core components: identifying "high-risk" containers, through the use of advance information, before they are loaded onto board vessels destined for America; prescreening the "high-risk" containers at the foreign CSI port before being shipped to the United States; using detection technology to prescreen high-risk containers, including radiation detectors and large-scale X-ray imaging equipment so that security inspections can be done quickly, without slowing down the flow of legitimate cargo; and using smarter, "tamper-evident" containers at the port of arrival that indicate to US Customs and Border Protection officers whether cargo has been tampered with after security screening overseas.

Ridge explained that CSI "involves stationing US Customs and Border Protection officers at foreign seaports to do the actual targeting and identification of high-risk containers," enabling America to "extend our zone of security outward, so that American seaports and borders become the last line of defense, not the first," as "we can't afford to focus exclusively on domestic ports."[7] Ridge noted that around 90 percent of all world cargo moves by container and that in the United States, almost half of incoming trade (by value) arrives by container ships—and "that means that almost 7 million cargo containers arrive and are offloaded at US seaports each year."[8]

Ridge noted that phase 1 of CSI "focused on implementing the program at the top 20 foreign ports," accounting for 68 percent of all cargo containers arriving at US ports.[9] He added that CSI is now operational at 13 ports worldwide and will soon become operational at the remaining 7 ports. According to Ridge, "CSI has emerged as a formidable tool for protecting America from the threat of terrorism."[10] With phase 2 underway, Ridge added that the United States will be able "to extend port security protection from 68 percent of container traffic to more than 80 percent—casting the safety net of CSI far and wide."[11] Bolstering CSI, Ridge said there will be "a significant level of program and funding support," including Operation Safe Commerce, a "pilot program, designed in conjunction with the Department of Transportation and the Bureau of Customs and Border Protection" that functions "much like a venture capital fund, the program will prompt private businesses, ports, and federal, state and local authorities to develop new technologies that can monitor the movement and integrity of containers as they move through the supply chain."[12] Ridge said that "true maritime security demands that government and industry work together—which is why we are continually collaborating with industry, states, and local authorities to secure our ports and waterways."[13]

IT on the border

Since its inception on January 24, 2003, DHS's Border and Transportation Security (BTS) Directorate has initiated a major reorganization of its component agencies, creating two new bureaus: the Bureau of Immigration and Customs Enforcement (BICE), and the Bureau of Customs and Border Protection (BCBP); deployed new technologies and tools at land, air, and sea borders; expedited distribution of billions of dollars in grant monies to states and cities—with more to come; and created a 24-hour Radiation/WMD Hotline to assist BCBP and BICE officers with scientific and technical needs regarding chemical, biological, radiological, and nuclear (CBRN) alerts along the border.

BCBP "is implementing the Free and Secure Trade Initiative (FAST)," as Asa Hutchinson, then–undersecretary of Homeland Security, testified to the House Select Committee on Homeland Security on June 25, 2003.[14] FAST will enable BCBP "to focus its security efforts and inspections on high-risk commerce while making sure legitimate, low-risk commerce faces no unnecessary and costly delays."[15] BTS was also in the first phase of developing the US-VISIT system with its initial deployment at air and sea ports of entry by December 31, 2003. It would eventually be capable of tracking the entry and exit of foreign visitors who require a visa to the United States, and make entry easier for legitimate travelers and more difficult for illegal entrants through the use of biometrically authenticated documents.

As Hutchinson described, BCBP deploys multiple technologies to support our layered inspection process, using various technologies in different combinations to detect the adversary who might defeat a single sensor or device. To date, Hutchinson noted, more than 250 "non-intrusive" inspection systems and/or portal radiation detection devices have been deployed to detect—and deter—the entry of radiological material into the country. BCBP provided all of its front-line (BCBP) inspectors across the country with personal radiation detectors that alert them to the presence of radioactive material. BCBP is also implementing the Customs-Trade Partnership Against Terrorism (C-TPAT), a public–private partnership aimed at securing the global supply-chain against terrorism, while also facilitating legitimate trade. And along with CSI, BCBP began enforcing the new 24-hour rule in February 2003, requiring submission of electronic advance cargo manifests by sea carriers 24 hours before US bound cargo is loaded aboard the vessel at a foreign port. The information obtained was used as a factor in determining which containers are high risk, in an effort to preclude a risk from ever arriving in the United States. BCBP continued to coordinate with the Coast Guard to have expanded Passenger Analysis Units at seaports around the country to target and identify high-risk travelers and immediately react to threats. BCBP cross-checked advance notice of arrival information provided to the USCG 96-hours prior to arrival at US ports, rather than the previous 24-hour notice—for potentially dangerous crew, passengers, and cargo—thus allowing USCG to act appropriately prior to arrival in the US port.

In the June 19, 2003, edition of Computerworld.com, Mark Willoughby reported that the BCBP is working to "secure the nation's borders with a state-of-the-art [IT] architecture," and its goal is to provide "'a single face at the border' for fast and efficient decision-making on the millions of visitors and billions of imports crossing US borders every week."[16] The result of this ambitious undertaking is large-scale effort to "encrypt information in storage and transit, authenticate users and provide rules-based authorization policies, single sign-on, radio frequency identification (RFID), content X-ray, and radiation detection with outsourced Internet threat monitoring and detection."[17] DHS is taking what Willoughby described as "a top-down, architectural approach to integrating disparate IT organizations," and that "security priorities extend from customs inspectors and border patrol agents in the field to foreign manufacturing plants and ports shipping goods to the US, and the layers of infrastructure required to support them."[18]

To help secure against threats originating at foreign ports, those "foreign points of origin for goods to be imported into the US are now viewed as an extension of US Customs jurisdiction, so that shipping containers can be inspected and sealed at the source. Containers then will be tracked and authenticated via RFID and other technologies. Insecure containers will be X-rayed and checked for radiation."[19] DHS has decided to use public-key infrastructure (PKI) to help deal with the chaos and risk of integrating encrypted and non-encrypted data resulting from the multiple sources of customs information emanating from this globally reaching extended border security program. As well, smart cards are being deployed by DHS to "provide multiple factor authentication and authorization for department personnel," supporting "a planned single sign-on system that will give a single view of data from multiple applications," enabling "agents in the field [to] access criminal, investigation, visa, tax and other point-of-entry decision support tools from remote systems via encrypted wireless links."[20]

New funding for port security

New port security programs require new dollars, and Ridge brought his checkbook along with him to Newark on June 12, 2003. There, he announced the release of an additional $170 million in port security grants, in addition to an earlier $180 million already committed "covering recent infrastructure security measures, training, exercises, information sharing and other protective measures."[21] So the total funding for port security grants will total $350 million. "Evaluated and selected by the Transportation Security Administration, the Coast Guard and the Department of Transportation's Maritime Administration" (MARAD), Ridge said, "this latest round of funding has been awarded to 198 state and local governments as well as private companies ... to help improve greater dockside and perimeter protections."[22] Ridge explained that these security dollars "will translate into upgrades such as patrol boats in the harbor, communications tools for better intelligence gathering and coordination, surveillance equipment at roads and bridges, the construction of new command and control facilities and much, much more."[23]

Ridge explained that these new port security measures "are about building on our capabilities—strengthening a vitally important system with additional layers of defense: information sharing, inspections, presence, technology, funding and, of course, vigilance at every turn, at every port, every day."

The 9/11 terror attacks were both a wake-up call to America to be more vigilant along its borders, as well as the sober realization that one of the country's worst nightmares could—and indeed had—come true. In October 2000, former US national security advisory Anthony Lake published a book called *Six Nightmares: Real Threats in a Dangerous World and How America Can Meet Them*.[24] In his book, Lake presciently examined half a dozen different nightmare scenarios for American security including a biological WMD attack—and in less than a year, 9/11 took place, proving that nightmares of the sort envisioned by Lake are not science fiction but sadly a reflection of the new risks and dangers that we face in this increasingly globalizing, interconnected world. As Lake wrote: "We have crossed the threshold to the era of high-tech terror, including the use of weapons of mass destruction."[25] There's no looking back, just ahead to the challenges of this new and dangerous world.

In the months and years since 9/11, America has been working in overdrive trying to solve its newly identified border security challenges. But securing US air, land, and sea borders "is a difficult yet critical task," as Asa Hutchinson explained to Congress when briefing lawmakers on a series of initiatives launched by DHS during the past six months.

Just how difficult? The United States has 5,525 miles of border with Canada—including its winding, mountainous border zone along the Alaska frontier with Canada's Yukon Territory and province of British Columbia, and 1,989 miles with Mexico. But its maritime border is nearly 15 times longer than its land borders, with 95,000 miles of shoreline, and a 3.4-million square mile exclusive economic zone. And, each year, more than 500 million people cross the borders into the United States, some 330 million of whom are noncitizens, through 317 different ports of entry.

Hutchinson explained that the BTS in partnership with the Coast Guard "watches over our nation's borders and transportation systems," and is responsible for "safeguarding US borders, ports of entry, and transportation systems; facilitating the flow of legitimate commerce; and enforcing US immigration laws."[26] To thwart any attempts to smuggle WMD or other contraband into the United States through US sea ports, Hutchinson said "the Container Security Initiative has established tough new procedures targeting high-risk cargo containers before they embark en-route to US ports," and so far 25 ports, including 3 in Canada, "through which approximately two-thirds of cargo containers coming to the US will pass—have agreed to participate in the program."[27] As Hutchinson testified: "Because of the efforts of the dedicated employees of the Border and Transportation Security Directorate—undertaken in partnership with the American people, our federal, state, local, private and international counterparts, and our other colleagues within the Department of Homeland Security—America is becoming safer and more secure every day."[28]

Maritime security through multilateralism

The twin terror attacks of 9/11 were a direct assault on our world of open borders, free trade, and the expanding zone of global economic integration. Ever since, as the United States has sought to tighten its border security, it has been pulled in two distinct and—on the surface—paradoxically irreconcilable directions: at once withdrawing inward, behind new layers of security protection, surveillance, and detection; while at the same time marching outward, into the world and all its dangers, to prevent and preempt terror at is very source. With such long and porous borders, America quickly realized in the aftermath of 9/11 that simply erecting electronic barriers and enhancing its perimeter defenses with the latest generation of biometric sensors, motion detectors, and IR scanners, along with biological, chemical, and nuclear detection devices and the like, would still leave the nation vulnerable to a variety of external threats.

By virtue of its continental scale, vast and dispersed infrastructure, long and porous borders, and economic dependence on the free movement of trade goods through its seaports, land border crossings, and airports, America remains frustratingly vulnerable to future mass-terror attacks, presenting any would-be terrorist with a long list of potential soft targets that are virtually impossible to secure. While that instinct to pull inward and withdraw from the world, like a tortoise under threat that retreats within his shell, is an understandable, indeed a naturally instinctive, reaction to the threat of terror, such a withdrawal cannot succeed in securing the American heartland.

At the same time, America has sought to reach outward, into the world, addressing the very source of its security challenges overseas. In so doing, it has effectively improvised its way back toward the very multilateralism that critics of American foreign policy say America has abandoned. Granted, America's "coalition of the willing" to oust Saddam, and its earlier enunciated concept of "shifting coalitions" as envisioned by the strategic planners in the Bush administration to prosecute the war on terror, is a far cry from multilateralism as it is conventionally understood (such as NATO-wide, UN-blessed "multilateral actions" not seen since the air war over Kosovo), the seeds of a truly multilateral response have now been planted by an administration long-criticized for forsaking multilateralism in favor of unilateral action.

Indeed, a look at the evolution of America's maritime and port security efforts since 9/11 shows that America's practical efforts to solve the riddle of post-9/11 border security has compelled it to reach out across the oceans that no longer insulate it from nefarious terror, and address its border security challenges multilaterally through greater security cooperation with its trading partners.

According to an overview of DHS port security strategy, "with 95 percent of our nation's international cargo carried by ship, port security is critical to ensuring our nation's homeland and economic security."[29] To successfully shield maritime borders and ports, "DHS is implementing an integrated and collaborative process among international, federal, state, local and private partners to protect our ports and maritime infrastructure by gaining the greatest intelligence about the people, cargo, and vessels operating in our waters and ports."[30] DHS recognizes that protecting America's ports and maritime borders "demands a comprehensive layered defense approach incorporating regulations, inspections, information sharing, vigilance, technology, and presence."[31] Such a "layered" approach extends beyond America's domestic efforts to enhance port and maritime border security to include bolstering security in transit as well as offshore, the latter requiring multilateral cooperation to succeed.

Indeed, on June 21, 2004, Homeland Security Secretary Tom Ridge announced that as part of his department's "Secure Seas, Open Ports" initiative, America would "build upon the layers of security that are already in place at the nation's ports" and to "add additional security protections," as "the oceans and ports of the world are vital to the economic livelihood of the US and countries throughout the world."[32] A layered approach to security thus enables DHS to "ensure there are protective measures in place from one end of a sea based journey to the other," and "to protect the three phases of the journey: overseas, in transit, and on US shores."[33] DHS thus commited to a "joint effort," since "securing our ports and waterways is a team effort," and "everyone, from local governments and private citizens to the international community plays an important role in ensuring that our waterways remain open for business."[34] Further, DHS noted "the US government does not have the resources to secure the ports and waterways alone," and as a consequence, "DHS must coordinate its efforts with the nation's trading partners" and at the same time "enlist the expertise of maritime industry and local government agencies, and use the eyes and ears of our citizens, to notice when something is amiss."[35] DHS said the goal was thus "to find the appropriate balance between security and freedom, between inspecting every container and keeping trade moving."[36]

The "overseas" layers involve several components, including the CIS, the International Ship and Port Facility Security Code, the International Port Security Program, the C-TPAT, the 24-Hour Advanced Manifest Rule, and Operation Safe Commerce.

Container Security Initiative, or CSI, discussed above, "incorporates side-by-side teamwork with foreign port authorities" and is "designed to identify, target, and search high-risk cargo."[37] Under CIS, the "screening of containers that pose a risk for terrorism is accomplished by teams of US Customs and Border Protection's (CBP) officials deployed to work in concert with their host nation counterparts," and "potential suspect containers are targeted and identified before being loaded onto vessels."[38] So far, "nineteen of the top twenty ports have agreed to join CSI and are at various stages of implementation."[39] These include LeHavre, Bremerhaven, Hamburg, Antwerp, Singapore, Yokohama, Tokyo, Hong Kong, Goetborg, Felixstowe, Genoa, La Spezia, Busan, Durban, Vancouver, Montreal, Halifax, and Port Klang—which, combined, account for over two-third of the containers heading toward the United States. The next phase of CSI will reach further, enabling DHS "to extend port security protection from 68 percent of container traffic to more than 80 percent" and expanding CSI to include "strategic locations beyond the initial 20 major ports to include areas of the Middle East such as Dubai as well as Turkey and Malaysia."[40]

According to the US Coast Guard, under CSI, CBP has stationed officers in these "major foreign ports, and is working side-by-side with foreign customs authorities to identify and target cargo containers that could present a potential risk for terrorism," and "foreign customs authorities then inspect those containers for possible terrorist weapons before the containers are placed on ships bound for the United States," with CBP officers observing these inspections. "The International Port Security Program will focus on improving the security of the vessels and port facilities that transport, stow, and handle cargo and people, including CSI containers."[41]

The *International Ship and Port Facility Security Code* (ISPS) is described by DHS to be "the first multilateral ship and port security standard ever created," and thus helps "prevent maritime related attacks by making ports around the world more aware of unusual or suspicious activity." It took effect on July 1, 2004, requiring "vessels and port facilities to conduct security assessments, develop security plans, and hire security officers."[42]

Under the *International Port Security Program* (IPSP), the US Coast Guard and host nations "work jointly to evaluate the countries' overall compliance with the IPSP code," allowing the Coast Guard to "use the information gained from these visits to improves the US' own security practices, and determine if additional security precautions will be required for vessels arriving in the United States from other countries."[43] The US Coast Guard announced the establishment of an IPSP on April 15, 2004, to "help the United States and its maritime trading partners better protect the global shipping industry by facilitating the implementation of security improvements in ports around the world," with implementation slated to begin later that year.[44]

Its objective was "to engage in bilateral or multilateral discussions with trading nations around the world to exchange information and share best practices to align port security programs through implementation of the ISPS Code and other international maritime security standards," and to promote "information exchange and collaboration with trading nations regarding implementation of established international maritime security standards," the "assignment of International Port Security Program Liaison Officers in three regions (Asia-Pacific, Europe/Africa/Middle East, and Central/South America) for world-wide coverage in order to assist other nations and facilitate the bilateral exchanges," and the "establishment of a Port Security Specialist Team based in Washington, DC, to conduct country/port visits to review and discuss security measures implemented and share 'best practices.'"[45] The Coast Guard pledges to "work bilaterally or multilaterally with countries to schedule visits" and "will work with countries to identify protective measures to help facilitate their compliance with the ISPS Code."[46] The Coast Guard is also "establishing a Port Security Training Program that will incorporate the Inter-American Port Security Training Program (IAPSTP) currently being offered to the Organization of American State member nations."[47]

At the time, Admiral Thomas H. Collins, the commandant of the US Coast Guard, explained that "shipping is a global industry and the economy of nearly every nation relies on overseas trade," and "by helping other nations evaluate security measures in their ports, we can help to ensure the safety and security of the global maritime transportation system."[48] As part of its effort, "the Coast Guard and the host nations will work jointly to evaluate the countries' overall compliance with the International Ship and Port Facility Security Code, an international agreement signed in December 2002," which came "into full force on July 1."[49] As well, "the Coast Guard will provide assistance with interpretation of the international code, as it has already done through discussions with representatives from over 50 nations."[50]

The Coast Guard also planned to work "very closely with Customs and Border Protection to ensure that this program, the Container Security Initiative and other programs are developed and executed in harmony."[51] The IPSP includes a traveling team that will visit approximately 45 countries each year; International Port Security Liaison Officers will be stationed around the world to share information on best practices and to provide assistance to the traveling team to "meet with appropriate national authorities to discuss the nation's maritime security regime and its interpretation and implementation of the international code," "jointly visit representative ports within the country to view implementation," "jointly verify with the host nation the effectiveness of the country's approval process for port facility and vessel security assessments and plans required under the international code," "provide technical assistance as necessary to assist countries with compliance," and "share information about best practices, both from within the country and around the world."[52]

The Coast Guard said those "vessels that make port calls at countries that are not participants or that are not in compliance with the requirements of the international code could be delayed when attempting to enter a US port as a result of additional enforcement actions," and "enforcement actions could include" such steps as "boarding the vessel at sea prior to entry into port," "controlling the vessel's movement with armed escorts," "conducting a comprehensive security inspection at the dock or at sea," and "denying entry into US waters." Such measures "will remain in place until the country demonstrates compliance."[53] As part of its multilateral approach to implementing IPSP, "the Coast Guard invites officials from other nations for reciprocal visits to the United States and select ports to observe the Coast Guard's procedures for implementing the international code."[54] This program is part of efforts within the DHS to develop and enhance international partnerships in order to create a more secure global shipping community, including US CBP's CSI. Other overseas initiatives are as follows.

- *The 24-Hour Advanced Manifest Rule*: This rule required that "all sea carriers with the exception of bulk carriers and approved break bulk carriers" should "provide proper cargo descriptions and valid consignee addresses 24 hours before cargo is loaded at the foreign port" via the "Sea Automated Manifest System."[55] Administered by DHS CBP, the 24-Hour Advanced Manifest Rule provides DHS with "greater awareness of what is being loaded onto ships" heading our way.[56]

- *Customs-Trade Partnership Against Terrorism*: The C-TPAT program ensured that the "thousands of importers, carriers, brokers, forwarders, ports and terminals, and foreign manufacturers have taken the necessary steps to secure their supply chains" and, by "providing verifiable security information," enable DHS "to devote more resources to high-risk shipments."[57]
- *Operation Safe Commerce*: Last, Operation Safe Commerce (OSC) was a pilot program that "analyzes security in the commercial supply chain and tests solutions to close security gaps," in an effort to identify technologies that "enhance maritime cargo security, protect the global supply chain, and facilitate the flow of commerce."[58]

These overseas initiatives were bound by a common theme: multilateralism. In order to succeed, these efforts required the participation of America's trading partners around the world, and thus could enhance the many new "in transit" activities such as the Smart Box Initiative, the Ship Security Alert System, Automated Targeting System, and 96-Hour Advance Notice of Arrival, as well as the even more plentiful "onshore" port and maritime border security programs implemented since 9/11, such as the High Interest Vessels Boarding, Operation Port Shield, Automatic Identification System, Port Security Assessment Program, Guarding In-Between the Ports, Operation Drydock, and Americas Waterways Watch; the establishment of a National Targeting Center, Maritime Intelligence Fusion Centers, Area Maritime Security Committees, and Maritime Safety and Security Teams; and the use of Port Security Grants, Non-Intrusive Inspection Technology, and Transportation Workers Identity Cards to enhance the security of our ports and maritime borders.[59]

The long journey toward secure ports and maritime borders

America was considering the challenges of maritime border and port security since long before 9/11. Indeed, in his July 24, 2001, speech presented before the Senate Committee on Commerce, Science and Transportation on port and maritime security, less than two months before 9/11, acting deputy maritime administrator Bruce J. Carlton presented the findings of an August 2000 report of the Interagency Commission on Crime and Security in US Seaports, whose "objective was to undertake a comprehensive review of seaport crime, the state of seaport security and the ways in which Government is responding to the problem," and which "identified threats to seaports and makes recommendations intended to reduce the vulnerability of maritime commerce, national security and the infrastructure that supports them."[60]

In his speech, titled "The Need for Heightened Port Security," Carlton observed that "terrorism is also a concern for seaport security," and that "the threat of such activity and the vulnerability of seaports are the reasons for concern."[61] Noting "US airports and land border crossings have well structured security measures," he explained "our ports do not enjoy the same level of security even though they offer unparalleled intermodal access to our nation's interior."[62] As a result, "addressing port vulnerabilities is key to ensuring that our ports are not targeted for terrorist and criminal activities."[63]

Carlton explained that "MARAD engages in outreach to foreign countries and their port authorities to enhance the efficiencies of global commerce, which in turn benefit our own maritime industry," and recalled MARAD's history serving "as Chair and Secretariat of the Technical Advisory Group (TAG) on Port Security of the Organization of American States (OAS) Inter-American Committee on Ports"—which seeks to "develop solutions and coordinate multilateral approaches to improving port security in the Western Hemisphere" by developing "a hemispheric approach to improving the security of the Inter-American maritime trade corridors," developing "a common port security strategy," devising "basic guidelines and minimum standards of security for ports of member countries of the OAS," and organizing and conducting "annual courses planned under the Inter-American Port Security Training Program, managed by MARAD."[64]

Inter-American collaboration

Carlton recalled how MARAD "has had an on-going port security program with the Organization of American States (OAS) since the 1980s, including port security outreach," and noted that "since 1995, MARAD has been conducting port security training courses in the Western Hemisphere," and during this period, "over 300 commercial port authority police and security personnel from the 34 member countries of the OAS have been trained."[65] So long before 9/11, America was well aware that "by its very nature, trade is an international business in which US companies rely upon the security and efficiencies of foreign ports."[66] The OAS website recalled that OAS "involvement with port related issues began in the 1950's through what was then known as the Inter-American Port Conference," and "at the time, the Member Countries visualized the creation of an Inter-American organism specialized in port area concerns" to "deal with port sector development issues, analyze the obstacles to such development, and propose possible solutions. At the same time, such an organization would reinforce hemispheric port cooperation."[67] The Inter-American Port Conference was renamed the Inter-American Committee on Ports in 1996.

Continued evidence of America's traditional use of a multilateral approach to port and maritime border security can be found in the post-9/11 era. For instance, consider the approval in 2004 of the Strategic Framework for Inter-American Port Security Cooperation by the OAS at the Western Hemispheric Port Security Conference, held on February 25–27, 2004. In all, 29 official delegations from the OAS member states attended, for a total of over 400 participants, including high-level port authority reps, security officials from OAS member states, and a variety of experts and executives from companies and NGOs active in the maritime port sector. As an OAS bulletin announced: "Considering that port security is a crucial component in the economic viability of the Americas maritime transportation system and international competitiveness, and that more than four-fifths of the region's trade is carried through these ports, the delegations of the OAS member states to this conference approved a 'Strategic Framework for Inter-American Port Security Cooperation,'" to "help member States in their efforts to combat terrorism and other threats, such as illicit trafficking of drugs, arms, and people, and other forms of organized crime, as well as other offenses affecting the cargo security and maritime traffic."[68]

The framework was developed by the Inter-American Committee on Ports of the OAS to foster an "interdependent network relationship among trade partner ports and associate countries, as well as adherence to a common international standard of security, to protect the flow of international trade and transshipment cargoes, as well as passenger transportation."[69] The framework served to "guide OAS Member States in developing the institutional readiness and technical capacity to implement necessary port security improvements foster the necessary."[70] It recognized that "those ports with substandard protective security measures are 'weak links' in the trade network and represent a vulnerability to the international marine transportation system."[71] It aimed to "improve and expand the multilateral mechanisms and work with other governments to implement a hemispheric port security framework," and to "strengthen cooperation" among OAS member states in order to "facilitate the flow of hemispheric maritime commerce unimpeded by the direct or indirect consequences of terrorism and transnational criminal activity in any of its variations."[72]

The framework recognized that "higher security standards" will "necessarily involve a fostering of stronger hemispheric cooperation so that the higher costs involved— improvement of physical and administrative infrastructures, equipment, training and improvement of capabilities, etc.—can be met by all the States as a means to guarantee the homogeneous implementation of new port security standards."[73] It advised member states to "examine existing bilateral and multilateral initiatives that have compatible purposes and structures, and evaluate how they may be used to foster this process."[74] By increasing "the priority and resources devoted to enhancing and maintaining port security in the hemisphere and trade partner seaports," the framework aims to "achieve greater effectiveness and synergy by improving internal and external coordination of national and regional agencies that deal with seaport security and the threats posed by terrorist and organized crime groups, and other malevolent non-state actors."[75]

Only by continuing to recognize this international dimension, and working multilaterally with our trading partners the world over, could our ports and maritime borders be protected, and thus prevent a "weak link" from unraveling our multilayered, and multilateral approach to port and maritime border security.

Notes

1 Office of the Press Secretary, Department of Homeland Security, "Remarks by Secretary Tom Ridge at the Port of Newark, New Jersey," June 12, 2003, www.dhs.gov/xnews/speeches/speech_0118.shtm.
2 Ibid.
3 Ibid.
4 Ibid.
5 Ibid.
6 Ibid.
7 Ibid.
8 Ibid.
9 Ibid.
10 Ibid.
11 Ibid.
12 Ibid.
13 Ibid.
14 Statement of Undersecretary Asa Hutchinson, Department of Homeland Security, Before the House Select Committee on Homeland Security, June 25, 2003, www.hsdl.org/?view&doc=17128&coll=limited.
15 Ibid.
16 Mark Willoughby, "IT to Provide Multifaceted Security at U.S. Borders," Computerworld.com, June 19, 2003.
17 Ibid.
18 Ibid.
19 Ibid.
20 Ibid.
21 "Remarks by Secretary Tom Ridge at the Port of Newark, New Jersey."
22 Ibid.
23 Ibid.
24 Anthony Lake, *Six Nightmares: Real Threats in a Dangerous World and How America Can Meet Them* (Boston: Little, Brown, 2000).
25 Ibid.
26 Statement of Undersecretary Asa Hutchinson.
27 Ibid.
28 Ibid.
29 Office of the Press Secretary, U.S. Department of Homeland Security, "Homeland Security Department Outlines Approach to Port Security," June 13, 2003, reposted at www.iwar.org.uk/news-archive/2003/06-13-3.htm.
30 Ibid.
31 Ibid.
32 Office of the Press Secretary, Department of Homeland Security, "Secretary Tom Ridge Announces New Nationwide Port Security Improvements," June 21, 2004, www.dhs.gov/xnews/releases/press_release_0440.shtm.
33 Department of Homeland Security, "Secure Seas, Open Ports."
34 Ibid.
35 Ibid.

36 Ibid.
37 "Homeland Security Department Outlines Approach to Port Security."
38 "Secure Seas, Open Ports."
39 Ibid.
40 "Remarks by Secretary Tom Ridge at the Port of Newark, New Jersey."
41 US Coast Guard Press Release, "Coast Guard to Begin International Port Security Visits," April, 15, 2004, www.piersystem.com/external/index.cfm?cid=651&fuseaction=EXTERNAL.docview&pressid=36578.
42 "Secure Seas, Open Ports."
43 Ibid.
44 "Coast Guard to Begin International Port Security Visits."
45 See International Port Security Program, www.uscg.mil/d14/feact/security.asp.
46 Ibid.
47 Ibid.
48 "Coast Guard to Begin International Port Security Visits."
49 Ibid.
50 Ibid.
51 Ibid.
52 Ibid.
53 Ibid.
54 Ibid.
55 "Secure Seas, Open Ports."
56 Ibid.
57 Ibid.
58 Ibid.
59 Ibid.
60 Acting Deputy Maritime Administrator Bruce J. Carlton, "The Need for Heightened Port Security," Speech presented before the Senate Committee on Commerce, Science and Transportation, July 24, 2001.
61 Ibid.
62 Ibid.
63 Ibid.
64 Ibid.
65 Ibid.
66 Ibid.
67 Ibid.
68 As cited by Barry Zellen, "Security through Multilateralism: U.S. Port & Maritime Border Security After 9/11," SecurityInnovator.com, August 3, 2004, http://securityinnovator.com/index.php?articleID=3550&sectionID=31.
69 Ibid.
70 Ibid.
71 Ibid.
72 Ibid.
73 Ibid.
74 Ibid.
75 Ibid.

10

Securing the Southern Front

Immigration, homeland security, and the border fencing debate

They called themselves the "Minutemen," named after the famed volunteer militia in the American colonies that started an armed rebellion against British rule two centuries ago, resulting in America's independence. But the mission of today's Minutemen was not to liberate occupied territory from colonial rule, or plant the seeds of democracy across new frontiers—but rather to prevent the flow of illegal immigrants across the US-Mexican frontier, many of whom are pursuing the very same dream of America that inspired the original Minuteman.

Like their namesake, however, they were a group of civilian volunteers, a contemporary militia that pledged to defend the US border from foreign infiltration, a task they believed the US government has not fulfilled. Initially brushed off by political elites as little more than a fringe group seeking vigilante justice, and portrayed as far outside the mainstream of public opinion, their persistence on this issue—and growing public alarm over America's long and under-secured border with Mexico during the continuing GWOT—propelled these new Minutemen onto the front pages of newspapers and onto the most prominent talk shows, as their issue unexpectedly soared to the top of the American political agenda in 2005 and 2006. Adding fuel to the political fire, America's huge population of Hispanic immigrants—with some 11 to 12 million illegals and many more times that number of legal residents from across the Rio Grande—recognized a unique political opportunity to assert their will, and instead of quietly lying low in fear of deportation, millions took to the streets in dozens of US cities, aligning with labor unions, the Roman Catholic Church, and politicians on the left, resulting in America's largest and most enduring mass protests since the Vietnam War.

A nationwide mass protest—scheduled for May 1, 2006—was expected to bring some 12 million immigrants and their supporters into the streets, closing factories, emptying schools, and in essence shutting down much of the American economy that depends upon cheap labor for their continued profitability. But in the days leading up to the "Day Without Immigrants" as the protest was widely known, rumors of government sweeps and a crackdown on undocumented workers in some southern cities quickly created a climate of fear, driving underground many of the illegals who just weeks earlier took to the streets, in fear of deportation.

Minutemen to the rescue

The Minutemen—whose full name is the Minutemen Civil Defense Corps—presented a conservative response to the immigration-related political discourse playing out along the border and throughout the cities and towns populated by millions of illegals across America, and they articulated a clear and simple solution to America's security dilemma along its southern frontier: fencing it off by building a security fence much like the Israelis have done to stop the flow of terrorists from the West Bank into Israel proper, and shutting down the virtual free-flow of illegal immigrants seeking a better life at the bottom rung of America's upwardly mobile economic system.

As reported by Associated Press reporter Arthur H. Rotstein: "If the government doesn't build security fencing along the Mexico border, Minuteman border watch leader Chris Simcox says he and his supporters will."[1] To that end, he has sent "an ultimatum to President Bush to deploy military reserves to the Arizona border by May 25 or his supporters will break ground for their own building project."[2] Simcox explained that his group intends on showing Washington "how easy it is to build these security fences, how inexpensively they can be built when built by private people and free enterprise."[3]

While the Minutemen are outspoken in their criticism of the government and its failure to protect America's southern border, their concern with security along the US southern frontier has rapidly blossomed into a mainstream issue—a weak flank in the war on terror that leaves much of America vulnerable to terrorist attack. Rotstein reported how the US Congress "has been debating immigration reform for several months," with one bill approved in the House of Representatives this past December that "calls for nearly 700 miles of fencing along the US-Mexico border."[4] The bill, HR-4437, proposed to erect a fence along much of the US-Mexico border, and to declare illegal immigrants as felons, subject to arrest and deportation.

The idea of fencing off the US-Mexican border has proven unpopular in Mexico, where remittances from Mexicans working in America sustain millions of Mexican families, so much so that Mexican president Vicente Fox has attacked the idea as "shameful." But the Minutemen remain undaunted, and appear to be gaining support on the ground. Simcox claims that "a half-dozen landowners along the Arizona-Mexico border have said they will allow fencing to be placed on their borderlands, and others in California, Texas and New Mexico have agreed to do so as well," while "surveyors and contractors have offered to help with the design and survey work," as well as to "provide heavy equipment for his Minuteman Civil Defense Corps to build fencing."

On April 19, Simcox spoke with Alan Colmes—cohost of the Fox News' *Hannity & Colmes* show. Simcox explained his group is "going to give the president an ultimatum to declare a state of emergency and deploy the National Guard and military reserves or by the 25th of May or Memorial Day weekend, we're going to break ground and we're going to start helping landowners to build a double layer security fence along their properties, because the federal government refuses to protect them."[5] He acknowledged that the Minutemen's efforts "would certainly be piecemeal, because the federal government, of course, has bought up a lot of the land along the border, as well as the state governments have bought land."[6] But despite the piecemeal nature of their fence building effort, Simcox explained that "it's symbolic of the frustration of Americans. Americans need to help other Americans along the border."[7] The Minutemen thus identified what became a hot-button issue, and moved forward to secure America's border through voluntarism, and some might argue, vigilantism. But their energized efforts and headline-generating moves were no longer those of a fringe movement cut off from the mainstream, but were now reflective of a broader movement to secure America's southern flank.

Momentum builds for a fence

As reported by reporter Mimi Hall in *USA Today*, the "once-radical idea to build a 2,000-mile steel-and-wire fence on the US-Mexican border is gaining momentum amid warnings that terrorists can easily sneak into the country."[8] Indeed, in the US Congress, "a powerful Republican lawmaker . . . proposed building such a fence across the entire border and two dozen other lawmakers signed on," and "via the Internet, a group called WeNeedaFence.com has raised enough money to air TV ads warning that the border is open to terrorists."[9] Hall noted that even at the DHS, which opposes building a fence along the entire border with Mexico, DHS secretary Michael Chertoff has "waived environmental laws so that construction can continue on a 14-mile section of fence near San Diego that has helped border agents stem the flow of illegal migrants and drug runners" there.[10] Like the Minutemen, the US government is starting to warm up to the idea of a security fence, at least as a piecemeal solution to a problem quickly dominating the political agenda.

As explained to Hall by Republican congressman Duncan Hunter of California, who serves as chairman of the House Armed Services Committee, and who has proposed building a longer fence all the way from San Diego, California, to Brownsville, Texas: "You have to be able to enforce your borders. It's no longer just an immigration issue. It's now a national security issue."[11] But Hall explained that fencing the border remains controversial, and noted that the Bush administration believes "a Berlin Wall-style barrier would be a huge waste of money—costing up to $8 billion."[12] She noted that Border Patrol Chief David Aguilar believes "it makes more sense to use a mix of additional agents, better surveillance, and tougher enforcement of immigration laws—and fences."[13]

Advocates of a border fence to secure America's southern frontier, like Representative Hunter, argue that San Diego's experience is proof positive that a fence can work, noting "the number of illegal migrants arrested is one-sixth of what it was before the fence was built."[14] Reminiscent of the Israelis, whose security fence along the West Bank was widely criticized the world over while at the same time drastically reducing the external security threat, Hunter explained that "people have made stupid editorial comments about the Great Wall of China," noting that "the only thing that has worked is that fence."[15]

Shutting down America

With the right calling for the construction of security fences, and for the deportation of America's millions of undocumented workers, many more left-leaning, pro-immigrant organizations—including the labor unions, civic organizations, and many Church groups—were calling instead for amnesty for America's illegals, and for maintaining an open border. In early 2006, a coalition of these organizations emerged, generating a mass movement that quickly spread across America, resulting in some of the nation's largest demonstrations since the Vietnam era. As reported by Reuters correspondent Dan Whitcomb, "pro-immigration activists say a national boycott and marches planned for May 1 will flood America's streets with millions of Latinos to demand amnesty for illegal immigrants and shake the ground under Congress as it debates reform," and that "such a massive turnout could make for the largest protests since the civil rights era of the 1960s."[16]

However, Whitcomb noted, "not all Latinos were comfortable with such militancy, fearing a backlash in Middle America."[17] Nonetheless, Jorge Rodriguez, a union official who helped to organize the massive rallies last month, expected there would be "2 to 3 million people hitting the streets in Los Angeles alone," adding "we're going to close down Los Angeles, Chicago, New York, Tucson, Phoenix, Fresno."[18] While massive, the immigration issue is nonetheless divisive—and Whitcomb explained that "immigration has split Congress, the Republican Party and public opinion."[19] On one side of the debate, conservative groups like the Minutemen "want the estimated 12 million illegal immigrants returned to Mexico and a fence built along the border," while those closer to the middle on this issue, "including President George W. Bush, want a guest-worker program and a path to citizenship."[20] On the other end of the political spectrum, progressives "want full amnesty, full legalization for anybody who is here," and as union official Rodriguez explained, "that is the message that is going to be played out across the country on May 1."[21] It's no surprise the national day of action was scheduled for May Day, as this is the traditional day "when workers around the world often march for improved conditions."[22] Organizers of the rallies expected that "America's major cities will grind to a halt and its economy will stagger as Latinos walk off their jobs and skip school."[23]

But opponents of the demonstrations, such as Minutemen founder, Jim Gilchrist, told Whitcomb that he believed "it's intimidation when a million people march down main streets in our major cities under the Mexican flag."[24] Consequently, he predicted that "this will backfire."

Potential for a backlash

Indeed, as reported by *Boston Globe* staff writer Yvonne Abraham on April 28, "across the country, hundreds of thousands of immigrants and their supporters are planning to stay away from work and school, avoid spending money, wear white, and join rallies and prayer vigils," but "despite that excitement, the plan has touched off an intense debate about whether the protest will backfire at a sensitive time in the immigration debate," and "some immigrant activists worry that it may undermine a hard-won image of immigrants as tireless workers who come to America seeking only jobs and better lives."[25] Some labor unions, such as the AFL-CIO and the SEIU, were even "discouraging their members from staying home from work, saying such work stoppages are justified only over contractual issues."[26]

In some communities, the days leading up to the protests sparked widespread anxiety throughout the immigrant community, as rumors of immigration raids and widespread arrests have driven many immigrants off the streets in fear. As reported by Alonfso Chardy in the *Miami Herald*, the so-called "Day Without Immigrants" planned for May 1 had "arrived early throughout South Florida, fueled by widespread talk on Spanish-language and Haitian-Creole radio shows of mass immigration arrests," and as a result "the festive atmosphere organizers hoped would prevail in the run-up to Monday's rallies has suddenly turned somber as immigrants believe they are being targeted everywhere and anywhere by immigration agents."[27] Indeed, "the climate reached such extraordinary proportions that it prompted the Mexican consul in Miami—Jorge Lomonaco—to call the *Miami Herald* Thursday and say that the situation has given rise to 'concerns by the Mexican government,'" and that "fears of raids had sparked confusion and a flood of calls to the consulate about sweeps and operations that his staff had yet to verify."[28] However, while "US Immigration and Customs Enforcement has acknowledged targeted operations in which wanted foreign criminal convicts or deportation absconders have been detained," Chardy reported the agency "has denied random raids."[29] But nonetheless, "fear was pervasive in immigrant communities from Homestead to Little Havana to Pompano Beach to Lake Worth," and "Homestead's streets were deserted, and many stores, nurseries and constructions sites in Miami-Dade, Broward and Palm Beach were missing workers and customers as many undocumented migrants stayed home for the fourth consecutive day fearing they will be swept up and deported."[30] Chardy believes these rumors have "helped to create an atmosphere of alarm in immigrant communities that almost certainly will have an impact on Monday's planned events," and noted "some organizers thought alarm would drive undocumented workers further underground, pre-empting participation in rallies and marches."[31]

But in spite of these fears, the May 1 actions were still expected to be huge. Indeed, as America braced for the May 1 demonstrations, businesses that depend on Hispanic workers expected to remain idle. As reported by Reuters, Cargill Meat Solutions, the second largest beef producer and third largest pork producer in the United States, said "five of its US beef plants and two hog plants will be closed this coming Monday due to the immigration rallies scheduled for that day."[32] A company spokesman explained: "We talked with employees and many wanted to participate in the May 1 activities. Because we share the concerns of many employees about HR-4437, we felt it was appropriate to change the schedules." Earlier mass protests held on April 10 reduced US meat production due to the absence of thousands of workers. Reuters reported how the US meat industry, "which relies heavily on immigrant labor, has been advocating immigration reform to ensure a legal and stable work force." The geographical reach of the meat industry suggests the issue is not just confined to the southwest states along the Mexican frontier, as the Cargill plants closing down were located from Texas all the way across the Midwest to Kansas, Nebraska, Colorado, Iowa, and Illinois.

Political complexity

With such large business enterprises finding their interests aligned with the aspirations of millions of America's illegal workers, it's no surprise to see the political debate over the US-Mexican frontier and the fates of the illegals becoming a complicated affair, causing fissures within both the Republican and Democratic parties. This complexity is reflected in an article authored by David Lightman, the Washington bureau chief of the *Hartford Courant*, from the northeastern and traditionally Democratic state of Connecticut. He reported how members of Congress had returned to the nation's capital after two weeks of recess back home, during which they had an opportunity to hear from their constituents "about what has become Washington's most pressing issue: illegal immigration." Lightman explained that "what members have heard . . . is a 'mixed bag of remedies.'"[33] Lightman observed that the US Senate had "thought it had a compromise on April 6 that would have toughened border enforcement while making it easier for the estimated 11 million illegal immigrants now in this country to gain citizenship," but "that plan fell apart because of parliamentary bickering."[34] Democrats were criticizing Republicans and the president for supporting "a plan that would criminalize immigrants, families, doctors and even churches just for giving Communion," while Republicans are fighting back against the Democrats for rejecting the Republican plan that envisioned a path to legal status for current illegals in America.[35]

Aiming for middle ground

Lightman pointed out that despite the partisan bickering in Washington, across America, "first and foremost, people want the border shut," and as explained by Connecticut Republican Congressman Rob Simmons, the people want "sensors, monitors, surveillance cameras, even a virtual fence: People want that done."[36] But according to Lightman, "few observers expect the 700-mile fence or the stringent penalties for illegal workers and their employers to survive" the next round of congressional compromise. He noted that Senate Majority Leader Bill Frist and House Speaker Dennis Hastert issued a joint statement "saying they intended to produce legislation 'that will not make unlawful presence in the United States a felony,'" and that Republican Senator and potential presidential candidate John McCain, "an architect of the compromise plan, says colleagues have three choices: 'the status quo, or send 'em all back, both of which are impractical,' or the kind of compromise that would allow guest workers to ease their way into this country," as has been envisioned by both President Bush and Senate Majority Leader Frist.[37] Lightman finds that politicians of all stripes appear to "agree on broad themes: secure the border, enforce immigration laws, and create a path to legal immigration."[38]

In the state of California—a predominantly Democratic state with a large population of illegal immigrants—its decreasingly popular Republican governor, Arnold Schwarzenegger, tried to find some middle ground. Schwarzenegger, himself an immigrant, who which eloquently speaks of the dream of America, has questioned the appropriateness of a security fence along the border with Mexico. He believes that a border fence with Mexico is both obsolete and economically disadvantageous to his state—as well as a potential political liability to the governing Republican Party in this traditionally Democratic state. Indeed, Governor Schwarzenegger "has come out strongly against tough immigration proposals . . . including the construction of a fence along the border with Mexico—an idea he called 'going back to the Stone Ages.'"[39] The governor told *ABC Television* that since "we are landing men on the moon and in outer space using all these great things," that he believes "other technology really can secure the borders" in a more effective manner than by building an old-fashioned wall.[40] As he explained: "If I say now, 'Yes, let's build the wall,' what would prevent you from building a tunnel? How many tunnels have been built in these last 10 years?"[41] He added "I mean, we've detected tunnels left and right that people can drive trucks through."[42]

Trying to maintain the middle ground on this divisive issue, Governor Schwarzenegger continued to oppose amnesty for America's 11–12 million illegal immigrants—one of the demands being articulated by the huge crowds at demonstrations held across the nation in 2006. But in contrast to those further to the right such as the Minutemen, he also has "lambasted calls for their immediate deportation"—citing the economic costs of such a large-scale deportation: "It would cost 500 billion dollars. Who's going to pay for that?"[43] Schwarzenegger, walks a unique tightrope on this issue. Associated Press reporter Michael R. Blood observed the governor's tightrope walk, noting how the governor had "backed a federal plan to build a stretch of border fence between San Diego and Tijuana," and then changed course, saying that "walling off hundreds of miles of the California-Mexico border is a strategy from the Stone Age."[44] Blood cites one political observer who explained "the governor's 'schizophrenic view' mirrors divisions among voters and within Schwarzenegger's own party," compounded by the increasing importance of the immigration issue on the political agenda. As Blood reported, a California statewide survey "ranked immigration as the most important issue in the state, overshadowing even education."[45]

Voting with their feet

Christian Science Monitor staff writer Danna Harman reported how as the political debate inside the United States "continues over immigration reform policy," down on the southern side of the border, "there seems to be consensus that enforcement measures will deter almost no one."[46] Can a fence stop the flow? Harman reported that "proponents of a fence argue that these preventative measures can be effective, and point to the San Diego sector as proof," where "after the creation of a fence and a beefing up of enforcement around the point of entry in the early 1990s," that region "saw the number of attempted crossings plummet."[47]

But Harman explained that "such measures only serve to push the human traffic elsewhere," just as Governor Schwarzenegger suggested in his comments on the proliferation of illicit cross-border tunnels.[48] So even though Operation Gatekeeper in California "did drastically cut down the number of illegal immigrants trying to cross near San Diego," Harman pointed out that "this only sent people to Texas."[49] Then, "beefed up patrols along the Texas border soon pushed the traffic away from El Paso and toward Nogales and Yuma"—so "today, close to half of all illegal crossings take place in Arizona."[50] And, Harman noted, "with increased vigilance near entry points and urban areas in this state, illegal immigrants try crossing in more difficult terrain—in locations where temperatures during the summer months often rise into the hundreds and never drop," and as a result, "a record 473 migrants died in 2005 while crossing the US-Mexico border, the most since the Border Patrol began tracking such deaths in 1999."[51] Harman noted that "the border patrol caught 1.2 million would-be illegal immigrants in 2005; that's an average of one arrest every 30 seconds."[52] Indeed, the dream of America, and its economic promise, continues to inspire millions of people to join the continuing exodus to the North. As Harman described: "They stream in. Today, the same as yesterday. The same as the day before. Backpacks are stuffed with bottled water, soap, chips, maybe an icon of the Virgin of Guadalupe. They wear sweaters and wool hats for the cold desert nights . . . travelers arrive from all over Mexico, Central America, even as far away as Colombia, and Brazil. They are going to 'El Norte.' They tell you that, straight out. And if they don't cross this time, they will simply try again."[53]

Drug war threatens to engulf southern front

When Americans headed to the polls in record numbers on November 4, 2008, one reason for the historic turnout was public concern with America's open-ended and budget-straining military commitments in Iraq and Afghanistan, as the GWOT entered its sixth year, with the nation's economy in free fall. Yet even as Americans voted for change, an issue closer to home ominously threatened to spiral out of control, with the potential to engulf its southern borderlands into chaos—and yet this gathering threat had been barely mentioned during the long 2008 presidential campaign. Over the preceding year, there had been a worrisome spike in violence on both sides of America's southern border, with over 5,000 casualties and a total body count approaching 30,000 by the end of 2010, the third year since President Felipe Calderón had launched an all-out offensive against Mexico's drug cartels in 2007—a situation so dire it still threatens to turn Mexico into a failed state, and as the chaos spreads, to turn America's southern border into a war zone. Tragically, on the very night of America's historic 2008 election, Mexico experienced a major setback in the war on drugs when its crime-fighting interior secretary Juan Camilo Mouriño and José Luis Santiago Vasconcelos, a senior security advisor to Mexico's president and formerly the top federal prosecutor for organized crime, were killed in a Mexico City plane crash. Only a few days earlier, acting federal police commissioner Gerardo Garaythe, had quit his post after allegations surfaced that the drug cartels had infiltrated senior levels of Mexico's crime-fighting agencies.

Then, Mouriño—the senior official in Mexico's war against organized crime—was killed, and though the cause of the crash of his government jet remains under investigation, its impact on Mexico's and America's war on drugs would no doubt be felt far and wide. As Ray Walser, a senior policy analyst specializing in Latin America with the Heritage Foundation, observed: "The loss of close, trusted associates of President Calderon in the fight against Mexico's drug cartels is certainly a serious one for the nation. If the crash of the aircraft was a result of sabotage or a bomb, it would be a very dangerous escalation in the fight against the drug cartels. Clearly US border security is very much linked to Mexico's capacity to reduce the threat posed by the cartels and their criminal associations with criminal elements and drug dealers in the US."[54]

Roots of chaos

I spoke with Dr David McIntyre, director of the Integrative Center for Homeland Security (ICHS) and professor of homeland security and terrorism at the Bush School of Government and Public Service at Texas A&M University. He noted there had now been over "5,000 deaths along the border in Mexico over the last 23 months," mainly from drug violence. As he calculated, "that's roughly one 9/11 of casualties each year, for two years in a row, along the border."[55]

And increasingly, that violence is spilling across the border into the United States. He recalled one "incident in Phoenix where three dozen people dressed as SWAT team members assaulted a house in Phoenix, the kidnapping of a six-year old in Las Vegas—again by people dressed as police." Dozens of Americans have been kidnapped south of San Diego in the border city of Tijuana, and over one thousand Mexican families have fled across the border to escape this epidemic of kidnappings back home. McIntyre finds it a "very important point" that there had been "no discussion of this in the 2008 presidential election—and almost no one is paying attention to this in the media." He noted that "there have been significant threats and even deaths against news media in Mexico," so journalists are "literally taking their lives in their own hands to do investigations of these topics."

McIntyre added that "within Mexico, the issue is not just violence but also corruption." That's why it has become a "regular practice when the army moves into an area along the border to disarm the police because the police are so uniformly in the pay of the drug cartels; it's not just once or twice, but a routine practice." McIntyre recalled "when the new president, Felipe Calderon, was inaugurated, he came to realize that a significant part of the Mexican government had been infiltrated, and that the legitimacy of the Mexican Government could soon be at risk." Indeed, "three of the most senior in Mexico's national anti-narcotic police were arrested and indicted for passing intelligence to the drug cartels." More alarming, the corruption has spread across the border. McIntyre recalled how in south Texas in 2008, Starr County Sheriff Reymundo Guerra was arrested on drug charges, and indicted for "providing security to drug shipments and acting as an informant, giving them the names of our informants. There is a very significant security issue that is developing along the border."

The problem is fostered by the huge of amount of money flowing across the US border to the drug cartels, a market he estimates to be $80–100 billion in size. By comparison, McIntyre explained, "the US provides $500 million to Mexico to support its drug effort," through the Merida Initiative, a drop in the bucket compared to the resources available to the cartels. Consequently, "the bad guys have better weapons, computers—better than our border patrol, better than Mexican officials. We've been arguing for years that our Defense Department will overwhelm any enemy. But down here, we're on the other side of that fence. And our appetite for drugs, our money, is fueling the problem."

Technology to the rescue

But despite this asymmetry of resources, American officials continue to wage the good fight, applying new technologies and old fashioned grit and determination in order to turn the tide. Michael J. Reilly, Field Operations supervisor of the DHS Border Security Operations responsible for the San Diego and Rio Grande Valley Sectors, who believes the situation is improving, told me that "US Border Patrol Agents improved border security, reducing the number of apprehensions at the borders by 17 percent in FY08. During FY08 Border Patrol apprehended 723,825, compared with 876,704 during FY07. Also, US Border Patrol seizures decreased significantly. In terms of weight, marijuana seizures are down in FY08 by 12 percent over FY07, and cocaine seizures decreased 35 percent. Heroin seizures declined 61 percent versus the previous year."[56] These declines, he believes, indicate that "smuggling organizations and criminals have become desperate to continue their illicit cross-border operations as a result of the Border Patrol's successes in gaining control of the Nation's borders. This desperation has led to violence."

As a result, Reilly observed, "the US Border Patrol has continued to experience an increase in assaults against frontline agents. Border-wide assaults continue on a record pace with 1,097 assaults occurring from October 1, 2007 through September 30, 2008, compared to 987 assaults for the same time frame last year; an 11 percent increase." To redress this rise in violence, Reilly explained that border patrol agents are equipping themselves with new technologies, including "less-lethal items such as collapsible steel batons, oleoresin capsicum (OC) spray, and pepper ball launching systems (PLS)," and "this year, the Border Patrol implemented the use of the FN-303, a less-lethal projectile launcher, in select sectors. These items are not a substitute for firearms; they give agents more options to respond to an assault before escalating to the use of deadly force. Ultimately, the agent will respond to an assault with the appropriate use of force as trained, equipped, and prepared."

In addition to these new weapons systems, Reilly noted another "initiative currently being utilized by the US Border Patrol is 'Operation Streamline,'" which he explained is "an enhanced law enforcement operation aimed at reducing illegal immigration in high-traffic or problematic areas. The Sector Chief Patrol Agent designates a 'zero tolerance zone' for all illegal entries and directs that all prosecutable aliens, regardless of nationality, apprehended within the geographic boundaries be prosecuted" for violating US Code Title 8, 1325, which forbids "improper entry by aliens" Another important initiative is the Secure Border Initiative (SBI), which Reilly described as "a comprehensive multi-year plan to secure America's borders and reduce illegal migration" that involves "more agents to patrol our borders, secure our ports of entry and enforce immigration laws; expanded detention and removal capabilities to eliminate 'catch and release' once and for all; a comprehensive and systemic upgrading of the technology used in controlling the border, including increased manned aerial assets, expanded use of UAVs, and next-generation detection technology; increased investment in infrastructure improvements at the border—providing additional physical security to sharply reduce illegal border crossings; and, greatly increased interior enforcement of our immigration laws—including more robust worksite enforcement."

A component of the SBI system is SBI*net*, which is a "unified border control strategy" designed to detect entries when they occur, identify what the entry is, classify its level of threat, effectively and efficiently respond to the entry, and bring the situation to the appropriate law enforcement resolution. As Reilly explained, SBI*net* "applies that comprehensive approach to securing the land borders at and between the ports of entry" and will "build a common operating picture (COP) of the border environment, within a command center environment, which will provide commonality within DHS components, and interoperability with stakeholders who are external to DHS. SBI*net* is the most comprehensive effort in the nation's history to gain control of its nearly 6,000 miles of international land border." Reilly added this "will provide the means to control and integrate sensors; identify and classify entries; and provide a functional, tactical display of the border that will be visible to command centers."

As for whether these new solutions are proving effective, Reilly observed: "Yes they are. In the Tucson Sector, where the technology is being tested, apprehensions have dropped from 378,239 in FY2007 to 317,696 in FY2008." But the drug cartels are reacting: "We were certain that when we increased our efforts to gain operational control of our nation's borders that the illegal cross-border traffickers would seek alternate routes to smuggle aliens and other contraband. Smuggling operations did seek to adjust their smuggling routes to other locations along the Southwest border. However, we were prepared with the implementation of urban, rural, and remote enforcement activities using a combination of personnel, technology, and infrastructure."

More work to be done

Jena McNeill, a homeland security analyst with the Heritage Foundation, has observed that "the US has made progress to secure the border but there is a lot of work to be done." She noted it "has recruited thousands more border patrol agents and is building the physical fence as well as deploying SBI*net*, the technological side to border security," with "radars, sensors, cameras, virtual fencing. But there is a lot to be done to make SBI*net* fully operational." McNeill believes "we have more work to do on border technologies," particularly since "sophisticated criminal enterprises can adapt."[57]

As she explained: "Criminals do change in response to security measures, the cartels are sophisticated, making law enforcement more difficult, but we still capture people in the process. And when you have flexible technology that can change along with adapting criminals, then it makes their job all the harder. They have to cross the border somewhere. And having quality border infrastructure can go a long way here to ensure that they are sneaking in merely because of easily secured gaps in infrastructure." Looking ahead, McNeill said "we need to have a systems approach to border security. The current layered system relies on instituting tons of layers, so that no one layer has to be perfect, but this mindset produces imperfect results across the board—and smart criminals, under this approach find a way around." She added that "we must integrate our border security strategy from the local government to the federal government, else efforts will be duplicative and not achieve real border security gains." And, she noted: "While we have made significant advances in some areas to secure the border and attack the problems, things could easily go the other way without adequate leadership in the next administration."

ICHS director McIntyre agrees that technology can play an important role in America's and Mexico's fight against the drug cartels, "but clearly technology alone is not going to solve this problem." He believes sustained political will and continued support to President Calderon will be required to stem the tide. McIntyre added: "Americans ought to be aching with admiration and supporting to the best of our abilities the President of Mexico and the honest members of his government, his army, and his federal police—doing their best against great odds, and at personal risk to them and their families, fighting our fight in many respects."

Pipeline terror on the rise across the Americas

September 11 will always be remembered as a day of infamy in the Americas, the day foreign terror reached across the vast and seemingly protective seas to inflict a lethal blow in 2001. But in 2007, September 10 became another day of terror—this time a day of homegrown terror, directed at a nation's energy supply. The attacks of September 10, 2007, took place across the Rio Grande, in Mexico, where a series of six explosions ripped apart Mexico's natural gas pipelines, ultimately disrupting a dozen separate lines, cutting the flow of natural gas to at least nine of Mexico's states, dealing what the *Economist* has described as a *triple blow* to Mexico—adversely affecting the hundreds of businesses that rely on natural gas for their operations; the state-owned Pemex (Petróleos Mexicanos) oil company, which depends on pipeline infrastructure to distribute its product and keep Mexico's economy firing; and the government of President Felipe Calderón, which found itself facing a shadowy insurgent threat capable of paralyzing the nation's energy supply. Some 20,000 residents fled their homes, and the total cost to Mexico's economy has been estimated to be in the hundreds of millions of dollars.

Taking credit for the attacks was the EPR—or Ejército Popular Revolucionario—a rural-based, Marxist guerrilla movement that came into public view in 1996 but which had become inactive in recent years, only to resurface during the protracted crisis in Oaxaca in 2006, when protestors lay siege to its city center for five months. This was EPR's second attack targeting Mexico's oil and gas infrastructure; their first took place in July 2007, and though that was on a smaller scale than their September 10 attacks, it successfully disrupted the operations of several major multinationals. After the July attacks, the Mexican government issued a statement in which it "categorically condemns the attacks against Pemex facilities. This criminal conduct aims to weaken democratic institutions, the patrimony of Mexicans and the safety of their families."[58] EPR has threatened further attacks, but so far, those threats have not yielded further action—but with Mexico's extensive oil and gas infrastructure increasingly important to its economy, the nation remains at risk.

I spoke with Scott Stewart, a senior security and counterterrorism analyst at Strategic Forecasting, Inc., better known as Stratfor, a private strategic intelligence company based in Arlington, Virginia. He explained that this summer's outbreak of terrorism targeting Mexico's energy infrastructure was "not a new form of terrorism at all," but that "economic targets have always been a part of warfare, and like armies, terrorist groups seek to attack critical economic nodes."[59] He added that "in Mexico, oil is an important economic target. The attacks against oil infrastructure should not be surprising not only when we look at the importance of oil to Mexico, but also when we view EPR in the historical context of Latin American Marxist and Maoist groups."

Terrorists have targeted oil and gas infrastructure throughout Central and South America for decades, and as Stewart noted: "Oil and energy targets have long been seen as natural, capitalist targets by guerrilla groups in Latin America. Oil and natural gas fields and pipelines have been attacked for many years in Bolivia, Colombia, Ecuador and Peru. Good examples are the Sendero Luminoso targeting of exploration efforts in Peru's Huallaga basin and their destruction of pipelines leading from the basin, as well as the FARC and ELN attacks on oil infrastructure in the Cano Limon oil field in Colombia and attacks on the Cano Limon-Covenas pipeline." Stewart views this summer's attacks in Mexico "as a natural outgrowth of Marxist revolutionary activity in the region," and "while the EPR is a domestic, Mexican group, such organizations are certainly inspired by the activities of their comrades in the region"—particularly as "oil is a very important source of revenue. Especially with prices being at the level they are now."

Dr James David Ballard, associate professor of Sociology at California State University, Northridge, and an expert on oil and gas infrastructure security, explained to me that "pipeline attacks have been common in Latin America," and while "the country by country patterns are not necessarily interrelated . . . groups learn from the experiences of other groups—they learn tactics and they learn vulnerabilities. So while past attacks in other countries may not directly affect what happened in Mexico—the learning curve is shortened by the experiences of other groups and public knowledge of what happened in those other countries."[60] He noted that "terrorist attacks, and sabotage attacks in general, on oil and gas infrastructure have a long history—beginning in the first oil fields where union disputes erupted. Terroristic attacks have been made against the well sites, pipelines, refineries—the totality of the infrastructure."

Ballard observed that the motivations, over time, for attacking energy infrastructure has varied, and terrorists "have been motivated by internal and external politics—some groups wishing a bigger share of the revenues, others seeking to take over the operations to gain total control of the revenues." For terrorists, he explained, "the strategic value of energy attacks may be rising. In recent years the economic value of oil and gas has risen and thus the symbolic profile of an attack against these assets has risen. With transportation attacks being thwarted, a logical step would be to move on to less hardened targets like oil and gas." But it's not just terrorists that have taken aim at oil and gas infrastructure, as "the military value of the infrastructure has always been critical also—in some cases sabotage of the infrastructure in advance of military operations being a significant historical trend." Ballard added that "on the military side, the value of oil and gas is that they provide the ability to wage war. Armies need fuel to fight—capturing that fuel means you do not have to import it into the theater of war wherever it is fought."

Preventing attacks on their oil and gas infrastructure presents a difficult challenge to oil producing states, as seen in many countries, such as Iraq and Nigeria, in addition to Mexico. However, Ballard believes that mitigation can reduce the consequence of such attacks, and noted that "states can, and have, used infrastructure redundancy as one means of mitigation—the more infrastructure that is present, the more redundant the infrastructure, the less vulnerability the state has to a single attack. The idea being that you can hurt me with an attack but you cannot halt the economic vitality of the nation."

Among the counterterrorism challenges facing oil and gas producing states, securing oil and gas infrastructure is a particularly "tough one because, by its very nature, oil infrastructure and pipelines are very exposed and vulnerable to attack," observed Stratfor's Stewart. "However, as seen by the history of systematic attacks in places like Peru, Colombia and Iraq, pipelines can be repaired fairly quickly. Because of this, security needs to be focused on protecting critical nodes and infrastructure that cannot be quickly repaired." While Stewart believes that "it is next to impossible to secure an entire pipeline or a field of wells," he noted that "when viewed in the big picture, militant attacks against oil infrastructure are very insignificant—the 2005 hurricane season destroyed far more US oil infrastructure than any militant group could ever have dreamed of."

Oil and natural gas is in many ways the lifeblood of Mexico's economy, as it's now the world's fifth largest oil producer. Its ability to secure its oil and gas supply, and its domestic distribution network, is of strategic importance. Ballard recalled how "Mexico started as a free market partner in the exploration of oil and gas, and then went to a state run form of business organization. Over the years this industry has increased in economic importance to the country, now being a major contributor to the economic stability of the country. This critical role of oil and gas to the economy of Mexico means that any disruption—be it natural (aging out of fields) or human initiated events (terrorism) could have a cascading effect on the fortunes of the whole country."

While America and its coalition allies have faced a similar rash of oil and gas infrastructure attacks in post-Saddam Iraq, Stewart does not believe they are related, and sees "no connection between the EPR and the GWOT." He explained that "the oil industry, by its very nature, is an attractive target for militants of any stripe," and that "in the jihadist context, you can go all the way back to bin Laden's 1996 declaration of War and see the emphasis he placed on oil then. It has been an oft-repeated theme since." While the "jihadists see it as stolen Muslim wealth," Stewart observed that "for Marxists like the EPR, it is seen as an economic soft spot that is believed to impact capitalists more than the peasants."

Ballard observed that "terrorism has and will continue to be a choice of certain activist groups worldwide," and while Mexico is facing the same sort of tactical threats that coalition forces and the Iraqi government are facing, he does not see a direct connection. As he explained: "The GWOT has been framed as a fight with Islamic extremists—an unlikely alliance in Mexico with respect to oil and gas attacks." But he added: "Where we do see connections is that groups of many varieties—extremists, separatists, radicals, etc.—see a value in using violence to further their agendas."

As a consequence, Ballard explained, "Mexico's experiences are not unique, and we as a global community will face similar mini-campaigns in the future. As energy increases in importance to the world community, such attacks need to be planned for, and oil and gas interests need to incorporate into their business planning a recognition of this fact."

Notes

1 Arthur H. Rotstein, "Minutemen Vow to Build Border Fence if U.S. Won't; Ultimatum: Group Says the Project Will Be Easy with Free Enterprise," *Salt Lake Tribune*, www. sltrib.com/cI_3737955.
2 Ibid.
3 Ibid.
4 Ibid.
5 Interview with Alan Colmes, "Minutemen May Help Build Fence along U.S.-Mexico Border," *Hannity & Colmes,* Fox News, April 20, 2006, www.foxnews.com/ story/0,2933,192521,00.html.
6 Ibid.
7 Ibid.

 8 Mimi Hall, "Momentum Builds for Fence along U.S.-Mexican Border," *USA Today*, November 17, 2005, www.usatoday.com/news/washington/2005–11–17-border-fence_x.htm.
 9 Ibid.
10 Ibid.
11 Ibid.
12 Ibid.
13 Ibid.
14 Ibid.
15 Ibid.
16 Dan Whitcomb, "May 1 Immigrant Boycott Aims to 'Close' US Cities," *ABC News* Go.com, April 27, 2006, www.abcnews.go.com/GMA/wireStory?id=1899370&gma=true.
17 Ibid.
18 Ibid.
19 Ibid.
20 Ibid.
21 Ibid.
22 Ibid.
23 Ibid.
24 Ibid.
25 Yvonne Abraham, "Planned Walkout Stirs Immigrant Debate," *Boston Globe*, April 27, 2006, www.boston.com/news/nation/articles/2006/04/28/planned_walkout_stirs_immigrant_debate/.
26 Ibid.
27 Alphonso Chardy, "Fears of Mass Arrests Keep Undocumented Immigrants Off South Florida Streets," *Miami Herald*, April 27, 2004, www.miami.com/mld/miamiherald/14443949.htm.
28 Ibid.
29 Ibid.
30 Ibid.
31 Ibid.
32 Reuters, "Some Cargill Meat Plants to Close Monday for Rally," April 25, 2006, http://today.reuters.com/news/articlenews.aspx?type=domesticNews&storyid=2006–04–25T154948Z_01_N25411823_RTRUKOC_0_US-FOOD-CARGILL-RALLY.xml.
33 David Lightman, "Border Back in Forefront: State's Lawmakers Listen to Constituents," *Hartford Courant*, April 24, 2006, www.courant.com/news/nationworld/hc-immigration0424.artapr24,0,7558793.story?coll=hc-headlines-nationworld.
34 Ibid.
35 Ibid.
36 Ibid.
37 Ibid.
38 Ibid.
39 "Schwarzenegger: Border Fence with Mexico Is Return to the Stone Age," *Monsters and Critics (M&G)*, April 24, 2006, http://news.monstersandcritics.com/northamerica/article_1158024.php/Schwarzenegger_Border_fence_with_Mexico_is_return_to_the_Stone_Age.

40 Ed O'Keefe, "Will Arnold Be Back after 06? Schwarzenegger on Global Warming, Immigration and Pumping up the Polls," *ABC News* Go.com, April 23, 2006, http://abcnews.go.com/ThisWeek/Politics/story?id=1879785&page=1.
41 Ibid.
42 Ibid.
43 Ibid.
44 Michael R. Blood, "Governor Teeters on Border: Schwarzenegger Speaks out on Immigration, but His Recommendations for Congress Are Nuanced at Best and Vague at Worst," Associated Press, www.contracostatimes.com/mld/cctimes/news/special_packages/governor_schwarzenegger/14449899.htm.
45 Ibid.
46 Danna Harman, "South of the Border, Fence Is no Deterrent: Would-Be igrants Say Nothing Will Stop Them from Working in US," *Christian Science Monitor*, March 29, 2006, www.csmonitor.com/2006/0329/p01s03-woam.html.
47 Ibid.
48 Ibid.
49 Ibid.
50 Ibid.
51 Ibid.
52 Ibid.
53 Ibid.
54 Barry Zellen, "All Chaos on the Southern Front: With America Embroiled in Overseas Terror War, the War on Drugs Threatens to Engulf Its Southern Flank," SecurityInnovator.com, November 15, 2008, http://securityinnovator.com/index.php?articleID=15850&sectionID=31. Subsequent quotations from Walser are from this article.
55 Zellen, "All Chaos on the Southern Front." Subsequent quotations from McIntyre are from this article.
56 Ibid. Subsequent quotations from Reilly are from this article.
57 Ibid. Subsequent quotations from McNeill are from this article.
58 Mark Stevenson, "Mexico Confirms Attacks on Pipelines," Associated Press, July 11, 2007, www.washingtonpost.com/wp-dyn/content/article/2007/07/10/AR2007071001102.html.
59 Barry Zellen, "Pipeline Terror on the Rise across the Americas: But Connection to Global Terror War Unlikely," SecurityInnovator.com, April 18, 2008, www.securityinnovator.com/index.php?articleID=15149&sectionID=27. Subsequent quotations from Stewart are from this article.
60 Ibid. Subsequent quotations from Ballard are from this article.

11

Securing the Northern Front

Securing the northern border: UAVs to the rescue

Across the many remote battle zones where the war on terror is being fought, the highly cost-effective and lethally precise UAV has delivered American military power to the isolated encampments of many an Al Qaeda and Taliban leaders—facilitating a remote-control and historically unprecedented air war aimed at decapitating the opponent's leadership. While controversial for the occasional miss and unfortunate collateral damage, the UAV has brought a degree of precision to air warfare that is historically unprecedented, surgical in its exactness. Such an innovative and effective tool of the warfighter is now being deployed along America's long, and traditionally un- or under-defended frontiers, with a recent field test taking place on the US-Canadian border along New York State's northern frontier in June 2009, where the Saint Lawrence River and Great Lakes form an internal maritime boundary that has been notoriously porous throughout American history.

According to a November 2008 report by the US Government Accountability Office (GAO) to Congress on Northern Border Security (GAO-09-93): "The US-Canadian border stands as the longest undefended border in the world, covering nearly 4,000 miles of land and water, most of which is sparsely populated with limited law enforcement presence," and while "historically, US attention and resources have been focused primarily on the US border with Mexico, where drug traffickers and illegal immigrants present a substantial challenge, to America's north, "the extensive volume of trade and travel between the two countries, and large expanse of areas with limited law enforcement presence, provide potential for terrorists and other criminal elements to enter the United States undetected at or between the northern ports of entry."[1]

While the GAO report was critical of the DHS efforts to secure the northern border—finding its attention had been largely focused on the southern front—it did note that DHS was "testing new technology that, if successful, may change the mix of technology and personnel deployed along the border, and partnerships among federal, state, and local agencies to coordinate information and operations may also create efficiencies that change resource requirements."[2] Among the new technologies being field tested was the UAV, or as it is known at the US Customs and Border Protection (CBP) agency, UAS—"unmanned aircraft system."[3]

Steve Hottman, associate dean and deputy director of the Physical Science Laboratory at New Mexico State University (NMSU), told me that a "UAS can increase the situational awareness of the personnel on the ground," and that it "can represent more of a persistent surveillance platform for monitoring larger areas using fewer personnel resources," while at the same time, it can "complement the existing tool box of capabilities that border agencies can employ for secure borders."[4] He described the components of a UAS, noting that "in very general terms there is an aircraft and some type of surveillance payload. The aircraft includes the airframe, ground control station, data links, operator/maintainer, training, etc which all represent part of the system. The payload can be based upon a variety of technologies which in some cases provide the capability to detect people or vehicles at night."

Hottman noted that "UAVs come in a variety of designs, capabilities, sizes, operational durations, and range to name a few parameters," and that a "variety of payloads can be mounted to a UAS for border security purposes," adding that "these technologies have the capability to 'see' through some weather, can function in the dark, or be based upon nonvisual technologies." Then, "the information from UAS is assessed in a variety of ways. One way is for a human payload operator to scan the image being transmitted back by the UAS. Additionally, algorithms exist that can seek out information automatically removing the human from the loop in some cases." A UAS may be "flown with the human directly in the loop in some cases," with the "human acting primarily as a monitor for highly automated systems. In some of these cases the UAS is in visual sight of the operator while the more sophisticated systems have the operator in a ground control station with no actual view of the UAS. Generally no matter how small a UAS might be, most of these systems have a capability to program waypoints that the UAV can fly to versus having the human constantly providing control inputs." Hottman noted there is a great variety of UAV types, and that "some UAS can remain loft for less than an hour. Others can be operated for well over 30 hours."

I also spoke with Juan Munoz-Torres, a spokesman for CBP, who observed CBP's Office of Air and Marine (CBP A&M) was currently operating the "MQ-9 Predator B unmanned aircraft system along the northern and southwest borders," and "along the northern border, CBP A&M operates the UAS out of CBP's UAS Operations Center—North Dakota at Grand Forks," where it "has a Certificate of Authorization (COA) from the Federal Aviation Administration (FAA) to operate along a 230 mile stretch of the Northern Border."[5] He added that "along the Southwest Border, CBP A&M operates the UAS out of our UAS Operations Center—Arizona, at Libby Army Airfield in Sierra Vista," where CBP "has a COA from the FAA to operate along 500 miles on the Southwest Border." CBP's southwestern UAV deployment dates back to 2005, when on August 30 it announced that it had "awarded General Atomics Aeronautical Services, Inc., of San Diego, California the contract to produce the 'Predator B' Unmanned Aerial Vehicle (UAV) to assist in protecting our nation's borders." The first Predator B was deployed the next month, on September 29, 2005, at Ft. Huachuca/Muni-Libby AAF in Sierra Vista, Arizona, "where previous UAV platforms were tested by CBP and home to the largest UAV training facility in the world."

CBP's more recent northern UAV deployment was announced on February 19, 2009, when CBP officially opened its Unmanned Aircraft Operations Center of North Dakota, "bringing enhanced security operations to the US-Canada border," as a CBP media release noted, adding that "along the US northern border, CBP processes more than 70 million international travelers and 35 million vehicles, makes approximately 4,000 arrests, and interdicts approximately 40,000 pounds of illegal drugs annually. The terrain, which ranges from densely forested lands on the west and east coasts, a significant maritime environment, then open plains in the middle of the country, is comprised of many sparsely populated lands with limited state and local law enforcement presence along much of the immediate border area. CBP's unmanned aircraft will serve as a valuable tool in securing US borders and supporting information sharing between and among law enforcement entities in this vast geography."[6] The November 2008 GAO report further noted: "Historically, these numbers have been significantly lower than those of the southwest border; however, DHS reports that the terrorist threat on the northern border is higher, given the large expanse of area with limited law enforcement coverage."[7]

In June 2009, CBP commenced UAS operations in the Great Lakes Region from Wheeler-Sack Army Airfield in Fort Drum, New York. Munoz-Torres explained that "the operation is designed to demonstrate UAS operations and evaluate law enforcement coordination concepts in both land and maritime environments at the Northern Border. Once operations are complete, the UAS will be moved to North Dakota." Munoz-Torres described other UAS activities to enhance America's border security. In March 2008, CBP and the US Coast Guard (USCG) "successfully conducted a demonstration of a maritime variant of the Predator B from Tyndall Air Force Base, Florida," which "paved the way for the development of a joint concept of operations and a preliminary operational requirements document for a maritime Predator that was jointly signed by CBP and the USCG. A charter for a CBP/USCG Joint Program Office was signed on November 6, 2008." Then, "During the 2008 Atlantic Hurricane Season, CBP A&M responded to a first-ever request from Federal Emergency Management Agency (FEMA) to support hurricane preparations and recovery operations with the Predator B. CBP A&M successfully flew several missions to map critical infrastructure before and then after the event, and to provide streaming video of the hurricane damage to aid first responders."

According to Munoz-Torres, CBP uses UAS "in support of law enforcement missions, as well as in prevention, response, and recovery of natural disasters," and it has become a "critical tool in situations where the level of risk to personnel might be too high to employ manned aircraft, including the following: Surveillance missions of long duration where crew rest and fuel limitations would prohibit manned flight; missions into areas of known or suspected radiological, biological, or chemical contamination; and situations where suspects might attempt to attack airborne law enforcement operations." He added that a UAS "also acts as a force multiplier when CBP A&M is called to support the homeland security and disaster relief efforts of its DHS partners, including the FEMA and USCG. Most importantly, the remotely piloted Predator B allows CBP A&M to safely conduct missions in areas that are difficult to access or otherwise considered too high-risk for manned aircraft or CBP personnel on the ground."

Munoz-Torres explained that CBP selected the Predator B "for its unique combination of cost, operational capabilities, payload capacity, pilot-in-the-loop mission flexibility, potential to accommodate new sensor packages, as well as for its safety and performance record with other federal entities, including the Department of Defense." So far, it has shown great potential. "Over a two-year period ending in March 2009," Munoz-Torres recalled, "the Predator B had flown more than 1,331 hours culminating in 60 arrests and the seizure of over 14,406 pounds of illegal drugs," adding "there is no peer to the Predator B among CBP A&M aircraft in terms of agility and flexibility while employed in long duration surveillance and interdiction missions." Accordingly, "demands for CBP A&M UAS support are increasing," and "CBP plans to expand across the entire Southwest Border, expand initial operations on the Northern Border, surge to the Great Lakes region, conduct sensor tests and demonstrations, and introduce a maritime variant of the Predator to the Caribbean and Eastern Pacific in support of long range surveillance and interdiction operations."

Munoz-Torres described the technology that makes the Predator B so helpful, noting it "consists of a medium altitude, high endurance remotely piloted aircraft; ground control station; ground data terminal; satellite and line of sight data and voice communications; as well as the ground support equipment required to operate, maintain, and sustain the system." It's also "uniquely modular and adaptable to a variety of land, sea, and air missions. The flexibility of the Predator B UAS platform allows CBP to affect the most appropriate response to ever-changing threats in homeland security and law enforcement environments." Predator B is "equipped with state of the art sensor and communications technology and is capable of flying 18 hour missions at altitudes up to 50,000 feet," and among its array of sensors are the Multi-Spectral Targeting System (MTS-B)" as well as a Synthetic Aperture Radar (SAR). The MTS-B "consists of multiple electro-optical and infrared sensors installed in a ball turret capable of rotating 360 degrees to provide ground imagery. Sensors can operate in both day and night to locate possible targets of interest to include people, vehicles, and to a lesser degree other aircraft. The system employs a laser marker for identifying points of interest and can operate effectively at altitudes over 15,000 feet."

For those missions that call for imagery that cannot be obtained by optical sensors, Munoz-Torres added, the Predator B employs the Lynx SAR that's "capable of providing clear ground images despite the presence of clouds or other natural or man-made atmospheric obstructions." The Lynx SAR is a "high-resolution synthetic aperture radar with Ground Moving Target Indicator capability" that "provides the capability to image vehicles, structures, and landscapes on the ground. The system provides coherent change detection by highlighting changes in the terrain via multiple passes over the same location." Added Munoz-Torres: "These systems allow CBP to effectively monitor terrain, identify possible criminal activity, and coordinate with ground forces in the apprehension of suspected criminals with little to no additional risk to CBP personnel. Electro-optical and infra-red sensors allow the Predator B to operate in both day and night conditions in support of its law enforcement and disaster relief partners, including the CBP Office of Border Patrol, FEMA, the Department of Defense, and local law enforcement agencies."

Reflecting on the many ways a UAV can contribute to border security, NMSU's Hottman explained that the UAS has "a wide variety of real and potential applications. Search and rescue functions can employ some of the same technology used to monitor border areas. Other UAS applications include fire monitoring, agriculture applications, traffic monitoring and other law enforcement functions to name just a few applications." He added that "reports from users have been positive regarding the application of UAS," and "based upon the capabilities that various technology provide us, UAS are envisioned to have a border security role for years to come."

Reflecting on the challenge of securing America's frontiers, Munoz-Torres noted that "the border is not merely a physical frontier. Effectively securing it requires attention to processes that begin far outside US borders, occur at the border, and continue to all interior regions of the United States. As such, CBP views the border as a continuum of activities that results in the physical border being the last line of defense, not the first. Consequently, CBP's strategies address the threats and challenges along the entire continuum." Munoz-Torres observed that "each of the nation's border regions provides a nexus point where three transnational threats converge: drug trafficking operations, alien and contraband smuggling, and terrorist activity. CBP A&M is committed to overcoming these threats by responding with the most rapid and focused use of its assets and resources." Within this context, he added, the Predator B "is considered a strategic air asset for homeland security, providing surveillance and information-gathering."

Securing America's "last frontier"

Alaska is no stranger to catastrophe, both man-made and natural. Among its most notable of man-made disasters was the March 24, 1989, oil spill in Prince William Sound, when the Exxon Valdez oil tanker struck Bligh Reef—spilling more than 11 million gallons of crude oil, causing both ecological and economic mayhem. The oil spill was an act of negligence, one of the most notorious acts of drunk driving ever—dumping 22 percent of the ship's liquid cargo into the pristine waters, creating a 1,776-square-mile oil spill, and damaging 3,167 miles of coastline, with oil from the spill reaching 470 miles to the southwest.

Economically, the Valdez oil spill cost a fortune: Exxon was forced to clean up the spill, spent $2.2 billion on cleanup work, and the total price-tag came to more than $4 billion. Exxon agreed to pay the state of Alaska and the United States a $900-million civil penalty over a ten-year period; as a criminal penalty, Exxon agreed to pay a $250-million fine—later reduced by $125 million for Exxon's cooperation during the cleanup, and upgraded safety procedures to prevent a reoccurrence.[8] On September 16, 1994, a jury in federal court returned a $5-billion punitive damages verdict against Exxon—which Exxon successfully appealed: the $5-billion verdict was overturned by a panel of the 9th Circuit Court in November 2001.

The ecological costs were also off the charts: between 100,000 and 600,000 birds were killed, as were 5,500 sea otters, 30 seals, and 22 whales.[9] As the US Environmental Protection Agency (EPA) website explained: "The spill was the largest in US history and tested the abilities of local, national, and industrial organizations to prepare for, and respond to, a disaster of such magnitude. Many factors complicated the cleanup efforts following the spill. The size of the spill and its remote location, accessible only by helicopter and boat, made government and industry efforts difficult and tested existing plans for dealing with such an event."[10]

What if? Alaska pipeline security after 9/11

With Alaska's huge North Slope oil and gas reserves and its long, hard-to-defend, 800-mile-long oil pipeline, the Exxon Valdez disaster revealed the scale of destruction that can be delivered upon America's resource-rich state by the hand of man. Trying to imagine the scale of destruction that could be caused by a terrorist attack in this post-9/11 era is enough to cause a chill to run down one's spine.

Many people think of Alaska as vast, untapped wilderness, but it's been a major oil producer for over three decades. As noted in a 2005 speech by Alaska's then–lieutenant governor, Loren Leman: "At 586,412 square miles of land, Alaska is one-fifth the size of the rest of the nation. That's larger than Washington, Oregon, California, Idaho and Montana combined!"[11] He added that "today Alaska provides 16 percent of the total US oil production."[12] And with vast, undeveloped natural gas fields with 35 TCF (trillion cubic feet) of known reserves in the North Slope, and plans for a new, natural gas pipeline in development to bring this treasure chest of natural gas to the market, the state's petroleum capacity may expand even further.

In early 2006, jihadist plans to attack the Alaska Pipeline were uncovered, and widely reported in the press. According to an article from the *Anchorage Daily News* on January 19, 2006, "a recent posting on a Web site purportedly affiliated with al-Qaida urges attacks against the trans-Alaska oil pipeline and Valdez tanker dock, calling on jihadists to either shower the pipe with bullets or hide and detonate explosives along its length. The unknown author encourages small cells of four or five mujahedeen, or Muslim guerrillas, living in the United States or in Canada or Mexico to mount the attacks."[13] As *Anchorage Daily News* reporter Wesley Loy explained: "The 10-page posting includes numerous links to Web sites providing maps and other basic information about the pipeline," and argues that by "attacking oil and gas targets in the United States and other countries is key to bringing down the economy of the 'American devils.'"[14] The posting "suggests mujahedeen hit pipelines and other oil and gas assets in the United States, as well as in Iraq and the Caspian Sea region, as a way to hurt the US economy and to gain payback for the war in Iraq," and that it "singles out the Alaska pipeline as a particularly valuable, and vulnerable, target for terror."[15] The posting also "notes that 300,000 gallons of crude oil spewed out of a bullet hole in 2001," when one intoxicated Alaskan shot at the pipeline with a .338 caliber hunting rifle.[16]

Shooting the pipeline: the 2001 incident

That 2001 incident was discussed in a series of press releases issued by Alyeska Pipeline in October 2001, the first act of sabotage against the pipeline since a 1978 explosion resulted in over 600,000 gallons of oil spilled. On October 4, 2001, Alyeska announced "the trans-Alaska pipeline was shut down at about 2:30 p.m. today after an Alyeska surveillance helicopter detected oil on the ground in the vicinity of milepost 400, about 15 miles north of pump station 7. The surveillance crew detected what appears to be a bullet hole in the pipe. Alyeska's Operations Control Center immediately began the process of shutting down the north end of the line, above the site of the incident." The company noted that "Alaska State Troopers have been dispatched to the scene," and "all appropriate government agencies have been notified."

The next day, on October 5, 2001, the company reported that "a suspect believed to be responsible for shooting the pipeline is in Alaska State Trooper custody." The company said it "immediately mobilized response crews, heavy machinery and a special land spill strike team to the scene to clean up the oil," which had sprayed "out about 75 feet from the pipeline."

Later on October 5, 2001, the company issued a release noting that "control, containment, and clean-up efforts continue at Milepost 400 of the trans-Alaska pipeline where a bullet hole punctured the pipe on Thursday, October 4, 2001," and that "oil continues to be discharged from the pipe although responders are 'recovering oil at a rate equal to, or greater than the leak rate,' said Bill Howitt, Unified Commander." The release noted that "of the estimated spill volume of 6,600 barrels, 371 barrels have been recovered," and that "personnel and equipment have been mobilized on site to repair the pipe" and that "more than 100 Alyeska and contract responders, working 12 hour shifts, are on the scene working to contain and recover the spilled oil with additional resources en route." On October 8, 2001, the company noted "an estimated total of 6,800 barrels or 285,600 gallons were spilled" but that "108,600 gallons have been recovered as of Monday morning."

On October 19, 2001, the company announced that "Alaska State Troopers notified Alyeska Pipeline Service Company Thursday evening that at least 4 additional bullet strikes had been discovered near MP 400," and this "discovery was approximately one mile north of where a bullet punctured the trans-Alaska Pipeline earlier this month" and that "these bullet strikes penetrated the outer insulation jacket and while they didn't cause any leaks, did cause sufficient damage to the pipe wall to require repair. That repair, consisting of two sleeves, will be done today." The company noted that it was "not known at this time whether the bullet strikes existed prior to the October 4 incident," adding that "Alyeska has documented more than 50 cases over the years in which bullets have struck the pipe," some of which "also required repairs to the pipe." Alaska State Troopers would eventually arrest a drunk hunter named Danny Lewis, who is now serving 16 years in jail for his crime in Fairbanks.

Securing the pipeline: The 2006 terror threat

The 2006 jihadist posting calling for an attack of the pipeline also "suggests attackers hit the pipeline with 'piercing bullets,' or better yet, place explosives alongside it, especially in rural and wooded places to slow response and create fires."[17] It adds that jihadis "should detonate the hidden explosives 'from time to time until they can receive news of the American devils' defeat."[18] It also suggests attacks "on the pipeline's pump stations, the oil tankers that carry the oil to the West Coast, and the storage tanks at the Valdez tanker dock, which are 'considered an ideal target.'"[19]

The posting, in Arabic, was "discovered and translated in late December [2005] by the SITE Institute, a Washington, DC, nonprofit organization that tracks international terrorists;" SITE's director, Rita Katz, found that "the posting was unusual and alarming in its length and detail."[20] SITE "has analyzed and translated many terrorism-related Web postings for its clients, including oil companies, and this one stood out."[21] As Katz explained: "When I saw this message, I was shocked. It was much longer, more thoughtful and more fully researched than the normal posting."[22]

As reported by *New Yorker* columnist Benjamin Wallace-Wells, "last December, Katz was reading a jihadist message board called Al Safanat when she discovered a manual describing how to attack the Alaska pipeline."[23] Wallace-Wells wrote that "she was struck by the level of detail: the manual recommended that an elite cell of four or five men equipped with armor-piercing bullets or explosives sneak across the border into Alaska from Canada."[24] According to Wallace-Wells, while "Katz conceded that her group doesn't check the scientific accuracy of each manual, or the legitimacy of every threat," she does try "to make sure that the Web site that a particular item appears on has produced credible threats in the past, and that the threat seems serious."[25] As she explained: "I'm telling people what terrorists are thinking. Wouldn't you rather know that they're thinking about the Alaska pipeline, even if this manual wouldn't work?"[26]

Anchorage Daily News reporter Loy reported that Curtis Thomas, a spokesman for the Alyeska Pipeline Service Co., "said his company also was aware of the posting, but that 'we're not aware at this time of any imminent threat' to the system."[27] The FBI's Alaska spokesman, Eric Gonzalez, told Loy that his agency was "in communications with state, federal and local law enforcement and private entities that would be affected by this," and added that "the posting did not seem to contain information beyond what is readily available to anyone with a little digging."[28] According to Gonzalez: "I don't think it's a secret to anyone that the trans-Alaska pipeline, the terminal at Valdez, is a critical asset not only to the state but the country."[29] Additionally, John Madden, deputy director of Alaska's Division of Homeland Security and Emergency Management, explained while "we take all of these matters quite seriously," that this posting was "'not any great, analytical document,' but rather a collection of information available from open sources."[30] Despite questions about the posting's tactical significance, Loy noted a month earlier that "federal pipeline regulators ordered Alyeska to develop new spill cleanup drills with 'terrorist attack scenarios' in mind."[31]

Alaska's isolation: Security or vulnerability

As reported by Associated Press reporter Mary Pemberton: the "trans-Alaska pipeline looks like it would be an easy target for terrorists intent on destroying a valuable American asset, but those responsible for its safekeeping say looks can be deceiving."[32]

Indeed, she noted, "terrorism experts say pipelines in general are easy targets, but tend to be low priority because they can be repaired so quickly," adding that "officials with an intimate knowledge of the pipeline say it's far less vulnerable than it appears—in part because of the difficulty a saboteur would have getting any weapon capable of serious damage into Alaska."[33] Alaska's Division of Homeland Security and Emergency Management deputy director John Madden told Pemberton that the Alaska pipeline has state, federal, and local agencies keeping an eye on it, and as a result, he dismissed the risk of firing a shoulder-mounted rocket at the pipeline, owing to "the difficulty of getting such a weapon near the pipeline."[34] Madden explained that "the very act of a shoulder-fired weapon suggests transport of that weapon," and that "agencies including customs, immigration, border control and state troopers, work to make sure that such a weapon would never make it into Alaska."[35] He added "there are quite a bit of those layers of defense and observation which the public will never see."[36]

Pemberton also cites Henry Lee, director of the Environment and Natural Resources Program at the Belfer Center for Science and International Affairs at Harvard University, who explained that "while the pipeline would be easy to blow up, it is not an attractive target for terrorists."[37] He explained that "terrorists blow up pipelines more as an irritant, pointing to a pipeline in Colombia blown up more than 100 times by rebels," and while "pipelines can be blown up, and they are fairly easy to blow up," the "problem is you would have it fixed in a matter of days."[38]

Oil as a global, strategic target

In an interview in *Family Security Matters*, former CIA chief R. James Woolsey explained that "the petroleum infrastructure is highly vulnerable to terrorist and other attacks," noting "the radical Islamist movement, including but not exclusively al Qaeda, has on a number of occasions explicitly called for worldwide attacks on the petroleum infrastructure and has carried some out in the Greater Middle East," and that a "well-planned attack could take some six million barrels per day off the market for a year or more, sending petroleum prices sharply upward to well over $100/barrel and severely damaging much of the world's economy."[39] Woolsey added that "domestic infrastructure in the West is not immune from such disruption" and noted "the Trans-Alaska Pipeline has been subject to several amateurish attacks that have taken it briefly out of commission" and that "a seriously planned attack on it could be far more devastating."[40]

As reported by Khalid Hasan in the *Daily Times of Pakistan*, "a leading expert on Al Qaeda has predicted that in the next phase of the terrorist group's war on the US economy, the number of attacks on oil infrastructure targets will increase."[41] Hasan cited Michael Scheuer, "who served the CIA for 11 years and was head of the agency's Osama Bin Laden unit," who explained that "Bin Laden's intention is to bankrupt the US economy, which is 'entirely likely' to lead to attacks on infrastructure targets inside the US by Al Qaeda, its allies and groups that may not necessarily be associated with either."[42] While such attacks "would probably focus on large targets that could cripple parts of the US economy," Scheuer added that "other groups, however, may be satisfied with staging small-scale attacks on pipelines, pumping stations, tanker trucks."[43] Scheuer explained: "Al Qaeda's February 2006 attack on the Abqaiq refinery in Saudi Arabia, the world's largest such complex, should be seen as the beginning of a new and more systematic phase of Al Qaeda's targeting of the oil infrastructure" and noted "the orders for the Abqaiq attack came direct from Osama Bin Laden" and that "two days later, there was a fatwa from the Al Qaeda-related cleric, Sheikh al-Anzi, which said that such attacks are legitimate and they must be conducted in a way that does not produce permanent damage to the Muslim community's ability to exploit and benefit from its energy reserves."[44]

Pipeline security is a global concern—according to Reuters, "Turkey plans tougher security measures to safeguard a $4 billion pipeline carrying Azeri crude from Baku to the Mediterranean port of Ceyhan."[45] Reuters observed that "the first oil arrived at Ceyhan on May 28 and the first loading onto tankers is expected to be completed by June 4, later than originally expected."[46] It added that Turkey's energy minister, Hilmi Güler, "met representatives of Turkey's state pipeline company Botas, national intelligence, the gendarmerie and the coast guard in Ankara on Wednesday to discuss ways of beefing up security."[47] Some measures to improve pipeline security "include increasing the number of police stations and special security teams charged with looking after the section of the pipeline, stretching 1,070 km (665 miles) out of the total 1,770 km, that crosses Turkish territory."[48] A week earlier, "Kurdish separatist guerrillas blew up part of a natural gas pipeline in eastern Turkey, disrupting the flow of gas and causing about $370,000 worth of damage."[49]

Turkish Daily News also reported that "specially equipped mounted police are to protect oil pipelines in Turkey, the Anatolia news agency reported," and that BOTAS "plans to strengthen its legal and security infrastructure due to the pipelines' inevitable expansion in length in the years ahead."[50] It added that "BOTAS currently has 2,500 kilometers of natural gas pipeline and 3,000 kilometers of oil pipeline in Turkey," and "another 2,500 kilometers are under construction."[51] *Turkish Daily News* added that "the mounted units will patrol uninhabited regions at night and will be equipped with night-vision systems, weapons, loudspeakers and sophisticated mean of communication," and that "guarding the pipelines on an around the clock basis, these units will immediately inform security forces when they encounter any suspicious situation."[52]

After 9/11

Anchorage Daily News reporter Loy reported that "security for the pipeline and Valdez tanker dock was heightened after the Sept. 11, 2001, terror attacks in New York City and Washington, DC," resulting in the creation of "a security zone the US Coast Guard enforces around the dock," which continues to this day, albeit "slightly downsized."[53] In a company announcement released by the Alyeska Pipeline Service Company on

September 11, 2001, Dan Hisey, the company's chief operating officer, observed that "operationally, Alyeska has ramped up security and focused on protecting our people, the terminal, and the pipeline" and that "we have been in constant contact with the military, the FBI, and the Coast Guard throughout the day and we will continue to maintain this level of security until we all agree it is safe to return to normal operations." He added that "based on information the Coast Guard had concerning a potential threat and in cooperation with the Coast Guard, we reduced staffing levels at the Valdez Marine Terminal," but "that threat did not materialize and we are now in the process of bringing full staffing levels back into the terminal."

Earlier in the day, the company had announced that "at the request of the United States Coast Guard, Alyeska Pipeline Service Company evacuated the Valdez Marine Terminal and is operating with a limited number of critical operations personnel," as "military officials considered a KAL airliner inbound to Anchorage a threat to the terminal, and the Coast Guard requested that Alyeska evacuate the terminal. At the request of the Coast Guard, loading operations have been shut down and tankers are being moved to sea. The airliner has been escorted by military planes to Whitehorse, Yukon Territory. Alyeska remains in a heightened state of security and preparedness. The pipeline is still operating."

Also on September 11, P.M. Coleman, commander of the US Coast Guard and captain of Prince William Sound, Alaska, announced that the US Coast Guard was "establishing a temporary security zone around the Trans-Alaska Pipeline (TAPS) Valdez Terminal Complex in Valdez, Alaska" and its boundaries would "encompass all waters approximately one mile north and east and two miles west of all terminal berths." According to a government announcement, "this security zone is necessary to protect the TAPS terminal and TAPS tank vessels from damage or injury from sabotage, destruction or other subversive acts" and that "entry into this security zone is prohibited unless specifically authorized by the Captain of the Port, Prince William Sound, Alaska." The announcement explained "the Coast Guard is taking this action for the immediate protection of the national security interests in light of terrorist acts perpetrated on September 11, 2001."[54] Originally, the regulation creating the security zone in Valdez was to remain "effective from 6 pm September 15, 2001 through June 1, 2002," but the zone remains in place to this day, albeit with reduced dimensions.

Budgetary realities

As noted by Alaskan journalist Bill McAllister, Capitol bureau chief for *KTUU-TV*, the NBC-affiliate in Anchorage, and a board member of Capitolbeat, the Association of Capitol Reporters and Editors: "Like other states, Alaska scrambled in the wake of the terrorist attacks to assess risk and heighten security around critical infrastructure. But despite recommendations by the governor for broad spending on new security measures, Alaska's looming budget deficit kept lawmakers from approving all but a fraction of funds targeted to ongoing homeland security projects."[55]

McAllister recalled that Alaska governor Tony Knowles "convened a "'terrorism disaster policy cabinet' and presented its recommendations in legislation carrying a $100 million price tag," and in November 2001 it issued a report noting: "Our geographical isolation from the 'lower 48' does not guarantee that . . . potential targets will have immunity from attack . . . as our nation improves its homeland security and targets become more difficult to attack, terrorists could well look to targets that are less protected."[56] However, "as the months went by, the sense of alarm seemed to ebb," and "with the state facing a $1 billion deficit in two years, based upon the projected depletion of budget reserves, lawmakers were in a penny-pinching mood."[57]

Indeed, "when the legislative session adjourned a month later, less than $2 million of state general funds—out of the governor's request for $46 million—was appropriated for ongoing homeland security purposes."[58] He noted this "legislative balking also stymied the state-run Alaska Marine Highway System's proposals to increase security aboard ferries, which are a critical transportation link, particularly in coastal communities that aren't connected to the road system. But with the lack of new legislative funding, the department scrapped tentative plans to search vehicles and baggage and to add on-board security personnel."[59] As for the pipeline, which "is considered the state's number one asset—not only because of its national importance, but also because oil revenue accounts for 80 percent of state general fund spending," McAllister pointed out that "there is both public and private security for the pipeline," and adds "the structure crosses hundreds of miles of unpopulated, difficult-to-traverse terrain." McAllister cited Drew Dix, Alaska's homeland security coordinator, who observed "that pipeline is a very difficult thing to defend—you can't guarantee anything. The terrorist has the advantage."[60]

Nonetheless, McAllister noted that "Alaska officials say they entered the post-9/11 world with some advantages," and that "the state's history of disasters, from the 1964 Good Friday earthquake to the 1989 Exxon Valdez oil spill to numerous fires and floods, has created 'integrated and effective emergency management and inter-agency procedures at all levels,' according to the governor's terrorism cabinet report."[61]

Indeed, Alaska's state government is "unusually centralized, with a chief executive that has as much power as any governor in the nation," so "even if new state funding is scarce, there's a different attitude in the Knowles administration."[62] As Alaska's Public Safety Commissioner Del Smith told McAllister: "Our focus has shifted to, when people tell us about something strange, we're more motivated to check it out."[63] Since 9/11, Smith added, "we're very wary. I don't think we can assume they don't know where Alaska is."[64]

Notes

1   US Government Accountability Office, *GAO-09–93: Northern Border Security: DHS's Report Could Better Inform Congress by Identifying Actions, Resources, and Time Frames Needed to Address Vulnerabilities*, November 2008, www.gao.gov/new.items/d0993.pdf.
2   Ibid.

3 Ibid.
4 Barry Zellen, "UAVs to the Rescue: Fresh from the Battlefield, Unmanned Aerial Vehicles Now Protect the Home Front," SecurityInnovator.com, June 30, 2009, http://securityinnovator.com/index.php?articleID=15845&sectionID=31. Subsequent quotations from Hottman are from this article.
5 Ibid. Subsequent quotations from Munoz-Torres are from this article.
6 "GA-ASI CBP Unmanned Aircraft Begins Operations in North Dakota: Aircraft Will Enhance CBP's Northern Border Security Mission," February 16, 2009, www.ga.com/news.php?read=1&id=180&page=3.
7 *GAO-09–93: Northern Border Security*
8 "The Exxon Valdez Oil Spill Disaster," March 24, 1999, www.explorenorth.com/library/weekly/aa032499.htm.
9 See http://library.thinkquest.org/26026/History/exxon_valdez.html.
10 See www.epa.gov/oilspill/exxon.htm.
11 "Why America Needs Alaska's Oil and Gas," April 11, 2005, in Bellingham, WA; www.ltgov.state.ak.us/speeches.php?id=2161.
12 Ibid.
13 Wesley Loy, "Web Post Urges Jihadists to Attack Alaska Pipeline: BULLETS OR EXPLOSIVES: Nameless Author Claims to Be Acting on al-Qaida Directives," *Anchorage Daily News*, January 19, 2006, www.adn.com/news/alaska/story/7371588p-7283808c.html.
14 Ibid.
15 Ibid.
16 Ibid.
17 Loy, "Web post urges jihadists to attack Alaska pipeline."
18 Ibid.
19 Ibid.
20 Ibid.
21 Ibid.
22 Ibid.
23 "PRIVATE JIHAD: How Rita Katz Got into the Spying Business," *The New Yorker*, May 29, 2006, www.newyorker.com/fact/content/articles/060529fa_fact.
24 Ibid.
25 Ibid.
26 Ibid.
27 Loy, "Web Post Urges Jihadists to Attack Alaska Pipeline."
28 Ibid.
29 Ibid.
30 Ibid.
31 Ibid.
32 Mary Pemberton, "Alaska Pipeline Not That Vulnerable," Associated Press, as reported in *The Detroit News*, February 10, 2006, www.detnews.com/apps/pbcs.dll/article?AID=/20060210/BIZ/602100432/1001.
33 Ibid.
34 Ibid.
35 Ibid.
36 Ibid.
37 Ibid.

38 Ibid.
39 "Exclusive: Jim Woolsey on Energy Security," *Family Security Matters*, June 13, 2006, www.familysecuritymatters.org/index.php?id=130423.
40 Ibid.
41 Khalid Hasan, "LATE NEWS: Al Qaeda Intent on Attacking US Oil Facilities," *Daily Times of Pakistan*, May 17, 2006, www.dailytimes.com.pk/default.asp?page=2006%5C0 5%5C17%5Cstory_17–5–2006_pg7_45.
42 Ibid.
43 Ibid.
44 Ibid.
45 "Turkey to Beef up Security for Ceyhan Oil Pipeline," Reuters, as reported in the *Turkish Daily News*, June 2, 2006, www.turkishdailynews.com.tr/article. php?enewsid=45088.
46 Ibid.
47 Ibid.
48 Ibid.
49 Ibid.
50 "Mounted Units to Guard Pipelines," *Turkish Daily News*, June 14, 2006, www. turkishdailynews.com.tr/article.php?enewsid=46136.
51 Ibid.
52 Ibid.
53 Loy, "Web Post Urges Jihadists to Attack Alaska Pipeline."
54 "Security Zone Declared after 9/11 by Coast Guard: Security Zone; Trans-Alaska Pipeline Valdez Terminal Complex, Valdez, Alaska," *Federal Register*, Volume 66, Number 216 (November 7, 2001), www.epa.gov/fedrgstr/EPA-IMPACT/2001/ November/Day-07/i27874.htm. In 2009, the fine for crossing the security zone's boundary increased from $250 to $1,000 for individual offenders. Commercial boats are fined $2,000, and repeat offenders can be fined up to $32,000. See: "Coast Guard ups Valdez 'trespassing' fine to $1,000," *Anchorage Daily News,* July 31, 2009, http:// www.adn.com/2009/07/31/883654/coast-guard-ups-valdez-trespassing.html.
55 "Alaska Won't 'Break the Bank' On Security Spending," Stateline.org, August 30, 2002,www.stateline.org/live/ViewPage.action?siteNodeId=136&languageId=1&content Id=14948.
56 Ibid.
57 Ibid.
58 Ibid.
59 Ibid.
60 Ibid.
61 Ibid.
62 Ibid.
63 Ibid.
64 Ibid.

Part III

Protecting the Populace

12

Air Rage: Aviation Insecurity after 9/11

September 11, 2001, has taught us a lot of lessons, but an important one was that the challenges of airplane cabin security must not be overlooked. These challenges were evident long before the mass-terror attacks of that day of infamy. Indeed, the phenomenon known as air rage has been long documented, and was even the title of a Hollywood action thriller released in July 2001, evidence that the risks and dangers of in-cabin misbehavior were widely known before that day of terror came to America's shores less than two months later. To understand the challenges of in-cabin security better, I spoke with world-renowned aviation security expert Dr Andrew R. Thomas, assistant professor of International Business at the University of Akron.[1] He is the founding editor-in-chief of the *Journal of Transportation Security* and a prolific author of several books, including *Aviation Insecurity: The New Challenges of Air Travel* (May 2003), and coauthor of *Air Rage: Crisis in the Skies* (September 2001). He is also editor of the three-volume book set *Aviation Security Management*, published by Praeger Security International in October 2008.

Thomas explained that the problem of cockpit intrusion, which was on the rise long before 9/11, was a time bomb waiting to go off. Indeed, his book *Air Rage: Crisis in the Skies* was researched and written well before the events of 9/11 transpired, and was released by its publisher (coincidentally, though seemingly prophetically) on September 11, 2001. Before 9/11, he explained, cockpit intrusions presented the biggest security problem facing the aviation industry. The terror masters who planned that day's events "knew all they needed was to get into the cockpits of those planes; they were studying out systems as criminals and terrorists do." He added that "the whole thing was predicated on getting in that cockpit door," something that had been "seen in practice some two dozen times before 9/11." Had the problem of cockpit intrusion been addressed before 9/11, and the terrorists had not gained entry to those cockpits that day, then "the world is a fundamentally different place today." Indeed, as Thomas observed, "there are so many outcomes of this, that shows you transportation security and post-9/11 aviation security, this is life and death stuff."

Today, Thomas observed, there are "still great challenges" with aviation security, and that "it's a question of where are we putting our resources, our efforts. So far, we're too often putting them in the wrong places," and consequently have created "a system with glaring vulnerabilities." Added Thomas, "when you have scarce resources, they need to be placed in an area where it reduces risk of attack to the system—by focusing so much on 9/11 and countermeasures to stop another 9/11, we have not focused resources on preventing or reducing the risk of the next round of attacks." He believes "we need vigilance, and to battle complacency—especially as it relates to the cockpit door. It still gets opened and remains opened far too much on these planes, and the further we get away from 9/11, that complacency just becomes more prevalent. That's where constant training and assessment matters."

Since 9/11, we've witnessed a series of catastrophic, and near-catastrophic, attacks of our aviation system by terrorists, including the unsuccessful December 2001 attack by Richard Reid, the infamous shoe-bomber; a deadly inflight arson attack in May 2003 of a China Northern Airlines flight, killing 112; the August 2004 attacks by Chechen suicide-bombers of two airborne Russian aircraft, killing 89. Several more attacks have been prevented in recent years, including a 2004 plot to ram a Mexicana flight into the Las Vegas strip, a 2006 plot to blow-up trans-Atlantic flights departing Europe using binary liquid explosives smuggled aboard as non-lethal components in bottles, and the attempted Christmas day bombing of Northwest Airlines flight 253 to Detroit by the infamous underwear-bomber, Umar Farouk Abdulmutallab, in 2009. As Thomas observed: "These guys are still thinking aviation is best way to make major impacts for them." He added that "this stuff has been going on for decades." Thomas noted the first confirmed bombing of a commercial airliner took place on October 10, 1933, when a United Airline Boeing 247 was destroyed by a bomb over Chesterton, Indiana. "This stuff goes back to the origins of commercial air travel."

Thomas described two types of technology solutions to boost in-cabin security: predictive modeling software, and closed-circuit television systems that enable the pilot or people on the ground to see inside the cabin 24/7. But he believes that "ultimately, technology can aid in the process, but this whole notion, and I think it's a wrong notion, that technology itself is the solution, is just wrong—if you look at how threats get thwarted, how potential threats get stopped, it's human interaction, someone taking initiative, somebody who is well trained." Recalling Richard Reid's 2001 attack high above the Atlantic: "You can't combat a human threat with mere technology. We try to do that, and I don't understand why—the threat is human, the response has to be human-led. Technology can help you, but at the end of the day the solution can't be technology-driven. It needs to be human-driven."

I also spoke with William McGuire, the CEO of New York–based Global Security Associates, who observed that "advancements in technology combined with an entirely new mindset are one of the biggest reasons for avoiding acts of terrorism in the aviation industry."[2] He added: "Companies involved with the growing needs of protecting our nation's aviation interests will agree—that the US has come along way" since 9/11. McGuire has found that "risk-based assessments at airports, and working with the airlines to understand where their vulnerabilities, was a great step forward," noting that "now this is an accepted way of thinking. As history has proven over and over again, you must stay several steps ahead. While there have been many advancements made in airport security in the last several years, the industry as a whole has more it can do—but it cannot do it alone."

McGuire believes that the "number one threat facing aviation is hijacking and other forms of terrorism," and that next in gravity—and "which is a more common occurrence—is civil disruption or public drunkenness which results in a diversion of the aircraft." Since 9/11, McGuire has found "there is more training for the flight crews to handle security situations, and also, there's more enhanced security measures on board the main cabin of the plane." But vulnerabilities remain, including "the risk of some item getting on the aircraft that can be harmful," such as "some sort of weapon, a gun, knife, liquid flammables, explosives of all kinds." Additionally, McGuire noted, is "the threat of an insider doing something harmful, for many reasons," such as being "unhappy with their job, or just simple mental illness."

To help combat the continuing risks to aviation security, McGuire's company "provides a wide range of courses and physical support to enhance the security posture of its clients," and noted "a few courses are identifying the threat, and a risk assessment of your flight. We also offer self defense training for flight crews. The final phase and the last line of defense is in-flight security." He noted aviation security has become a priority for Washington, and that under the DHS there will be an 8 percent increase in funding over FY2007, with a total request of $46.4 billion in funding for 2008. An April 15, 2008, report, "Transportation Security: Efforts to Strength Aviation and Surface Transportation Security Continue to Progress, but More Work Remains," issued by the US Government Accountability Office, has found while "efforts have helped to strengthen the security of the transportation network, DHS and TSA still face a number of key challenges in further securing these systems."[3]

While technology alone may not solve the problems associated with in-cabin security, it can play an increasingly important role. John A. Dolan, vice president of Business Development at AD Aerospace, a UK-based aviation security provider, explained to me that "the main threats facing aviation today are terrorism, smuggling, security threats, and lately the price of aviation fuel."[4] He includes the high cost of fuel because "the US majors are having a very difficult time making a profit with the large rise in aviation fuel costs," which puts pressure on the availability of resources for aviation security. When it comes to in-cabin security, Dolan noted, "there is always the threat of air rage, drunkenness, the threat of someone trying to take over the plane and customers as hostages, as well as blowing the plane up and the fallout from the skies."

Since 9/11, Dolan explained, "many countries have mandated the need for aircraft having a video cockpit door surveillance system (CDSS) on the larger aircraft, and thus, the cockpit crew can identify 'friend or foe' outside the cockpit door as well as the main cabins, provided there are the appropriate cameras in location." Additionally, "due to possible smuggling and thievery of valuables in baggage, some airlines are using video in the cargo holds to nab airline employees or companies that are hired as contractors." But, Dolan added, "not all countries mandate CDSS," and this includes the United States. Consequently, "the US majors rely on procedural measures to inform the cockpit crew of who is approaching the cockpit door using the intra-phone and the spy-hole in the cockpit door. This means that at all times there must be two crew on the flight deck—and when a pilot needs to leave the cockpit, their place must be taken up by a member of the cabin crew. This method has been rejected by most of the major airlines outside the US." Dolan added that he "would feel much more secure on US airlines if video surveillance was mandated by the US Government. In addition, smuggling and baggage thievery is a much larger problem than perceived by the general public, and thus the need for video surveillance in the cargo holds of aircraft." Dolan explained that whether as a result of terrorism, criminal misbehavior, or air rage, "there is always the possibility of some individual creating problems while in flight."

To help airlines meet their in-cabin security challenges, Dolan noted, "AD Aerospace offers video safety and security systems that can provide additional information to the pilot on activities both in the main aircraft cabins, the cargo areas, and external cameras on the aircraft—as well as the use of video motion detection to detect movements of personnel. In addition, we make cameras that have infra-red LEDs that allow you to 'see' at night. These cameras allow better decision-making by the flight crew and therefore better control of any adverse situation." Additionally, AD Aerospace's IP addressable video servers "allow for wireless transmission of video both into the airport if the aircraft is at a gate, or we can offer wireless transmission of data anywhere the operator wants it provided there is the correct communication link. We currently do this for VIP-type aircraft."

Dolan has found that in the years since 9/11, "most airline travelers have accepted the security problems and hassles that come along with the long lines from TSA," but added that "traveling has not gotten any easier." However, thanks to solutions like those provided by AD Aerospace, it has gotten safer.

Private aircraft face increased security as TSA tackles general aviation sector

Members of the noncommercial, general aviation (GA) community were abuzz after the US Transportation Security Administration (TSA) announced in late 2008 that it will be escalating its efforts to improve America's aviation security by expanding its oversight from just the commercial aviation sector to now include the general aviation industry.

William McGuire, president and CEO of Global Security Associates, noted in an interview with me that "TSA officials had begun a serious town hall meeting to discuss the upcoming changes to security of the general aviation (GA) community. While many of the rules are necessary, the general aviation community says that they can regulate security themselves, and they are the best ones to do this. Some of the proposed rules are screening of all passengers, running the names of all crew and passengers through government watch lists, and securing aircraft when they are parked."[5]

McGuire added that "some are calling the new security measures the '12,500 rule.' and its date of implantation is late spring/early summer. The pros and cons are simple: we need to do a better job at securing general aviation, it is a wide open door. But it is not that easy to close the door, there are many reasons why. There are people and corporations that own and operate their own aircraft and they do everything they must to keep their aircraft (asset) safe and out of harm's way. Could they be doing more? I guess that could be said about a lot of industries. Then there are the charter operators and they are and need to be competitive, and run a business—so if there are no rules, then they won't do anything. Simple economics: if the other guy is not doing it (security measures), then you can compete if you want to provide some level of security."

McGuire observed that the years since 9/11 have "seen a dramatic increase in general aviation," with an increase in GA traffic "of approximately 30 percent, and this has a lot to do with charter outfits and timesharing operations. These give the everyday person, who does not have the means to own their own plane, but now can share-own as if they did own one. So the market came up quick, and now general aviation is the soft target and can be used as a weapon. In some cases, the general aviation aircraft are easier to fly and carry more fuel than a commercial airliner. So you don't need a bomb, the plane is a bomb or a guided missile."

Dr James Jay Carafano, a Senior Research Fellow at the Washington, DC–based Heritage Foundation, explained to me in an interview that the TSA's new rules "are focused on first trying to keep someone from using a large non-commercial passenger (general aviation) aircraft (like a FedEx cargo plane) as a faux 'cruise missile' similar to a 9–11-style attack, or smuggle bad things or bad people into the country. For smaller, craft, the enhancements really just dovetail with programs for sound safety and good law and order practices."[6] Carafano noted that "since the 9–11 terrorist attacks, air security has focused overwhelmingly on commercial aviation, and on passenger airlines in particular" but that "also flying in America's skies every day, however, are thousands of small airplanes, many of them owned and operated by individuals. So it was important that the government look at risks in this area as well." He added that GA "is an industry that comprises 5,288 community airports in the United States and supports 1.3 million jobs, totaling just over 1 percent of GDP. The approximately 219,000 general aviation aircraft in the United States account for 77 percent of all US air traffic."

Carafano was confident the new rules would be accepted by members of the GA industry. "My guess is that most of them will be accepted. There was a lot of discussion and outreach to the community and the department was seeking reasonable solutions that provide real security benefits without unduly burdening the community. Most important the government did not adopt a 'one size fits all' approach. The sheer size and diversity of the general aviation sector makes it difficult to craft a single comprehensive security policy for the industry. Of the over 200,000 general aviation aircraft registered in the US, 90 percent are powered by a single engine and have a short travel range."

In the decade plus since the September attacks of the US commercial aviation system, aviation security has come a long way. As Global Security Associate's CEO McGuire explained: "A lot of this has to do with capabilities of the TSA, and their gathering of intel and the sharing of information. Pre 9–11, the aviation security sector did not talk to each other, even if they were a mile apart. Now they do, with a central command center, and reporting and monitoring." Now, he added, the "TSA and the aviation security community can and are better equipped to do their jobs more effectively. There is always a risk of attack (IED) or otherwise, but we harden the target.

We change the methods. We keep them guessing, so we don't get hit again." McGuire is upbeat about the capabilities of the TSA, and noted, "in my opinion it seems as if the TSA now has the commercial aviation well locked down, and they are not letting their guard down in this area by all means. But now they are focusing on the softer targets, such as general aviation, cargo, and even the rail system to strengthen these areas," while "never losing focus on their job, and that is transportation security."

Heritage Foundation analyst Carafano observed that the TSA has adopted "a sound 'risk-based' approach to looking for threats. People can still sneak things through, but the point is that even an imperfect system represents a powerful deterrent to the terrorists." Its risk-based approach to aviation security has "focused on the measures that give the most security at reasonable cost. It is less about 'atmospherics.' Remember having National Guard troops in the airports after 9–11, that was a worthless security measure but it made people 'feel safer,' now we are more interested in making people safer than making them 'feel' safer."

University of Akron's Dr Andrew R. Thomas, described in the evolution of the TSA and its approach to security in America's aviation system.[7] He observed there have been "two forces which, although separate at times, do intersect," pulling the agency in competing directions: "On one hand," noted Thomas, "is the slow, arduous agency-building process that began with the creation of TSA," as illustrated during its first and second generations of leadership, which "were primarily dedicated to expanding the agency's reach and influence within the federal bureaucracy, especially as it related to annual funding increases." Thomas added that the "rules regarding GA aircraft have been developing for a number of years, and these most recent incursions are examples of the expansive aspect of TSA culture."

"Conversely," Thomas explained, "there has been an emerging realization in the last few years that TSA can't simply buy its way to security. There are limits to bureaucratic largesse and it starts with funding constraints. This is what seems to be driving the risk-based agenda. In other words, the realities of transportation security mandate a smart allocation of limited resources to places where it will make the most impact." Thomas added: "This is what should have happened from the beginning: a risk-driven strategy which would reduce the impact of attacks on the system. And that is the key word, system. Instead, TSA came right out of the box seeking to protect all things for all time. This is simply not possible given the complexity and scope of the global air transport system."

Thomas observed there's "been great fear within the GA community after 9–11 that TSA would come in and mandate measures which would dramatically restrict the freedom they have enjoyed as owners and operators of small aircraft. Recall that Mohammed Atta had expressed interest in crop dusters and applied to the USDA for a loan." But Thomas added that "the GA community is tight-knit and incredibly protective of their lifestyle," and cautioned not to expect a tectonic shift in aviation security. "My belief is that the new GA rules are the result of a compromise between the GA community and TSA after years of back-and-forth on what those measures would be"—and though "they may not admit it publicly, I believe they are pretty happy with what came out of the process. Smaller planes under 12,500 [pounds], which are the majority of GA aircraft, came out pretty much unscathed. From a security perspective, the new policy seems to make sense, although I doubt TSA will do much beyond some window dressing."

The shift toward a risk-based strategy means addressing real vulnerabilities of the aviation system, and allocating limited resources in a manner that is both effective and cost-efficient. This means focusing less upon technological quick-fixes, and more on making substantive changes to the nation's aviation security system, thereby deterring future terror attacks or increasing the likelihood of thwarting attempted attacks. As Heritage Foundation analyst Carafano explained: "I don't think you need super advanced technologies to provide a sufficient deterrent." However, new technologies can enhance the passenger experience. For example, Carafano noted that "full body scanners offer an advantage to passengers who otherwise would have to experience the discomfort of a body-search in secondary screening. The body scanners are completely non-intrusive." However, Global Security Associates CEO McGuire believes "the role of technology is huge," especially "the advancement in scanning for prohibitive items, liquids, trace detection, etc., but this just one tool in the tool box," albeit a "very big tool." Nonetheless, you still "need intelligence and human assets using the equipment."

University of Akron's Thomas pointed out that "some of the biggest threats come from plastic-based explosives/IEDs," and he cautioned that "the current technology is not designed to deal with this reality. X-ray devices—which are overwhelmingly the baggage and checkpoint machines at use today—are a nineteenth-century process which are pretty useless to detect plastic explosives and items." Thomas believes "technology will never be the solution to transportation security challenges. The threat is human and the responses must be as well. Technology can certainly help. But human intelligence, innovation, and action, led by an accountable management structure, is the real only way to provide the level of acceptable risk reduction to the system."

Looking ahead, Thomas said, he's "not very confident that TSA will be able to move to a true risk-based strategy over the coming years. New, properly focused leadership at DHS and TSA would certainly help. Still, many of the mid-level managers who run the day-to-day operations will remain holdovers. They don't seem either willing or able to make the changes necessary." Thomas said that "at the core of this doubt is the critical lack of organizational learning and knowledge-building which is sorely missing from the transportation security profession. At present, there are almost no recognized programs, certifications, or training programs which validate someone's abilities as a transportation security professional. Barbers go through more formal processes to become certified in their profession than those who do transportation security. This has to change."

Thomas added: "Moreover, we know that transport networks in general and aviation in particular remain the most prized targets for terrorists and criminals around the world. Another major attack, which is almost a certainty, will lead to emotional decisions, as happened after 9–11. This would likely retard any move towards professionalization."

The lingering liquid bomb threat

Long before the improvised underwear explosive of Umar Farouk Abdulmutallab nearly downed Northwest Airlines flight 253 on Christmas day in 2009—using a syringe to inject a liquid trigger to detonate his wearable IED, packed with 80 grams of pentaerythritol tetranitrate (PETN)—airline passengers and aviation officials have been worried about the lingering liquid bomb threat, and its continued potential to thwart currently deployed security systems. Abdulmutallab's explosive-laden skivvies were actually not a liquid bomb proper, but a binary explosive that required liquid acid to detonate the otherwise powdered explosive compound. It would only take one such detonation to paralyze one of the foundations of globalization: the international aviation system.

A sweeping series of arrests over three years earlier, in August 2006, revealed a nefarious and even more dramatic plot by Al Qaeda sympathizers to use improvised binary liquid explosives to bring down ten America-bound passenger jets departing the United Kingdom, whose destinations included Washington, New York, Chicago, San Francisco, Toronto, and Montreal. That plot was so horrific that security officials quickly imposed substantial carry-on limitations, and in the early days when confusion reigned, hundreds of flights were either cancelled or delayed. Two years on, seven of the eight accused liquid bomb plotters faced a retrial. One was cleared of all charges, and seven pled guilty to creating a public nuisance. Just three plotters were found guilty of conspiracy to commit murder; those three had pled guilty of conspiracy to cause explosions, though they argued in court that their intent was not to bring down the jetliners, but instead to cause a political spectacle.

While the outcome of the trial was certainly a disappointment to all those whose lives were disrupted by their plot, and the incalculable economic costs of so many cancelled flights, delays, lost luggage, long queues, and resulting anxiety and frustration among the traveling public, it does not mean the liquid bomb plot was any less menacing, or that the liquid bomb threat has been alleviated. Indeed, the enduring lesson of the 2006 liquid bomb plot is that the aviation sector remains a top target to terrorists the world over, and if vulnerabilities are found in the aviation security system, terrorists will invariably take aim at those points of weakness.

Two days after the liquid bomb plot burst into the public's imagination, the *New York Times* opined in its editorial titled "The Liquid Bomb Threat": "The most frightening thing about the foiled plot to use liquid explosives to blow up airplanes over the Atlantic is that both the government and the aviation industry have been aware of the liquid bomb threat for years but have done little to prepare for it."[8] That would quickly change. The initial response was an outright ban on carry-on items, including liquids of all sorts; but over time these restrictions were eased, and are now generally limited to what is known as the 3–1-1 rules, with exceptions allowed for baby bottles and meds. All other bottles must be three ounces or less by volume; they must be contained in one quart-sized, clear, zip-locked. plastic bag; only one such bag per passenger is allowed to be carried on.

According to Doug Kahn, the chairman and CEO of Ahura Scientific, Inc.: "One of the key lessons from the 2006 liquid bomb threat was a greater awareness of liquids as a potential threat. Prior to that time, most threat screening technologies at aviation checkpoints focused on plastic explosives and weapons. With this awareness was the knowledge that volume matters, and by limiting the quantity of liquids brought onto an aircraft, security agencies were able to minimize the threat, leading to the 3–1-1 policy in the US."[9] As described on the TSA website, the increasing acceptance of the 3–1-1 limits "demonstrates the international understanding of the threat to aviation from liquid explosives," and today 60 countries have "currently harmonized with TSA's rules for carrying liquids through the checkpoint."[10] One consequence of the 3–1-1 rule is that it reminds the public that the liquid bomb threat remains. As the TSA website noted: "You arrive at the checkpoint to the sound of a transportation security officer reminding travelers to remove liquids, gels and aerosols from carry-ons. To the seasoned traveler this is old news, but to the seasonal traveler it might be a surprise. Regardless of your personal travel experience, the international traveling community agrees—TSA's 3–1-1 for liquids makes security sense."[11] Kahn noted that for the traveling public, "this was a big change which had tremendous potential to impact their travel experience in a much more personal way. That led to another key lesson that came from the 2006 threat. New technology and procedures introduced to address the liquid explosives threat can be onerous and time-consuming—for the inspectors, the public, duty-free—virtually everyone in the security chain. The importance of creating sound and effective security processes, while mitigating inconvenience to passengers, is incredibly important when developing a sustainable and widely accepted program."

Mike Moore, the manager of transit systems at ICx Technologies, was formerly contracted to serve as program manager to the TSA's Liquid Explosives Program, observed the liquid bomb plot primarily demonstrated "terrorists were getting more adept at not getting caught.[12] The fact that certain liquid mixtures can be used to cause an explosion was nothing new to security experts, but terrorists tend to use what's most readily available to them, which on a global scale had mainly consisted of more conventional bomb making ingredients like TNT. Additionally, making liquid explosives detonate at the time and place you want them to—and with enough force to cause damage—requires some chemistry expertise, which had served as somewhat of a barrier until recently." He added that the quickly implemented 3–1-1 rule that was "adopted by many countries really does work as a basic deterrent, however inconvenient it may be," but noted it was just "a stopgap, not a permanent solution. Security agencies must continue to explore technologies to address the category of liquid threats."

In addition to 3–1-1 rule, there has been a renaissance in technology research in the search for solutions to liquid bomb threat. Moore pointed out that "many countries have deployed handheld devices for use at airport checkpoints which scan passenger's bottles for threat materials. One technology replicates a dog's olfactory senses, and 'sniffs' the vapors from a sealed bottle to determine if it is harmful. A reaction inside the device occurs when the chemical comes into contact with a particle of the harmful material." An example of what might be coming down the pike, added Moore, "would be the path security agencies in many counties are aggressively taking to advance the current Checkpoint and Checked Baggage Screening equipment at airports with algorithms which can find a bottle in a person's bag and identify if the liquid is a threat, as each mixture has a unique 'signature.' This process, when coupled with those aforementioned handheld devices, provides layers of security and help to streamline passenger flow."

As Ahura Scientific's CEO Kahn explained: "Current technology deployed for liquid explosives is geared toward detecting the presence of liquids in baggage," and that "this is a critical first step in addressing the liquid explosives threat, but emerging technologies will go even further, providing confirmed identification of threats, not just general detection of liquids in bottles. New screening technologies can very rapidly provide an accurate, reliable identification, even through sealed glass or plastic containers. As technology continues to evolve, this could potentially alleviate the restrictions required by the 3–1-1 guidelines, without sacrificing public safety." He described Ahura Scientific's TruScreen solution, which was designed to "rapidly and accurately screen for specific threats" and which in its current release is "optimized for liquid explosives and provides trained operators with the ability to quickly distinguish (less than 20 seconds) between threat-listed materials, such as explosive substances and precursors, and benign substances that are safe to carry onboard an aircraft. TruScreen is very easy to use and maintain and requires no consumables." TruScreen, he explained, "uses light and spectroscopic analysis to identify the contents of glass or plastic containers, requiring no direct contact with the substance in question. This non-invasive screening technology helps maintain uninterrupted passenger throughput at security checkpoints." Kahn added, TruScreen is "part of extensive laboratory and operational trials globally and is now shipping with limited availability."

ICx Technologies' Moore described his company's Fido Paxpoint solution, noting it was the "primary bottled liquid scanner deployed today," and "uses the 'sniffing' technique" that he described above. To date, he observed, "TSA has deployed the Fido Paxpoint to many airports in the US so far." Other technologies he mentioned were undergoing further testing by TSA before they are considered suitable for deployment, such as "raman spectroscopy, which is another handheld device that uses an infrared laser beam to identify the spectra or 'signature' of the liquid in the bottle." He also described "technologies in development by national labs and private companies for liquid threat detection," which "include the use of electromagnetic wavelengths which 'excite' the particles in the bottle to determine what's inside based on the response. Also acoustic technologies can tell what's in a container by sonically sending out a pulse through the container, and receiving a unique echo." Moore pointed out that a liquid bomb could bring harm not only to the aviation sector, but to other sectors as well. Liquid bombs are thus "like any other threat, in that a terrorist, if successful, can detonate it in any public venue. As their objective is typically to cause as much damage, fear and casualties as possible, all transit systems and locations with large crowds are considered vulnerable. The value of mobile, handheld liquid scanners is just that—they can be used anywhere. What's difficult is enabling screeners to access a suspicious bottle."

Ahura Scientific's Kahn noted while "the screening application may be most familiar to aviation travelers," that "we've seen a great deal of interest for chemical identification and screening in a variety of applications. Rail and subway systems, ports and border crossings, power stations and other mission critical infrastructure, government facilities, stock exchanges, sports stadiums and high profile events all have unique security requirements which could benefit from threat screening. Operational considerations will be very different for each of these, so security personnel must have a solid understanding of their goals—and what is deemed acceptable by those using the facility." Kahn observed that "technology has been hampered in the past because it was typically very expensive, slow and difficult to maintain," and that "as newer technologies emerge, these challenges are being addressed. New innovations are making equipment faster, more accurate and easier to operate." He believes that technology "certainly has the potential to ease the boarding process for the traveling public while enhancing security and safety. TruScreen, for example, enables very fast screening of liquids without even opening the container. When used in concert with complementary technologies such as x-ray and IMS, this provides an additional layer of security with minimal impact on the public, whether it's used to confirm the safety of milk, medications or other items allowed in greater quantities, or as a way to alleviate 3–1-1 regulations."

Kahn described "the tremendous coordination required in order to ensure public safety in aviation," as "airports, airlines and aviation security regulatory bodies globally must work closely together to ensure the greatest levels of security with minimal passenger inconvenience." Kahn added, "there is no one single technology or 'magic box' that spans the breadth of aviation security requirements, so security authorities select complementary and confirmatory products from a number of vendors. This provides a layered approach to security screening, enabling stronger security protocols than could be possible from a single vendor." He noted that "global aviation security agencies have been extremely thorough in their evaluation of technology and the acceptable level of passenger inconvenience through operational trials, showing a high level of concern for both accuracy and passenger experience."

In addition to taking a layered approach, ICx Technologies' Moore believes that "expandability is the key. The direction that liquid screening, as well as screening for all other types of threats, is heading is that the technologies will apply an easily expandable library of threats to screen against. Therefore if a new threat is developed by a terrorist group, a few lines of code adding that threat to the device's library can be transmitted over the Internet to all of the equipment across entire countries with the click of a button." Moore noted that "factors such as cost and the speed of technological development will keep these capabilities from being deployed everywhere large crowds may be, and even now we see terrorists changing their tactics, as in Mumbai. So the agencies study the intelligence reports and respond according to an assessment of risk, which is really the only practical approach."

Notes

1   Barry Zellen, "Cabin Fever: Despite Major Gains in Aviation Security since 9/11, In-Cabin Insecurity Persists," SecurityInnovator.com, June 15, 2008, http://

securityinnovator.com/index.php?articleID=15210&sectionID=27. Subsequent quotations from Thomas are from this article.

2 Ibid. Subsequent quotations from McGuire are from this article.

3 Cathleen A. Berrick, "Efforts to Strengthen Aviation and Surface Transportation Security Continue to Progress, but More Work Remains," United States Government Accountability Office, April 15, 2008, www.gao.gov/new.items/d08651t.pdf.

4 Zellen, "Cabin Fever." Subsequent quotations from Dolan are from this article.

5 Barry Zellen, "Aviation Security at a Crossroads: Private Aircraft Face Increased Security as TSA Broadens Its Reach from Commercial to General Aviation Sector," SecurityInnovator.com, January 15, 2009, http://securityinnovator.com/index.php?articleID=15849&sectionID=31. Subsequent quotations from McGuire are from this article.

6 Ibid. Subsequent quotations from Carafano are from this article.

7 Ibid. Subsequent quotations from Thomas are from this article.

8 New York Times Editorial Board, "The Liquid Bomb Threat," *New York Times*, August 12, 2006, www.nytimes.com/2006/08/12/opinion/12sat1.html.

9 Barry Zellen, "The Lingering Liquid Bomb Threat: Two Years on, New Technologies and Continued Carry-On Restrictions Promise to Make Air Travel Safer," SecurityInnovator.com, April 17, 2009, http://securityinnovator.com/index.php?articleID=15840&sectionID=27. Subsequent quotations from Kahn are from this article.

10 See www.tsa.gov/311/.

11 See www.tsa.gov/311/.

12 Zellen, "The Lingering Liquid Bomb Threat." Subsequent quotations from Moore are from this article.

13

Truck Bombing Shifts into High Gear

News headlines continue to tell a depressing tale of car bombs and truck bombs going off across Iraq, Afghanistan, and Pakistan with alarming frequency, even as our opponents in the war on terror find themselves on the run, its principal architects either dead, in detention, or in hiding. While not with the same intensity or ferocity as witnessed a few years ago when insurgency spread like wildfire across post-Saddam Iraq, the enduring popularity of this classic tool of terror remains worrisome to those tasked with protecting the populace as well as our armed forces, both here and abroad.

A look at the history of such weapons shows they've been a weapon of choice for a wide variety of actors for much of this century, including terrorists, governments, and organized crime, gaining notoriety during Lebanon's long civil war as a weapon of mass terror as well as assassination. Like the bombs of Beirut, the bombs of Baghdad have proven both lethal and ubiquitous, causing near constant bloodshed in an effort to spread chaos and fear.

Most experts call car or truck bombs VBIEDs (Vehicle Borne Improvised Explosive Devices), and as the insurgency in Iraq gained momentum, it became an oft-used tool against coalition forces, our new Iraqi allies, and even the United Nations, whose Iraq headquarters was destroyed on August 19, 2003, by a VBIED—killing the UN's administrator and 21 of his colleagues. But VBIEDs aren't a new phenomenon. According to *Wikipedia*, a car bomb or truck bomb is an "improvised explosive device that is placed in a car or other vehicle and then exploded. It is commonly used as a weapon of assassination, terrorism, or guerrilla warfare, to kill the occupant(s) of the vehicle or people near the blast site or to cause damage to buildings or other property."[1] A truck bomb acts as its very own delivery vehicle, delivering a substantial bang for not only a minimal buck, but also in a tremendously stealthful manner.[2]

VBIEDs have been a fact of life since the very first vehicles appeared. Records indicate an early truck bomb—more accurately, a horse-drawn carriage bomb—was detonated on Wall Street back in 1920 by anarchists. As reported by InfoPlease.com, on September 16, 1920, a "TNT bomb planted in unattended horse-drawn wagon exploded on Wall Street opposite House of Morgan, killing 35 people and injuring hundreds more. Bolshevist or anarchist terrorists believed responsible, but crime never solved."[3]

From Beirut to Baghdad

Until the 1980s, VBIEDs were relatively infrequent; but this changed with the disintegration of Lebanon during its long civil war, especially after US forces entered the fray in a peacekeeping capacity. During the 1980s, at least four VBIED attacks took place against American targets in the Middle East, as chronicled by InfoPlease.com.[4] On April 18, 1983, a massive truck bomb destroyed the US embassy in Beirut, killing 63 people, including 17 Americans. Then on October 23 of that year, Shi'ite suicide bombers exploded a truck bomb disguised as a delivery truck outside US military barracks at the Beirut airport, killing 241 Marines. And just a few moments later, a second bomb killed 58 French paratroopers in their barracks in West Beirut. On December 12, 1983, in Kuwait City, Shi'ite truck bombers attacked the US embassy and other targets—killing 5 and injuring 80. And on September 20, 1984, in East Beirut, a truck bomb exploded outside the US Embassy annex, killing 24.

In the 1990s, truck bomb attacks were launched on American soil as well as against US military and diplomatic targets overseas. Among the most notable was on February 26, 1993, in New York, when Ramzi Yousef joined forces with Sheikh Omar Abdel Rahman, deploying a truck bomb using ammonium nitrate fertilizer mixed with fuel oil in the basement garage of the World Trade Center, in a failed effort to topple the Twin Towers and kill tens of thousands. In the end, only six were killed but over a thousand were injured, and the towers stood, untoppled.

Two years later, on April 19, 1995, when Timothy McVeigh and Terry Nichols decided to bring their personal war against the US government to Oklahoma City, a truck bomb was detonated outside the Alfred P. Murrah Federal Building, killing 268 people, and injuring many more. Just over six months later, on November 13, 1995, a VBIED bomb exploded at US military headquarters in Riyadh, Saudi Arabia, killing five US military servicemen, and around a half year later, on June 25, 1996, a truck bomb exploded outside Khobar Towers military complex in Dhahran, Saudi Arabia, killing 19 American servicemen, and injuring hundreds more. Two years after that, Al Qaeda used truck bombs to simultaneously attack the US embassies in Nairobi, Kenya, and Dar es Salaam, Tanzania, on August 7, 1998, killing 224 in all (213 in Kenya, and 11 in Tanzania), and injuring nearly 5,000 more. In many ways, the September 11, 2001, attacks were the mother of all VBIED attacks—with the vehicle delivering the deadly payload escalating from truck to jumbo jet, and instead of packing a plane with explosives, the perpetrators harnessed the vehicles' own full fuel tanks as the explosive agent.

In the ongoing low-intensity slugfest that has defined the GWOT since 9/11, the truck bomb has continued to be a weapon of choice by Al Qaeda and its sympathizers around the world—especially since increased airport and cockpit security has made a repeat of the 9/11-styled airborne IED attacks far more difficult to execute. But inside Iraq, VBIEDs became alarmingly frequent, including the August 7, 2003, truck bomb attack of the Jordanian Embassy, which killed ten people, and the notorious attack of the UN headquarters on August 19, killing the top UN envoy to Iraq, Sergio

Vieira de Mello, and sixteen others, and injuring over a hundred more "when a bomb-laden cement truck exploded beneath the window of his office in the Canal Hotel at about 4:30 p.m."[5]

Historical VBIED trends

Wikipedia has compiled a long list of VBIED attacks through the end of 2005—including mass-terror attacks and more specific VBIED assassinations (such as those portrayed in the above-noted films). A big spike in VBIED attacks in Iraq corresponds with the start of the insurgency against the Coalition. In May 2003, intelligence officials report a pivotal planning meeting took place in a car in Baghdad—where, according to CNN, Saddam Hussein's deputy, Izzat Ibrahim al-Duri, and four other top Saddam loyalists, "decided to activate an insurgency."[6]

From May 2003 through the end of 2005, there were 51 VBIED mass-terror attacks worldwide—of which 37 took place in Iraq and only 12 elsewhere, including 3 attacks in Saudi Arabia; 2 attacks in Egypt, Pakistan, Turkey, and Russia (including Chechnya, which is fighting Moscow for independence); and 1 attack in Lebanon, Indonesia, and India during this period. Of the Iraqi attacks in this period, 13 used multiple, often simultaneous or near-simultaneous, VBIEDs—with as many as 11 vehicles used in a single attack, though most multiple vehicle-borne IED attacks use far fewer (four Iraqi attacks used four vehicles, three used three vehicles, and four used two vehicles, while only one attack used five vehicles, and only one used 11.) Outside Iraq, only two other nations experienced multiple-VBIED attacks during this period: India with a 2-vehicle attack on August 25, 2003; and Saudi Arabia with a 4-vehicle attack on May 12, 2003.

Interestingly, from the start of 2000 until May 2003, there were only 16 VBIED mass-terror attacks around the world. There was just 1 VBIED attack in 2003 before the Iraq insurgency began—on February 7 in Colombia. And in 2002, there were 11 VBIED terror attacks around the world—2 in Pakistan, 2 in Israel, 1 in Chechnya, 1 in Kenya, 1 in Indonesia, 1 in Afghanistan, 1 in Tunisia, 1 in Colombia, and 1 in Peru. In 2001, there were only 3 attacks—1 in Russia, 1 in Chechnya, and 1 in Kashmir. And in 2000, there was only 1 VBIED attack recorded—in Chechnya. In only 4 cases were more than 100 people killed in a single attack since 2000.

In contrast to the past few years of prolific VBIED attacks, during the entire 1990s there were only 28 attacks worldwide, far fewer than the 37 VBIED attacks recorded in the 1980s. In the 1990s, there were: 1 attack in 1999, 4 in 1998, 2 in 1997, 4 in 1996, 6 in 1995, 2 in 1994, 6 in 1993, 2 in 1992, and 1 in 1990. Only 3 of these attacks resulted in over 100 people killed. In the 1980s, there were 4 VBIED attacks in 1989, 3 in 1988, 5 in 1987, 3 in 1986, 5 in 1985, 1 in 1984, 9 in 1983, 4 in 1982, and 3 in 1981. Only 2 attacks in the entire 1980s resulted in over 100 killed.

For the six decades from 1920 to 1980, there were only 8 VBIED attacks in total around the world, including 3 in 1948 in Palestine. The most lethal VBIED attack in this period resulted in 52 deaths. As for VBIED assassinations of the sort portrayed in mafia films, 24 are recorded—9 in Lebanon, 4 in Iraq, 3 in the United States, 2 in the United Kingdom, 2 in Turkey, 1 in Argentina, 1 in Spain, 1 in Greece, and 1 in Qatar.

DHS responds with frequent advisories and bulletins

The threat of VBIEDs is now so ubiquitous that the DHS routinely issues Homeland Security Threat Advisories and Information Bulletins as part of the Homeland Security Advisory System often relating to the VBIED threat, and responding to changes in tactics observed in overseas attacks.

DHS' Homeland Security Threat Advisories "contain actionable information about an incident involving, or a threat targeting, critical national networks or infrastructures or key assets," whereas its Homeland Security Information Bulletins "communicate information of interest to the nation's critical infrastructures that do not meet the timeliness, specificity, or significance thresholds of warning messages."[7]

An Information Bulletin issued on July 30, 2004, was titled "Potential Threat to Homeland Using Heavy Transport Vehicles," which was a joint DHS and FBI information bulletin whose aim, according to the Ryder Safety Services September/October 2004 newsletter, was "to sensitize state and local authorities and the private sector responsible for security of critical infrastructure and key resources to the potential for terrorists to use heavy transport vehicles as vehicle-borne improvised explosive devices (VBIEDs) against a range of attractive targets in the US."[8]

And, a joint DHS and FBI advisory from August 1, 2004, titled "Homeland Security Advisory System Increased to ORANGE for Financial Institutions in Specific Geographical Areas" raised the US Homeland Security Advisory System (HSAS) level for the financial services sectors in New York City, Northern New Jersey, and Washington, DC, from "YELLOW—ELEVATED" to "ORANGE—HIGH."[9] The advisory noted that "recent credible and specific intelligence reporting indicates terrorist operatives have done extensive research and reconnaissance activity against major US and international financial institutions in Washington, DC, Northern New Jersey and New York City," including the Citigroup buildings in the New York City area, the New York Stock Exchange Building in New York City, the International Monetary Fund and the World Bank Buildings in Washington DC, and the Prudential Insurance Company of America in Newark, New Jersey.[10] The advisory pointed out that "the reporting provides a level of detail that is unusually specific, to include information about the interior configurations of these buildings, as well as infrastructure, services, and buildings that surround the targets of interest." While it "does not specify the timing or mode of attack. Based on the nature of the reconnaissance information," the advisory states "the most likely means of attack would be a Vehicular-Borne Improvised Explosive Device (VBIED), to include limousines, large vans, trucks, and oil tankers which could be placed in underground parking areas or near highly populated entrance ways."[11] The advisory refers to an earlier joint DHS/FBI Information Bulletin "Potential Threat to Homeland Using Heavy Transport Vehicles," issued on July 30, 2004, that "outlines terrorist use of VBIEDs overseas as well as in the United States."[12]

A year earlier on May 15, 2003, DHS issued a Homeland Security Information Bulletin specifically on VBIED prevention titled "Potential Indicators of Threats Involving Vehicle Borne Improvised Explosive Devices (VBIEDs)," which explained that DHS "believes that a truck bombing by terrorists may be preempted if the general public remains alert for certain indicators," and as such aims "to provide general information to assist in efforts to recognize potential VBIED-related threats or incidents based on recent Riyadh bombings."[13] It noted tactics used in that week's May 11 Riyadh attack include "multiple targets," "simultaneous attacks," "multiple vehicles per target," and "an assault/breaching cadre armed with small arms/weaponry accompany the VBIED to clear security personnel and gain access to the compound."[14]

The bulletin includes a detailed tactical analysis of the Riyadh attack, and explained that "while the ability to conduct multiple, near simultaneous attacks against several targets is not new for terrorist groups such as Al-Qaida, the manner in which these attacks was conducted indicates a more refined capability," noting how "in each attack a number of armed terrorists was used to eliminate the security elements guarding the compounds so suicide cadre could drive a vehicle borne improvised explosive device to the desired location and detonate it."[15] The bulletin presented some "potential VBIED indicators," including: Purchase or theft of explosives or chemicals may be a precursor to terrorist attacks; rental of self-storage units and the delivery of chemicals to such units; chemical fires, toxic odors, brightly colored stains, or rusted metal fixtures in apartments, hotels rooms, or self-storage units; theft of truck or van with minimum 1 ton carrying capacity; modification of smaller capacity vehicles to accept a minimum 1 ton load; small test explosions in rural or wooded areas; treated/untreated chemical burns or missing hands and/or fingers; purchase of, or illicit access to, blue prints of the targeted facility; and, nearly every major terrorist attack is preceded by a thorough surveillance of the targeted facility.[16]

A July 22, 2003, DHS Information Bulletin, titled "Potential Terrorist Use of Official Identification, Uniforms, or Vehicles," warns that "Al-Qaeda and other terrorist groups likely view the theft or other illegal acquisition of official identification, uniforms, or vehicles as an effective way to increase access and decrease scrutiny in furtherance of planning and operations."[17] It observed that "terrorist groups have utilized police or military uniforms to mask their identities and achieve closer access to their targets without arousing suspicion. This was illustrated in the December 2002, suicide bombings that targeted the Chechen Government Headquarters in Groznyy, Russia."[18] As well, it recounted how "terrorists in South America, the Philippines and Pakistan have commandeered or stolen emergency medical services vehicles and uniforms (or cleverly designed imitations) to facilitate the execution of their attacks on key facilities."[19] DHS noted that "in an effort to understand the extent of official identification, uniform, and vehicle thefts, DHS conducted a survey of selected members of the law enforcement community in five states," which "revealed that from February to May 2003 hundreds of official identification cards, badges, decals, uniforms, and government license plates were reported stolen or lost."[20] At the same time, DHS found "a number of private companies have reported receiving suspicious inquiries about renting official delivery vehicles and emergency services representatives have received unusual requests for detailed vehicle descriptions."[21]

A DHS Advisory issued on September 4, 2003, titled "Maintaining Awareness Regarding Al-Qaeda's Potential Threats to the Homeland," aimed at federal departments and agencies, homeland security advisors, first responders, and information sharing and analysis centers noted that based upon "a recent interagency review of available information leading up to the September 11th anniversary, we remain concerned about Al-Qaeda's continued efforts to plan multiple attacks against the US and US interests overseas."[22] In its advisory, DHS noted the continued threat to critical infrastructure, and that "Al-Qaeda views critical infrastructure targets in the US as attractive attack options because of their potentially significant economic and psychological impacts."[23] It explained that a "demonstrated capability of Al-Qaeda and other terrorist organizations against an infrastructure-type target involves the use of a vehicle carrying a large amount of explosives, commonly referred to as a car or truck bomb," as "this tactic allows for attacks to be conducted without entering a facility and requires a protective strategy to include areas outside the controlled perimeter."[24]

DHS observed that there's "no standard type of vehicle associated with vehicle borne improvised explosive devices (VBIEDs)" and that "vehicle selection depends on vehicles common to and available in a region as well as the security posture of the intended target."[25] DHS explained "the typical tactic for the employment of a VBIED is to drive a single vehicle to the target, park the vehicle, and allow the vehicle to detonate via time delay or by remote control" and that "another tactic is the use of suicide drivers, driving up to the target and detonating the vehicle by use of a 'dead-man' switch."[26] DHS also noted "in the case of the Riyadh, Saudi Arabia compound bombings this May, we saw a change in tactics from the 'traditional' tactic of driving a single VBIED to a target, to confronting security personnel with assault teams equipped with small arms to gain access through the perimeter in order to allow suicide VBIEDs to gain entry to the target area."[27]

VBIEDs are now such a regular part of our threat landscape that the US Bureau of Alcohol, Tobacco, and Firearms (BATF) has prepared a table that presents the relative size and effective range of various sizes of VBIEDs—from the compact sedan, whose maximum explosive capacity is 500 pounds and lethal air blast range is 100 feet, with a falling glass hazard of 1,250 feet; all the way up to the semi-trailer, whose maximum explosive capacity is 60,000 pounds, and whose lethal air blast range is 600 feet—with a falling glass hazard of 7,000 feet.

An elusive shield?

The rising frequency of VBIED attacks suggests they are, for terrorists, a magic bullet, a weapon of choice that cannot be easily thwarted. Efforts have been made to reduce the threat, such as DHS' detailed lists of VBIED indicators and protective measures.

On August 8, 2004, Spencer S. Hsu and Sari Horwitz authored a detailed article as part of "The World after 9/11" series in the *Washington Post*, titled "The Truck Bomb Threat: Impervious Shield Elusive against Drive-By Terrorists."[28] They reported on government efforts across the United States to measure and assess the potential destructiveness, and thereby mitigate and prevent VBIED attacks. They calculated that the United States had spent over $1B by the summer of 2004 on "efforts to stop a single threat: the explosion of a car or truck bomb at a government installation or other structure."[29] And yet, some "11 years after Muslim extremists used an explosives-laden van to attack the World Trade Center and nearly three years after the Sept. 11, 2001, terrorist attacks, even senior federal agents acknowledge that the country has virtually no defense against a terrorist barreling down the street with a truck bomb."[30]

However, there has been steady progress—and "since the 1993 World Trade Center bombing, the government has hardened federal buildings and military facilities at home and abroad; passed laws restricting the sale of explosives and shipments of hazardous materials; inspected thousands of people who deal with explosives; and researched explosive-detection and vehicle-disabling technology."[31] Around Washington, they noted, "blast walls, barricades and setbacks at sensitive buildings have become the last line of defense," and "the Pentagon, White House and Capitol increasingly resemble fortresses."[32] Accordingly, "defensive measures costing hundreds of millions of dollars are proposed or underway at more than 20 facilities, and the government has adopted a 100-foot setback as a guideline for high-security new construction in the United States and overseas."[33] But as evidenced in Iraq, "hardening some locations might redirect terrorists to 'softer' ones, including hotels, malls or stadiums."[34]

Other methods to reduce the threat of VBIEDs in America include the Transportation Security Administration's (TSA) $19M grant to the American Trucking Association (ATA), which in 1933 was established by a national affiliation of state trucking organizations, to expand its Highway Watch program, described by Hsu and Horwitz as a "computerized instant-reporting network through which professional drivers and highway workers can report accidents, thefts, hazards and suspicious incidents nationwide."[35] Even fertilizer, a common ingredient in VBIEDs, is more closely watched now. Hsu and Horwitz report that in July 2004, "the fertilizer industry urged ammonium nitrate sellers to voluntarily track sales and require buyers to show identification," part of its steady "history of voluntary initiatives"—like its 1996 "Be Aware for America" campaign after the Oklahoma City bombing; its 2001 "Be Secure for America" campaign; and its 2004 "America's Security Begins with You" campaign. Another preventive effort is the Safe Explosives Act, which "requires users and sellers of explosives to submit photographs and fingerprints and undergo criminal background checks."[36]

But despite these efforts, the very magnitude of the problem remains uniquely challenging. As Hsu and Horwitz explained, "there are 23.8 million trucks used for business purposes in the United States and 70 million more in personal use," none registered by a single federal agency."[37] As well, there are "600,000 trucking companies, which have 2.6 million tractors, 3.1 million big-rig drivers and 5 million trailers."[38] As for fertilizer, "nearly 5 million tons of ammonium nitrate fertilizer are sold each year in the United States." That's why Hsu and Horwitz cautioned that "at the end of the day, the nation's security experts say they expect terrorists will get their hands on the weapon and that keeping bombers away from buildings is their best hope."[39]

Notes

1 *Wikipedia*, "Car Bomb," http://en.wikipedia.org/wiki/Car_bomb.
2 http://en.wikipedia.org/wiki/Car_bombs.
3 InfoPlease.com, www.infoplease.com/ipa/A0001454.html.
4 Ibid.
5 www.cnn.com/2003/WORLD/meast/08/19/sprj.irq.main/index.html.
6 www.cnn.com/2005/WORLD/meast/10/12/schuster.column/index.html.
7 Homeland Security Advisory System, Department of Homeland Security, www.dhs.gov/files/programs/Copy_of_press_release_0046.shtm.
8 www.rydersafetyservices.com/eNewsletter/rssflash401.html.
9 DHS Advisory, "Homeland Security Advisory System Increased to ORANGE for Financial Institutions in Specific Geographical Areas," Department of Homeland Security, August 1, 2004, www.homelandsecurity.ms.gov/pdf/pr_threatlev_change_8-1-04.pdf. On April 20, 2011, Homeland Security Secretary Janet Napolitano announced the implementation of a new DHS National Terrorism Advisory System (NTAS) to provide timely information to the public about credible terrorist threats, replacing the earlier HSAS color-coded alert system.
10 Ibid.
11 Ibid.
12 Ibid.
13 Homeland Security Information Bulletin, "Potential Indicators of Threats Involving Vehicle Borne Improvised Explosive Devices (VBIEDs)," Department of Homeland Security, May 15, 2003, www.iwar.org.uk/homesec/resources/dhs-bulletin/vbieds.htm.
14 Ibid.
15 Ibid.
16 Ibid.
17 Homeland Security Information Bulletin, "Potential Terrorist Use of Official Identification, Uniforms, or Vehicles," Department of Homeland Security, July 22, 2003, www.iwar.org.uk/homesec/resources/dhs-bulletin/uniforms.htm.
18 Ibid.
19 Ibid.
20 Ibid.
21 Ibid.
22 Homeland Security Information Bulletin, "DHS Advisory to Security Personnel, No Change in Threat Level," Department of Homeland Security, September 4, 2003, www.dhs.gov/xnews/releases/press_release_0238.shtm.
23 Ibid.
24 Ibid.
25 Ibid.
26 Ibid.
27 Ibid.
28 www.washingtonpost.com/wp-dyn/articles/A48677-2004Aug7.html.
29 Ibid.
30 Ibid.
31 Ibid.

32 Ibid.
33 Ibid.
34 Ibid.
35 Ibid.
36 Ibid.
37 Ibid.
38 Ibid.
39 Ibid.

14

Underground Tremors: Securing the Metro

Ever since the March 20, 1995, sarin attack on the Tokyo subway system by Aum Shinrikyo, which targeted five separate lines in a coordinated attack, killing 12 people and injuring some 6,000 others, subway terrorism has been a fact of life. Indeed, since the Tokyo subway attacks, there have been several other assaults on subway systems around the world—including the February 18, 2003, Daegu, Korea subway arson-attack that killed 130 and injured 139 more; the February 6, 2004 attack in Moscow that killed 40 subway riders; and the July 7, 2005, London subway attack that simultaneously destroyed 3 subway cars and killed 52 riders and injured over 700. On top of this, there was the mass-terror attack of Madrid's commuter rail system on March 11, 2004, involving 10 separate bombs and 4 separate trains resulting in 195 deaths and 1,240 injuries.

In the spring of 2006, Dan Tangherlini was appointed interim general manager of the DC Metro, the premier public transportation system in the United States serving over 700,000 riders each day. I had the opportunity to interview Tangherlini and his colleague Polly Hanson, chief of the Metro Transit Police, in Washington, DC.[1] Among the many challenges confronting any Metro chief is the ever-present specter of terrorism. But the very nature of subway systems—their sprawling networks of underground tracks, their multiple entry and exit points, and the hundreds of thousands of passengers, most of whom are reluctant to endure delays associated with mandatory individual searches and screenings such as employed by airports—make them exceedingly difficult to protect. Though just on the job, Tangherlini brought fresh ideas to the top post at the DC Metro, and joined an experienced team of security professionals that has been grappling with the omnipresent threat of terror for many years.

Tangherlini was not just head of the DC Metro; he was also a DC resident and commuted daily by Metro along with over half a million other people. Accordingly, I asked if he was worried about the danger of a terror attack while riding on the Metro. "I ride Metrorail and/or Metrobus everyday, and feel safe and secure while I ride," he replied. "However, because of the times we live in, the threat of terror is always upon us. I wouldn't say that I worry about a terror attack on Metro daily, but I am keenly aware that it could happen. We emphasize to our employees and 1 million-plus riders the importance of staying aware and being prepared for any kind of emergency situation."

He described for me the DC subway system, and some of the unique challenges of keeping this system secure, noting "the 30-year-old Washington Metro system covers 106 miles. There are 86 station stops in Washington, DC, and the close-in suburbs of Virginia and Maryland. As with any mass transit system, Metro has an open environment with multiple entrances/exits, unlike airports that can funnel people through one point. We're responsible for getting 700,000 people to and from their jobs, homes, schools, tourist spots and entertainment locations every weekday, in a safe, efficient and timely manner."

With municipal budgets always tight, and the system growing older with each passing day, I asked how one juggles competing priorities such as maintenance, renovations, system upgrades, and counter-terrorism efforts. "We do have to juggle," Tangherlini noted. "However, the FTA requires that 1 percent of the budget is spent on security. Beyond that, we look for federal opportunities for funding, primarily from the Department of Homeland Security. Since fiscal year 2003, we've received about $5 million a year in transit funding grants from the Department of Homeland Security. In addition, we tap into regional DHS funding through the Urban Area Security Initiative program." Tangherlini noted the DC Metro's proposed operating budget for fiscal year 2007 was $1.1 billion, and added: "There is no single line item in the budget for terror prevention," reiterating that "funding for terror prevention efforts from training and equipment to personnel come from a variety of sources."

In the FAQs on the DC Metro website, some of the concerns raised by the 2003 Korea subway attack are directly addressed, and I wanted to find out if the Metro has responded as well to the Moscow and London subway bombings, and the lessons learned from these attacks. Tangherlini responded that the DC Metro "is different than the Korean subway that would make an attack like theirs less likely here. One major example: the interiors of our rail cars are made with fire-retardant materials, making an arson attack as in Korea, unlikely. Well before the Moscow, Madrid and London bombings, we knew that explosives posed a significant threat and that explosives are a weapon of choice for terrorists. Metro has a robust Explosives Ordnance Detection team and K9 program to detect, identify and disrupt explosives."

During visits to DC, I've noticed that at several stations underground I can receive a strong cell phone signal, and have seen riders enjoy making calls while traveling beneath the city. But ever since the use of cell phones as triggers in the Madrid commuter rail bombings, which enabled the remote and simultaneous detonation of multiple bombs at multiple targets, some analysts have expressed worry about the inherent dangers of cell phone coverage being available at potential mass-terror targets. I asked if the Metro has considered cell phone-jammers or the suspension of cell phone service to mitigate this risk, and Chief Hanson replied: "We do have the capability to shut down cell phone service in Metrorail tunnels. However, there is a disadvantage in doing so. In the event of an emergency, we would be cutting off a valuable source of information, as people—employees and riders—on an incident train would not be able to call out with information."

I also noticed there was visible, and seemingly widespread, use of surveillance cameras and wondered how pervasive the system is. Chief Hanson replied: "We have surveillance cameras in all 86 rail stations and will have them on 525 of our 1,500 buses this spring. The digital cameras record information and the recordings are kept for a certain number of days and then are recorded over. All new Metrobuses will come equipped with security cameras." I asked if the DC Metro has experimented with and/ or deployed biometrics technologies to automate the matching of facial-geography with terror suspects, and if so what has this experience been like? Tangherlini replied: "We have looked at biometrics and it's very challenging in our environment. The technology is very expensive and right now we have other spending priorities."

As for other types of solutions deployed, Chief Hanson explained, "we currently have a chemical, biological and radiological detection program in our system. Last year, we reinstalled bomb-containment trash cans to rail station platforms. In addition, our Explosives Ordnance Detection team uses a variety of tools, including a team of bomb-sniffing dogs, portable x-ray machines, and a robot to investigate suspicious packages and disrupt explosive devices." In the wake of the March 20, 1995, sarin attack on the Tokyo subway system, it has been reported that the DC Metro subsequently implemented a bioterror detection system at key stations called PROTECT that integrates bio/chem sensors with traditional surveillance and monitoring systems. I asked for an update on the PROTECT system and any additional technologies and systems that have been deployed to help prevent or mitigate such an attack, but Chief Hanson could only note: "We have a chemical, biological and radiological detection program in our system, but do not discuss specifics of those programs for security reasons."

Sometimes, counterterrorism efforts depend more on the human factor than on new technology. For instance, Richard Reid, the would-be shoe-bomber, was defeated by an alert air crew and hypersensitive fellow passengers whose suspicions helped to prevent him from completing his mission. In Israel, effective profiling and well-honed instincts by security screeners and security-conscious civilians have foiled many an attack. I asked about ways to enhance security consciousness among Metro staff, as well as Metro riders, through training, public service announcements, and the like, to which Tangherlini responded: "We regularly work with our customers and employees, reminding of the need to remain vigilant and to report any suspicious activity or behavior to the Metro Transit Police. We refresh the message to keep riders' attention and we are ready to launch a new campaign reminding customers to stay aware and not become complacent. We have posters with security and emergency preparedness messages in trains and stations and on buses and make security-related announcements throughout the system. We offer training for riders, employees and regional emergency responders. In addition, our Web site (www.MetroOpensDoors.com) has a wealth of safety/security information, including an animated video that shows viewers how to evacuate a Metrorail train in the event of an emergency."

Tangherlini also observed that "Metro's Department of System Safety and Risk Protection in conjunction with the Metro Transit Police hold drills to test our emergency response and coordination with regional emergency responders. The most recent drill was held in February 2006 and included 100 participants from local fire, rescue and police agencies, as well as federal agencies. One very important element and lesson is the coordination among the various entities that respond to an emergency and the ability for the various first responders to communicate with each other." When asked about using random searches as a deterrent to would-be terrorists as tried in

New York City during a 2005 terror alert, Tangherlini commented: "We have studied random bag searches. It is not something we are pursuing at this time."

Ever since the creation of the Homeland Security Advisory System, we've all kept an eye on terror alerts, changes in the threat level, and on occasion system- or site-specific terror threats. But as time goes by, people seem less and less worried and pay less and less attention to the general threat environment. I asked if the DC Metro has a system in place to communicate with its riders the fluctuations in the terror threat level. Tangherlini replied: "We continuously refresh our safety and security messages. As mentioned earlier, we're getting ready to launch a new campaign that reminds riders not to become complacent and to report suspicious items and/or activity to the Metro Transit Police or any Metro employee. We regularly change the security message so that it remains fresh for our customers." Chief Hanson also commented: "We keep in touch with our riders through various methods—advertising, system announcements, information on the Web site, demonstrations and customer outreach sessions. We continually ask our riders to be extra sets of 'eyes and ears' for the Transit Police, asking them—the people who ride the system everyday—to report anything that seems suspicious, out-of-place or out-of the-ordinary. We also cannot emphasize enough the importance of having an emergency plan and being prepared. We work with the Red Cross and Homeland Security to promote preparedness at home and in the workplace."

As for how the Metro coordinates the flow of information with other branches of the government, Chief Hanson explained that "Metro works with the FBI and has a Transit Police Officer on the FBI's National Terrorism Task Force, and we work closely with the Washington local field office. We also work closely with the Department of Homeland Security, the (DC) Metropolitan Police Department and other regional and local policing agencies." Further, she noted, "we partnered with federal air marshals to provide increased security in January for the president's 2006 State of Union Address. We will look for other opportunities to work with federal air marshals in the future."

I asked Tangherlini if he had any advice for riders on the DC Metro on how best to protect themselves from the risk of terror. He did: "Be prepared and make a plan. Know what to do and where to go in the event of an emergency. Figure out an alternate route to get home, including taking different Metrorail lines or Metrobus routes in case part of the rail system is closed, and know different routes to take in the event of road closures. Most importantly, make an emergency plan with your family that includes an emergency meeting place and an out-of-town contact person. Go to www.makeaplan.org to get started."

Note

1   Barry Zellen, "Securing the DC Metro: A Q&A with Dan Tangherlini," SecurityInnovator.com, March 31, 2006, www.securityinnovator.com/index.php?arti cleID=6483&sectionID=27. Subsequent quotations from Dan Tangherlini and Polly Hanson are from this article.

15

Courtroom Violence and the War against the US Government

In recent years, there has been a rise in courthouse violence, bringing America's system of justice into the line of fire of an increasingly potent convergence of vigilantism, terrorism, and domestic violence. Having "your day in court" has taken on an unprecedented lethality, and while terror trials were anticipated for some of Al Qaeda's incarcerated operatives and terror planners, it was possible that we might see a convergence of courtroom violence and Jihadist rage. Indeed, so worried were officials, Democratic and Republican, about the dangers of of holding a trial in Manhattan for the architect of 9/11, Khalid Sheikh Mohammed, that local and state leaders pushed back against the President Obama's 2008 campaign promise to bring the prisoners held offshore in Guantanamo to trial in civilian courts, where the rule of law and the supremacy of the US Constitution would no longer be in doubt. But the billion dollar price tag for security, on a scale required to host an Olympics, as well as the expectation of some sort of terror plot, reinforced by a new antiterror vigor that was precipitated by the failed Christmas Day airplane bomb plot, forced the White House to reconsider. Looking back just a few years, we can see how, even without the added element of international terrorism thrown into the mix, courtroom insecurity and violence has become widespread.

Indeed, in just a single month during the spring of 2005, a wave of courthouse violence swept across America, shocking the nation and stimulating a widespread debate on how to secure its courtrooms so that justice can be properly served. This month-long orgy of courthouse violence started on February 24, 2005, when David Hernandez Arroyo opened fire on his ex-wife and son on the steps of the Smith County Courthouse in Tyler, Texas—killing his wife and a resident who sought to intervene. Arroyo's son was injured as were three law enforcement officers. Four days later, on February 28, the family of Federal District Judge Joan Lefkow was murdered in Chicago. And just two weeks after that, an even more violent incident took place inside the Fulton County courthouse in Atlanta, Georgia, on March 11, 2005. There, Brian Gene Nichols escaped from custody and fatally shot Judge Rowland W. Barnes in his private chambers, where he also killed court reporter Julie Brandau. He also shot and killed Sergeant Hoyt Teasley and injured several other law enforcement and court officials. Nichols' courthouse shooting spree generated widespread debate across America on courtroom security.

Of course, the most shocking and destructive attack of all took place a full decade earlier—when on April 19, 1995, the Alfred P. Murrah Federal Building was destroyed in Oklahoma City, with 168 dead and over 800 injured. This domestic terror attack resulted in the immediate deployment of Jersey barriers along the perimeters of all federal buildings, and led to legislation designed to secure federal buildings, calling for all new federal buildings to be constructed with truck-resistant barriers and deep setbacks from the street to reduce the threat of vehicle-borne IEDs. Whether from a terrorist attack, an external assault on the courthouse steps, or a violent attack of its inner sanctum, the problem of courthouse security has been painfully revealed. According to security consultant and professor of criminal justice Todd Bell, "the problem is huge, due to the fact that many arrests and confrontations end up and are decided in the courtroom, where security staff can be substandard."[1] Bell has over 18 years of law enforcement experience, and is cofounder and vice president of RL Security Solutions and criminal justice professor at Westwood College in Anaheim and Santa Ana College, both in California.

Bell told me that "courtroom and Courthouse violence is not a new phenomenon, it goes back years. The problem was that it was not taken seriously, and staffing levels were inadequate. It has become more problematic due to the nature of the proliferation of weapons on the streets." He reflected that the 2005 courthouse shooting in Atlanta, Georgia, "was a prime example for the need to enhance courthouse security, and update training for law enforcement." Additionally, Bell has found that "violence in the courthouse is primarily happening in Family Law Court where emotions run high. Issues such as child custody, child support, and asset division bring out the worst in people. We have a saying in law enforcement: 'Criminal Courts are for bad people on good behavior, and Family Law Court is for good people on bad behavior.'"

Bell believes "the primary risk and challenges that need to be addressed to secure the courthouse and courtrooms is the need get everyone up to speed on the reality of courthouse violence. Many times, judges, administrators, and court officials feel there is an over reaction and fall into a false sense of security. Getting everyone to buy-in to preventable security measures is paramount."

There are numerous solutions available to help secure the courts. "Some of the solutions for securing courtrooms and courthouses include developing partnerships with regional law enforcement, updating training for personnel, and sharing intel that is vital. Also, technological advances such as sensors, x-ray machines, surveillance cameras, hand-wands, automatic door locks, and emergency notification systems are important steps," and when deployed can be "proactive measures to ensure courthouse safety." In order to maintain courthouse security, Bell believes a collaborative effort must be taken: "Usually, the sheriff of said county is responsible for the lead on security issues of the courthouse. However, judges, courthouse administrators, and court personnel are vital to discussion and input."

I also spoke with Captain (ret.) Tim Quinton, who teaches court security at Sam Houston State University's Correctional Management Institute of Texas (CMIT) in Huntsville, Texas, a program he's taught since, coincidentally, the day after 9/11: "It was ironic, but I had a class set up for the 12th of September, 2001. With the events of

9/11, we thought at first we should cancel the class." But, "the more I thought about it, the more I knew we needed the class more than ever."[2] And so the class took place, as scheduled, on the day after: "We had a great training the next two days. I have been teaching the class ever since." As Quinton recalled: "The morning after was one of the most difficult classes I have ever taught. We started with a moment of silence to honor our brothers and sisters of law enforcement, our country's men and women and their families. I then addressed the obvious and let the class discuss the issues. We finally got into the lesson plan after lunch." Quinton travels around Texas to "teach parts of the class around the state" and has "also presented at several national conferences" where he addressed the continuing challenges of making the operation of America's justice system a more secure experience. He also provides consulting services to "one of the companies that build all kinds of security systems," which "we customize for each customer."

In order to ensure that the security solution fits the specific requirements of the client, "I will usually walk the courthouse, jail, or school that we want to secure. We then make recommendations to the customer. They then make the call on what we install." Among the ingredients they may select are "the latest in cameras, recorders, access control door locks, metal detectors, x-ray machines, etc. Most courthouses are going to an upgraded system." As well, there is growing interest in "virtual arraignments" using remote video systems. "We're also now installing the video arraignment to do several things: it is much safer to keep the inmates in the secured areas when possible, it is cost effective not to transport when you don't need to, and it is time effective." Quinton observed that "overall, these technologies are very effective if they are monitored correctly and responses to problems are co-coordinated properly."

But technology alone cannot solve the problem of courthouse security. Proper training, to ensure a full awareness of the threat and to prepare court officials to respond swiftly to security problems when they arise, is also essential. Quinton has found that "some courts do better than others" when it comes to their security preparedness. He believes that "the bailiffs and support staff must develop a street cop attitude," since "the street in many cases has moved to the courthouse."

With the rise in courthouse shootings across the country in recent years, Quinton recalled how "the court used to be a place of high respect," and was to a large degree protected by its widely held sanctity as the house of justice. But now, there has been an erosion in that respect. As Quinton put it: "People do not hold it in that kind of esteem." Now, he finds, "people will get away with what you let them. I can go into a courtroom and tell you in a few minutes if the staff is doing a good job or a poor one by the way business is being done. Poorly run courthouses and courtrooms lead to tragic events." Quinton believes that to redress the uneven nature of courtroom operations, and the uneven level of court security, we "need to be consistent with all aspects of security," and that standards are necessary to ensure a steady level of security is maintained across the state and country. "All staff must be standardized so nothing gets missed," Quinton observed, and "the best place to start is with policy and procedure."

Quinton cautions that the "court staff has to keep up with the rest of law enforcement. I feel they have been left behind in many areas. The mindset has been this is a retirement job." And that mindset has contributed to the persistence of lax courthouse security. But Quinton believes that "well trained staff can stop a lot of problems by being pro-active and on top of what is going on around them," and that "better trained staff is the answer. I also think we should include all court personnel for training. Judges, clerks, DAs (district attorneys), even defense attorneys should receive different types of training." Given the chance, Quinton noted, "I would train them with what to do in a crisis issue. The way the other staff responds in a crisis can help or hurt the security response." As Quinton explained: "Courthouse security and the response to a crisis takes all of the things we mentioned, technology plus support and response from first responders and the civilian population working the courthouse on a daily basis. I always recommend that a courthouse develop a security committee. This committee is made up of at least one person from each department. The committee will set guidelines for the staff. These guidelines will mandate what is expected of the staff in a crisis. The response here will make the job easier for the law enforcement response."

Courtroom violence has become common across America, and is not just associated with violent inner cities where gangs, guns, and drugs are rampant. "Big city or urban area, it does not matter. Threats and drama in court happen everywhere," from the smallest rural community to the largest megalopolis. The real differentiator is whether there is adequate funding for training and the installation of security solutions such as metal detectors and video surveillance systems. "Money versus security will always be the biggest test," observed Quinton. In the state of Texas, "the sheriff, by law, is in charge of courthouse security." But, he noted, "the catch is the court commissioner has the right to fund him or not. If the sheriff does not have the support, it is hard for him to secure the courthouse." Fortunately, Quinton has found, funds for courthouse security training are on the rise. "Training costs time and money, but we have seen an increase."

Looking back on major incidents of courthouse violence, as well as acts of terror directed at the federal government that magnified awareness of the threat to government operations including the system of justice, RL Security Solutions' Bell commented: "The Oklahoma City bombing, the first World Trade Center bombing, 9/11, the Texas courthouse shooting, and the Atlanta courthouse shootings, unfortunately have caused us to reevaluate security measures in the courthouse. In the midst of tragedies like these, we can ensure to the best of our abilities, that incidents like such can be prevented, and a proper response to a critical situation will be met with competent tactics and a reliable course of action that gives the public and personnel, confidence in public safety officials to keep them safe from future incidents in the courthouse."

But as CMIT's Quinton observed, in the years since 9/11, security consciousness has begun to decline as those attacks recede in time. "Security in courthouses follows the trend: after 9/11 everyone was aware. Years go by and awareness declines." Added Quinton: "We can be better in all aspects. This will always be a work in progress. Key word: Progress."

Notes

1 Barry Zellen, "Order in the Court, or Murder in the Court? Technology, Training, and Vigilance Help Tackle Rise in Courtroom Violence," SecurityInnovator.com, August 14, 2008, http://securityinnovator.com/index.php?articleID=15522&sectionID=31. Subsequent quotations from Bell are from this article.
2 Ibid. Subsequent quotations from Quinton are from this article.

16

Black Sunday Redux

It seemed straight out of Hollywood's darkest imaginings, reminiscent of the plot line of the 1977 Hollywood thriller *Black Sunday*, when terrorists targeted the Super Bowl with a hijacked blimp ingeniously transformed into an aerial IED, or of Tom Clancy's 1991 suspense novel of nuclear terrorism, *The Sum of All Fears*, in which the Super Bowl was brought to an early, and unexpectedly radioactive, end. But it wasn't a Super Bowl that was attacked; more ominously, in real life, on American soil, it was an ordinary college football game, one of hundreds that takes place on any given Saturday in the autumn. At around 7:30 pm on October 1, 2005, just before half-time festivities began, a suicide bomber detonated a backpack explosive just outside the Oklahoma Memorial Stadium, which was filled to capacity with 84,000 spectators watching the evening game between the Oklahoma Sooners and the Kansas State Wildcats.

The would-be terrorist was a suicidal student named Joel "Joe" Henry Hinrichs III, a 21-year-old Oklahoma University mechanical engineering student with an avid interest in explosives, who built his bomb with triacetone triperoxide, known as TATP, described by GlobalSecurity.org as "a new terrorist explosive" that "has recently appeared as a weapon in the Middle East," and used by suicide bombers around the world, including the July 7, 2005, London Subway bombings, and the failed December 2001 attack by infamous airplane "shoe-bomber," Richard Reid. Among its most worrisome features is that TATP is nearly undetectable by either sniffer dogs or conventional bomb detection systems.

But fortunately for all but Hinrichs, TATP is highly sensitive to impact, temperature change, and friction, and the bomb detonated at a safe distance from the stadium, leaving just Hinrichs' lower body intact after he rummaged around his backpack. FBI and local police have concluded the perpetrator acted alone, with no assistance from any terrorist group, and was a loner suffering from severe depression. A suicide note left on his computer said: "None of you are worth living with. You can all kiss my ass." But there is speculation that he sought to enter the full stadium and to kill as many fans as possible, but was turned away at the gate because backpacks were forbidden. More ominous: just two days before his TATP bomb went off, Hinrichs was overheard by an off-duty police officer as he inquired about purchasing a large amount of ammonium nitrate from a feed store—the highly destructive ingredient used in the 1995 Oklahoma City mass-terror attack.

This suggests that America came perilously close to a real-life *Black Sunday* type attack. While this seems to be as loud and clear a warning of the risks and dangers faced by stadium security professionals, media coverage of the 2005 Oklahoma Attack was minimal, and there was no public panic or outcry to follow. But to those tasked with protecting stadiums and their stunningly large number of spectators from terrorist attack, Hinrichs' failed attack is a cautionary tale that cannot be forgotten, since next time, luck may be on the side of the perpetrator, and the scale of destruction as extreme as that imagined by the author of *Black Sunday*.

James McGee, the director of Programming at the Center for Spectator Sports Security Management (CSSSM) at the University of Southern Mississippi, served as the FBI security coordinator for the 2004 Athens Olympic Games. He told me that "the current terrorist threat specifically targets stadiums and arenas during planned events as a viable and attractive target."[1] McGee added that "it is estimated 43 million fans attend college football games during a given season," and noted, "two of the primary criteria by terrorists are body count and high profile events. Sport venues meet both of these. The scale of the effort to secure stadiums and arenas is monumental and a critical tasking." Indeed, McGee spent two years working with Greek Olympic officials "to ensure their games occurred without incident," and is pleased to report: "We succeeded." He explained that "security at an event as large as the Summer Olympics is synonymous to preparing for a Super Bowl every day for three weeks. It is a monumental, multi-national endeavor and can't be accomplished by one country alone."

An Olympic event represents one end of the scale, with the most sophisticated and extensive of security arrangements provided, but for the millions of sports fans that attend high school, junior college, National Association of Intercollegiate Athletics (NAIA), or National Collegiate Athletic Association (NCAA) games, they face a wide disparity in security solutions. As McGee explained: "Currently Universities generally exist as a 'softer' target for attack. The professional leagues have a greater amount of revenue to dedicate to security at professional venues." This disparity is "why the CSSSM is addressing the NCAA university environment first. Research revealed that this is where the biggest gap exists, in terms of security awareness, mitigation, preparedness, response, recovery. The next area of concern includes NAIA, Junior Colleges and high schools." Added McGee, "there are well over 1,000 stadiums and arenas that cause concern" and "currently, security measures vary from venue to venue."

According to William McGuire, the president and CEO of Global Security Associates, a provider of executive protection and security services: "One of the biggest challenges is the sheer size of the event. Let's, for example, look at a football game held in the US, Europe or South America. The volume of people entering the stadium at one time, or over a short period of time, can present a security challenge as any one of those attending could use the simplest item, such as a glass bottle and turn it into a weapon. In a stadium, everyone is at risk; players and fans. As a result, the approach is to ban all items and set up areas where all patrons are checked as well as all equipment entering and this also involves physical searches because the potential is very real."[2]

McGuire said that he's seen "a lot of progress made to keep attendees safe. Stadium officials have a big job to do and are accomplishing the ability to keep events safe." On the whole, he has found that fans seem to be cooperating. As McGuire noted, "there are some similarities in the security approach" taken by airports and by stadium officials: just as airline passengers have gotten used to the extra security layer and now routinely take their laptops out and their shoes off. McGuire has found that "there does not seem to be any resistance on anyone's part to boosting security. Everyone is in a post-9/11 world mindset and the dangers are real." And so they are getting used to new restrictions on forbidden items and behaviors at the stadium and even submitting to pat-down searches, though a legal challenge in Tampa, Florida, temporarily suspended pat-downs in that one venue.

But according to the StubHub website, Yankee Stadium prevents "backpacks, briefcases, attaché cases, coolers, glass or plastic bottles, cans, large purses, bags or video cameras" from being "permitted into the ballpark," and that in addition, "no laptops are permitted into the stadium."[3] An even more detailed list appears on the N.Y. Yankees website: "Any soft-sided bag larger than 16 inches by 16 inches by 8 inches, including diaper bags, backpacks and purses; Briefcases, coolers and hard-sided bags and containers; Glass, cans and plastic bottles; Laser pens; Video cameras; Laptop computers; Firearms or knives; Beach balls, blow horns and all other distracting noisemakers; Any other devices that may interfere with and/or distract any sports participant, other patron, audio or audio/visual telecast or recording of the game or any technology-related service provided in Yankee Stadium."[4] At Tampa, Florida's Raymond James Stadium, a similar list of items is also forbidden: "backpacks, duffel bags or large bags; food, drinks, cans, bottles, glass; seat cushions; banners/flags with sticks or poles; video cameras; umbrellas or anything that would obstruct a fan's view; coolers; horns/air horns (artificial noisemakers); lasers; weapons/fireworks; items that could be missiles or projectiles; cameras with lenses longer than 12-inches; chucky dolls; thunder sticks; footballs; strollers; large bags; pets (except assistive animals); skates, skateboards, skate-shoes, all cycles and Segways."[5]

McGuire observed that there is "a huge difference between a professional and or college level event, and the security plan that is developed for such venues as the Olympics or international events such as the World Cup and other international sporting events." To help its clients protect themselves, "Global Security Associates incorporates a threat assessment approach to every event. Our team of security professionals will review the location of the event, the size and where the event sits on the world stage. When we protect individuals attending, such as VIPs or government officials, additional security protocols are put into place such as having many layers of security in place to always ensure their safety."

Even with the events of 9/11 now many years behind us, most Americans still recognize the need to take more proactive measures to ensure stadium security. As CSSSM's McGee has commented: "Our experience shows that the general public is aware of the potential risk to stadiums and arenas, and are generally in favor of increased security at these venues. However, the security efforts at sport venues must be more transparent then at airports so that the spectator experience is not tainted by security measures that manifest in the form of long lines and significant inconvenience. The security needs to be mostly 'behind the scenes.' Some visible security is generally applauded by spectators, who take comfort in knowing the environment is secure."

He added: "Transparency is the key so that security efforts do not significantly have a negative impact on the spectator experience. This is a tough challenge to meet."

McGee said that the University of Southern Mississippi's CSSSM "is addressing this issue on a variety of fronts" and is "working to standardize security efforts through the 'Sport Event Security Aware system,'" and so far, "all seven public universities have been through the process during the pilot stage." He added: "We have developed our own tool called the Sport Event Security Awareness Model and we provide this tool and the service of conducting risk assessments to universities." As well the DHS introduced an online Vulnerability Self-Assessment Tool (VSAT) for stadiums in 2005, and McGee observed that "the DHS self assessment is a good start but generally a self assessment does not reveal all of the potential vulnerabilities requiring corrective action."

Essential to successful terrorism prevention is awareness of the threat. McGee added that "awareness is a necessity upfront," and explained "this is an All Hazards Awareness," and "not just terrorism but weather-related issues, natural disasters, crowd control, and criminal activity. Mitigation and prevention can be accomplished through numerous physical protection systems and cyber security systems. Keeping backpacks out and limiting alcohol consumption are both good starts for any stadium/arena." He noted as well the requirement for "some degree of 'Game Day Employee' training so the ushers/ticket takers/vendors know what to look for and how to respond." With the rise in fatal campus shootings, security is increasingly on the minds of students, faculty, and staff at universities around the country.

McGee believes that these "recent campus shootings have absolutely placed our efforts specific to campus sport venues in the spotlight. Having a secure stadium/arena on campus requires the campus to be concurrently secure. Many of our systems can be adopted for the campus in general." Hinrichs' failed Oklahoma Memorial Stadium attack in October 2005 was a chilling reminder of what might have been. "This is a prime example of the potential threat," noted McGee, "and as the facts in this matter reveal, an attempt has already happened in this country. Had the perpetrator gained access to the stadium, the results could have been catastrophic. I am at a loss as to why this story was not circulated more widely. Apparently the media did not see the need. Maybe you can change that."

Olympic security in an age of mass terror

Emmy Award–winning film producer Bud Greenspan, who specializes in films about the Olympics, has observed how for over a century, "thousands of young men and women have answered the call to enter the arena to compete in friendly competition for the honour and glory of sport . . . fulfilling the philosophy that is still paramount today, to improve the human race, to strengthen understanding and friendship among all peoples, and to promote the Olympic spirit."[6] But just as (and one might argue *because*) this global, biannual sporting event brings the entire world together, as friends and not foes, the Olympics present an ideal target for terrorists.

Olympics command one of the world's largest television audiences: during the Athens Olympics in 2004, 3.9 billion individuals watched the televised events at least once—exceeding the 3.6 billion viewers of the 2000 Sydney Olympics—with a cumulative total of 40 billion views. During August 8–24, 2008, the Beijing Olympics enjoyed an even larger television audience, totaling around 4.7 billion viewers worldwide as reported by *Xinhua*, making the event a prime-time opportunity for terrorists.[7] Terrorism has struck at the Olympics at least twice, most famously in September 1972 when the Black September Organization, an offshoot of the Palestine Liberation Organization (PLO) formed after Jordan's King Hussein expelled the Palestinian militants after they had failed in a putsch to take over the Kingdom, kidnapped and murdered 11 Israeli athletes and officials in their attack of the Olympic Village, now known as the Munich Massacre. The horrific event, televised for the world to see, riveted audiences to their TV sets, and has been credited for thrusting the cause of Palestinians onto the world stage, thus launching the contemporary era of live, televised international terrorism.

In July 1996, terror struck again during the Atlanta Olympics, when a small backpack bomb went off at the Centennial Olympic Park, killing one spectator directly, and causing the fatal heart attack of a Turkish camera operator while injuring over 100 others. The late hour of the attack—well past midnight—and the fact the perpetrator called in a warning to the police some 20 minutes before the explosion, suggests the aims of this attack were more modest and homegrown. But it was nonetheless a fatal reminder that terror could still strike the Olympics, despite spending over $150 million on security there. The price tag for securing the Olympics has been rising steadily ever since, especially after 9/11: it cost $310 million to secure the 2002 Salt Lake games, and by the Athens Olympics in 2004, the cost had spiraled to $1.5 billion. In Torino in 2006, the price was a slightly more modest $1.4 billion. While Beijing's preliminary budget for Olympics security was only $300 million, the final price tag for securing the 2008 Olympics was substantially higher—though no accurate budget has been released.[8] The IT budget alone for that event was estimated to have cost $400 million.[9]

With the price tag for Olympic security so high in the post-9/11 world, some observers have started to wonder if it's worth paying such a high price: when terrorists struck the London transit system only one day after it was announced that the 2012 Olympics had been awarded there, the danger of terrorism and the high price tag for its prevention was on many peoples' minds. Before the blasts, officials estimated the price tag for security to be $400 million. After the blast, as *Business Week* published an August 15, 2005, article titled "For London, What Price Olympic Security? After the bombings, London's estimate for the 2012 games seems way too low."[10]

But as former head of the Salt Lake City Olympic organizing committee, retired Massachusetts governor, and defeated Republican presidential candidate Mitt Romney told a May 2004 hearing on Olympic security held by the US Senate Commerce Subcommittee on Competition, Foreign Commerce and Infrastructure: "I was asked many times whether or not it made sense to continue holding the Olympics, considering the increased security risks and the enormous expense of housing the Games. My answer then, as now, is that it is more important than ever that the Games continue and that the United States play a major role in the continuation of the Olympic movement."[11]

With the Olympic spirit still high and states the world over clamoring to host the high visibility event, the challenge becomes how to secure the Olympics in the age of live, televised international terrorism? I spoke with several security consultants in order to better understand the challenges inherent in securing a post-9/11 Olympics. I first spoke with William McGuire, president and CEO of Global Security Associates, LLC, a corporate security firm that has been engaged to execute security operations for numerous high-profile events—including the 50th Anniversary of the UN General Assembly, the 43rd United States Presidential Inauguration, and the 2006 Torino Olympic Games.[12] He observed that the Olympics are "a massive undertaking that requires special security protocols to be designed" that "address a myriad of potential threats in order to keep athletes, VIPs, visiting executives and spectators safe while also being aware of the local political environment." McGuire noted that the Olympics serves as "an international stage and one where different groups of individuals with agendas would look to make their political, religious or other issues known." Securing an Olympics requires not only protecting those attending the event, McGuire said, but also great deal of coordination with the authorities and security personnel tasked with securing the event."

McGuire finds that the Olympics "make an attractive target for individuals and groups with sinister intentions to draw attention to themselves or their cause," and he recalled that "past threats that have been carried out included small suitcase bombs to the devastating hostage taking in 1972." While "current preparations for security will also cover this," he noted they "will also take into account the growing concern for suicide bombers, concealed explosive devices, biological threats and all possible scenarios meant to injure or kill a single person or a group of people attending the Olympic Games." Olympic organizers will have to keep an eye out for a wide spectrum of security challenges as "threats from petty crime to international terrorism will be very real and prevalent to the organizers, and their ability to respond to all types of threats will need to be prepared for. There is a dire need for the security forces to remain highly adaptable to the changing security climate—what may not be identified as a threat now during the assessment period may well become very real, specific and credible threat just days or even hours before the events commence." Further, McGuire noted that "aside from purely security threats, there is a need to focus on other potentially life-threatening issues such as health risks" associated with such hazards as Avian flu, which "may well prove to become a pandemic for which the authorities will need to have contingency plans for."

McGuire cautioned in advance of the 2008 Olympics in Beijing that they "may pose significant risks to the IOC, Olympic athletes, and their audiences. This is despite the assurances from the local government and the Mayor Liu Qi that the 'New Beijing' is changing and more open than it was." McGuire added that "the potential for social unrest and disaffected populations could present a challenge to city and national officials," as "there are stresses evident in Chinese society which could also be a challenge to IOC including: worker strikes making it difficult for the venues and transportation systems to run smoothly, labor and pro-democracy demonstrations that challenge government policies," as well as "ethnic unrest in the occupied territories of Tibet, Inner Mongolia and Xinjiang which has contributed to increased social instability." McGuire pointed out that "China has not been free from transnational terrorist acts, with some Chinese minorities spurred into armed protest against the central government by ethnic separatism, Islamic fundamentalism and al-Qaeda's networks," adding that "the over 100 million Muslims in China, many of whom maintain strained relations with central authorities whose chauvinist tendency in the past planted seeds of discontent among minorities, proved a major attraction to bin Laden and his terrorist networks. The confluence of al-Qaeda and the ethnic independence fighters within China was natural to some extent." McGuire added "there is little doubt that these networks would view the Beijing Olympics as a perfect venue for bringing world attention to their cause by staging attacks." McGuire also expected that the Darfur issue would catalyze protests at the Beijing Olympics, as already "campaigns to use the Olympics to put pressure on Beijing to do more to stop the violence in Darfur have been gathering steam," and this "will present a challenge to security professionals."

According to Victor Anderes, VP of Special Operations at Global Security Associates: "Given China's position on the world stage, the Chinese Government is going to make every effort to ensure that the Olympics are not just successful from a sporting perspective, but also from a security perspective."[13] Around half of China's 70,000 Olympic volunteers will be involved in security, and a series of dry runs were held during 26 sporting events during the second half of the preceding year to test out the security system before the 2008 Olympics took place.

In Torino, McGuire recalled, the security effort involved "thousands of police officers deployed to patrol potential targets around the Olympic venues," including "some 300 police officers on ski equipment patrolling the ski courses after closing hours, and the Italian government's option of suspending the European open-borders treaty to control borders during the games." And "in addition to the athletes," McGuire added, "some 21 heads of state, six royal families and 15 heads of government were confirmed to participate. More than a half-dozen countries, including the US, Britain and Israel, helped Italy prepare for this massive security effort." The total number of organizations and agencies involved was thus most likely "in the hundreds or more," and "there are so many areas that security will cover and this will branch out to the local police, national police, the military including: air support, ground activities and port security. Local municipalities will be involved and the host country will dictate all of this as well as providing security for all the provisions such as food, medicine, power, border security throughout the country. During the event, there will be a deployment of thousands of individuals tasked with security—both overtly and covertly."

Global Security Associates spent over six months preparing for its role at Torino, where it provided personal protection to executives from corporations that sponsored the games, "gathering intelligence and working with local Italian law enforcement agencies, the US military and the US consulate. Our goal was to coordinate the logistics of our personnel in and around the country." So by the time the games began, "we had spent a tremendous amount of time planning and studying the physical area in the event of something going wrong and being able to extract our clients on short notice from the area."

McGuire anticipated that being host city for the 2008 Olympics would "present many challenges from a security perspective," and "this massive undertaking will involve 100 percent participation of all the security departments from around the city and indeed the entire country." McGuire added that "as with the Games in Italy, every country will have a vested interest in making sure their dignitaries and athletes are safe." McGuire credits Beijing's approach as being "most prudent as the need for cooperation on an international scale is crucial to ensuring an environment where athletes, spectators and other visitors are secure." As reported by *China Daily,* a meeting of the International Permanent Observatory on Security Measures During Major Events (IPO), which was set up in February 2003 by the United Nations Inter Regional Crime and Justice Research Institute (UNICRI) and the European Police Office (EUROPOL), took place in Beijing in May 2005, and twenty-four foreign security experts representing ten different countries and four international organizations were in attendance.[14] IPO promotes the identification of security best practices and aims to strengthen international cooperation and information exchanges in security. The Beijing Olympic Security Coordination Group had been set up in December 2004, and in March 2005, Beijing's Olympic security master plan was officially unveiled.

McGuire expected China's Olympic security program would include security technology similar to that used in Athens, where "a vast computer surveillance network with thousands of hidden cameras and microphones that analyzed dozens of languages" was deployed. McGuire noted "China has strict border controls, and I believe we will see a large part of the security effort being pushed back to the borders and ports of entry into the country. Utilizing international databases of known terrorists combined with facial recognition technology and fraudulent document detection technology, every attempt will be made to control access to the country prior to and during the games." On top of this, he added that "security screening equipment, explosive detection technology and radiation detectors are likely to be deployed at numerous locations both overtly and covertly. There will also be a significant deployment of access control technology around the venues and residential quarters of the athletes," including facial recognition systems to weed out potential troublemakers.

I also spoke with Bruce Schneier, security expert and prolific author of eight books, including *Beyond Fear: Thinking Sensibly about Security in an Uncertain World, Secrets and Lies.* With its past history of terrorism, it's hard not to equate Olympic security with counterterrorism, and as Schneier explained: "The security threat everyone will be thinking about is terrorism, of course, because that's what's on people's minds." But he's confident that "the authorities will be on top of that, to be sure."[15]

Schneier posits that "the real threats are more pedestrian in nature." Schneier explained that "the biggest threat at any large event is always crime. Crime against the Olympics: theft, ticket forgery, and so on. And theft against the fans: again, petty crime. The Olympics is basically a large city full of people descending on another city for a short time, and that always strains the local police. And the solutions are pretty much what you'd expect: more eyes and ears on the street, more investigative muscle, and a coordinated system to deal with all the incidents." Thus, while "the Olympics will almost certainly be focused on anti-terrorism security," Schneier believes that "this is almost certainly to be a waste of money, as it focuses so narrowly on one tactic. Defending the Olympics against terrorism is only valuable if the terrorists are targeting the Olympics. If they're targeting something else, it's a waste. If they were targeting the Olympics and switch their target because of the massive security, it's still a waste." Schneier said he "would much rather see all that money be shifted to intelligence and investigation: security that is effective regardless of what target the terrorists have chosen, and what tactic they're going to use to attack it."

As Beijing prepared to welcome the world's top athletes, government and business leaders, and millions of spectators, Schneier counseled Beijing's Olympic organizers to "study the security from previous Olympics," pointing out that "the world does this every two years—once in the summer and once in the winter—and there's a lot of experience and expertise to be learned from those who've done it before. Both about what the common threats are, and about what threats are exaggerated. That being said, China will have its own internal politics to worry about as well." As Schneier pointed out, technology is both a source of the problem as well as part of the solution. The threat itself does not change, he noted, "they rarely do. What does change are the tactics, and they change because of technology. Technology will make tickets easier to forge, or will make some Internet-based Olympic fraud easier. Watch the real world, and you'll see the criminal tactics that will be used at the Olympics." As Schneier observed: "Technology is an important tool for the attacks, but it's an important tool for the defenders as well. I expect you'll see a lot of high-tech anti-fraud technology. I expect you'll see a lot of cameras as well," and "this application, a massive temporary high-profile event, they're a smart security technology. Mostly the best technology will be working behind the scenes, though, making the human security organization more effective."

Schneier noted that the Olympics present some unique security challenges: "The Olympics are a large event, meaning that a lot of security is required for the duration, but the need evaporates when the event ends. But unlike a lot of other large events, the Olympics lasts over several weeks. And it consists of many, many individual pieces: venues, spectacles, living quarters, and so on. This, and the international nature of the Olympics, makes it a unique challenge." And McGuire believed with the right preparation, this challenge can be met. He recalled how the British Special Air Service uses the term "Train hard. Fight easy," and added, "while the athletes will be doing this in preparation for the Games, so too should the security services—robust planning, intensive training and reliable intelligence networks will make the difference."

Lessons of Beijing 2008

Tragedy did indeed strike during the 2008 Beijing Olympics when a knife-wielding man stabbed and killed Todd Bachman, the father-in-law of the US women's indoor volleyball coach Hugh McCutcheon, and seriously injured Bachman's wife while wounding their Chinese tour guide. The assailant then jumped to his death from the thirteenth-century Drum Tower, a popular tourist destination. The first word to come to mind for many that day was *terrorism*, but it soon became clear that the crime was a random act of violence; the perpetrator was a disgruntled, unemployed 47-year-old from Hangzhou intent on committing a very public act of suicide, a scenario eerily similar to Schneier's prescient prediction during our pre-Olympics interview that it would be random crime in the populace tourist-filled city and not political terror that we would most likely witness.

But apart from this one act of violence, the 2008 Olympics passed without incident, with over 400,000 foreign and more than 1 million Chinese spectators attending, 17,600 accredited journalists covering, and 10,708 athletes competing in events held in 37 separate venues, with 31 spread out across the sprawling capital city, and 6 located outside the city—football in Qinhuangdao, Shanghai, Shenyang, and Tianjin; sailing in Qingdao; and equestrian events in Hong Kong. Beijing spent an estimated £20 billion or more on the event, constructing new roads, subway lines, an airport terminal, a high-speed intercity rail line, as well as 12 new sports venues. The Olympic stadium, the famed Bird's Nest—slated to become a shopping and entertainment complex due to its limited sports use after the Olympics concluded—was built at a cost of $450 million.

To ensure the Olympics remained secure, a 100,000-strong security force was assembled and deployed around Beijing. The government also installed 300,000 surveillance cameras, and an antiaircraft system was set-up at the Bird's Nest. Authorities increased identity inspections, and boosted the reward to citizens who reported a security threat. Over 400,000 citizen-volunteers were recruited, more than a million cars were taken off the streets, and some 200 local factories were shuttered to clear the air. In short, the Olympics reflected a massive effort at social engineering, transforming the face of Beijing for all the world to see. And top on officials' minds, long before the opening ceremonies began, was ensuring the security of the Games.

To understand how Beijing scored when it came to its Olympic security effort, I spoke with Ray Mey, an expert on Olympic security and trainer at the Center for Spectator Sports Security Management (CSSSM) at the University of Southern Mississippi. Mey has worked every Olympic Games since 1984, gaining a first-hand perspective on the unique challenges of securing an Olympics.[16] Mey said "the biggest security challenges of the Olympics are for the country's government to make a strategic and financial commitment to the security requirements for an event like the Olympic Games," as "the event requires the highest levels of the government to pledge its commitment early on to deliver a safe and secure Games and to make it one of the highest priorities in the initial stages of planning."

He found that "the Chinese Government took the security planning and operations for the 2008 Olympic Games very seriously," and noted that he, "along with many entities, was involved in providing information on best practices and lessons-learned to the Chinese." As Mey observed: "Essentially, the Chinese government expanded their security exponentially by co-opting the public and mobilizing a volunteer force of thousands to be the eyes and ears of security threats or individuals attempting to disrupt or sabotage the Games." Additionally, with regard to team security, "extensive efforts are taken by each respective country to protect their team members from harm. This, combined with extremely high security at the Olympic Village and at the venue sites, provided optimal security for the various Olympic teams."

In 2006, Mey was a representative of the United Nations Institute of Criminal Research's (UNICRI) International Permanent Observatory on Security for Major Events, where he, "along with several international law enforcement representatives provided several days of training and information pertaining to Olympic Security," and he "participated in additional briefings to the Chinese at FBI Headquarters in Washington, DC two years before the Games."

Mey noted that it is important to recognize that "intelligence and investigation are the critical first line of defense against criminals and terrorists targeting the Games," and observed that "the Chinese engaged in extensive efforts to identify and minimize these threats. This combined with a huge security force and technical capabilities, created a strong security effort." And while hindsight shows "there are always other approaches to planning and securing major events such as an Olympic Games, however the security effort must be adapted to the culture along with political, economic and sociological considerations." Mey found that Beijing's investment in Olympic security "absolutely" paid off, and that Beijing "proved to the world that they could plan, implement and manage a safe, secure and successful Olympic Games."

As the Drum Tower stabbing demonstrated, "there is no such thing as 100 percent security," but Mey noted "this was a random act of violence and it was by chance that one individual, a westerner was killed in the attack. A Chinese person and the deceased victim's wife were also seriously injured in the attack." Helping to limit the fatalities, "the Chinese response to this was quite good, and the medical attention to the deceased's wife were second to none. The Chinese EMTs and doctors who provided emergency medical care to her saved her life." Apart from this one incidence of violence, Mey reflected, "to the best of my knowledge, there were no other security incidents during the conduct of the games worth mentioning."

Mey recalled the Centennial Park bombing at the 1996 Olympics, noting that this sort of case "poses one of the most difficult challenges, where a 'lone wolf' individual evades the efforts of law enforcement and targets a non-venue location, such as Centennial Park where thousands of people gathered, and lesser security screening and hardening measures of official Olympic venues had been taken." He noted Centennial Park "had not been designated as an official Olympic venue site in Atlanta," while "today, that type of location would have been designated an official venue site, and afforded the same level of protection as any other Olympic venue location."

But with over 30 venues spread out across a vast capital city of 17 million, chock-full of popular tourist destinations outside the official Olympics sites, there is little that can be done to thwart a random act of violence. As William McGuire noted in a follow-up interview after the event, "the stabbing event was a tragic event," but preventing this kind of random violence is exceptionally challenging, "unless the coach and his family were traveling with personal security." But even then, "I am not sure this would have helped, this individual was a mentally unstable person, and this is hard to protect against random violence."[17]

McGuire noted that securing an Olympics is a "huge" challenge, and like "all major sporting events that bring media coverage from all over the world, is a bad guy's dream." Furthermore, "the different nationals represented pose many security logistics issues," and "the diplomacy to handle two hundred-plus nations is a great challenge," as is the challenge inherent in "the IOC working with the host nation." But Beijing's organizers, the IOC, and the participating teams overcame these challenges—and Beijing's investment of time and resources to secure the Games "definitely paid off. There were no major or minor terrorist events that we know of, and the amount that was spent was close to the amount spent on the Athens games," though he added that "this was a soft number at best as the Chinese were reluctant in disclosing the numbers or measures taken to secure the Games."

Much can be learned from China's effort to secure the Games. Overall, McGuire said he "would rate their effort a B+," noting Beijing's effort to secure the Games included using "volunteers, and the proper training of those volunteers and the communications that was needed to keep the volunteers in touch with the volunteer command center that was staffed by police and military. Along with the volunteers, the Chinese used an enormous amount of cameras and all tied into their central command center." In addition, McGuire noted, "most of the larger countries send some sort of security team with their athletes, along with engaging with local assets"; to "help insure the teams safety these efforts also need to follow all local laws of the country."

McGuire pointed out that "every event has its pros and cons," as they are all "different in their challenges." In his assessment of Beijing's effort to secure its Olympics, "I feel the that the use of volunteers in the security sector was a huge success, and is a good best practice or lesson-learned for the IOC to bring to the next site location, and also for other large scale or multi-national events." McGuire added that "with the IOC as an independent entity, they bring the best practices of what worked last and modify it to work at the next location." He also noted China's efforts to manage uprisings in its restive Tibetan and Xinjiang autonomous regions in the days and weeks leading up to the Olympics, and reflected on how "everything is timing, and if the uprisings occurred a year earlier, the world news media might not have even given it a mention." Terrorism, he added, "is staged for a reason: events, dates, anniversaries all play a role."

And, as CSSSM's Mey observed, "like other countries that have hosted an Olympic Games in the past, law enforcement agencies and respective government intelligence agencies must take early efforts years before the actual conduct of the games to identify and assess the potential threats to the Games. Once the threats are identified, efforts must be directed at strategies and operations to minimize and neutralize these threats." Mey found that in Beijing's case, "China was well aware of these threats before the Games and early efforts and continued efforts were ongoing over a period of approximately two years to step up operations to contain these threats to the Games." He reiterated that "the best way to address such risks and threats is through intelligence gathering, investigation and the arrest of identified criminals and terrorists. The hardening of the venue sites with physical security countermeasures is the final dragnet that will hopefully catch those who have eluded the investigative effort."

Looking ahead to the London 2012 Olympics, Mey identified several valuable lessons learned: "Start planning early, strong coordination between all public safety agencies, robust exercise and training, early commitment of personnel, resources and funding, stand up operational activities months before the event, seamless coordination and integration with the host organizing committee, identify the best and most talented people early and who will be in place for the duration of the planning and operations." Boiling these down to the bare essentials, Mey identified "planning, training and exercises" as the fundamental lessons of Beijing for future Olympics security preparation.

Notes

1 Barry Zellen, "Stadium Insecurity: America's next 9/11 might Be a Mass-Casualty Attack of a Sports Stadium Packed with Fans," SecurityInnovator.com, April 21, 2008, www.securityinnovator.com/index.php?articleID=15150&sectionID=27. Subsequent quotations from James McGee are from this article.
2 Ibid. Subsequent quotations from William McGuire are from this article.
3 As posted at www.stubhub.com/yankee-stadium-tickets/ details/?venue_config_ID=333389.
4 As posted at http://newyork.yankees.mlb.com/nyy/ballpark/security.jsp.
5 As posted at www.raymondjames.com/stadium/policies_security.htm.
6 As posted at www.olympicspirit.org/mission.php.
7 *Xinhua*, "Beijing Olympics Attracts Record 4.7 Billion TV Viewers," September 6, 2008, www.chinadaily.com.cn/olympics/2008–09/06/content_7005208.htm.
8 Jeff Lee, "2010 Olympic Security Will Cost between $400 million and $1 billion; The Cost of Securing the 2010 Olympic Games Will Be more than Double the Original Estimate," *Vancouver Sun*, October 10, 2008, www.canada.com/vancouversun/story.html?id=ef1ab251–5f23–43e4-be4c-411a02ed8791.
9 Dan Nystedt, "IT at Beijing Olympic Games to Cost US$400 million," *PC World*, August 15, 2007, www.washingtonpost.com/wp-dyn/content/article/2007/08/15/AR2007081501047.html.
10 "For London, What Price Olympic Security? After the Bombings, London's Estimate for the 2012 Games Seems Way Too Low," *Business Week*, August 15, 2005, www.businessweek.com/magazine/content/05_33/b3947076_mz054.htm.
11 Testimony of the Honorable Mitt Romney, Governor, The Commonwealth of Massachusetts, "Lessons Learned from Security at Past Olympic Games: Given at a Competition, Foreign Commerce, and Infrastructure Hearing," May 4 2004, http://myclob.pbworks.com/w/page/21958442/Lessons-Learned-from-Security-at-Past-Olympic-Games.
12 Barry Zellen, "Olympic Security in the Age of Mass Terror," SecurityInnovator.com, June 15, 2007, www.securityinnovator.com/index.php?articleID=11944&sectionID=27. Subsequent quotations from William McGuire are from this article.
13 Ibid. Subsequent quotations from Victor Anderes are from this article.

14 Lei Lei, Raymond Zhou, and Li Jing, "Firms Eye 2008 Olympic Security Budget," *China Daily*, May 10, 2005, www.chinadaily.com.cn/english/doc/2005–05/10/content_440848. htm.
15 Zellen, "Olympic Security in the Age of Mass Terror." Subsequent quotations from Bruce Schneier are from this article.
16 Zellen, "Securing the Olympics." Subsequent quotations from Ray Mey are from this article.
17 Ibid. Subsequent quotations from William McGuire are from this article.

Special Delivery: Letter-Bombs Continue to Deliver a Lethal Message

Far less dramatic but much more common than imploding a federal building, unleashing mayhem on a crowded sports stadium, or downing a commercial jetliner, the old-fashioned letter-bomb remains an enduring tactic, an inexpensive, improvised weapon wielded in pursuit of various goals for more than two centuries. It would be a modern counterpart to the timeless letter-bomb that would be selected by Al Qaeda in the Arabian Peninsula (AQAP) in its effort to bring down at least two and potentially many more jets cleverly disguised as ordinary commercial air freight, but which contained hidden within the enclosed HP laser printers reconfigured ink cartridges filled with the high explosive compound pentaerythritol tetranitrate (PETN) with at least one set to explode mid-air over US soil—a nefarious but in the end unsuccessful plot to disrupt America's worldwide freight industry and to paralyze its global supply lines.[1]

One of the first known letter-bomb attacks was made in 1764, as recorded by Danish historian, privy-councillor, and avid book collector Bolle Willum Luxdorph. In his diary, he wrote that on January 19, 1764, a Colonel Poulsen was mailed a box which when opened was found to contain gunpowder and a firelock to ignite it—but which apparently failed to cause harm. The next month, a letter was sent containing a threat from the perpetrator to increase the amount of powder next time. That same year, Luxdorph also noted a similar letter-bomb was used in Italy. In June 1889, another well-known attack was attempted by the 61-year old Edward Richard White, a disgruntled designer from Madame Tussaud's wax museum, who sent a gunpowder-laden bomb to John Theodore Tussaud, the son and biographer of its famous founder, Marie, with the intent to "do him grievous bodily harm," as described in a police report in the July 20, 1889 edition of *The Times*. Fifteen years later, on August 20, 1904, Martin Ekenberg sent a mail-bomb rigged with bullets and explosives to Swedish business executive Karl Fredrik Lundin in Stockholm.

T. Lamont Green, group program manager for Homeland Security at the US Postal Inspection Service (USPIS), told me that that "letter-bombs are usually intended for specific targets"—in contrast to the more widely used weapon of choice by jihadist terrorists, suicide bombs, whose users "are attempting to cause mass havoc and disruption."[2] The intent of letter-bombers has been more precise, primarily to kill, or maim, or scare in pursuit of economic or political change. Green added that letter-bombers' "motives can range from domestic disputes, religion, revenge and terrorism." These motives are as old as history itself, and a recurring source of conflict since the letter-bomb first appeared. Green noted "the mechanics of letters bombs and IEDs have not changed," though he added "the components and explosive the bombers are putting in devices has changed based on their availability to secure materials and knowledge of using materials such as HMEs," or homemade explosive. And so, for over two centuries, the letter-bomb has relentlessly delivered its explosive message, across the very breadth of time. As Green described: "Bombers are creatures of habit; if they become comfortable with a certain type of device and it accomplishes the mission, they'll continue to use it." And so they have.

In more recent times, Mossad twice tried to assassinate Alois Brunner, Adolf Eichmann's assistant, by letter-bomb, once in 1961 and again in 1980, succeeding in maiming but not killing him. More widely known in America is its homegrown "Unabomber," Ted Kaczynski—the Harvard-educated whiz kid who became a math professor at Berkeley at 25, and later waged a one-man, protracted terror campaign from 1978 and 1995 against America's technologists from his isolated cabin in Lincoln, Montana, sending some sixteen mail-bombs in all, killing three people and injuring twenty-three others, and nearly downing an American Airlines commercial jet.

Since the Unabomber was brought to justice, letter-bombs have continued to be sent: Franz Fuchs, an Austrian letter-bomber, killed four people and injured fifteen more in the 1990s, and Icelandic pop star Björk was sent a letter-bomb from an obsessed fan in 1996, which was intercepted by police. In February 2007, a series of letter-bombs mailed in the United Kingdom injured nine, while around the same time a mail-bomber named John Patrick Tompkins, who signed his letters "The Bishop," was arrested after targeting US investment firms with lethal parcels that included pipe-bombs. As Peter R. Rendina, the National Public Information Officer (PIO) for USPIS, told me: "Tompkins sent parcels to financial institutions in an attempt to manipulate stock prices."[3]

But letter-bombs have become part of the arsenal of the Islamist terror, and not just a tool of American grudges, whether against technology or to manipulate markets. Just across the Canadian border, in August 2007, the greater Toronto area experienced its own letter-bomb campaign, which resulted in the arrest of Adel Mohamed Arnaout, an immigrant from Lebanon, who manufactured at least six letter-bombs—three of which were mailed to recipients in bubble-wrapped envelopes, properly addressed complete with courier receipts, containing an explosive mix of petroleum-based fluids, resulting in one injury. Three more of these mail-borne IEDs were found in the trunk of a rental car stopped in Toronto prior to his arrest.

To reduce this enduring risk, and threat to our security, through the ubiquity of our postal networks, USPIS National PIO Green advises the following: "Know your mailers, especially if you receive an unexpected piece of mail or parcel," and "be cognizant of the characteristic of suspicious parcels, such as, excessive postage."

A poster produced by the US Postal Service provides guidance on what to look for with regard to "Suspicious Mail or Packages," and to "Protect yourself, your business, and your mailroom."[4] It cautions to look out for such notable features on a letter or parcel as: no return address; restrictive markings; sealed with tape; misspelled words; badly typed or written; unknown powder or suspicious substance; possibly from a foreign country; excessive postage; oily stains, discolorations, crystallization on wrapper; excessive tape; strange odor; incorrect title or addressed to title only; rigid or bulky; lopsided or uneven; or protruding wires. If there is anything suspicious such as these features, it counsels the following action: "Stop. Don't handle"; "Isolate it immediately"; "Don't open, smell, or taste"; "Activate your emergency plan. Notify a supervisor"; "Isolate area immediately"; "Call 911"; and "Wash your hands with soap and water."

According to Rendina, "vigilance is a key component to reduce the threat of letter-bombs by first the postal employee and then customer/addressee. The Postal Service in conjunction with Aviation Security, a department within the US Postal Inspection Service, enforce policy that any parcels mailed 13 ounces and above must be taken to a post office and shipped in person. This eliminates the potential for an individual to mail a dangerous item anonymously." Rendina added that "due to processing and delivering over 200 billion pieces of mail every year, it is difficult to use any of the existing technology to screen mail generically for explosives," as the volume is simply too great. But US Postal Inspectors do "use a Real Time Radiography (RTR) mobile x-ray to identify suspicious parcels, mail, packages or items left on postal property such as backpacks and briefcases."

Rendina recalled how "for over 150 years, postal inspectors have been investigating suspicious and dangerous items sent via the US mail. Through this experience we have found that improvised explosive devices are designed to be 'victim' initiated," as "the perpetrators understand that the device will be handled by many employees of the US Postal Service and transported in many cases great distances. The goal or objective is to injure the intended recipient." He noted USPIS inspectors have found "these devices need to be triggered by some action of the recipient such as adding a power supply (battery), tripping a wire by opening the box or flipping the on switch to an electronic that appears to be harmless." But this was not the case during the October 2001 anthrax-letter attacks, what can be considered the first WMD attack on American soil, distributed by an age-old method: letter mail. Rendina noted "the biological that was sent through the mail in October of 2001 was not intended to escape the envelope it was placed in. Due to the size of the biological and the microscopic holes in the weaving of the paper envelopes the biological escaped and contaminated mail facilities and other mail pieces around the envelopes carrying the biological substance."

The anthrax-letters were sent in two waves, the first involved five letters sent to the New York offices of *ABC News, CBS News, NBC News,* and the *New York Post,* as well as the *National Enquirer* in Boca Raton, Florida. The second wave, which involved two more anthrax-bearing letters, went out three weeks later, addressed to two US Senators, Tom Daschle of South Dakota and Patrick Leahy of Vermont, effectively shutting down US government mail. In total, twenty-two people developed anthrax infections, with eleven considered life-threatening. Five people died. Heritage Foundation senior research fellow and terrorism expert, Dr James Jay Carafano, told me that even with the anthrax-letter attacks, there wasn't a fundamental change in the letter-bombs, as letters remained "just a delivery platform." He added that terrorists "tend to stick with what they know, and when they innovate they tend to try do what they do better or with a slight twist." Even after the anthrax-letter attacks, which brought US government mail to a standstill, and frightened much of the nation, there's been "no significant increase in letter bombs." He thus described the letter-bomb to be "mostly a nuisance," and noted it's still "not used by serious terrorist groups."

But as worrisome as this new threat seemed to American officials and to the public at large, Rendina noted that "sometimes good can come of bad events." He observed USPS "responded to the 2001 biological attacks with a solution to screening mail for such substances. The solution is the Biological Detection System. In over 271 Processing and Distribution Centers across the country, the BDS is set up to screen the air above mail processing machines as an early detection device. Since the system was put into place in 2003 there have been over seven million tests. Not one of those tests put the BDS into a positive or false positive alarm." Rendina noted that the USPS processes and delivers over 200 billion items every year, and pointed out that "we had four letters laced with a dangerous biological in 2001. The chances of someone receiving something dangerous in the mail are very low."

In addition to addressing the bioterror threat with the BDS deployment, USPS has sought to increase the security of commercial mailing centers, which account for some 85 percent of those 200 billion items mailed annually in America. In October 2003, USPS introduced its B.2.2 Security Initiative for Commercial Mailers, a voluntary mail security initiative that "focuses on national and premier account mailers" and which "is designed to reduce the risk of an injurious article being sent through the US Mail by a commercial mail source"; it is named for Appendix B.2.2 of the US Postal Service (USPS) Emergency Preparedness Plan of March 2002, "which describes the process of examining and strengthening mail security controls for the commercial mailstream." As the USPS explained: "By examining security controls at large-scale, commercial mailers, we will be better able to protect the American public, postal employees, and members of the mailing industry. The initiative also allows the US Postal Inspection Service to concentrate more security resources on the relatively anonymous collection mailstream."

Such efforts appear to be making an impact. Rendina noted there have been "no recent campaigns to speak of" since the 2007 arrest of Tompkins, a.k.a. "The Bishop." But there continue to be threats and hoaxes, and these can cause great disruption, diverting attention and resources from more salient risks. Indeed, as recently as February 3, 2009, the DoJ announced the arrest of Richard Leon Goyette, a.k.a. Michael Jurek, in New Mexico, for mailing 65 threatening letters to financial institutions in October 2008. Sixty-four of his letters contained a white powder, with the threat that those breathing the powder would die within ten days. Though ultimately testing negative for hazardous materials, these mailings "caused emergency responders and hazardous response teams immense unnecessary labor and expense, diverted personnel from actual emergencies, completely disrupted business at these financial institutions, and caused untold emotional distress to those who received the letters," said acting US attorney James T. Jacks. "Those who send threatening letters, whether they contain white powder or not, even if their threat is a hoax, will be prosecuted with the full resources of this office."[5]

The countermeasures taken in response to the bioterror attacks of 2001, its mix of new technologies and greater vigilance, combined with other mail-acceptance and mail-screening procedures adopted in the years since, have helped to lower the risk of letter-bombs. But while the USPS has taken measures to ensure the safety of its system, USPIS inspector Green noted that the growth of "private shipping companies [does] increase the possibility of distributing IEDs outside of the postal system"—ensuring that the long-lived letter-bomb, a threat dating back to the eighteenth century, will remain with us a while longer.

Notes

1   Con Coughlin, "Yemen: The New Breeding Ground for Terror," *The Telegraph*, October 30, 2010, www.telegraph.co.uk/news/uknews/terrorism-in-the-uk/8099469/Yemen-the-new-breeding-ground-for-terror.html.
2   Barry Zellen, "Special Delivery: After Two Centuries, Letter-Bombs Continue Their Lethal Legacy," *SecurityInnovator.com*, March 6, 2009, http://securityinnovator.com/index.php?articleID=15842&sectionID=27. Subsequent quotations from Green are from this article.
3   Ibid. Subsequent quotations from Rendina are from this article.
4   See USPS, "Suspicious Mail Poster," www.usps.com/communications/news/security/suspiciousmail.htm.
5   US Department of Justice Press Release, "Richard Leon Goyette Arrest Press Release," Justice.gov, February 3, 2009, www.justice.gov/usao/txn/PressRel09/goyette_white%20powder_arrest_pr.html.

18

Bracing for Bioterror

Deep in America's heartland—where our country's vast agricultural system sustains not only the nutritional requirements of nearly 300 million people, but contributes over $50 billion each year to America's export economy—a new, lingering worry would haunt our security experts' minds after 9/11. This new, dark fear was of a deliberate terror attack of America's food supply. Indeed, this fear was articulated publicly—and clearly—by outgoing secretary of Health and Human Services (HHS) Tommy Thompson during a candid question period following the announcement of his resignation on December 3, 2004, during which he shared his grave concern about the possibility of a terrorist attack on the nation's food supply: "For the life of me, I cannot understand why the terrorists have not attacked our food supply because it is so easy to do."[1]

Such a deliberate attack of our nation's food supply would be a unique and nefarious form of terrorism, called *agriterror* by some, which could include the biological infection of our livestock; the contamination of our food processing and distribution systems through exposure to chemical, radiological, or biological agents; and/or the physical destruction of our crops—whether through introduction of pests, destruction of irrigation systems, or the intentional setting of a prairie fire. While the very scale of America's food production system and its vast, continental expanse suggests an inherent invulnerability, as 9/11 has shown, it only takes one successful, symbolic attack of our infrastructure to paralyze our nation, shake our confidence, and spread fear across the land.

Agriterror is not a new invention. Some believe that agriterror is, ironically, an American invention, and during the world's first truly modern total war, the US Civil War—which introduced a potent form of mechanized warfare by wedding the power of industrialization with the mass-mobilization of the nation—that resulted in the near total destruction of the secession-minded Confederacy's economic infrastructure. During General Sherman's infamous march to the sea, his troops intentionally torched Confederate cities and set aflame its farms, destroying the rebellious South's capacity to feed itself while at the same time destroying the backbone of its agrarian economy, King Cotton.

Destroying an enemy's food production capability is an ancient tactic, dating back to the days of Rome's conflict with Carthage, whose fields it salted to render them forever barren and unproductive. But with General Sherman, the scale and speed of destruction achieved a new level, bringing agriterror into the modern age—as a tool of total warfare. In our new age of international terrorism, it no longer requires an army of mechanized armor and mobile infantry to destroy a nation's infrastructure and food production capabilities. Now, one well-placed and virulent bioweapon could do the trick.

Even as the SARS outbreak—which revealed how real the bioterror threat is, and how easily a new pandemic can spread globally—quickly settled down, an even newer threat emerged, this time right in the American heartland: monkey pox, a close but less-deadly cousin of the dreaded smallpox. Monkey pox had its very first outbreak in the western hemisphere last spring, an ominous and in some ways fortuitous warning of the dangers we face in this new world of boundless terror. As Steve Mitchell, medical correspondent for United Press International (UPI), reported, over the course of just a few weeks, dozens of Americans were infected with monkey pox. Doctors in Wisconsin saw the first patient on May 22, 2003, when a four-year-old girl developed a rash similar to that caused by smallpox.[2] In spite of the risk of potential spread, local health officials as well as the national Center for Disease Control and Prevention (CDC) in Atlanta were not notified until 13 days later. Mitchell reported that the CDC, in turn, did not make the case known publicly until June 7, three days after it had learned of the case in Wisconsin. By then, there were 19 suspected monkey pox cases in Wisconsin, Indiana, and Illinois. Mitchell observed that despite the CDC's claim "that the nation has improved its preparedness to respond to a bioterrorist attack and emerging infectious diseases, the monkey pox experience indicates there still is no rapid communication system to alert physicians and health agencies around the country."[3] Indeed, the "outbreak of monkey pox in the United States, and the delay in alerting healthcare personnel to its spread, highlights the need for a national communications system to alert physicians and public health officials rapidly about bioterrorist attacks or emerging diseases such as SARS and West Nile virus."[4]

Mitchell said "quicker notification of the country's medical community might have been particularly prudent because monkey pox has spread, now infecting as many as 54 people in several additional states, including Texas, New Jersey, Pennsylvania and South Carolina. The outbreak has become such a concern the CDC is taking the unprecedented step of recommending experimental use of the smallpox vaccine—which can have severe side effects, including death—in infected people, healthcare workers and those who were exposed to sick prairie dogs, which appear to be the source of the monkey pox."[5] Mitchell sounds the alarm over monkey pox because it "could have been smallpox."[6] And, he added, "some bioterrorist experts have expressed concerns terrorists could try to use monkey pox itself as a bioweapon."[7]

So how can America protect itself from future biothreats? The Bush administration's solution, announced in January 2003 during the president's State of the Union, was Project BioShield. In his speech, President Bush called on Congress to bolster America's biodefenses, but in the months to follow, legislation went in circles in the US Congress.[8] An editorial six months later published by the *Washington Times*, the conservative DC daily, castigated Congress for dawdling, arguing that "it appears unlikely to pass before Congress returns from its July 4 recess—if at all," as both the House and Senate versions of the bill have been held up in committee.[9]

Without a Congressional mandate to secure America from this invisible but worryingly potent threat, the *Washington Times* noted that pharmaceutical companies saw little commercial potential in searching for treatments to the plague, anthrax, or ebola, and have avoided the necessary investment of time and resources to equip America with the defensive tools it needs. The *Washington Times* argued that "while lawmakers have made holding the line on spending a top priority, terrorists are making it their first priority to develop biological weapons. Congress needs to move quickly to support Project BioShield, an essential component of US defense against bioterrorism."[10]

Both the House and Senate agreed that BioShield was needed, but not on the amount to spend. President Bush didn't want to impose a cap on spending, but some in Congress did. It would take another year before a deal was concluded, and on July 21, 2004—more than a year after the *Washington Times* accused Congress of dawdling—President Bush signed Project BioShield into law, providing "new tools to improve medical countermeasures protecting Americans against a chemical, biological, radiological, or nuclear (CBRN) attack."[11] It allocated $5.6 billion over ten years for developing the necessary vaccines and medicines to protect Americans from a bioattack—guaranteeing government purchase of the new biomedical products.

According to the terms of the final legislation signed into law, Project BioShield was designed to: Expedite the conduct of NIH research and development on medical countermeasures based on the most promising recent scientific discoveries; give FDA the ability to make promising treatments quickly available in emergency situations—this tightly controlled new authority will enable access to the best available treatments in the event of a crisis; and ensure that resources are available to pay for "next-generation" medical countermeasures. Project BioShield will allow the government to buy improved vaccines or drugs. The FY2004 appropriation for the DHS included $5.6 billion over ten years for the purchase of next generation countermeasures against anthrax and smallpox as well as other CBRN agents.[12]

As a result of the Project BioShield legislation, the US government quickly began the process of acquiring several new medical countermeasures, including: 75 million doses of a second generation anthrax vaccine to become available for stockpiling beginning next year; new medical treatments for anthrax directed at neutralizing the effects of anthrax toxin; polyvalent botulinum antitoxin; a safer second generation smallpox vaccine; and initial evaluation of treatments for radiation and chemical weapons exposure.[13] With these new BioShield authorities, the White House announced that Secretary Thompson "will launch multi-year initiatives to develop advanced treatments and therapeutics for exposure to biological agents and radiation poisoning," adding that signing Project BioShield into law "is just the latest step the President has taken to win the War on Terror and protect our homeland."[14]

Al Qaeda's agriterror ambition

Al Qaeda computer records, abandoned on hard drives found in safe houses scattered across Afghanistan during Operation Enduring Freedom, suggest that the terror network was keenly interested in bioweapons prior to 9/11, as they are widely considered to be the *poor man's WMD*, requiring far less technical and financial investment to produce than nuclear weaponry. As well, Al Qaeda had developed an interest in America's agriculture, and its training manual examined methods to commit agricultural terrorism.

As reported by GovExec.com's Katherine McIntire Peters: "It shouldn't be surprising that a determined enemy like al Qaeda would consider ways to disrupt US food supplies."[15] She adds that the "history of warfare is full of examples of burned crops, poisoned wells and slaughtered herds. Agriculture is an obvious target for terrorists: infecting plants or animals with deadly disease is easier, cheaper and less risky than infecting humans directly; the economic consequences of a widespread attack would be enormous; and the panic and fear such an attack might reap could lead to wide-scale social disruption."[16]

She noted that Al Qaeda "left behind many clues to their aspirations in "hundreds of pages of US agricultural documents that had been translated into Arabic," and that "a significant part of the group's training manual is reportedly devoted to agricultural terrorism—the destruction of crops, livestock and food processing operations."[17] As a consequence, McIntire Peters said US state and federal governments "have beefed up security and increased inspections of food and agricultural facilities across the country" but that given the vast scale and complexity of the agricultural system in the United States, "security is an elusive concept. From sprawling farms to feed lots, from state fairs to food processing plants, there are countless points at which terrorists could access the food supply system with relative ease."[18]

The US DoD has conducted high-level crisis simulations, McIntire Peters reported, noting that a RAND Review article last summer observed that "the farming and food industries are highly vulnerable to both deliberate and accidental disruption for several reasons."[19] The National Defense University has identified five potential targets of agricultural bioterrorism: field crops, farm animals, food items in the processing or distribution chain, market-ready foods at the wholesale or retail level, and agricultural facilities. Officials of the RAND Corporation "estimate that no major US city has more than a seven-day supply of food,"[20] revealing an Achilles heel that Al Qaeda has already recognized.

According to McIntire Peters, 20 states have passed—or are considering—legislation related to agriterrorism, according to data compiled by the Council of State Governments. Many states have also hired more farm and food inspectors, developed guidelines for improving physical security at agricultural facilities, and are building more effective disease surveillance networks. Federal responsibility for agricultural security is shared by the Department of Agriculture (DoA), the Department of Health and Human Services (DHHS), and the DHS. At DoA, the Food Safety and Inspection Service monitors meat and poultry products, and plans for responding to outbreaks of food-borne illness, while a division of the Animal and Plant Health Inspection Service (APHIS) is responsible for protecting agricultural crops and plants from disease. At DHHS, the Food and Drug Administration (FDA) is responsible for ensuring the safety of seafood, plant and dairy foods, beverages, and other food products. DHS has taken over the inspection of food and agricultural products entering the United States, formerly the responsibility of APHIS' Agricultural Quarantine Inspection program.

To ensure the security of America's food supply, there is the need for greater federal interagency cooperation, though McIntire Peters noted that in the "last 18 months, agencies have taken steps to boost their inspection and analysis capabilities."[21] Further, the USDA has hired 20 new "import surveillance liaison" inspectors, to reinspect imported meat and poultry products. Additionally, as a result of the 2002 Public Health Security and Bioterrorism Preparedness and Response Act, the FDA is tightening food safety regulations—by requiring food processing facilities to register with the agency, mandating that companies provide advance notice of imported food shipments, and maintaining better records to make it easier to trace tainted food to its source.[22]

As McIntire Peters reported, many agricultural experts believe the greatest threat to US agriculture would be the deliberate or accidental introduction of foot-and-mouth disease—a "highly contagious viral disease that attacks cloven-footed animals, including cattle, swine, sheep, deer and elk" that is "so swift and debilitating that milk and meat production could be severely cut nationwide."[23] Indeed, in 1997, foot-and-mouth disease appeared in pigs in Taiwan, and "spread throughout the island within six weeks, forcing authorities to slaughter more than 8 million pigs and halt pork exports."[24] The origin of the disease has been traced to a single pig from Hong Kong—"and China was suspected of deliberately introducing the disease into Taiwan." The total cost of this outbreak to Taiwan: $19 billion. At the time, some speculated this was a case of bioterror directed against Taiwan by mainland China. And every bit as worrisome as a foot-and-mouth disease attack of America's livestock would be an attack of America's crops, which "make up more than half the total value of American farm commodities and contribute more to exports."[25] So how can America secure its foodstuffs?

With over half a million farms and 57,000 food processing facilities spread across the vast continental United States, the challenge is huge. New policies, and interagency and interdepartmental cooperation is one key, spreading the burden across various government departments. Technology is another.

Toward a bioterrorism surveillance system

As Tom Ramstack reported in the *Washington Times*: "Continuing bioterrorism scares are breathing new life into obscure scientific projects as the nation gropes for a way to defend itself from deadly microbes."[26] One solution that is emerging is a handheld microarray system that "tests white blood cells to detect viruses within 36 hours of exposure, sometimes even before victims know they are sick. The device is supposed to be an early warning system against biological bombs. It was developed by the Walter Reed Army Institute of Research for the malaria soldiers might encounter in other countries," and the "Army plans to refine the system to detect anthrax, smallpox and other diseases."[27] Another case of technology innovation is the use of radar to detect bioterror attacks. In one test of such a use of the US national weather radar grid, "a crop duster released a mixture of grain alcohol, clay dust and water and polyethylene glycol over central Oklahoma on March 24. The Army and the Environmental Protection

Agency were testing whether radar could detect a bioterrorist attack."²⁸ Ramstack said that "they hope to develop computer technology for a nationwide bioterrorism detection program," and that the "EPA has done similar tests in Maryland, Utah and Florida since 2001."²⁹

Federal Computer Week's Sara Michael reported that "in an effort to detect bioterrorism attacks at an early stage, Centers for Disease Control and Prevention officials are studying ways to access and analyze prediagnostic health data for indications of a disease outbreak."³⁰ BioSense is a new proposal being discussed with CDC's parent agency, DHHS. "By examining syndromic data from several national sources, public health officials may be able to detect a trend, allowing for a more rapid response. BioSense would draw on several national data sources, such as requested lab tests, over-the-counter drug sales and managed care hot lines that patients call with questions or concerns."³¹ *CIO Magazine*'s Sarah D. Scalet observed: "Health officials are working toward a sophisticated IT network that could detect the early warning signs of bioterrorism, but formidable obstacles remain."³² She cited Rosemary Nelson, chairman of National Preparedness and Response, a new bioterrorism task force created by the Healthcare Information Management and Systems Society (HIMSS), who said such a system, to "sound the alarm in that precariously short window of time when the spread of disease could be stopped," is now "being defined and created."³³ Scalet reported that today "it might take weeks or months for the CDC to gather sufficient information to spot a bioterrorist attack"—but "with a sophisticated IT network, it would take just days."³⁴ At New Mexico's Sandia National Labs, Scalet observed researchers have developed a system called the Rapid Syndromic Validation Project, which "requires health-care providers to actually log on to a secure website and type in information about a patient's symptoms in return for trend and treatment information," nearly instantly.³⁵

As well, the CDC has developed the National Electronic Disease Surveillance System (NEDSS), which "lays out a sort of meta-standard for both healthcare information and IT standards," and all state health department systems must be NEDSS-compatible "if they want a piece of the $918 million in bioterrorism grants that the CDC is handing out this year."³⁶ With such "pocketbook persuasion," Scalet believes things could get better—but currently, "a national bioterrorism surveillance system seems far off, indeed."³⁷ In addition to technology, new policies are being crafted to help America cope with the new threat of bioterror. Ramstack reported that "Congress responded to the October 2001 anthrax scare by passing the Public Health Security and Bioterrorism Preparedness and Response Act of 2002, known as the Biopreparedness Act," which created "new restrictions on who can handle dangerous microbes, which ones they can handle and how and where they can be used. In addition, industry must follow stricter procedures to prevent contamination of food and water supplies."³⁸

The $500 billion food-processing industry must now "register facilities and give prior notice of any imports companies accept"; the FDA has "also increased its inspections of foods that could be contaminated with anthrax or other toxins."³⁹ Other provisions of the Biopreparedness Act impose criminal penalties on unauthorized handling of organisms and chemicals, some of which are commonly used in academic research. With this evolving mix of new, and proactive, policies to more thoroughly monitor the US food supply, and emerging technologies to better detect and track a bioattack from its earliest stages, America is getting into a better position to respond to a the nightmare scenario of bioterrorism if it has to. As Secretary Ridge has pointed out, this could effectively deter such an attack from ever happening. As they say, an ounce of prevention is worth a pound of cure. When it comes to agriterrorism, one might argue that an ounce of prevention is worth a ton of cure, maybe more.

Bioterror reboot

As the swine flu quickly circled the earth In 2009, the Obama administration shifted from the rhetoric of "hope" to a genuine effort to "cope" with the real dangers of bioterrorism. The Obama administration had been rethinking the war on terror from its start. Issue by issue, step by step, it's been reexamining each piece of the complex mosaic that defined America's post-9/11 strategic environment, from Iraq to missile defense. And so it came as no surprise that the administration turned its attention to the nefarious threat of bioterrorism—convening its first meeting of bioterrorism experts at the White House Conference Center on August 13, 2009, to partake in a round table discussion cochaired by National Security Council (NSC) senior director for WMD terrorism Laura Holgate.

One participant at that summer's White House meeting on bioterrorism was Brian D. Finlay, a Senior Associate at the Washington, DC–based Henry L. Stimson Center, who found few concrete takeaways from this first meeting on bioterrorism, but explained to me that "when you get 40 experts on bioterrorism in a room, you're going to hear 50 different opinions on how to address the threat—this is testament to the complexity of meeting this challenge."[40] And "because the White House discussion was designed to be one-way," Finlay added, "we don't yet have a sense as to where the administration is going at this point." While it's "clear that the administration is in the midst of a top-down review of the US government's bioterrorism strategy," he found "there is much less clarity on what the path forward might look like."

Finlay observed that "not only has the President not spoken out as vociferously on this subject, which necessarily depresses its priority within the bureaucracy, but early indications of the administration's commitment based upon the FY2010 budget request are less than promising." For biological threat reduction programs, Finlay noted, "the President's request is $33.4 million below the FY2009 appropriated level." Finlay recalled in December 2008 a "bi-partisan Congressional Commission declared a 50% or greater chance of a terrorist attack involving a nuclear or biological weapon. Shockingly, these odds represented the probability of an attack over the next five years. In light of these findings, the President's reductions to bio-threat activities at the Department of Defense are a distressing indication of flagging commitment to preventing bioterrorism."

Finlay believes "there are two critical steps" the administration should pursue going forward: the first is to "develop tighter partnerships with the biotech and pharmaceutical sector," and the second is to "break down the barriers within government between the public health agencies and the national security agencies." An encouraging indicator of the government's commitment to bioterror prevention is its new FDA commissioner, Margaret Hamburg, "a brilliant choice by the White House," who during the Clinton administration "led the US government's efforts to build a biodefense plan," and who after leaving government "led a non-profit effort that sought innovative public-private responses to the same." She thus has the "capacity to bridge the unnecessary and dangerous divide between the public health and national security communities in Washington," but "the question will be how much time and effort she is able to dedicate to this important effort."

One of the greatest difficulties in developing a response to bioterrorism is determining whether an outbreak of a pathogen is an act of terror or just an unfortunate natural event. Dr Anne Clunan, an editor and coauthor of the 2008 Stanford University Press book on bioterrorism, *Terrorism, War, or Disease? Unraveling the Use of Biological Weapons*, and associate professor at the US Naval Postgraduate School in Monterey, California, explained to me that her book "is about how can governments determine whether the appearance of a biological or toxin agent was deliberate or naturally-occurring, and if deliberate, how to credibly establish who was responsible. This question is the 'attribution problem'—how do we know who is responsible for a suspicious outbreak of disease?"[41] She explained the attribution problem has three parts: The first is "identification of which bio agent is responsible for the illness that appears." The second is "characterization of that outbreak as intentional or unintentional." And the third is "attribution: if the outbreak is the result of intentional introduction of a bio-agent, who is to blame for that introduction?"

Clunan believes "that managing biological warfare attribution and other problems arising from nontraditional threats requires shifts in how governments acquire and use information. The first shift requires changing the understanding of information, from intelligence, as something to be kept secret in order to gain relative advantage over an adversary, to information, as a resource to improve government management of and response to threats. In other words, governments must move from 'need-to-know' limitations on intelligence sharing to a 'need-to-share' paradigm of information sharing." This in turn requires the "development of networks for information sharing," and "addressing the challenges of establishing trust among members of such networks and between networks and the public."

Such networks "include health and medical professionals and other first responders, epidemiologists, entomologists, toxicologists, animal and public health experts"— agencies such as the CDC, the World Health Organization (WHO), and the World Organization for Animal Health (OIE), as well as "biotechnologists in industry and academia, law enforcement officials, military personnel, and policymakers." Clunan noted there are "a lot of efforts to collect and in some cases, share, information that are underway" and that "governments have made recent efforts to improve technical and technological capacity to aid in biological warfare detection, including early detection and warning systems. For example, in 2003 the United States adopted a nationwide system of sensors to detect pathogens in 31 US cities, called the BioWatch program."

As well, the US Centers for Disease Control and Prevention (CDC) "actively promote the wider adoption of US technical standards to increase international interoperability of information systems that address biological warfare information needs," and CDC's Epi-X program "was developed to help public-health professionals nationwide share preliminary health surveillance information." In the private sector, Clunan noted, "the Google foundation is supporting surveillance of flu outbreaks with its Flu Trends website."

Additional efforts are taking place at the global level, such as the WHO's Global Outbreak Alert and Response Network (GOARN), and—in conjunction with Health Canada—its open-source Global Public Intelligence Network. And in 2006, the OIE, the UN Food and Agriculture Organization (FAO), and the WHO "jointly created the Global Early Warning and Response System (GLEWS)." Clunan adds that "many countries have also adopted 'syndromic surveillance' for early detection of both biological terrorism incidents and newly emerging diseases, such as SARS and avian influenza. The US has BioSense and National Biosurveillance Integration System (NBIS); the UK has the NHS Direct Syndromic Surveillance Project." Clunan observed that "globalization tremendously increases the consequences of the intentional or unintentional spread of pathogens and toxins. With SARS, we saw the transmission of the disease from China to 6 countries in 24 hours, and to 28 over 5 months. Swine flu this year spread to over 141 countries in just 3 months. Similar results could occur with intentionally introduced diseases that were highly contagious." Clunan added that "a key consequence of bioterrorism is not only illness and death, and this is the other way in which globalization enters into the risks associated with a bio-attack. Globalization has increased every country's exposure and dependence on foreign commerce. A bio-attack or a disease outbreak in one country will have tremendous economic costs to that country and to those that do business with it and travel to it."

I also spoke with Dr Laurie A. Garrett, Senior Fellow for Global Health at the New York–based Council on Foreign Relations, and the Pulitzer Prize–winning author of the bestselling books *The Coming Plague: Newly Emerging Diseases in a World Out of Balance* and *Betrayal of Trust: The Collapse of Global Public Health*.[42] Garrett also noted the challenges inherent in globalization, and explained that a key lesson of the global spread of swine flu was that "globalization of risk, as well as economics and benefits, has occurred." She found the response by governments to the H1N1 pandemic indicates "the world community is still in early, even primitive, stages of maturation in global governance. When pushed by a real threat, countries still retreat to old-fashioned nation-state 'solutions' that are based on the false promise of controlling microbes along human national borderlines. We still have a very long way to go, as a world community." She recalled how "following 9/11 and the anthrax mailings, significant amounts of money poured into public health and bioterrorism-related drug development in the US and some European and Asian societies. It was slanted toward anti-terrorism. After SARS, more money poured in, slanted towards surveillance and international transparency. After Katrina, still more money was directed in the US towards a homeland security model. Following the spread of H5N1 flu attention and funds shifted toward control of that bird virus. And now the world is reacting to

H1N1." As she explained: "Each of these 'moments' has infused cash and attention to an element of public health, in one country or another. Still missing is a systematic and strategic approach to global public health infrastructure. The key missing element is personnel."

Garrett observed that "overall, the Obama Administration is seeking a more nuanced approach to all forms of terrorism than Bush's 'War on Terrorism.' This affects everything from nuclear proliferation to the war in Afghanistan. My sense is it is still evolving." Her advice to the administration as its policy continues to evolve is to "seek evidence, and base policy on empirical realities. That would be very refreshing." While many people worry about the risks of terror, she believes the greater threat is from a naturally evolving plague, and noted that "nothing beats the threat of virulent pandemic flu, e.g., a reassortment of H5N1 and H1N1." But she believes we can reduce the risk, whether from a virulent pandemic flu or a malicious act of biological terror, through more "surveillance and rapid diagnostics." As she elaborated: "We need far more sophisticated RT-PCR (reverse transcription polymerase chain reaction) going on, affordably and on a mass basis, not just in US but all over the world. Right now RT-PCR for unknown and mass-platform organisms is still too costly and difficult for developing country routine use. Worse, insurance companies are not reimbursing their cost in US hospitals. This needs to get fixed. Frankly, if the US insurance piece gets fixed, massive use in our hospital system will pull cheap, easy technologies out of the pipeline, taking care of the developing country side of the problem."

Clunan also has some advice for the Obama administration as it began to build its bioterrorism response: "The bumper-sticker version would read: 'Discourage use and deny effect.' Or 'make health, not war.' The bottom line for policymakers is to focus on consequence mitigation—on measures to prevent, resist and withstand the impact of a bio attack. Instead of deterring a potential attacker by threat of physical punishment, the best defense is to have a robust public health and first responder system in place to protect your population from harm, which discourages attacks, and if one comes, significantly mitigates the health effects and any public panic." She added that "robust national and transnational networking, information exchange, standard setting and collaboration among first responders, health workers, the biotech industry, academics, and non-proliferation, intelligence and law enforcement officials is critical for successful mitigation and attribution." Clunan believes "we also need to strengthen international laws and norms against biological warfare and to discourage and de-legitimate the development and use of biological and toxin weapons," and "to develop international standards for monitoring the development, movement, and use of agents with the potential for warfare uses."

By taking these actions, Clunan presents us with a comforting solution to the question raised by her bioterrorism book's title: *Terrorism, War, or Disease?* With a diligent effort to prevent or reduce the consequences of bioterrorism, we just might be able to add a fourth choice to consider: None of the above.

Notes

1 Robert Pear, "U.S. Health Chief, Stepping Down, Issues Warning," *New York Times,* December 4, 2004.

2 Steve Mitchell, "Monkey Pox Shows Gap in Bioterror Readiness," United Press International (UPI), June 12, 2003.

3 Ibid.

4 Ibid.

5 Ibid.

6 Ibid.

7 Ibid.

8 For a transcript of the president's 2003 State of the Union, you may view a transcript at "Transcript of State of the Union" on *CNN's* website.

9 "Still No Bioshield," *Washington Times,* June 22, 2003.

10 Ibid.

11 "Project Bioshield" Progress in the War on Terror," July 21, 2004, http:// georgewbush-whitehouse.archives.gov/infocus/bioshield/.

12 Ibid.

13 Ibid.

14 Ibid.

15 Katherine McIntire Peters, "Officials Fear Terrorist Attack on U.S. Food Supply," GovExec.com, June 10, 2003.

16 Ibid.

17 Ibid.

18 Ibid.

19 Ibid.

20 Ibid.

21 Ibid.

22 Ibid.

23 Ibid.

24 Ibid.

25 Ibid.

26 Tom Ramstack, "Germ Research Gets Urgent," *Washington Times,* June 8, 2003.

27 Ibid.

28 Ibid.

29 Ibid.

30 Sara Michael, "BioSense Would Sniff Out Bioterror," *Federal Computer Week,* June 16, 2003.

31 Ibid.

32 Sarah D. Scalet, "Immune Systems," *CIO Magazine,* June 2003.

33 Ibid.

34 Ibid.

35 Ibid.

36 Ibid.

37 Ibid.

38 Ramstack, "Germ Research Gets Urgent."

39 Ibid.

40 Barry Zellen, "Bracing for Bioterror," SecurityInnovator.com, September 30, 2009, http://securityinnovator.com/index.php?articleID=15847&sectionID=29. Subsequent quotations from Brian Finlay are from this article.

41 Ibid. Subsequent quotations from Anne Clunan are from this article.

42 Ibid. Subsequent quotations from Laurie A. Garrett are from this article.

19

Nuclear Terrorism Post-9/11: Rethinking the Unthinkable

It's been a decade now since the Twin Towers collapsed and with it America's sense of post–Cold War invulnerability. While the dramatic scale of devastation and the high loss of civilian life caught many off guard, there were two groups closely watching that day's horrific events who were not surprised at all: the Al Qaeda terror masters who conceived, planned, and executed the 9/11 attacks; and those strategic and military planners who have long pondered the risk of WMD and mass-terror attacks against America's heartland—but who until that fateful day were largely ignored by the press, public, and policymaking elites responsible for protecting America from such external threats.

The age of mass casualty terror

Interestingly, the 9/11 attacks were not WMD attacks. No radiological, biological, or chemical weapons were deployed. Indeed, this stands in contrast to the view shared by many analysts of the first World Trade Center (WTC) attack on February 26, 1993. The goal of the attack was to "devastate the foundation of the north tower in such a way in that it would collapse onto its twin," as the bomber "foresaw Tower One collapsing onto Tower Two after the blast would occur." The 600-kg truck bomb was built for just $300—using "urea pellets, nitroglycerin, sulfuric acid, aluminum azide, magnesium azide, and bottled hydrogen," with sodium cyanide added "to the mix as the vapors could go through the ventilation shafts and elevators of the towers." WTC bomber Ramzi Yousef "wanted to prevent smoke from escaping the towers, therefore, catching the public eye by poisoning people inside."[1]

As such, the 1993 WTC attack can be viewed as a dual conventional/chemical weapons attack whose primary mission was conventional—to topple the towers— while its secondary mission was to deliver what its Al Qaeda terror masters hoped would be a horrific and lethal mix of airborne cyanide, to not only instill terror in the hearts of the thousands of employees working in the vast and towering office complex but to also kill and injure as many innocents as possible. As noted by Laurie Mylroie, "according to the presiding judge in last year's trial, the bombing of New York's World

Trade Center on February 26, 1993 was meant to topple the city's tallest tower onto its twin, amid a cloud of cyanide gas."[2] Mylroie adds that "had the attack gone as planned, tens of thousands of Americans would have died. Instead, as we know, one tower did not fall on the other, and, rather than vaporizing, the cyanide gas burnt up in the heat of the explosion. 'Only' six people died."[3] Yet Mylroie observed how "few Americans are aware of the true scale of the destructive ambition behind that bomb."[4]

However, not all observers of the 1993 WTC attack agree that the bombers intended to deliver a deadly chemical payload. As written by John V. Parachini, while "the February 1993 bombing of the World Trade Center in New York City marked the beginning of an ugly new phase of terrorism involving the indiscriminate killing of civilians," he "refutes the claim that the WTC bombing involved the terrorist use of chemical weapons."[5] But he concedes that "substantial evidence indicates that Ramzi Yousef, the mastermind behind the attack, seriously considered employing chemical agents in the WTC bombing and in subsequent attacks."[6] And even if lacking a chemical weapons component, he agrees with the consensus view that 'the World Trade Center bombing was motivated by the desire to kill as many people as possible."[7] However, the terrorists were thwarted from their goal to inflict mass casualties, and in the end "the explosion killed six people and injured more than 1,000." More worrisome than this relatively modest level of casualties was the undisputable fact that "the consequences could have been far worse."[8]

Richard K. Betts has observed that "WMD present more and different things to worry about than during the Cold War," and with the proliferation of chemical and biological weapons know-how, "there is less danger of complete annihilation, but more danger of mass destruction."[9] So even though there's now "less chance of an apocalyptic exchange of many thousands of weapons," Betts believes "the probability that some smaller number of WMD will be used is growing."[10] As WMD "no longer represent the technological frontier of warfare," he suggests they will inevitably become more readily accessible to smaller states and non-state entities, and thus "will be weapons of the weak-states or groups that militarily are at best second-class."[11]

The 1993 WTC attack was but a hint of the emerging dangers of the post–Cold War era, and along with the more sophisticated coordinated attacks of 9/11 reveal both the destructive capabilities as well as the relatively inexpensive operational costs of conducting mass-casualty terror attacks. And yet both WTC attacks were relatively benign when compared to both the anticipated casualty figures that the bombers sought as well as to what can now be readily imagined should more destructive WMD devices be employed. Indeed, the fact that the number of casualties of both attacks combined was less than 5,000 dead and injured is much less significant than the fact that the planners of those two WTC attacks audaciously plotted to attack America's heartland using an improvised WMD/mass casualty device.

America was now on notice that its enemies would try to offset their strategic inferiority in terms of conventional military power with their own force-de-frappe. But unlike France's minimally sufficient nuclear stockpile whose primary mission has been to deter a future military attack of its territory, the terror planners of Al Qaeda viewed their coveted WMD capabilities first and foremost as warfighting tools, an extension of their traditional terror tactics—though on a much more destructive scale. Tools that, they hoped, would prove capable of breaking the will of the world's sole remaining superpower, forcing a withdrawal of American military power from Middle East just as the relentless guerrilla warfare of the anti-Soviet jihad drove the defeated Red Army out of Afghanistan, contributing to the liberation of Central Asia from Soviet domination.

When Al Qaeda's second strike against the WTC took place eight years after its first, the attackers struck from the air, using improvised cruise missiles (commandeered jumbo passenger jets) whose full fuel tanks provided the incendiary agent, and whose massive, high-velocity impact would—they hoped—convey the necessary momentum to either knock the towers over (as originally planned by the 1993 attackers), or set them on fire—killing as many people as possible, cutting off the means of escape for those civilians on the upper floors.

There is no evidence to suggest that Al Qaeda sought to induce an implosion of the Twin Towers, and thus their hauntingly graceful vertical collapse that day no doubt struck its planners as an unexpected—though in no way disappointing—surprise. Likely unaware of the building's unique architectural attributes, including its innovative dampening shock-absorbers designed to absorb the energy of the tower's natural swaying movements, the 9/11 architects could not have foreseen that the momentum transferred by the commandeered jets' impact would initially be absorbed. However, having learned in 1993 that the towers were harder to knock over than they had at first imagined, the terror planners no doubt suspected they could again fail to topple the towers laterally. As such, one can deduce that their *plan B* was to watch the towers burn, with those on higher floors trapped, doomed—awaiting certain death. As such, the implosive collapse of the Twin Towers was likely an unexpected bonus—a powerful and symbolic articulation of Al Qaeda's desire to foster what they hope to be a collapse of American military and economic power, much like the Soviet empire experienced a decade earlier (and for which many Al Qaeda members, veterans of the anti-Soviet jihad, take credit.)

Preparing for the unthinkable

America thus had eight years to plan for Al Qaeda's second WTC strike—and to digest the lessons of 1993, which revealed Al Qaeda's unambiguous strategic objective to deal a potentially decisive strategic coup d'oeuil against its enemy. Some of America's strategic thinkers used this time well, as illustrated by the US Commission on National Security/21st Century, more commonly known as the Hart-Rudman Commission, named for the two US senators who chaired the commission, Gary Hart and Warren B. Rudman.[12]

In the preface to their Phase 1 report (their first of three to be released over the next two years), "New World Coming: American Security in the 21st Century," issued on September 15, 1999, they observe that "the world has changed dramatically in the last fifty years, and particularly in the last decade," and that "institutions designed in another age may or may not be appropriate for the future."[13] They note "the mandate of the United States Commission on National Security/21st Century to examine precisely that question," which it did in three distinct phases: "the first to describe the world emerging in the first quarter of the next century, the second to design a national security strategy appropriate to that world, and the third to propose necessary changes to the national security structure in order to implement that strategy effectively."[14]

Among the 14 conclusions of the Hart-Rudman Commission's Phase I report, their very first—and in the wake of 9/11, eerily prophetic—conclusion is: "America will become increasingly vulnerable to hostile attack on our homeland, and our military superiority will not entirely protect us."[15] They explain that "American influence will increasingly be both embraced and resented abroad, as US cultural, economic, and political power persists and perhaps spreads. States, terrorists, and other disaffected groups will acquire weapons of mass destruction and mass disruption, and some will use them. Americans will likely die on American soil, possibly in large numbers."[16]

As noted on the website of the New York Times Company Foundation, which hosted a five-day immersion course for a dozen journalists in July 2002 at the Homeland Security Institute—a joint program of the New York Times Company Foundation and the Council of Foreign Relations to "explore in-depth complicated issues surrounding current proposals to create a more secure homeland," the Hart-Rudman Commission was created to "re-examine the world today and to analyze the implications of this world for future US national security," and recognized that "national security strategies and institutions that existed at the time of the commission were created before the fall of the Berlin wall and during communism."[17] The Commission "believed a new global environment existed—and American institutions and strategies needed to be altered."[18] With a budget of $10.4 million, the Commission's research took three years to complete, incorporating the ideas of "a diverse group of prominent Americans: southern democrats; republicans; captains of industry; retired military officers; Ambassadors; the press; academics; and foreign and intelligence officers," who "represented a spread of individuals with a basic understanding of national security and with experience in government."[19]

Laying a foundation for much of the national security debate that took place in the anxious months following 9/11, the Hart-Rudman Commission aimed to "describe the world emerging in the first quarter of this next century," to "propose a national security strategy that reflects this world," and to "examine the nature and structure in which the nation executes its national security strategy and suggest reforms."[20] Its work stretched from July 1998 until February 2001—but ironically, it was not until after the 9/11 attacks that the Commission's findings found a widespread audience—helping to guide the post-9/11 security debate, including the movement to create a new DHS. As Charles Graham Boyd, USAF (ret.) and CEO and president, Business Executives for National Security observed, America's "security for the twenty first century does not lie in great armies and navies, but with changes at home."[21] Ironically, he added, "most of the recommendations made by the commission were taken seriously" but while "many have been put into practice, some before 9/11," most were implemented after the Twin Towers fell.[22]

Having decided during its first of three phases that "the world was a dangerous place and that the US was not secure," the Hart-Rudman Commission "made fifty recommendations," the very first of which was "developing a Homeland Security Department that consolidates and refines the missions of nearly two dozen agencies and departments that play a role in securing the nation," and which would "be responsible not only for protecting the lives of Americans, but also overseeing the protection of the nation's critical infrastructure, including information technology."[23]

The fog of peace

While America's strategic thinkers began to prepare for the unthinkable between the 1993 WTC attack and 9/11, their efforts proceeded slowly—driven by subsequent Al Qaeda orchestrated terror attacks against US military and diplomatic targets around the world. As former White House counterterrorism advisor Richard Clarke testified on March 24, 2004, to the National Commission on Terrorist Attacks Upon the United States, "the 1993 attacks and then the terrorism in the Tokyo subway and the Oklahoma City bombing caused the Clinton Administration to increase its focus on terrorism and to expand funding for counter-terrorism programs"—with the 1996 attack on US military barracks in the Kohbar Towers complex in Saudi Arabia, the 1998 near-simultaneous US Embassy bombings in Kenya and Tanzania, and the 2000 attack of the USS Cole in Yemen adding greater impetus to the administration's counterterror activities.[24] In 1998, Clarke recalled he was "appointed by the President to a newly created position of National Coordinator for Security, Infrastructure Protection and Counter-terrorism," though even then—after years in Al Qaeda's crosshairs, he still "had no budget, only a dozen staff, and no ability to direct actions by the departments or agencies."[25]

He told Congress—and the family members of the 9/11 victims—"we tried to stop those attacks," and "some people tried very hard."[26] But while "there were people in the FBI, CIA, Defense Department, State Department, and White House who worked very hard to destroy al-Qaeda before it did catastrophic damage to the US," Clarke commented, "there were many others who found the prospect of significant al-Qaeda attacks remote"—and in "both CIA and the military there was reluctance at senior career levels to fully utilize all of the capabilities available."[27] Indeed, Clarke believes the "FBI was, throughout much of this period, organized, staffed, and equipped in such a way that it was ineffective in dealing with the domestic terrorist threat from al-Qaeda."[28] Clarke explained that "at the senior policy levels in the Clinton Administration, there was an acute understanding of the terrorist threat, particularly al-Qaeda" and this understanding "resulted in a vigorous program to counter al-Qaeda including lethal covert action," but he noted this understanding among top levels of the administration "did not include a willingness to resume bombing of Afghanistan," and that "events in the Balkans, Iraq, the Peace Process, and domestic politics occurring at the same time as the anti-terrorism effort played a role" in limiting America's response to the threat Al Qaeda posed.[29]

After the Democrats lost the White House in 2000, Clarke observed that "the Bush Administration saw terrorism policy as important—but not urgent—prior to 9/11."[30] Indeed, his own "difficulty in obtaining the first Cabinet level (Principals) policy meeting on terrorism and the limited Principals' involvement sent unfortunate signals to the bureaucracy about the Administration's attitude toward the al-Qaeda threat."[31] Such official indifference to the gathering mass-casualty terror threat against America came to a sudden, albeit belated, end on 9/11 with that day's unforgettable glimpse of the potent lethality of mass-casualty terrorism.

The gathering threat—Al Qaeda's nuclear ambition

In "Current WMD Challenges in the Middle East," in the March 2002 edition of the US Naval Postgraduate School's *Strategic Insights* e-newsletter, authors Peter Lavoy, Jack Boureston, and James Russell examine Al Qaeda's WMD potential, and observed that "Osama in Laden and his network al-Qaeda have been seeking to develop chemical, biological, and perhaps nuclear weapons capabilities for at least a decade," citing "evidence that they have considered developing biological agents such as anthrax, botulinum toxin and ricin."[32] Indeed, they point out that "US troops inspecting terrorist training camps in Afghanistan have uncovered rudimentary laboratories for developing biological weapons," and that "at the abu-Khabab terrorist camp, al-Qaeda elements may have conducted tests on animals to investigate the effects of these agents."[33] However, "in terms of a nuclear weapons capability, there is little evidence to suggest that al-Qaeda ever developed a nuclear explosive device," though there are "several known instances in which al-Qaeda members attempted to acquire uranium."[34] The authors observed that "troops investigating one camp close to the Kandahar airport found a substance in jars that is suspected to be depleted uranium" and if so, this could indicate that "al-Qaeda was attempting to develop a so-called 'dirty bomb' intended to expose a large area to radiation."[35]

The authors concluded that while it's "difficult to assess al-Qaeda's capacity to develop biological, chemical, or nuclear weapons, it seems probable that the group would direct its efforts toward biological and chemical weapons—since these are easier to develop and simpler to deploy."[36] While "it remains to be seen how successful US efforts to stop al-Qaeda from creating a WMD capability will be," they noted that ongoing and vigilant "intelligence collection and analysis, and the cooperation of the international community, will be essential in this endeavor."[37]

David Albright, a physicist and the president of the Institute for Science and International Security in Washington, DC, examined Al Qaeda's efforts to acquire WMD in "Al Qaeda's Nuclear Program: Through the Window of Seized Documents," published by the Nautilus Institute.[38] He observed that Al Qaeda developed "only limited technological capabilities in Afghanistan to produce WMD," but he believes that had Al Qaeda "remained in Afghanistan, it would have likely acquired nuclear weapons eventually."[39]

He recalled how after the Taliban fell in late 2001, "intelligence agencies and the media scrambled to find documents and other information about al-Qaeda and its next potential targets," and a top priority "was uncovering information about al-Qaeda's progress on acquiring weapons of mass destruction (WMD), including nuclear weapons."[40] According to Albright, "al-Qaeda views the acquisition of WMD as a religious obligation," and while al-Qaeda only developed "limited technological capabilities in Afghanistan to produce WMD," he believes that "al-Qaeda's determination to get nuclear weapons along with its increased ability to obtain outside technical assistance, lead to the conclusion that if al-Qaeda had remained in Afghanistan, it would have likely acquired nuclear weapons eventually."[41] And while Al Qaeda's WMD efforts appear to now be "in disarray, it remains determined to get WMD." As such, Albright believes that "preventing al-Qaeda and other terrorist groups from getting nuclear weapons or other WMD must be an overarching goal of the United States and the international community."[42]

After the Taliban fell, Albright recalled that "Western and Northern Alliance intelligence officers scoured houses, caves, and training camps for documents, booklets, personnel records, videos, equipment, materials, and other evidence of WMD programs."[43] As well, "many members of the media, who arrived in Kabul soon after the fall of the Taliban in mid-November 2001, uncovered many al-Qaeda and Taliban records."[44] According to Albright, "captured documents reinforce assessments that al-Qaeda is highly determined to obtain nuclear weapons and other weapons of mass destruction," and he cited US Defense Secretary Donald Rumsfeld who said, during a January 16, 2001, Defense Department briefing: "We have found a number of things that show an appetite for WMD."[45] CNN reported on December 4, 2001, that authorities found a "hand drawn diagram found either in a Taliban or al-Qaeda facility [that] showed a design for a 'dirty bomb,'" and "US officials also saw evidence that al-Qaeda was also seeking to acquire or develop a nuclear explosive device."[46] Albright also reported that former CIA chief George Tenet informed the US Congress in late January 2002 "that the United States uncovered rudimentary diagrams of nuclear weapons in a suspected al-Qaeda house in Kabul," which, "while crude, describe the essential components—uranium and high explosives—common to nuclear weapons."[47]

In November 2001, Albright noted, "CNN found an Arabic document titled 'Superbomb' in the home of Abu Khabbab, the code-name of a senior al-Qaeda official," which in "over 25 neatly hand-written pages, the author discusses various types of nuclear weapons, the physics of nuclear explosions, properties of nuclear materials needed to make them, and the effects of nuclear weapons."[48] And though the document's accuracy revealed incomplete knowledge about nuclear weapons, Albright wrote "this documents shows that al-Qaeda was interested in developing a deeper understanding of nuclear weapons," and that "some of the information in the document suggests that the author understood short cuts to making crude nuclear explosives."[49] More ominously, Albright observed that "other records imply that al-Qaeda had a more sophisticated understanding of atomic bombs than what is suggested by the Superbomb document," and "several documents reportedly described the manufacture of nuclear weapons and their effects."[50] Albright cites other documents that "support the view that al-Qaeda's leadership understood its limitations and was taking steps to improve its ability to create an industrial infrastructure to make WMD," and that "foreign assistance would allow it to overcome its weaknesses and be more efficient and economical in making WMD."[51]

Albright explained that "documents found in Afghanistan show that al-Qaeda members are neither supermen nor morons," and while "their efforts in making nuclear weapons were far less sophisticated than known state programs," he believes "their determination to get nuclear weapons is astounding and their apparent willingness to use them is terrifying."[52] And "because many of these terrorist groups will never give up in their quest for nuclear weapons and other WMD, the world cannot let down its guard either."[53]

Preventing the unthinkable

In November 2003, Jack Boureston, managing director of FirstWatch International, a private WMD proliferation research group, and Charles Mahaffey, a graduate student pursuing a degree in International Policy Studies and Nonproliferation at the Monterey Institute of International Studies, authored "Countering the al-Qaeda WMD Threat," published by the US Naval Postgraduate School in its November 2003 edition of *Strategic Insight*.[54] They argued that "the threat of al-Qaeda's use of weapons of mass destruction is real," noting how "during the 1990s, al-Qaeda used its significant financial resources and global support network to pursue the acquisition of nuclear, biological, chemical and radiological weapons."[55] Indeed, "as the terrible events of September 11, 2001 demonstrated," the authors pointed out that "the attacks on New York and Washington DC also reveal the group's ability to use the infrastructure of the target country as a weapon," and an attack of America's vulnerable critical infrastructure "could result in casualties even beyond what the world witnessed on September 11, with or without weapons of mass destruction."[56]

However, the authors argue that "no matter how much work goes into making an area more secure, it can never be made invulnerable," as "the sheer volume of radioactive, biological, and chemical material transported and stored in the United States alone makes it nearly impossible to ensure the security of such shipments at all times."[57] Hence, in order for America to prevent a future attack, the authors believe—as put forth by Dr Joshua Sinai in "How to Forecast and Preempt al-Qaeda's Catastrophic Terrorist Warfare," in August 2003 edition of *The Journal of Homeland Security*—that "we need to begin thinking like the enemy—always anticipating and preparing to counteract new types of attacks and targeting."[58] The authors concluded that "this can only be done through greater intelligence, analysis, preemption, and protection."[59]

Once the smoke and debris of 9/11 cleared, America's strategic planners realized the futility of depending upon deterrence theory and its associated Cold War–incubated doctrine to protect America from the emerging mass-casualty terror threat, and decided that the most effective defense against such a foe would be offense. America thus felt compelled to regain strategic initiative, and to use force to preempt future attacks. However, this shift toward more aggressive, preemptive action was, at least in part, designed to enhance America's capacity to deter future mass-casualty terror attacks—something it failed to do prior to 9/11—and as such suggests that deterrence was not yet obsolete. Preemption became America's strategy by default—and to formalize this strategic shift, America put forth its new doctrine of preemption in The National Security Strategy of the United States of America, issued by the White House in September 2002—one full year after the 9/11 attacks and nearly a decade after the 1993 WTC attack.

Indeed, Section V of the September 2002 National Security Strategy of the United States of America, "Prevent Our Enemies from Threatening Us, Our Allies, and Our Friends with Weapons of Mass Destruction," begins with a quotation from President Bush who, on June 1, 2002, told the very first graduating class at West Point to graduate after 9/11: "The gravest danger to freedom lies at the crossroads of radicalism and technology. When the spread of chemical and biological and nuclear weapons, along with ballistic missile technology—when that occurs, even weak states and small groups could attain a catastrophic power to strike great nations. Our enemies have declared this very intention, and have been caught seeking these terrible weapons. They want the capability to blackmail us, or to harm us, or to harm our friends—and we will oppose them with all our power."[60]

As 9/11 proved beyond a doubt, with the collapse of the Soviet Union and the end of the Cold War, "America's security environment has undergone profound transformation"—and "new, deadly challenges have emerged from rogue states and terrorists."[61] And while "none of these contemporary threats rival the sheer destructive power that was arrayed against us by the Soviet Union," the new National Security Strategy explained that "the nature and motivations of these new adversaries, their determination to obtain destructive powers hitherto available only to the world's strongest states, and the greater likelihood that they will use weapons of mass destruction against us, make today's security environment more complex and dangerous."[62] Henceforth, the United States would remain committed to being "prepared to stop rogue states and their terrorist clients before they are able to threaten or use weapons of mass destruction against the United States and our allies and friends."[63] Its strategic response would thus "take full advantage of strengthened alliances, the establishment of new partnerships with former adversaries, innovation in the use of military forces, modern technologies, including the development of an effective missile defense system, and increased emphasis on intelligence collection and analysis."[64]

America's new strategy promised to take a "comprehensive" approach to combat WMD threats—including "proactive counterproliferation efforts" to "deter and defend against the threat before it is unleashed"; "strengthened nonproliferation efforts to prevent rogue states and terrorists from acquiring the materials, technologies, and expertise necessary for weapons of mass destruction"; and "effective consequence management to respond to the effects of WMD use, whether by terrorists or hostile states."[65]

The new doctrine recognized that "it has taken almost a decade for us to comprehend the true nature of this new threat"—and acknowledged that "given the goals of rogue states and terrorists, the United States can no longer solely rely on a reactive posture as we have in the past," noting America's "inability to deter a potential attacker, the immediacy of today's threats, and the magnitude of potential harm that could be caused by our adversaries' choice of weapons," which "do not permit that option."[66] Going forward, American strategy fully digested the implications of 9/11: "We cannot let our enemies strike first." Indeed, unlike during the Cold War, when "weapons of mass destruction were considered weapons of last resort whose use risked the destruction of those who used them," the new American strategy recognized that "today, our enemies see weapons of mass destruction as weapons of choice."[67]

In a press release issued on March 9, 2002, the Pentagon released a "Statement on Nuclear Posture Review," which confirmed that the Defense Department was conducting its legally mandated review of US nuclear strategy, "the latest in a long series of reviews since the development of nuclear weapons."[68] Reflecting the transformed international milieu of the post–9/11 world, it noted: "This administration is fashioning a more diverse set of options for deterring the threat of WMD. That is why the Administration is pursuing missile defense, advanced conventional forces, and improved intelligence capabilities. A combination of offensive and defensive, and nuclear and non-nuclear capabilities is essential to meet the deterrence requirements of the 21st century."[69] As Secretary Rumsfeld told the media during a press conference: "The Cold War is over. The whole orientation of the United States of America for many decades was to the Soviet Union, properly so . . . We don't consider them an enemy today, so the orientation of our nuclear posture is significantly different today than it needed to be during the Cold War. Other countries are interested in developing nuclear weapons and engaged in activities that demonstrate their intent and their purpose. And the United States is perfectly—it's perfectly proper for the United States to take note of those things and be sensitive to them."[70]

In December 2002, the United States articulated its new National Strategy to Combat Weapons of Mass Destruction, which blends interdiction, preemption, deterrence, and enhanced intelligence into a multifaceted strategy to secure our homeland from WMD attack.[71] In the years since, America has waged one war of preemption, overthrowing the regime of Saddam Hussein, and it has successfully interdicted at least one high-seas shipment of ballistic missile technology exported by North Korea under the joint operating mission of the Proliferation Security Initiative (PSI). On the home front, America has enacted broad legislation to protect its ports and frontiers, setting up the necessary pieces to both defend America from a WMD attack and—yes—to more persuasively deter both terror organizations and rogue states from again attacking our homeland.

The December 2002 National Strategy to Combat Weapons of Mass Destruction examined the evolution of deterrence theory as part of America's evolving strategy to counter the proliferation of WMD, stating: "Today's threats are far more diverse and less predictable than those of the past. States hostile to the United States and to our friends and allies have demonstrated their willingness to take high risks to achieve their goals, and are aggressively pursuing WMD and their means of delivery as critical tools in this effort. As a consequence, we require new methods of deterrence. A strong declaratory policy and effective military forces are essential elements of our contemporary deterrent posture, along with the full range of political tools to persuade potential adversaries not to seek or use WMD. The United States will continue to make clear that it reserves the right to respond with overwhelming force—including through resort to all of our options—to the use of WMD against the United States, our forces abroad, and friends and allies."[72]

In addition to conventional and nuclear responses, the new WMD strategy explained that "our overall deterrent posture against WMD threats is reinforced by effective intelligence, surveillance, interdiction, and domestic law enforcement capabilities. Such combined capabilities enhance deterrence both by devaluing an adversary's WMD and missiles, and by posing the prospect of an overwhelming response to any use of such weapons."[73]

The continuing WMD threat

With Al Qaeda on the run since the fall of the Taliban—its training camps in ruins and its leadership either dead, captured, or dispersed to some of the world's remotest regions—there has been little chance for the terror network to develop and articulate a new strategy in response to America's reinvigorated counterterrorism strategy. One can thus logically conclude that those remaining terror cells—and new ones that are emerging amidst the current leadership vacuum—are continuing to operate from the old playbook, hoping to inflict yet another deadly blow against America, this time achieving truly mass casualties.

Having tried to topple the Twin Towers in 1993, and failed—only to succeed on 9/11, but with relatively modest casualties (certainly well below the attackers' best-case scenario after having patiently plotted for nearly a decade to inflict mass casualties), one can imagine that at least one Al Qaeda cell, or that of a successor organization, is eager to try again. And next time, they may succeed in delivering a truly catastrophic blow, delivering what they can only hope will be the long-awaited strategic coup d'oeuil that Al Qaeda has long planned to bring to our shores.

With 3,000 dead on 9/11, America was psychologically devastated, and its economy briefly paralyzed. But that was in the era of WMD and mass-casualty terror, a mere pinprick. A single thermonuclear weapon of the sort developed during the height of the Cold War could incinerate an entire metropolitan area—the largest built is capable of unleashing a 100-megaton yield, the explosive equivalent of 100 million tons of TNT—and would be vastly more destructive. A much smaller atomic fission weapon—of the sort used by America against Hiroshima and Nagasaki—would result in a fraction of the yield, but would also be quite lethal. For instance, a 20-kiloton atomic weapon would be just one five-thousandth, or one fiftieth of a percent, as powerful as a 100-megaton thermonuclear weapon. But as reported by the United Nations Office on Drugs and

Crime, "if a 20-kiloton nuclear fission weapon exploded on Wall Street at noon on a business day, it could kill an estimated 1 million people. Hydrogen bombs are many times more powerful."[74]

So even if a relatively small atomic weapon were utilized by Al Qaeda, the fatalities could be as high as 1 million—nearly 333 times as lethal as on 9/11, and over 166,667 times as lethal as the 1993 WTC attack. No doubt, Al Qaeda would love to acquire an atomic weapon from the former Soviet arsenal, or from one of the new nuclear arsenals in South Asia. More plentiful, of course, are the many thousands of smaller yielding tactical nuclear weapons and *mini-nukes* that proliferated during the Cold War, which are more portable and thus easier for a terror cell to deploy. Other potential WMD weapons exist—in addition to nuclear weapons—including improvised radiological weapons (dirty bombs), whose explosive yields are nominal but whose psychological effects and economic costs would be notable, as well as biological and chemical weapons, which have the potential to kill many thousands of civilians or more.

In the coming years, America must thus remain vigilant—knowing that the die is cast, and that it's only a question of time before we're struck again. Next time, Al Qaeda or its offshoots may well succeed in its long-term mission to deliver a truly mass-casualty blow—unleashing what until only recently would have been unthinkable devastation to our homeland.

Notes

1 WordIQ.com, "World Trade Center Bombing," www.wordiq.com/definition/World_Trade_Center_bombing. Originally posted in Wikipedia.org.
2 Laurie Mylroie, "The World Trade Center Bomb: Who Is Ramzi Yousef? And Why It Matters" *The National Interest*, Winter 1995/96.
3 Ibid.
4 Ibid.
5 John V. Parachini, "The World Trade Center Bombers (1993)," Chapter 11, in Jonathan B. Tucker, ed., *Toxic Terror: Assessing Terrorist Use of Chemical and Biological Weapons* (Cambridge, MA: MIT Press, 2000), 185–206.
6 Ibid.
7 Ibid.
8 Ibid.
9 Richard K. Betts, "The New Threat of Mass Destruction," *Foreign Affairs* Volume 77, Number 1 (January/February 1998).
10 Ibid.
11 Ibid.
12 U.S. Commission on National Security/21st Century (Hart-Rudman Commission), www.au.af.mil/au/awc/awcgate/nssg/.
13 "Major Themes and Implications: The Phase 1 Report on the Emerging Global Security Environment for the First Quarter of the 21st Century," *New World Coming: American Security in the 21st Century*, September 15, 1999, www.au.af.mil/au/awc/awcgate/nssg/nwc.pdf. Also available at FAS.org, www.fas.org/man/docs/nwc/nwc.htm.

14 Ibid.
15 Ibid.
16 Ibid.
17 The New York Times Company Foundation Website, "Homeland Security," www.nytco. com/company/foundation/homeland_security.html.
18 Ibid.
19 Ibid.
20 "Major Themes and Implications: The Phase 1 Report."
21 Barry Zellen, "Nuclear Terrorism: Re-Thinking the Unthinkable after 9/11," SecurityInnovator.com, September 26, 2005, http://securityinnovator.com/index.php?a rticleID=5428&sectionID=29.
22 Ibid.
23 Ibid.
24 Richard Clarke, "9/11 Prepared Testimony," March 24, 2004, www.msnbc.msn.com/ id/4595173/.
25 Ibid.
26 Richard Clarke, "9/11 Prepared Testimony," March 24, 2004, www.msnbc.msn.com/ id/4595173/.
27 Ibid.
28 Ibid.
29 Ibid.
30 Ibid.
31 Ibid.
32 Peter Lavoy, Jack Boureston, and James Russell, "Current WMD Challenges in the Middle East," *Strategic Insights* Volume I, Number 1 (2002).
33 Ibid.
34 Ibid.
35 Ibid.
36 Ibid.
37 Ibid.
38 David Albright, "Al Qaeda's Nuclear Program: Through the Window of Seized Documents," Nautilus Institute Special Forum 47, November 6, 2002, www.ncsparks. com/riskmanagement/library/VirtualLibrary/albright2002.pdf.
39 Ibid.
40 Ibid.
41 Ibid.
42 Ibid.
43 Ibid.
44 Ibid.
45 Ibid.
46 Ibid.
47 Ibid.
48 Ibid.
49 Ibid.
50 Ibid.
51 Ibid.
52 Ibid.
53 Ibid.

54 Jack Boureston and Charles Mahaffey, "Countering the al-Qaeda WMD Threat," *Strategic Insights* Volume II, Number 11 (November 2003).
55 Ibid.
56 Ibid.
57 Ibid.
58 Ibid.
59 Ibid.
60 Section V, "Prevent Our Enemies from Threatening Us, Our Allies, and Our Friends with Weapons of Mass Destruction," *National Security Strategy of the United States of America*, September 2002, http://georgewbush-whitehouse.archives.gov/nsc/nss/2002/nss5.html.
61 Ibid.
62 Ibid.
63 Ibid.
64 Ibid.
65 Ibid.
66 Ibid.
67 Ibid.
68 Department of Defense, "Statement on Nuclear Posture Review," March 9, 2002, www.fas.org/news/usa/2002/dodnpr031002.htm.
69 Ibid.
70 Ibid.
71 SPD-17/HSPD 4: National Strategy to Combat Weapons of Mass Destruction, December 2002, www.fas.org/irp/offdocs/nspd/nspd-17.html.
72 Ibid.
73 Ibid.
74 Zellen, "Nuclear Terrorism."

Part IV

Ensuring Our Survival: Thinking about the Unthinkable after 9/11

20

Nuclear Weapons and the War on Terror: Halting the Spread

After a half century of international stability maintained by a strategy of extended nuclear deterrence, we now find ourselves in a new, chaotic, and menacing world. Once the smoke and debris of 9/11 cleared, we've embarked upon an odyssey that began when America's defense-planners realized we were up against an adversary that had not been effectively deterred from attacking our homeland. With clarity borne of the horror of that day, America's strategic planners realized the most effective defense against such a foe would be offense. So instead of deterring aggression, we felt compelled to seize the strategic advantage, and to use force to preempt future attacks.

Operation Iraqi Freedom

Having lost an opportunity in the first decade of the post–Cold War era to transform, rebuild, and democratize Iraq under the benign military occupation of the 1991 American-led Gulf War Coalition, we instead left Saddam in power; Kuwait liberated only "halfway" (and still not free of its own corrupt tyranny); an angry, seething, disaffected Arab youth culture marginalized by our own undemocratic Arab Middle Eastern partners, Saudi Arabia and Egypt; and—a few years later—a collapsing peace process between democratic Israel and the undemocratic Palestinian Authority. While visionary former Soviet premier Gorbachev pulled the plug on further subsidizing tyrannical, one-party regimes in Central Europe (paving the way for a sudden, quick, and democratic transformation of the former Communist bloc a decade ago), it appears that America—in a land where our military power was largely unchallenged—missed an historic opportunity to bring an end to continued tyranny and stagnation in the Middle East by maintaining the status quo after the first Gulf War, and as a result, the seeds of 9/11 were planted in fertile soil. Yes, we easily crushed the Republican Guard, and destroyed 4,000 Iraqi tanks in a 100-hour battle while losing just 10 of our own tanks in 1991. But we failed to translate our military victory into political change, losing a moment in history to export our values to a land craving them. For the next ten years, we sought to apply a strategy of containment to Iraq—leaving one more open, festering wound in the Middle East that begged to be healed.

The region became a breeding ground of terror and that terror, starting in 1993, was clearly aimed at America—and after Osama bin Laden's 1996 "Declaration of War Against the Americans Occupying the Land of the Two Holy Places," and his 1998 *fatwah* urging *jihad* against Americans, it was clear a holy war was being waged against us. From the first World Trade Center attack, to the US Embassy bombings in Kenya and Tanzania, to the near-sinking of the U.S.S. Cole in Yemen, the attacks against us grew bolder—and more sophisticated. In hindsight, an attack on the scale of 9/11 looks to be inevitable—but part of this inevitability, I believe, is our failure to articulate a credible strategy of deterrence of terror, or successfully adapt and extend our Cold War systems of deterrence to the emerging threat of mass terror.

That is why, after 9/11 and the loss of so much innocent blood on American soil, we were compelled to mobilize for a preemptive war, and finally address this failure by "finishing the job" left incomplete in 1991. With the menacing regime of Saddam Hussein quickly crushed by conventional US armor, the process of democratization and reform was at last under way in the Gulf region—and though the road ahead would be rocky, there is now the promise that the roots of terror will be stamped out as hopelessness is replaced by hope, and despair is replaced by opportunity and inclusion. The Bush administration's bold Middle East policy, and its vision to transform the region's breeding grounds of anti-American hate and terror into nascent democracies, offered a real opportunity to make deep, and lasting, change. But elsewhere in the world, chaos still reigned, and America continued to face grave risks. Most notable was the renewed nuclear showdown on the Korean Peninsula, and the simmering dispute with Iran over its concealed nuclear weapons research program—suggesting we may again face an emerging nuclear nemesis. As well, the remnants of Al Qaeda are still out there, hidden in the shadows—and as such continue to present a WMD threat to us. It's therefore conceivable that we could again face another acid-test, this time against a nuclear-armed rogue state or WMD-equipped terror group.

Rethinking the unthinkable

In a press release on March 9, 2002, the Pentagon released a "Statement on Nuclear Posture Review," which noted that the DoD was conducting its legally mandated reviews of US nuclear strategy, "the latest in a long series of reviews since the development of nuclear weapons."[1] Reflecting the transformed international milieu, it noted: "This administration is fashioning a more diverse set of options for deterring the threat of WMD. That is why the Administration is pursuing missile defense, advanced conventional forces, and improved intelligence capabilities. A combination of offensive and defensive, and nuclear and non-nuclear capabilities, is essential to meet the deterrence requirements of the 21st century."[2] As Secretary Rumsfeld told the media during a press conference: "The Cold War is over. The whole orientation of the United States of America for many decades was to the Soviet Union, properly so . . . We don't consider them an enemy today, so the orientation of our nuclear posture is significantly different today than it needed to be during the Cold War. Other countries are interested in developing nuclear weapons and engaged in activities that demonstrate their intent and their purpose. And the United States is perfectly—it's perfectly proper for the United States to take note of those things and be sensitive to them."[3]

The strategic environment had indeed changed profoundly, and America appeared to finally be preparing to develop, and later deploy, its nuclear forces for both defensive and offensive purposes in pursuit of its military objectives in the post–Cold War anarchy. And, because of the inherent contradictions of nuclear strategy, by being so prepared, perhaps we may well have reduced the very likelihood of ever having to do so. Just as they did during the Cold War, our war planners now hoped that by preparing options for the unthinkable, and considering choices for nuclear warfighting—even against asymmetrical threats like those we face today—that it will contribute to a more credible deterrent, and thus reduce the likelihood of ever having to break the long nuclear taboo. By being ready and willing to use nuclear weapons as tools of preemption and not just tools of deterrence, perhaps our strengthening credibility will of itself elicited change— fostering, perhaps, the emergence of a more benign North Korea prepared to back from the nuclear brink. One may even speculate that the Iranian acknowledgment of its long secret nuclear program might have been the result of America's proactive strategy of preemption, and the fact of its military deployment along two of Iran's frontiers.

During the Cold War, America flip-flopped between the cold logic of MAD— Mutual Assured Destruction—and the more credible doctrine of flexible response, where nukes, just like our conventional armory, were merely another warfighting tool to be deployed as we worked our way up the escalation ladder. We never really knew for sure which strategy we preferred nor which was the more effective. MAD—for all its madness—in theory perpetuated peace, since the threat of massive retaliation would surely deter aggression. But as we articulated our MADness, we never really knew if our adversaries believed our threat. Were we angry enough, crazy enough, stupid enough to push the button? Would we risk the end of the world to protect the freedom and independence of Western Europe? So NATO hoped—and the quietude of the central front during the Cold War was testimony to the fact that MAD seemed to successfully extend deterrence to our European allies. The risks were high but the payoff—a half century of peace—was likewise a prize worth risking much for.

But far from the Central Front, the hotspots of the Cold War—from Korea to Vietnam and Central America and South Asia—showed that outside the democratic, western, liberal club of NATO, deterrence was a lot harder to extend, and the probability of war was much higher, as was the risk of nuclear escalation in battle. That might be why during North Korea's nearly successful conquest of the Korean peninsula in 1950 —and the final, successful offensive of the North Vietnamese Army in 1975—old-fashioned conventional blitzkriegs were the tools of choice and why, in the end, we either fought and won the peace (as we did in Korea) using only our conventional might, or backed away and surrendered our freedom-aspiring ally (as we did in Vietnam) after we proved unwilling or unable to do the job with conventional force. Then—even as we worried about the credibility of deterrence, the sanity of MAD, the dangers of flexible response—we were clear to draw a line between what we would and would not use our nuclear firepower for.

In the back of our war planners' minds was no doubt the legacy of Hiroshima and Nagasaki, where the desperation to end a long and bloody war and the anger that festered since Pearl Harbor led us to do the unthinkable against civilians, committing an act of atomic urbicide against our attackers in our final, angry act—not once, but twice. We showed the world then and the memory remains that yes, we will, we can, we did drop atomic bombs and incinerate hundreds of thousands of men, women, and children, all defenseless—and that to bring peace, end war, redress injustice, or purge the anger in our veins would become so terrible and terrifying that perhaps we would never again be so challenged. The success of our nuclear wrath in 1945 likely contributed to the stability of the post–World War II world.

It no doubt taught NATO and the Warsaw Pact to limit their hostility and better understand one another's moods so war would not break out and quickly escalate beyond control. But far from the Central Front, where the risks of escalation were lower, wars did break out and millions died in proxy wars on battlefields fought in the name of competing ideologies and economic systems that seemed out of place, whether in the jungles of Central America, the deserts of Arabia, or the drought-ridden plains of the Horn of Africa. Before outsourcing was in vogue, the Cold War's logic and the balance of terror helped to offload the warfighting and death to proxy armies far from the true origins of the conflict. So powerful was the nuclear stalemate that it carved out a little sanctuary of peace and stability, within which, during the European revolutions of 1989 and 1990, one side simply joined the other—and there was no more talk of defeat.

The Global War on Terror

A decade after the Cold War's end, we found ourselves in a new world—where all great powers, whether communist or democratic, freedom loving or tyrannical, or a little bit of both, were now aligned in the GWOT (though clearly unaligned on our extension of the war on terror to our preemptive regime change in Iraq). Russia—fearing much from Islamic rebels on its southern flank—quickly joined forces with us, knowing that now we shared a common enemy for the first time since World War II. Even China—in many ways our greatest strategic threat, with its own robust nuclear arsenal and its giant modernizing economy and conventional army, knows well our fears, as it struggles to keep its union together and to fight entropy, internal corruption, and a variety of rebellions and insurgencies on its flanks—is part of the grand coalition. This war was pitched as a war against evildoers, a war against evil, something pure and insidious in a way the threat of communism never really could claim. That evil was nothing short of international terrorism—and the host countries that nurture and sustain it.

Fighting this war would require new ways of thinking. It started with a brilliant and daring attack upon us by 19 men armed with simple box-cutters. With these tools—which cost pennies and which are available at any convenience store—they seized commercial jetliners, each worth hundreds of millions of dollars. They gained entry to their cockpits, and took control—turning them into guided missiles. And with those missiles, they destroyed two giant office towers, America's largest; killed thousands of civilians; and inflicted severe damage upon the Pentagon—the source of American military command and control and symbol of our military power. In short, they harnessed our own technology and know-how and turned it into a lethal weapon, unleashing destructive power well beyond their own offensive capabilities. Now, we wait—and wait—until we learn what they are up to next. Likely, they will again turn our own technology against us—and figure out a way to, for instance, destroy a dam, flooding a city below, crippling its source of power Or, they may find their way onboard another jetliner and smash through a nuclear plant's outer concrete wall, exposing widespread areas and millions of their inhabitants to lethal radiation without needing their own nuclear capability. Or, taking their cue from nature, they might unleash an endless wave of forest fires upon us, choking our cities with smoke, knowing a single spark can start a prairie fire.

We found ourselves up against a foe that we greatly outgunned, but which we could not readily find and destroy. They set up camps in foreign countries and when those are shut down, they disappear over the mountains to hidden sanctuaries. Once, Al Qaeda was based in Sudan—but we persuaded the Sudanese to evict them, and they ended up in Afghanistan. After 9/11, we engineered the collapse of their new hosts and they once again fled, into the chaos of Pakistan and beyond. Now, we face a scattered foe, but one still lethal. We have captured or killed a significant portion of their leaders, but as Secretary Rumsfeld's leaked October 16, 2003, memo suggested: "We are having mixed results with Al Qaida, although we have put considerable pressure on them— nonetheless, a great many remain at large."[4] He additionally noted that we've "made reasonable progress in capturing or killing the top 55 Iraqis," but "somewhat slower progress tracking down the Taliban."[5] Rumsfeld noted that we lack the necessary "metrics to know if we are winning or losing the global war on terror. Are we capturing, killing or deterring and dissuading more terrorists every day than the madrassas and the radical clerics are recruiting, training and deploying against us?"[6] He considered the long-term need "to fashion a broad, integrated plan to stop the next generation of terrorists."[7] But in the meantime, hidden and reconstituted terror cells continued to plot and plan—as we waited, and watched, and wondered where and when and how they might strike next.

The logic of preemption

Enter our formidable nuclear arsenal. During the Cold War, that arsenal was mainly a weapon of dissuasion—a tool to persuade the communists to stay on their side of the iron curtain. And for the most part, it succeeded. During the first post–Cold War hot war, Operation Desert Shield/Storm, we faced a new enemy: Iraq. Once our would-be friend, the secular bulwark that used its own blood and steel (and our intelligence) to defend the West (and the oilfields of the Gulf) against the spread of radical Shi'ite fundamentalism after the 1979 Iranian Revolution, Iraq—upon invading Kuwait and standing massed along the Saudi border, the world's oil supply in dangerous proximity to its army—crossed the line and became a threat to international stability and the security of the West. After all the risks and fears of the Cold War's nuclear madness, it turned out that old-fashioned conventional military power deployed along the world's largest oil and gas fields could potentially cripple the West in ways the Soviets never imagined.

With Iraq, we faced a new threat from a small but menacing state. In addition to the conventional might it deployed along the Kuwaiti-Saudi border, it possessed a robust stockpile of chemical and biological weapons—and was pursuing an ambitious nuclear weapons program. And yet, as we fought Iraq and expelled its army from Kuwait in 1991, we did not bring the battle to Baghdad, nor did we threaten to topple the regime of Saddam Hussein. On the eve of Desert Storm, then secretary of state James Baker told Iraq that if it used chemical or biological weapons, we would consider them WMD and use our nuclear weapons in response. And having once used such weapons against an earlier enemy, our threat of nuclear retaliation was perceived by the Iraqis to be credible. Iraq was deterred and though it launched conventionally tipped ballistic missiles against Israel and our forces scattered throughout the Gulf, it refrained from launching chemical-biological warfare (CBW) payloads. Iraq, in its rationality, did not call our bluff—and once the war was over and Kuwait free, we quickly withdrew and left Saddam in power, his regime unchallenged. Even as the Kurds and Shi'ites rose up against Saddam, we betrayed our new friends and let Saddam crush their rebellions and their aspirations for freedom, as if we, too, were deterred—unwilling to inspire suicidal madness from Saddam's regime, which, if pushed into a corner and threatened with collapse, would have nothing to lose. Once we achieved our stated goals, we avoided mission creep, and took no more risks of crossing the abyss. We let Saddam withdraw, and remain in power.

In the years since—and particularly in the aftermath of 9/11—we came to view the lingering threat from terror groups and their sponsoring rogue states in a new light. This perspective was captured by America's post-9/11 doctrine of strategic preemption. As encapsulated by the 2002 *National Security Strategy of the United States of America*, the problem of rogue states was explained as follows: "In the 1990s we witnessed the emergence of a small number of rogue states that, while different in important ways, share a number of attributes. These states: brutalize their own people and squander their national resources for the personal gain of the rulers; display no regard for international law, threaten their neighbors, and callously violate international treaties to which they are party; are determined to acquire weapons of mass destruction, along with other advanced military technology, to be used as threats or offensively to achieve the aggressive designs of these regimes; sponsor terrorism around the globe; and reject basic human values and hate the United States and everything for which it stands."[8]

The 2002 *National Security Strategy* identified Iraq and North Korea as the two most menacing rogue states, arguing that "these states' pursuit of, and global trade in, [mass destruction] weapons has become a looming threat to all nations." To combat this threat, the new strategy noted, "we must be prepared to stop rogue states and their terrorist clients before they are able to threaten or use weapons of mass destruction against the United States and our allies and friends." The comprehensive strategy to combat WMD included the following. (1) Proactive counter-proliferation efforts. We must deter and defend against the threat before it is unleashed. We must ensure that key capabilities— detection, active and passive defenses, and counterforce capabilities—are integrated into our defense transformation and our homeland security systems. (2) Strengthened nonproliferation efforts to prevent rogue states and terrorists from acquiring the materials, technologies, and expertise necessary for weapons of mass destruction. (3) Effective consequence management to respond to the effects of WMD use, whether by terrorists or hostile states. Minimizing the effects of WMD use against our people will help deter those who possess such weapons and dissuade those who seek to acquire them by persuading enemies that they cannot attain their desired ends.

The new doctrine recognized that WMD in the hands of rogue states is the new salient threat, in contrast to the relative stability of the Cold War, when WMD were considered to be "weapons of last resort whose use risked the destruction of those who used them." In contrast, today "our enemies see weapons of mass destruction as weapons of choice," as "tools of intimidation and military aggression against their neighbors," and as "their best means of overcoming the conventional superiority of the United States." According to our new doctrine, "traditional concepts of deterrence will not work against a terrorist enemy whose avowed tactics are wanton destruction and the targeting of innocents; whose so-called soldiers seek martyrdom in death and whose most potent protection is statelessness. The overlap between states that sponsor terror and those that pursue WMD compels us to action." But while "traditional concepts of deterrence" may not work, since mutual deterrence depends on states acting rationally, and mutually fearing the destruction that would follow from deterrence's failure—a less "traditional" and more controversial concept of deterrence might be quite effective, one based on the doctrine of nuclear warfighting.

In the 2002 *National Strategy to Combat Weapons of Mass Destruction*, one section articulated America's evolution of deterrence theory as part of its evolving strategy to counter the proliferation of WMD.[9] It stated: "Today's threats are far more diverse and less predictable than those of the past. States hostile to the United States and to our friends and allies have demonstrated their willingness to take high risks to achieve their goals, and are aggressively pursuing WMD and their means of delivery as critical tools in this effort. As a consequence, we require new methods of deterrence. A strong declaratory policy and effective military forces are essential elements of our contemporary deterrent posture, along with the full range of political tools to persuade potential adversaries not to seek or use WMD. The United States will continue to make clear that it reserves the right to respond with overwhelming force—including through resort to all of our options—to the use of WMD against the United States, our forces abroad, and friends and allies." In addition to traditional conventional and nuclear responses, the 2002 WMD strategy observed that "our overall deterrent posture against WMD threats is reinforced by effective intelligence, surveillance, interdiction, and domestic law enforcement capabilities. Such combined capabilities enhance deterrence both by devaluing an adversary's WMD and missiles, and by posing the prospect of an overwhelming response to any use of such weapons."

Preemption in action

After our homeland was attacked on 9/11, we traced the roots of terror throughout the Middle East and South Asia, and began to hunt down the many terror cells arrayed against us and our friends. And we looked at Iraq—unrepentant—and wondered: what shall we do? We knew Iraq had long aspired to possess WMD, and we feared what Iraq might do with its WMD know-how, and the remnants of its arsenal, in the post-9/11 world. That is why the president and his defense advisors made Iraq's WMD program— real or imagined—a target in the war on terror. It was its potential that scared us, not its imminent threat. As JCS chairman General Richard B. Myers told students at the Harvard Kennedy School of Government in 2002 "After 9/11, I sat in situation room, and we set our goals: destroy and degrade as best we can international terrorism; make it hard for states to harbor terrorists, so they don't get a place to train, finances, and so forth; and third, that weapons of mass destruction should not fall into the hands of terrorist groups."[10] While it did not really fit, the administration knew there would be no better opportunity, no better time, to use its military power to topple Saddam and replace his government with something a little less menacing, and a little more pro-Western.

After 9/11, the new and inescapable logic of preemption led to America's highly mobile blitz to Baghdad, and in the face of certain military defeat, the regime of Saddam Hussein collapsed as silently and quickly as the communist collapse a decade earlier. No WMD were used against our advancing wall of steel—indeed, no credible defense was waged at all. Preemption worked, much to the surprise of almost all observers. In 1991, we respected the regime's right to exist, and in exchange, the conflict did not escalate to WMD use. This time, we used our military power to crush a government, to topple its leadership, raising the risk that Saddam's regime would have nothing to lose this time, nothing to fear from using the tools in its arsenal that had deterred us before. So this time, we carefully communicated a message to the same military leadership, noting that we would retaliate in kind, and view the use of WMD as a crime against humanity—and thus a legitimate trigger for our own WMD retaliation.

That is why President Bush and Secretary of Defense Rumsfeld articulated a new nuclear doctrine, one that suggested we were shifting toward nuclear warfighting and away from pure deterrence—a plan that required developing a new generation of nuclear weapons, such as mini-nukes and deep earth-penetrating bunker-busting weapons, as tools of military preemption against targets such as underground weapons labs, terror command and control centers, and WMD armories. As we learned from Operation Enduring Freedom in Afghanistan, this war on terror can—and likely will continue to—yield high-value military targets that conventional weapons can barely reach.

Nuclear ambiguity

This new, post-9/11 rethinking of the unthinkable was no longer just talk of deterrence and the diplomacy of dissuasion—or was it? Just as our Cold War talk of flexible response and nuclear warfighting doctrines were meant on one level to increase credibility and thus extend, and shore up, our ability to deter aggression—more recent doctrinal debates over the articulation of a new, post-9/11 nuclear warfighting as a tool to preempt and destroy the emerging threat potential of an aspiring nuclear power could, ironically, result in the resurrection of deterrence as a strategy for the post-9/11 world—this time saying, "We will crush you not only if you use WMD against us, but also if you strive to obtain WMD that can be used against us in the future."

Once again, it was the threat of us using nuclear weapons first, in an act of preemption, and to bring the war to the enemy—nuclear war, not just conventional—in order to rid the world of a future nuclear threat, that gives us the credibility to make deterrence work. That's why pursuing research and development of a new generation of mini-nukes and bunker-busting, deep earth-penetrating nuclear weapons could help to ultimately win the war on terror. And just as we refused to declare a policy of "No First Use" during the Cold War—not wanting to erode our own credibility and thereby increase the risk of war—we now proclaimed that we, the world's most advanced nuclear power with the largest and most modern nuclear arsenal, remain prepared to use those weapons for more than just deterring an attack against us.

Indeed, our nuclear umbrella provided no protection against the unconventional and asymmetrical attacks of 9/11. Against terrorists, against shadow warriors operating from within the cracks of the international system, our ability to deter aggression failed. But that doesn't mean deterrence itself can't work—just that we need to develop the right nuclear force structure to make deterrence more credible against our new foes. At times during the Cold War, when the rationality of our Soviet opponent was questioned, or when the credibility of our will to reciprocate in the event of a nuclear exchange was questioned, deterrence theorists shifted from traditional deterrence toward a strategic warfighting doctrine that sought to make nuclear warfare fightable and winnable, dictating the development of a wide panoply of nuclear forces so that flexible nuclear responses were possible in combat, so America could work its way up the escalation ladder—avoiding an overwhelming nuclear response at the outset of hostilities.

After the dust and debris of 9/11 started to settle, we began shifting back in this direction, but in a new, asymmetrical world, against our new asymmetrical foes. That's why we turned to a doctrine of nuclear use and preemption, so that something a little bigger, with a little more bite than what we tasted on 9/11, does not emerge as the next threat against our security and values. But therein lay the trick: if we are prepared to use our nuclear weapons to take out emerging nuclear arsenals from rogue states, perhaps they will not bother pursuing such programs in the first place? Or, perhaps those heading down that path might be talked into abandoning their nuclear weapons programs, as Libya did during the War on Terror. Now, our willingness once more to go beyond deterrence to a more proactive strategy of nuclear use might just end up achieving what we wanted in the beginning: successful deterrence of further aggression and terror against us—now, and in the future.

It seems to have worked in the Gulf during Operation Iraqi Freedom. As our armor bore down on Baghdad, the regime quietly slipped away into the night, dissolving with a whimper and not a WMD bang. With our proactive, preemptive military strike, the regime certainly knew we were in it to the finish. And up against our nuclear arsenal, guided by a new proactive nuclear strategy, a quick and quiet collapse was perhaps the most logical choice. That was our goal.

But we can only hope that it works as well next time. With North Korea now across the nuclear chasm and Pyongyang periodically demonstrating that it was now a bona fide member of the nuclear club, the risks next time will surely be much greater. But as Libya's willingness to renounce its errant nuclear ambition demonstrated, our willingness to preemptively engage Iraq could perhaps suggest with some persuasiveness to rogue states that stepping back from the nuclear brink could be their wisest course of action. Conventional US weaponry—whether the potent if indiscriminate Massive Ordnance Air Blast (MOAB, also known as the Mother of All Bombs) or the more refined, unprecedentedly precise, and increasingly omnipresent UAV—cannot convey the same cold logic and commitment as can a firm but flexible nuclear response capability. Hence the belief, held by many in the George W. Bush administration from the earliest moments of the war on terror, that we must augment our nuclear assets too, and develop a robust arsenal of both mini-nukes and conventional bunker-busting munitions to ensure our reach is not only global but also capable of both pinpoint accuracy and lethal potency. With America at war, and our willingness to consider reinvigorating a flexible nuclear response to combat emerging nuclear and CBW threats on the rise for the first time since the Cold War's successful end, it was hoped that our ability to deter WMD proliferation would also rise concomitantly—as the credibility of our newfound will to strike back with a long-unseen lethality sunk in.

Notes

1   Department of Defense (DoD) News Release, No. 113–02, "Statement on Nuclear Posture Review," March 9, 2002, www.dod.mil/releases/2002/b03092002_bt113–02. html.
2   Ibid.
3   DoD News Transcript, "DoD News Briefing—Secretary Rumsfeld and Gen. Pace," March 15, 2002, 11:15 am, www.dod.mil/transcripts/2002/t03152002_t0315sd.html.
4   As reprinted in "We Have Not Yet Made Truly Bold Moves," on SecurityInnovator. com, October 22, 2003, http://technologyreports.net/securityinnovator/index. html?articleID=2142.

5 Ibid.
6 Ibid.
7 Ibid.
8 *The National Security Strategy of the United States of America,* September 2002, www. globalsecurity.org/military/library/policy/national/nss-020920.pdf.
9 *National Strategy to Combat Weapons of Mass Destruction*, December 2002, www.state. gov/documents/organization/16092.pdf.
10 General Richard B. Myers, Chairman, Joint Chiefs of Staff, "An Update on the Global War on Terror," SecurityInnovator.com, November 24, 2002.

21

False Alarm: Saddam, WMD, and the GWOT's First Sideshow

The simmering clash of wills between US president George W. Bush and Iraqi strongman Saddam Hussein was presented to the world community in 2002 and 2003 as phase two of the GWOT, marking a distinct strategic shift from dismantling Al Qaeda's worldwide terror network to the implementation of America's newly articulated doctrine of strategic preemption, designed to prevent rogue states from acquiring WMD. However, the selection of Iraq as the first testing ground for strategic preemption, while other aspiring nuclear powers, such as North Korea—which had recently admitted to pursuing a secret nuclear program in clear violation of its international agreements—continue to seek their own WMD arsenals, suggests that much more was at play than simply proactive WMD prevention.

The White House's preoccupation with Iraq suggests a confluence of several factors, including the saliency of oil politics in the Bush White House to the feeling expressed openly during the 2002 presidential campaign that the United States had erred in 1991 by leaving Saddam in power, and must now "finish the job." With the United States rapidly building up troops and war materiel in the Gulf Region, and the White House dismissing apparent Iraqi compliance with the current UN sanctioned weapons-inspection regime, it appeared that a Third Gulf War would shortly begin—demonstrating that world politics, like classical Greek theater, can often be a tragedy in three acts.

As critics of the Bush administration's bellicose policy toward Iraq argue, the White House seems to have judged Iraq guilty of WMD proliferation even before the current weapons-inspection "trial" had concluded—suggesting that the US efforts to win a UN Security Council resolution sanctioning the current weapons inspections might be political theater on the global stage—paving the way for the third tragic act in the Gulf drama that has continued for a generation.

The First Gulf War: A US-Iraq axis

Ironically, Iraq's aggressive efforts to develop WMD date back to an earlier era in US-Iraq relations, when America tilted toward Iraq in its own long war against Iran from 1980–88. Initiated by Saddam Hussein upon consolidation of an expansionist Islamist theocracy in Iran following the 1979 revolution, Saddam's invasion of Iran was in fact driven by Iraq's own strategy of preemption against a revolutionary, expansionist movement that threatened the security of the Iraqi state—and by extension—the oil fields of the Gulf and the world economy.

This US partnership with Iraq, more tactical than strategic, was very much a "lesser of two evils" choice—common during the Cold War to contain Soviet expansionism and easily applied to post-revolution Iran. As reported by Reuters in August 2002, the United States gave Iraq "vital battle-planning help during its war with Iran as part of a secret program under President Ronald Reagan even though US intelligence agencies knew the Iraqis would unleash chemical weapons."[1] According to Reuters: "The highly classified covert program involved more than 60 officers of the US Defense Intelligence Agency who provided detailed information on Iranian military deployments, tactical planning for battles, plans for airstrikes and bomb-damage assessments for Iraq."

In addition to this sharing of satellite intelligence and vital strategic information on Iranian troop movements, there was also a transfer of weapons technology that resulted in the transfer to Iraq of technology with dual-use for biological and chemical weapons development. As Matt Kelley reported in the Associated Press in October 2002: "Iraq's bioweapons program that President Bush wants to eradicate got its start with help from Uncle Sam two decades ago, according to government records getting new scrutiny in light of the discussion of war against Iraq."[2] Kelley continued: "The Centers for Disease Control and Prevention sent samples directly to several Iraqi sites that UN weapons inspectors determined were part of Saddam Hussein's biological weapons program." He added: "The CDC and a biological sample company, the American Type Culture Collection, sent strains of all the germs Iraq used to make weapons, including anthrax, the bacteria that make botulinum toxin and the germs that cause gas gangrene, the records show. Iraq also got samples of other deadly pathogens, including the West Nile virus. The transfers came in the 1980s, when the United States supported Iraq in its war against Iran."

During the First Gulf War between Iran and Iraq, Iraq faced potential military defeat by the more highly motivated, if technologically less well-armed, Iranian military—and Saddam's development of, and later use of, chemical and biological weapons—took place within this context of strategic asymmetry, military vulnerability, and later on, internal political instability along the Iranian frontier.

According to Samantha Power, in her Pulitzer prize–winning book *A Problem from Hell: America and the Age of Genocide*: "Unwilling to see an Iranian victory, the Reagan administration began in December 1982 to intervene to offset Iranian gains. In what Secretary of State George Schultz called 'a limited form of balance-of-power policy,' the United States provided Iraq with an initial $210 million in agricultural credits to buy US grain," and soon thereafter "removed Iraq from its list of countries sponsoring terrorism."[3] By November 1984, Power wrote, "the United States and Iraq restored diplomatic relations," even though "US officials had detailed knowledge of Hussein's reliance on torture and executions."[4] Power added that the United States "did not even complain when Hussein acquired between 2,000 and 4,000 tons of deadly chemical agents and began experimenting with the gases against the Iranians," eventually using chemical weapons "approximately 195 times between 1983 and 1988, killing or wounding, according to Iran, some 50,000 people."[5]

Power believes the mute US reaction to Saddam Hussein's use of WMD further encouraged him: "Once Hussein saw he would not be sanctioned for using these weapons against Iran, the Iraqi dictator knew he was onto something."[6] According to Power: US officials justified their soft response to Iraqi chemical weapons use on several grounds. They portrayed it as a weapon of last resort deployed only after more traditional Iraqi defenses were flattened. Although Iraq carried out first-use attacks, the operations were frequently presented as defensive attacks designed mainly to deflect or disrupt Iranian offensives, not to gain ground. This, of course, was a fine line to walk, as proponents of the preemptive, defensive rationale might have applied the same logic to rationalize nuclear first use.

As reported by Patrick Tyler in the *New York Times*: US intelligence officers "never encouraged or condoned the use of chemical weapons by Iraqi President Saddam Hussein's forces, but also never opposed such action because they considered Iraq to be struggling for its survival and feared that Iran would overrun the crucial oil-producing Gulf states."[7] The *New York Times* quoted an unidentified former Defense Intelligence Agency official as saying: "Having gone through the 440 days of the hostage crisis in Iran, the period when we were the Great Satan, if Iraq had gone down it would have had a catastrophic effect on Kuwait and Saudi Arabia, and the whole region might have gone down. That was the backdrop of the policy."[8] Ironically, the United States paid a high price for its balance-of-power policy in the Gulf—which has resulted in a region engulfed by war, and the simmering threat of its reappearance, for two decades. To preempt Iran's revolutionary expansion, and prevent the collapse of the conservative oil monarchies in the Gulf under a tidal wave of Islamist revolution, international terrorism, and multi-front jihad, America helped to equip Saddam Hussein's regime with its WMD capability to offset its strategic asymmetries, and to help reverse Iraqi military setbacks. The success of Iraq's use of chemical and biological weapons against Iran—and the muted response from US officials—further encouraged Saddam Hussein. As reported by Power: "These weapons instilled such psychological terror that even well-equipped troops tended to break and run after small losses."[9]

Though "the battle was won" by uncorking the WMD genie from its bottle, in the end, the seeds of the next Gulf War were planted.

The Second Gulf War: Axes to grind

When Saddam blitzkrieged across Kuwait and his army stood poised along the Saudi frontier in 1990, it was partly in response to a series of unresolved border disputes with Kuwait that had lingered since the end of the First Gulf War—over issues that included war reparations payments, claims by Iraq of Kuwaiti oil overproduction, Iraq's desire to swap territory with Kuwait for a Gulf seaport with direct access to the Shatt el-Arab sea lanes, and simmering tensions over oilfields straddling the Iraq-Kuwait border.

With Iran militarily and economically exhausted after a decade of war and the turmoil and disruption of its Islamist revolution, Iraq was now unthreatened throughout the region, and armed to the teeth. Thus, the Second Gulf War, 1990–91 became inevitable—as the self-proclaimed (and in many ways true) "savior" of the Gulf from the previous decade, had now become an undisputed menace to those very same oil fields and very same oil monarchies.

With the added specter of Saddam expanding his WMD program to include a nuclear capability, in addition to his potent biological and chemical capabilities, and his well-known willingness to use WMD to suppress internal revolt by Iraq's Kurdish minorities and border communities sympathetic to Iran during the First Gulf War, America and its allies felt compelled to roll Saddam's armies out of Kuwait, away from the Saudi border, and to restore the status quo ante—leaving the oil sheiks in charge and guaranteeing the free flow of oil from the Gulf. As the same time, a driving motivation was to defang Iraq's military and dismantle its WMD programs, while leaving the Saddam regime intact and strong enough to deter Iran from renewing hostilities.

The post–Gulf War (II) environment was thus dominated by a strategy of "dual containment," simultaneously containing Iraqi military capabilities while deterring the expansion of Iranian-backed extremism and state-sponsored terrorism. But everything would change on 9/11, in a fiery instant, when the collapse of the Twin Towers, the blow to the Pentagon's edifice, and the heroic prevention of a fourth assault that day, perhaps aimed at the White House, the Capitol Building, or CIA headquarters, no one can now be sure. But on that fateful morning, America was shaken by its newly exposed vulnerability. US officials quickly redefined world politics in Manichean terms, for the first time since the Cold War had divided the world into "East" and "West," a "them" and an "us." After 9/11, the world was perceived to be uniquely dangerous, and the old Cold War preference for more "timid" strategies of deterrence and containment was suddenly superseded by a new and aggressive desire for more proactive strategies including "compellance" and "preemption."

The Third Gulf War: The Axis of Evil

Within this context of the GWOT, a new global coalition of relatively stable states aligned against a handful of sources of globally reaching, international terror. The new US doctrine of preemption sought to further link the threat of international terrorism with the emerging WMD threat from the three rogue states defined by the White House to form an "Axis of Evil," linked apparently only by the intensity and endurance of their hostility to Washington.

However, as much as the White House insisted there was an Al Qaeda-Iraq connection, there appears to have been, at best, a tenuous link between Iraq and any globally reaching international terror movement including Al Qaeda. And while support in Iraq was strong for the ongoing Palestinian intifadah, support was every bit as strong among the US Gulf allies such as Saudi Arabia, making it very hard to persuade any rational observer of a credible link between Iraq and international terrorism—leaving much of the world skeptical that a Third Gulf War should have been fought in the name of combating global terrorism.

But the Bush administration remained committed to including in its war on terror its newly articulated strategy of preemption against rogue states seeking WMD—believing that such states pose a long-term strategic threat to the United States, its oil-producing allies in the Gulf, and its oil-consuming allies throughout the Western world—a threat every bit as menacing, perhaps more so, than the threat of international terrorism. The war on terror thus appears to have been mostly a rhetorical and diplomatic rationalization— thinly veiled—for a Third (and "final") Gulf War designed to depose Saddam's regime, and install a friendly government as it did in Afghanistan—simultaneously solving the long-term WMD threat while securing Western access to Gulf oil.

It is ironic that the United States first tilted toward Iraq in the 1980s to prevent Iranian sponsored international terrorism and the spread of radical Islamist instability across the Gulf, thus threatening the world economy that depends so much on Gulf oil. Then, the United States helped Saddam fight a war of preemption designed to defang a pan-Islamist movement of global terror. Now, the United States was poised to fight a war against Saddam for these very same reasons—presenting its war plan to topple Saddam as a war of preemption, designed to defang a pan-Islamist movement of global terror.

In the First Gulf War, the United States helped to uncork the WMD genie from its bottle; in the Second Gulf War, the United States started to put the genie back; and in its Third Gulf War, the United States sought to put the cork back in that bottle once and for all, only to find that it had largely succeeded in the prior war, and its postwar effort at containment, to rid Iraq of an active WMD program.

The Fourth Gulf War: A "Final Act"?

Many would speculate what might happen after the Third Gulf War, after a "friendly" pro-Western regime was emplaced in Iraq. Would the United States continue its proactive, preemptive march—expanding the war on terror to the other members of the Axis of Evil? Would it focus its energy and military power on protecting Saudi Arabia and the smaller oil kingdoms from both the threat of internal Islamist rebellion as well as external threats? Would the United States pursue a goal of democratic transformation of the entire Gulf and Middle East regions, in a wave of democratization on a scale unseen since the 1989 revolutions freed Eastern and Central Europe from Soviet communism?

For a while this last, more ambitious policy would be asserted, laying a foundation in President Bush's second inaugural address for a major transformation of the region, and the world, consolidating the democratic expansion underway since communism's collapse. But then the tide of war turned, and an insurgency against America's transformed military, with too light a footprint to ensure postwar stability and order, erupted across Iraq, as Saddam's harsh but stable order gave way to an unexpectedly lethal form of chaos.

Ironically, to preserve regional stability and guarantee the free flow of Gulf oil to the West, there was in fact little motivation for the United States to support a rapid democratization of the Gulf region—as democracy would likely bring into power Islamist parties hostile to US interests, as had happened in other elections across the Islamic world, from the parliamentary elections in Pakistan and Turkey, to the earlier and suppressed Algerian elections a decade earlier, and even evident in the pro-Iran sentiment of many in Iraq's newly democratic order, an order that favored the long-oppressed Shi'ite majority, many who had found sanctuary in Iran during the long years of Saddam's rule.

But if American power were to be used to delay the region's democratization, the results of the Third Gulf War could in the end plant the seeds of a potential Fourth Gulf War, resulting in a revolutionary upheaval throughout the Gulf modeled on the Iranian revolution that led directly to the First Gulf War—and indirectly paved the way to the Second and then Third, as the Arab street rose up to overthrow its many unpopular and repressive governments, and in so doing, deliver a blow to their pro-Western stance. This tragedy in three acts could thus result in one, final prologue of cataclysmic proportions—thrusting the entire Gulf region into an anti-Western rebellion, deposing the oil monarchies dependent upon US military and financial support for their survival.

Ironically, that was the goal of Osama bin Laden and his followers, who sought to unify the Gulf under an Islamist banner of theocracy, albeit one that favored Sunni interests, and who have articulated a long-term strategy of bringing jihad to the Gulf and dislodging US military power while at the same time liberating what they perceive as occupied Palestinian land. They linked US military plans for Iraq to their global struggle against American power, which they believe is the source of the oil monarchies' endurance. And for a while, it looked like they might see their wish fulfilled, as early on, Iraq erupted into flames, and ironically, Al Qaeda established a toe-hold in what it hoped would become the Islamic Republic of Iraq and which took every ounce of American strategic ingenuity to counter.

Saddam Hussein, in his prewar and inflammatory "apology" to Kuwait for his 1990 invasion, had similarly urged Kuwaitis to rise up and expel US troops, and to join a jihad against "the occupation of infidel armies," a call to arms that "rattled neighboring Arab governments, who are struggling to control rising anger and frustration among their populations over what is widely seen as US bullying in the region," according to Toronto's *Globe and Mail* newspaper.

By linking the GWOT to the efforts of rogue states to acquire WMD, and toppling the secular-minded if undemocratic Saddam in a Third Gulf War, the United States seemed to be playing straight into the hands of both Saddam as well as the Al Qaeda terror movement that opposed him—perhaps providing them with a reason to join forces, and potentially creating a real, and menacing, axis where none had hitherto been.

In the early days of the insurgency such an alignment looked possible, as disgruntled Baathists, toppled from power, found common cause with the very Islamists they had oppressed when in power. By declaring war against Iraq under the banner of its war on terror, the United States seemed to be putting into motion a self-fulfilling prophecy—making it more likely that a new generation of young Muslims will heed the call of jihad, and perpetuate terror throughout this region that has been so long "en-Gulfed" by a state of perpetual war. That was why the war degenerated into a "Fiasco," as described by Thomas Ricks in his classic work of war reporting.

But in the end, the liberating power of democracy would help to tame and channel the chaos that had erupted, and with much effort, and great sacrifice, American forces and their allies managed to reclaim Iraq, and to restore a new order on that fractured land. With the seed of democracy thus planted in the cradle of human civilization and the very heart of the Arab world, it would only take the passage of time and the arrival of a new administration in the White House to nurture forth the wider democratic transformation that President Bush had so boldly imagined, but then so recklessly set in motion.

Notes

1   Reuters, "Report: U.S. Aided Iraq Despite Chemical Weapons," August 18, 2002.
2   Matt Kelley, "Iraq Got Germs for Weapons Program from U.S. in, '80s," Associated Press, October 1, 2002.
3   Samantha Power, *A Problem from Hell: America and the Age of Genocide* (New York: Basic Books, 2002), 176.
4   Ibid, 177.
5   Ibid, 178.
6   Ibid, 179.
7   Patrick E. Tyler, "U.S. Aided Iraq Despite Gas Warfare," *New York Times*, August 18, 2002. Reprinted by the San Francisco Chronicle, online at www.sfgate.com/cgi bin/article.cgi?file=/c/a/2002/08/18/MN92685.DTL.
8   Ibid.
9   Power, *A Problem from Hell*, 178.

22

Power Vacuum: Saddam's Fall and the Rise of Iran

General William Tecumseh Sherman—the American Civil War strategist whose march to the sea (including his infamous burning of Atlanta) destroyed the economic infrastructure of the Confederacy, and with it the secessionist government's war-making capacity—knew better than most that "war is hell," a phrase oft-attributed to him. As he told the Mayor of Atlanta (while rejecting his appeal not to burn that city), "you might as well appeal against the thunderstorm as against these terrible hardships of war."[1] And so it is in the post-9/11 maelstrom of continuing warfare, a new era of endless shadow wars against non-state actors operating outside the rules of war. In such an age as we now find ourselves, a contemporary (and appropriate) variant of Sherman's infamous dictum would be "peace is hell." And so it was for Coalition forces in the time that has passed since President Bush announced, perhaps somewhat prematurely: "Mission Accomplished."

The infamous "Bombs of Basra" were a case in point—ushering in a worrisome rise in the level of violence and in the destructive capabilities of Iraq's troublesome insurgents during the peak of their insurgency. But even more worrisome than the tactical lethality of that generation of IEDs deployed by the insurgents was the speculation at the highest levels of both US and British leadership that Tehran's fingerprints could be found in the bomb-makers' new designs—suggesting a regional escalation and internationalization of this internal conflict, as proxy war threatened to overtake civil war, and with that, to increase the risk of Iraq's disintegration.

So while the original strategic objective—the overthrow of the tyrant Saddam Hussein and the consequent eradication of the longer-term threat he posed both to his neighbors and to the West—was quickly and decisively achieved, the early achievement of this strategic objective ushered us into a long twilight period of uncertainty and instability in the new Iraq—where a violent and growing insurgency against the victors and the young democracy that the victors have fostered grew in intensity as the occupation continued.

After Saddam, chaos

Politics, like nature, abhors a vacuum, and the post-Saddam era has been proof positive that the Laws of Thermodynamics are true not just in the world of physics but also in the world of military politics. In the absence of Saddam's secular authoritarian rule, Iraq quickly proved to be a fractious land, a nation forged of asynchronous components that seem at times quite incompatible—whether in the democratic Kurdish north, the theocratic Shiite south, or the seething, disempowered Sunni heartland trapped in between, lacking in both natural resources and political power. And that was just the local neighborhood.

Cross Iraq's borders, and you would find yourself in hostile territory—whether in Baathist-run Syria, Shiite theocratic Iran, Sunni oligarchic Saudi Arabia and Kuwait, or even secular-democratic Turkey, which viewed the empowerment of Iraq's Kurds with trepidation, owing to its own restive Kurdish minority along the border. And in all the porous nooks and crannies, there emerged the new menace of Abu Musab al-Zarqawi, and his ambitious Al Qaeda in Iraq (AQI) organization, which took it upon itself to meet President Bush's "bring it on" challenge head-on, and help fulfill the president's self-fulfilling prophecy that turned Iraq from a stable, though highly repressive, dictatorship, into the frothy and turbulent central front in the war on terror. Iraq's only truly friendly neighbor was the Hashemite Kingdom of Jordan, whose citizens and rulers alike seem quite relieved to be flanked on both its eastern and western frontiers by young democracies—even though it soon found itself in the terrorists' sights.

With such external and internal chaos initially confronting the new Iraq, it was no wonder that the quickly won peace was so Shermanesque.

Containing Iran

With the fall of Saddam, the theocratic regime in Tehran now found itself boxed in, with US-dominated Coalition forces dug in along both its eastern frontier with Afghanistan, and its western frontier with Iraq. One can quite logically speculate that Tehran's strategists would have liked nothing more than to give the Coalition forces a bloody nose, perhaps even to drive Coalition forces from those frontiers, by raising the cost paid in blood by Coalition troops, and thus ratchet up political pressure back home to bring the boys home.

While still lacking proof, both US and British intelligence analysts and political leaders publicly chastised Tehran for its role in the festering Iraqi insurgency—and for seemingly escalating the destructive power of the tool-of-choice used in the shadow war that is the Iraqi insurgency: IEDs, or improved explosive devices. When Saddam's army melted into the night on the eve of the Coalition invasion in March 2003, it left unguarded vast caches of military armaments and explosives. With a light invading army lacking the manpower to secure these many weapons depots, supporters of the old guard and opponents of the new found free and easy access to a treasure trove of destructive tools for their insurgency. With the right engineering know-how, these leftovers from Saddam's arsenal could be jury-rigged to unleash a devastating and hard to control plague of irregular attacks, targeting stray platoons and isolated military convoys with alarming frequency—and making Iraq increasingly difficult to pacify.

The victorious Coalition forces faced no credible opponent in its march to Baghdad, but when they got there they found they did face the specter of an elusive new foe, and its irritatingly destructive IEDs. On the ground, over time, Coalition forces have learned to cope with this threat—up-armoring its tactical wheeled vehicles, co-opting locals whenever possible to break the terror cells operating from the shadows, and deploying new detection technologies to help find IEDs before they are detonated. Were Iraq's borders sealed off entirely, the IED threat may well have begun to fade— but because the new Iraq was so fractious and its frontiers both porous and adjacent to regimes that viewed democracy as anathema, external tactical knowledge appears to have worked its way into Iraq, inspiring a new generation of bomb-makers—and boosting the lethality of their IEDs.

As reported by Eric Schmitt of the *New York Times* on August 5, 2005: "Many of the new, more sophisticated roadside bombs used to attack American and government forces in Iraq have been designed in Iran and shipped in from there, United States military and intelligence officials said Friday, raising the prospect of increased foreign help for Iraqi insurgents."[2] US military commanders were thus expecting that "deadlier bombs could become more common as insurgent bomb makers learn the techniques to make the weapons themselves in Iraq." And, Schmitt added, "just as troubling is that the spread of the new weapons seems to suggest a new and unusual area of cooperation between Iranian Shiites and Iraqi Sunnis to drive American forces out—a possibility that the commanders said they could make little sense of given the increasing violence between the sects in Iraq."

Schmitt explained that "unlike the improvised explosive devices devised from Iraq's vast stockpiles of missiles, artillery shells and other arms, the new weapons are specially designed to destroy armored vehicles," and "feature shaped charges, which penetrate armor by focusing explosive power in a single direction and by firing a metal projectile embedded in the device into the target at high speed." Schmitt noted this "design is crude but effective if the vehicle's armor plating is struck at the correct angle." He cites an unnamed military official who explained "these are among the most sophisticated and most lethal devices we've seen," adding that "it's very serious." However, Schmitt pointed out that there has been "no evidence that the Iranian government is involved."

Schmitt reported that "American commanders say they first saw the use of the new explosives in the predominantly Shiite area of southern Iraq, including Basra, but their use by insurgents steadily migrated into Sunni-majority areas north and west of Baghdad," adding that "the influx of the new explosives comes as allied commanders are stepping up efforts to stop the infiltration of fighters, weapons and equipment along Iraq's porous borders with Iran and Syria." Schmitt explained that "American troops and the insurgents have been engaged for months in an expanding test of tactics and technology, with the guerrillas building bigger and more clever devices and the Americans trying to counter them at each turn." He cited US Brig. Gen. Donald Alston, who explained "the terrorists are trying to adapt to that level of protection that our forces have; they have been motivated to try to find a way to get advantage." Alston admitted "such bombs remain the No. 1 killer of American troops in Iraq."

Blaming Iran

On September 20, 2005, the *Times of London* reported that "Tehran's involvement may be linked to Britain's hardening position on its nuclear programme"—and noted while "attention has been focused on the Sunni Muslim insurgency against US-led forces further north," that "the British have been facing a sharp rise in attacks from an increasingly sophisticated and deadly foe."[3] According to the *Times*, "there are strong suspicions that the bloodshed is being orchestrated with weapons and encouragement from Iran," and that "British officials are convinced that Iran is implicated in the upsurge in violence and suspect it may be connected to Britain's hardening position against Tehran's nuclear programme."[4] The *Times* cited a "secret report" in which "military intelligence warned commanders that attacks on British forces were being deliberately intensified using a new armour-piercing bomb developed in Iran"—and such bombs proved lethal against British troops since the July 16 deaths of Second Lieutenant Richard Shearer, and Privates Phillip Hewett and Leon Spicer.[5]

On September 25, 2005, the *Sunday Times* reported on a "'secret war' against insurgents bringing sophisticated bombs into the country from Iran," and that ever "since the increase in attacks against UK forces two months ago, a 24-strong SAS team has been working out of Basra to provide a safety net to stop the bombers getting into the city from Iran," in an effort to "seal the notoriously porous border using high-technology sensors that monitor movement by night."[6] On October 12, BBC reported that "Iran's military are accused of links to Shia militias in Iraq" and in particular that "specialist bomb-makers targeting British troops in southern Iraq are being trained by an elite arm of Iran's armed forces."[7] BBC cited as its source "UK defence sources" who believe "insurgents making tank-busting explosives, which have killed eight UK soldiers in recent months, are being trained in Iran and Lebanon."[8] Though Tehran denied these claims, BBC reported that British Prime Minister Tony Blair has made the case there is evidence linking the tank-busting IED attacks "either to Iran or its militant, Lebanese allies Hezbollah, but added that officials could not be sure."[9] As BBC quoted Blair, who told a London press conference in London with Iraqi President Jalal Talabani, "there have been new explosive devices used—not just against British troops but elsewhere in Iraq"—and that "the particular nature of those devices lead us either to Iranian elements or to Hezbollah . . . however, we can't be sure of this."[10] Blair's qualification suggested an absence of hard proof—and BBC cited a MoD official who confirmed there is still "no clear proof Iran's Revolutionary Guard was involved."[11] And Tehran denied the British claims, calling them "baseless," and it has "demanded the UK government produce evidence to back up the claims," the BBC reported.[12]

Despite the lack of a smoking gun, Con Coughlin reported in London's *Telegraph* on October 29, 2005, that "Iran's Revolutionary Guards have set up a network of secret smuggling routes to ferry men and equipment into Iraq for attacks on Coalition troops, according to an exiled opposition group"—and that this "smuggling is said to be orchestrated by the guards' elite Quds Force, which has its HQ in the southern Iranian city of Ahwaz."[13] Coughlin specified that "the National Council of Resistance of Iran (NCRI) says commanders are sending a steady stream of agents and bomb-making equipment from a base codenamed 'Fajr' into Iraq, where roadside attacks are carried out against Coalition troops."[14] Coughlin recalled how in August, the *Sunday Telegraph* had reported "Iran was supplying infra-red bombs to Iraqi insurgents," and as such, the British government has "held the Iranians responsible for the deaths of at least eight British soldiers."[15] It noted: "Western Intelligence agencies have reported a sharp increase in Iran's involvement in insurgent operations since Mr. Ahmadinejad was elected in June," and adds that Prime Minister Blair "condemned Iran as a 'threat to world security' after President Mahmoud Ahmadinejad, a former Revolutionary Guards commander, declared that Israel should be 'wiped off the map.'"[16]

On November 1, even *Al Jazeera* reported the rise of a new generation of "sophisticated bombs" and that "US commanders have been voicing increasing concern at the power and sophistication of roadside bombs, the biggest killers of their troops."[17] It added that "devices capable of penetrating armoured vehicles have become more common this year, based on technology US and British officials say has been introduced from Iran."[18]

At a joint press conference with US defense chief Don Rumsfeld and British secretary of state for defense, John Reid, on November 7, 2005, one reporter asked Reid to discuss his "concerns, especially in southern Iraq, with these explosives coming across the border?"[19] Reid replied that "it is our belief that the nature of the devices being used against British troops and possibly elsewhere in Iraq in recent months bear the hallmark of groups like Hezbollah and may well be connected with elements within Iran."[20] But he added that "we don't have the evidence that says this is being backed by the Iranian government, but it is nevertheless worrying, and we've made representations to Iran, because it would obviously not be right for a country to be publicly supporting democratic self-determination in Iraq at the same time as it was allowing or in any way encouraging the use of terrorism or violence."[21] He further added that "we will take the necessary steps to protect our troops" and that "we hope that anyone on the borders of Iraq—whether it's Syria, Iran or anyone else—will desist and make sure that no one is supporting terrorism inside Iraq, or indeed, elsewhere."[22]

At a news briefing on November 29, 2007, with Secretary of Defense Donald Rumsfeld and General Peter Pace, a reporter asked General Pace for his "overall assessment right now of the IED situation? Are attacks up, down? What kinds of new IEDs are you seeing?"[23] Pace replied: "They're increasing the numbers they're using in an attempt to intimidate the Iraqi population. Interestingly, the numbers of IED explosions has gone up. The numbers of casualties from those explosions has stayed level and/or gone down a little bit, which means that our protection mechanisms—our own force protection mechanisms are working. However, we still have a lot to do because this is a thinking enemy, and we need to be thinking through our tactics, techniques and procedures as they change how they employ the IEDs."[24]

News reports have challenged the claims made of an Iran connection to the rising IED threat. In a UPI article published in January 7, 2006, Hannah K. Strange reported that "British parliamentarians and soldiers' families have accused the government of making politically motivated accusations that Iran was involved in killing troops in southern Iraq, after government officials reportedly admitted there was no evidence for doing so."[25]

Strange reported that "government officials have now reportedly acknowledged that there is no evidence, or even credible intelligence, connecting the government in Tehran to the sophisticated bombs which have killed 10 British soldiers in the past eight months"—and that this "apparent U-turn comes three months after Blair told a Downing Street press conference there was evidence to suggest that a type of infra-red triggered explosive device used in deadly attacks against British troops 'and elsewhere in Iraq' did originate in Iran."[26] According to Strange, former Labor defense minister Peter Kilfoyle "accused the Blair government of following President George Bush's obsession with Iran," suggesting this "is part of an almost unconscious urge to support whatever the American policy of the moment might be."[27] Indeed, according to Strange's article, "British officials will now only say that the devices were similar in design and technology to those used by the Lebanese guerilla group Hizbollah, which has ties with Iran and Syria" but while "parts for making explosive devices may have been smuggled over the porous Iran-Iraq border, there was no reliable evidence that the Iranian Revolutionary Guard were the suppliers."[28]

Iran denials

Echoing Strange's report, Iran's *Islamic Republic News Agency* (*IRNA*), which serves as the Foreign Ministry of Iran's official news outlet, reported on January 7, 2006, that "the British government is being accused by MPs and families of soldiers killed in Iraq of politicizing allegations raised against Iran last year similar to the false intelligence used to overthrow Saddam Hussein's regime," also citing the claims made by former Labour defence minister Peter Kilfoyle.[29] *IRNA* reported "his accusation comes after the *Times* reported on Monday that Britain had dropped its high-profile charges of Iranian involvement in supplying sophisticated explosive devices responsible for insurgents killing a series of British soldiers in southern Iraq last summer" and that "government officials were said to now admit that there was no evidence, or even reliable intelligence, connecting the Iranian government to the infra-red triggered bombs which killed 10 British soldiers in the past eight months."[30] However, *IRNA* added that "the Foreign Office in London rejected the latest report in the *Independent* newspaper, saying it was 'simply wrong,' and 'that remains our position. There has, therefore, been no U-turn.'"[31] *IRNA* has reported that it "learned from a party of British journalists visiting Basra" that "commanders on the ground dismissed the allegations against Iran amid suggestions they had been politically motivated."[32]

Whether or not Iran's fingerprints would ever be found on the bombs of Basra, the insurgency would continue to fester and its lethality to grow. And with theocratic Iran next door, threatened by the sudden emergence of American-imposed democracy to both its east and west and increasingly defiant in its pursuit of nuclear weapons, whether or not Tehran was behind the bombs of Basra would in the end be beside the point: so long as Iran's government opposed the democratic movements whose seeds were taking root on both its flanks, and instead pursued its menacing nuclear and ballistic missile programs, peace in the new Iraq, and beyond, could soon again become a Shermanesque hell.

Notes

1 William Tecumseh Sherman, *Memoirs of General W.T. Sherman* (New York: Penguin Classics, 2000), 495.
2 Eric Schmitt, "Some Bombs Used in Iraq Are Made in Iran, U.S. Says," *New York Times*, August 5, 2005.
3 "Iran Blamed as Militias Step Up Basra Attacks," *Times of London,* September 20, 2005.
4 Ibid.
5 Ibid.
6 "SAS in Secret War against Iranian Agents," *Sunday Times*, September 25, 2005.
7 "Iran 'Is Training Basra Killers,'" *BBC News*, October 12, 2005.
8 Ibid.
9 Ibid.
10 Ibid.
11 Ibid.
12 Ibid.
13 "Smuggling Route Opened to Supply Iraqi Insurgents," *Telegraph,* October 29, 2005.
14 Ibid.
15 Ibid.
16 Ibid.
17 "Many Killed in Basra Car Bomb Blast," *Al Jazeera*, November 1, 2005.
18 Ibid.
19 Joint News Briefing with Secretary of Defense Rumsfeld and British Secretary of State for Defense Reid, November 7, 2005, www.defense.gov/transcripts/transcript. aspx?transcriptid=1459.
20 Ibid.
21 Ibid.
22 Ibid.
23 Joint News Briefing with Secretary of Defense Rumsfeld and British Secretary of State for Defense Reid, November 29, 2005, www.defense.gov/transcripts/transcript. aspx?transcriptid=1492.
24 Ibid.
25 Hannah K. Strange, "U.K. 'U-Turn' on Iran Bomb Claims," UPI, January 7, 2006.
26 Ibid.
27 Ibid.

28 Ibid.
29 "UK Politicizing Allegations against Iran: MPs, Families," *Islamic Republic News Agency* (*IRNA*), January 7, 2006.
30 Ibid.
31 Ibid.
32 Ibid.

23

Nuclear Ambitions:
Emergent Ballistic Missile Threats

As Tehran marches closer to the nuclear club,
its neighbors anxiously await the world response

In recent months, Iran's intensifying nuclear ambition has become a critical concern to policymakers around the world, not only to its Gulf neighbors and Israel, which lie within range of Tehran's current missile reach, but also to the United States and Europe, which view a nuclear Iran with trepidation. With the change of helm in Washington, and President Obama's at-times frustrating diplomatic efforts to reengage Tehran in dialogue in the hope of dissuading it from joining the nuclear club, many hoped Iran's determined effort to cross the nuclear chasm could be slowed, and perhaps reversed.

But in response to the White House's extended olive branch, Tehran seemed intent to follow down the path blazed earlier by North Korea, which boldly test-fired a long-range missile on April 5, 2009 in the face of global condemnation. Pyongyang claimed to have successfully launched a Unha-2 rocket carrying the Kwangmyongsong-2 communications satellite into orbit, but Western officials believe it was in fact another test launch of the long-range Taepodong-2 ballistic missile. Just six weeks later, on May 20, Tehran announced it had successfully tested a new medium-range, two-stage solid-fuel missile, the Sejil-2, capable of delivering a nuclear payload 2,500 km—far enough to threaten not just Israel, which views a nuclear Iran as an existential threat, but also American forces deployed across the Middle East and Persian Gulf region, as well as parts of Europe. Like the DPRK a month earlier, Tehran sent its own missile message to the Obama administration, rebuffing its engagement effort and reaffirming its determination to develop its own nuclear deterrent, and thus become immune to the risk of externally imposed regime change of the sort that quickly toppled Iraqi strongman Saddam Hussein six years ago.

Israel responded with its own symbolic counterstatement to Iran: the Israeli Air Force conducted large-scale air exercises, with Iran among its several designated targets. And on Capitol Hill, chairman of the US Joint Chiefs of Staff Admiral Mike Mullen testified on May 21 before the Senate Foreign Relations Committee that he was "one who believes that Iran getting a nuclear weapon is calamitous for the region and for the world," and that a nuclear-armed Iran "generates neighbors who feel exposed, deficient and then develop or buy the capability themselves. The downside, potentially, is absolutely disastrous."[1] He added that the world community must "come together to arrest this growth or the long-term downside for the people in the world is really, really tragic and drastic."[2]

US Secretary of State Hillary Clinton echoed Admiral Mullen's pessimism, telling the US Senate Appropriations Subcommittee a day earlier that a "nuclear-armed Iran with a deliverable weapons system is going to spark an arms race in the Middle East and the greater region," and reminding the senators that President Obama had "made it clear that he is committed to preventing Iran from obtaining nuclear weapons with all of the consequences that that would entail."[3] In a silver lining, she described the emergence of an "alliance which has come together of Israel and many of her Arab neighbors against Iran obtaining nuclear weapons," and she believes this alignment of strategic interests among traditional foes presents "an opportunity that will enable us both to move forward with our engagement regarding Iran and our commitment to pursue diplomacy and to build a multilateral coalition."[4]

James Russell, associate professor of National Security Affairs at the Naval Postgraduate School in Monterey, California, and prolific author and renowned expert on Middle East and Persian Gulf security, has observed that "Iran's Gulf neighbors are extremely concerned that Iran will acquire a nuclear weapon," and as a consequence, "we can expect that they will take steps to ensure that Iran cannot use its nuclear superiority to create a coercive bargaining framework designed to ensure Iran's regional military and political ascendance."[5]

On whether a regional arms race of the sort predicted by Secretary Clinton will result, Russell said he was "reluctant to predict that regional reactions will take the form of a nuclear arms race, but we can expect that states will take corresponding steps to ensure their security. I don't think it's a coincidence that the region's renewed interest in nuclear power has occurred as Iran is demonstrating apparent technical progress in its own enrichment program." Russell added that "we can expect states to take a variety of steps in response to Iran crossing the nuclear threshold. I wouldn't rule anything out. But I'd also say that not all the states will seek a nuclear weapon." Russell explained that America's Gulf allies "have implied security commitments from the United States in the form of defense cooperation agreements that form the legal basis for the forward deployed presence in the Gulf," and that "in those states that are host to significant numbers of US troops, the United States has repeatedly stated that it will use all means at its disposal to protect its troops. The umbrella is thus two-fold: it extends to the states with whom we have defense cooperation agreements as well as to those states that host US forces. This includes such countries as Kuwait, Bahrain, the United Arab Emirates, Jordan, Oman, and—most recently—Iraq. We have commitments conveyed in other ways to Saudi Arabia."

On why Tehran is pursuing the bomb, Russell noted this remains a "source of genuine disagreement, which is really an argument between different theoretical approaches to international relations." He explained that the realist approach, which reflects his view, argues "that Iran is a status quo regional power that is taking rational steps to protect itself and further its influence over regional rivals." But "others argue that Iran is motivated by an ideology and religious fervor stemming from the Islamic revolution." Russell believes that Iran's nuclear ambition is motivated "mostly from its analysis of its security dilemma. Iran feels both threatened by the US military presence and the US relationships with its regional rivals in the Gulf and is looking for ways to counter this threat while simultaneously searching for ways to increase its leverage in the regional balance of power."

As an adherent of the realist school of international relations, Russell said he is "less drawn to cultural and religious factors in explaining regional tensions and conflict. Clearly, however, in the Gulf region, religious and ideological differences form part of the narrative that frames the mutual suspicion between Iran and Sunni states of the Arabian peninsula." In his view, "Iran's relationships with Hizbollah and Hamas are examples of a realist-oriented regional power that seeks to use a variety of different levers to enhance its power and influence over regional rivals. Hamas, for example, has little ideological or religious connection with Iran. It is purely a tactical alliance of convenience for both parties."

Just how close Iran is to becoming a nuclear weapons state remains difficult to ascertain. Russell commented that "it seems clear that Iran eventually will achieve the ability to build a nuclear power infrastructure that includes an indigenous uranium enrichment capability. They are marching towards this objective." But "as for weaponizing the program, that's a more difficult call in terms of timelines—but there is again enough circumstantial evidence to suggest their intent to weaponize." But for the moment, it appears Iran has yet to cross the nuclear chasm: "I don't believe they have reached the point yet where they could declare 'virtual' arsenal," and Iran already has a weapon, but has not yet tested it. And while some observers suggest America's preemptive actions in Iraq, overthrowing Iraqi strongman Saddam Hussein, has fueled Iran's nuclear ambition, Russell pointed out that "Iran's interest in nuclear power goes back to the 1970s," and that "Ayatollah Khomeini re-started the program in the mid-1980s during the Iran-Iraq war." Russell thus believes we "must see Iran's interest in nuclear issues as part of an historic continuum."

On the potential emergence of an Israel-Arab alliance, or at least an alignment of strategic interests in response to a nuclear Iran, Russell noted that "there is now speculation to this effect—that a Saudi/Egyptian/Jordanian rapprochement with Israel is being encouraged by the prospect of a nuclear Iran. Some even believe that these states would tacitly support Israeli strikes on Iran's nuclear infrastructure." But while such a rapprochement may be a diplomatic silver lining to the darker nuclear cloud hanging over the region, Russell cautions that we should not be overly optimistic at this juncture. "My view is that the world is closer than it thinks on an escalation spiral that could lead to the use of nuclear weapons in the Middle East. This is an outcome I hope never happens. It would be a global catastrophe." As Russell explained: "Israel is committed to maintaining its nuclear monopoly and will tolerate no existential threat to the state—or at least, that's what the leadership keeps saying. Iran appears implacably committed to its right to enrichment and frankly has a history that draws into question its peaceful intentions. Thus you have two parties with two objectives that are in no way symmetrical and neither shows any inclination to negotiate away their objective. If Israel attacks Iran, we face the prospect of a wider regional war that could involve non-state actors, non-conventional weapons, and terrorist-type attacks. It's a lethal mix and one that could prompt escalation by Israel and/or the United States." Russell thus concluded that the region was "marching towards a confrontation that somehow must be defused by the US."

North Korea's emergent ballistic missile threat

America traditionally celebrates its July 4 Independence Day holiday with brilliant displays of fireworks, often choreographed to live orchestral music ending with the thunderous finale of Tchaikovsky's *1812 Overture*. Never subtle, the world's lone superpower proudly celebrates its independence from colonial rule with an explosive fervor. Back in 2006, however, America's explosive Independence Day fireworks took a more ominous form, as the emergent nuclear power, the Democratic People's Republic of Korea (DPRK), defied warnings from the international community, breaking its eight-year-old moratorium on ballistic missile testing with a series of well-timed, and highly symbolic, ballistic missile tests scheduled to coincide with America's beloved Fourth of July celebration.

The DPRK fired seven missiles over a two-day period starting in the wee hours of July 5, 2006, local time—or mid-day on July 4, 2006, in the United States half a world away. According to the *Power and Interest Report*, which issued an "intelligence brief" on North Korea's missile tests on July 5, Pyongyang's intent for its missile tests was "to coincide with the Independence Day holiday in the United States, and also possibly with the Discovery space shuttle launch in Florida," firing off a "series of short- and medium-range missiles and also apparently test[ing] its new Taepodong-2 multi-stage missile with a range of 3,500–4,300 kilometers (2,190–2,690 miles), enough to hit Alaska — that rocket, however, failed shortly after launch," much like its more recent launch effort.[6] According to Michael Needham, director of the Asian Studies Institute at the Heritage Foundation: "At approximately 3:30 AM local time (2:30 PM EDT, just minutes after the launch of the space shuttle Discovery), North Korea began its testing of seven missiles. Six appear to have fired successfully; these were Scud and Nodong missiles, which have been part of the North Korean arsenal—and available for sale on international markets—for years. The remaining missile was a Taepodong 2, which has been on its launch pad since May."[7]

Heritage Foundation policy analyst for Northeast Asia Balbina Y. Hwang believes the DPRK's actions, which were "in violation of North Korea's international agreements," were "designed to goad the United States into direct bilateral talks." She believes "the US must not take the bait," as "no good will come from rewarding North Korea for its belligerent behavior."[8] So far, the United States has refrained from rewarding Pyongyang for its resumption of ballistic missile testing, and continues to promote the resumed Six-Party Talks as the one appropriate mechanism for resolving regional security issues on the Korean Peninsula, and more broadly in Northeast Asia, in the wake of Pyongyang's nuclearization and its increasingly robust ballistic missile capabilities.

Yet while parties to the Six-Party Talks—China, Russia, South Korea, North Korea, the United States, and Japan—all have much to gain from the continued pursuit of a multilateral solution to this regional problem, their individual reactions to the July 4 missile tests reveal a wide diversity of opinion on how best to respond to Pyongyang's provocation—revealing fault lines within this six nation group that could result in a fracture of the Six-Party process, which in turn could lead to unilateral action such as preemptive military action again the DPRK. As reported by DefenseTech.org, the resumption of ballistic missile testing by Pyongyang in 2006, it was feared, could "ignite a political chain reaction in Japan, the United States and China, which have been trying to re-engage North Korea in stalled talks about its nuclear weapons program," and the result could be that "the Bush administration might step up financing for missile defense; Japan might increase its missile defense efforts as well, while militant Japanese politicians might push to reconsider the nation's nuclear weapons options."[9]

China's *Xinhua* newspaper reported that NATO called for "a firm response from the international community," as Pyongyang's "development, deployment and proliferation" of ballistic missile technologies "pose a serious threat" to both Northeast Asia and the world. NATO expressed "grave concern" about the missile tests, noting Pyongyang's "missile programs and provocative actions necessitate a firm response from the international community."[10] NATO called on Pyongyang to "immediately cease the development of long-range missiles," and to return to the Six-Party Talks "without precondition," and to "completely and verifiably eliminate its nuclear weapons and related programs."[11] *Xinhua* reported that Italy's Foreign Minister, Massimo D'Alema, responded to the DPRK's missile tests by noting he was "deeply disturbed and very concerned" with Pyongyang's resumption of ballistic missile testing, telling the Italian News Agency *ANSA* that "Pyongyang's actions will certainly complicate the current deadlock in negotiations regarding North Korea's nuclear potential to which Italy has offered and will continue to offer its contribution."[12] And Belgian Foreign Minister Karel De Gucht said in a statement that the July 4 missile tests were "a dangerous provocation," which would boost regional tensions and threaten the peace; De Gucht called for economic and above all, political sanctions, to be taken against the DPRK.[13] Even Russian President Vladimir Putin responded critically to the DPRK missile tests, telling an interactive webcast that "we are disappointed over what is happening in that area," as did China, which had sought to persuade Pyongyang not to test-launch its barrage of missiles. As China's Foreign Ministry spokesman Liu Jianchao said in a press release on July 5: "We are seriously concerned with what had happened." *Xinhua* also reported South Korea's concerns, citing President Roh's spokesman, Jung Tae-ho, who said "President Roh and President Bush talked on the telephone between 7:50 a.m. local time and 8 a.m. local time and agreed to make joint diplomatic efforts to solve the missile problem," adding that "Seoul and Washington would resolve the problem through close consultations with China, Japan and Russia."[14]

Much to the concern of its neighbors, one of the nations to come out swinging most aggressively was Japan, whose pacific, post-WWII policy of non-militarization seemed to now be at risk. As *New York Times* reporter James Joyner explained in his July 10 article: "Japan was badly rattled by North Korea's missile tests last week and several government officials openly discussed whether the country ought to take steps to better defend itself, including setting up the legal framework to allow Tokyo to launch a preemptive strike against Northern missile sites."[15] As then chief cabinet secretary Shinzo Abe, later to be Japan's prime minister and now leader of Japan's opposition Liberal Democratic Party, bluntly announced: "If we accept that there is no other option to prevent an attack . . . there is the view that attacking the launch base of the guided missiles is within the constitutional right of self-defense. We need to deepen discussion.'"[16]

Appeasing the DPRK?

Caught between an increasingly bellicose Japan and a nuclear-armed North Korea, South Korea quickly condemned the Japanese rhetoric of preemption. As reported in the *International Herald Tribune*: "South Korea angrily accused Japan of arrogant and reckless remarks Tuesday, a day after Japanese leaders raised what South Koreans consider a chilling scenario: a pre-emptive strike on North Korea that would violate Japan's Constitution."[17] Jung Tae Ho, a spokesman for President Roh Moo Hyun, pledged that South Korea "will strongly react to the arrogance and senseless remarks of Japanese political leaders who intend to amplify a crisis on the Korean Peninsula with dangerous and provocative rhetoric such as 'pre-emptive strike.'"[18]

Oddly, South Korea seemed less concerned about the increased lethality of the DPRK's missile force—which was now poised to threaten the homeland of the United States, South Korea's principle military ally and protector, potentially undermining America's half-century-long policy of extended deterrence. China similarly responded to Japan's bluster with criticism. On the government of China's website, Gov.cn, China's Foreign Ministry spokeswoman Jiang Yu "criticized on Wednesday Japanese remarks of making 'a preemptive strike' against the Democratic People's Republic of Korea (DPRK), calling the move 'extremely irresponsible.'"[19] Jiang explained that Japan's "remarks made at a time when the international community is trying all efforts of peaceful diplomacy are 'extremely irresponsible' and hard to understand." According to Gov.cn, Jiang described Japan's move to be "like adding fuel to the flames, and it would only severely interfere with the international diplomatic efforts and aggravate tensions in Northeast Asia, which is what the people of all countries would not want to see."[20]

However, prior to the missile tests, Beijing played a more even hand in its reaction to the DPRK's preparations to resume ballistic missile tests. Professor Lyman Miller, an Asia expert on the faculty of the US Naval Postgraduate School, recalled how "before the North Korean missile launches, Beijing's public posture in response to apparent preparations to test a Taepodong-2 long-range missile had sought both to discourage Pyongyang from escalating tensions on the Korean peninsula by proceeding with its test launch and to encourage restraint on the part of Washington and other capitals in the region."[21]

Miller noted that "lower level Chinese commentary made it plain that Beijing was irritated at Pyongyang and saw renewed missile firings as a serious obstacle to the

Six-Party Talks," as illustrated by a commentary in the June 21 edition of the Shanghai party newspaper *Wen Hui Bao* that stated "it is not good to play with fire, and pouring oil on a fire is an act that should not be adopted. If a gun goes off accidentally, peace and stability in northeast Asia is bound to be threatened, and other countries in the region will also be involved."[22] As well, Miller noted, the "Canton newspaper *Guangzhou Ribao* carried a commentary by China Institute of International Studies analyst Zhao Qinghai" on June 21 that "predicted that a North Korean missile test would 'create new factors of uncertainty in northeast Asia . . . Should the DPRK carry out the test, it will cause an anti-DPRK wave among the public in Japan, the United States, and elsewhere, and it is possible that US and Japanese policy toward the DPRK will harden.'"[23] And on June 24, Miller noted, "the PRC-owned communist Hong Kong newspaper *Wen Wei Po* carried a commentary by Phoenix television commentator Qiu Zhenhai suggested that Pyongyang's resumption of missile testing would 'not only complicate the regional security situation, but also put China and Russia in a more difficult situation and encourage hard-line forces in the United States and Japan.'"[24]

Miller observed that "low-level Chinese commentary also made plain the hopes Beijing's official statements conveyed implicitly that Washington would respond calmly to the North Korean missile test preparations and firings," such as the June 21 commentary in the Shanghai newspaper *Dongfang Zaobao* by Fudan University's Institute of International Studies vice president Shen Dingli, "a politically well-connected academic well known to American counterparts, that urged both Pyongyang and Washington as 'stakeholders' to avoid steps that exacerbate the situation," singling out the United States, "in particular, Shen observed, 'as a big and powerful country should be better able to keep its cool and keep the situation under control, rather than be driven by the situation.'"[25]

Sanctioning sanctions

Both Japan and the United States called for a resolution to toughen sanctions against North Korea after the missile tests, efforts strongly opposed by both China and South Korea. As reported in *The Australian*, "Japan is poised to impose financial sanctions next week aimed at hurting the high echelons of Kim Jong-il's regime. Japan will follow Washington in freezing assets and bank accounts of 12 North Korean or Pyongyang-aligned business groups and an unnamed individual."[26] *The Australian* noted these efforts are opposed by South Korea, which seeks to avoid increasing tensions between the two Koreas.[27] Even more strenuous in its rejection of sanctions was China. As Chinese foreign minister Jiang told a press conference, "if approved, [sanctions] will aggravate contradictions and increase tension," and "will harm peace and stability in the Korean Peninsula and Northeast Asian region and hurt efforts to resume six-party talks as well as lead to the UN Security Council splitting."[28]

South Korea's angry rebuke of Japan's determined, and one might argue, appropriately defensive, response to Pyongyang's latest round of missile testing eclipsed its own muted reaction to the tests, suggested that Seoul was more worried about the survival of the DPRK than about the external military capability of the DPRK. Similarly, China's vociferous rejection of sanctions suggests it was similarly more concerned with the economic viability of the DPRK—this may well be a result of the fact that both South Korea and China would bear the greatest burden should the DPRK collapse, with massive flows of refugees likely to stream across both borders, and a staggering price-tag accompanying the regime's collapse.

So while Japan and the United States fear most the potential lethality of an ICBM-armed DPRK, South Korea and China—both unlikely to be on the receiving end of a DPRK nuclear assault given Pyongyang's goal to reunite with the former, and its dependence on the continued friendship and economic support of the latter—are most worried about the economic and political survival of the DPRK itself, since the alternative would prove costly to both neighbors.

The return of Japanese militarism and the specter of a nuclear Japan

With North Korea once again upping its nuclear ante, and its concerted determination to develop a truly intercontinental capacity to lob nuclear weapons, there is speculation that Japan might be pushed to an even more aggressive posture—beyond mere talk of preemption to bolder action, such as crossing the nuclear chasm itself. According to a "Review & Outlook" article from the *Wall Street Journal* (*Opinion Journal*) on July 16, 2006, for "60 years Japan has refrained from becoming a nuclear power and remained militarily quiescent," even though Japan has the capacity to quickly nuclearize, with estimates ranging from mere days to weeks for it to do so.[29] According to the *Wall Street Journal*, "that particular sun may be rising again, however, thanks to the support by China and South Korea for the military threats of North Korean dictator Kim Jong-il."[30]

While Article 9 of Japan's 1946 Constitution "bars military force in settling international disputes and prohibits Japan from maintaining a military for the purpose of warfare," Japan nonetheless "has 243,000 men under arms and one of the world's most technologically capable militaries," and "only the US, Russia and China spend more on defense."[31] The *Wall Street Journal* recalled how "North Korea's first Taepodong missile test, in 1998, shocked many Japanese and elevated national security as a political issue, leading to the election of hawkish Prime Minister Junichiro Koizumi in 2001."[32] Indeed, as *Voice of America* reported on September 3, 1998:

> Clearly, one of the week's major foreign policy issues was the unexpected test of the latest North Korean medium-range missile, the Taepodong One, which has a range of about 1930 km. That's far enough to hit all of South Korea, almost all of inhabited Japan, and even the capital of Taiwan, Taipei, with a nuclear warhead or poison gas. If the North Korean goal was to get the world's attention, in the midst of the Monica Lewinsky scandal in the United States, and the meltdown of the Russian economic and political systems abroad, that goal was achieved. Very

few dailies of any size around the world, failed to comment on the significance of the test.[33]

Voice of America described Japan's response to the 1998 DPRK's missile test, which the Japanese viewed to be both "regrettable" and "dangerous,"[34] and commented that Japan's "reaction was quite strong as well, in part because the missile flew over the main island of Honshu, before falling into the Pacific."[35] Tokyo's daily *Yomiuri* editorialized that "Japan remains in utter shock following North Korea's test-firing."[36] And, *Nihon Keizai* editorialized that "whatever the reason, we cannot but call the North Korean motive extremely regrettable."[37] Interestingly, the 1998 missile test took place just a few days prior to the 50th anniversary of the founding of the DPRK—a point noted by *Voice of America,* which reported that "some newspapers saw this as a kind of advertising campaign for North Korean missile sales, while others figured it was a sort of show of force or celebration marking the 50th anniversary of the founding of North Korea on September 9th."[38] If anything, the North Koreans know how to celebrate Independence Day with a bang—whether its own, as it did in September 1998, or America's, as it did on July 4, 2006, or as it more recently celebrated the 100th year anniversary of the birth of its founder, Kim Il-Sung.

The *Wall Street Journal* pointed out after the 2006 missile tests how "virtually every poll since the North Korean test also shows overwhelming public anxiety about North Korea and support for a strong response."[39] And despite Japan's "pacifist constitution, to which Mr. Koizumi has proposed major revisions, including jettisoning Article 9," the *Journal* noted Mr Abe—who was widely quoted in the world's press on the possibility of a preemptive strike by Japan—was "the leading contender to succeed Mr. Koizumi as PM" and who "also favors constitutional revision."[40] The *Journal* thus believes that "North Korea's provocations have introduced a threatening new instability," and explained "the combination of China's strategic cynicism toward a client dictatorship and South Korea's naive appeasement is making that neighborhood a much more dangerous place."[41] As a consequence, the *Journal* believes that "if North Korea continues to defy the world and the world continues to do nothing, a more militarily assertive, and probably nuclear-armed, Japan is inevitable."[42]

Even if a nuclearized Japan seems far-fetched to more moderate analysts, the prospect of a militarily more aggressive, and rhetorically more bellicose, Japan, is likely. As the Heritage Foundation's Hwang recalled: "North Korea's Taepodong 1 test over Japan in 1998 was a wake-up call that led Tokyo to cooperate with Washington on a missile defense system," and "a new launch would not only bolster Japanese efforts to erect defensive capabilities against North Korea but would also likely spur the US Congress to increase its support for missile defense efforts."[43] As well, Hwang anticipated that "such aggression from North Korea could play a role in selecting the future leadership of Japan."[44] Hwang noted Japanese Prime Minister Koizumi is "preparing to step down in September, and polls indicate that Shinzo Abe, who has taken a strong stance against North Korea and China, trails moderate candidate Yasuo Fukuda. A North Korean missile test could aid Abe's campaign, reducing the possibility of a diplomatic reconciliation between North Korea and Japan."[45]

An end to Japanese pacifism

While Japan openly contemplated preemption in the wake of the July 4 missile tests, the United States considered it before the test took place—with some prominent defense policy experts and elder statesmen calling on the US government to act preemptively with force. Among the most influential of these calls for preemptive military action was an op-ed article published by the *Washington Post* on June 22, less than two weeks before the missile tests, by two former top defense officials in the Clinton administration—former defense secretary William J. Perry, and his assistant secretary, Ashton B. Carter.[46]

In their widely discussed and controversial article, the authors recalled how "last time North Korea tested such a missile, in 1998, it sent a shock wave around the world, but especially to the United States and Japan, both of which North Korea regards as archenemies," and both "recognized immediately that a missile of this type makes no sense as a weapon unless it is intended for delivery of a nuclear warhead."[47] Even more worrisome, in the eight years that have passed since its 1998 missile test, North Korea has become a more menacing military threat, and today "openly boasts of its nuclear deterrent, has obtained six to eight bombs' worth of plutonium since 2003, and is plunging ahead to make more in its Yongbyon reactor."[48] Perry and Carter thus asked, rhetorically: "Should the United States allow a country openly hostile to it and armed with nuclear weapons to perfect an intercontinental ballistic missile capable of delivering nuclear weapons to US soil?"[49]

Their response: "We believe not."[50] They argued that if the DPRK "persists in its launch preparations, the United States should immediately make clear its intention to strike and destroy the North Korean Taepodong missile before it can be launched"—perhaps by means of "a cruise missile launched from a submarine carrying a high-explosive warhead," whose "effect on the Taepodong would be devastating."[51] While such a bold act "undoubtedly carries risk," Perry and Carter believe that "the risk of continuing inaction in the face of North Korea's race to threaten this country would be greater."[52]

Overhyping the DPRK missile threat; echoes of the "missile gap"?

Missile anxiety has long been a tool in the war chest of American politicians, dating back to the dawn of the missile age. Indeed, as a young presidential candidate, John F. Kennedy sought to win votes with some tough talk of his own about what he and his team described as a "missile gap," leaving the United States vulnerable to the Soviet Union's strategic nuclear superiority. After the election, it turned out that there was indeed no missile gap at all, and that the United States had in fact enjoyed a substantial strategic advantage over the Soviet Union at the time. But the fear was so great that America ramped up its ballistic missile force, pushing the Soviet Union to react in kind—driving a major escalation in the Cold War's arms race.

With North Korea's missile testing and emerging nuclear capability, some critics sense a similar hype-cycle at work. These critics of a bellicose reaction to North Korea's aggressive missile diplomacy believe the military threat from Pyongyang has been vastly overstated. Indeed, one expert, Dartmouth College associate professor David Kang, coauthor of *Nuclear North Korea: A Debate on Engagement Strategies,* who was a visiting professor at Korea University, argued the July 4 missile test was in fact a failure—and an embarrassing one at that.[53] As Kang explained: "No matter what the cause of the missile test, its failure—within the first minute of flight—was a major setback for North Korea," and "if North Korean leader Kim Jong-il was hoping to impress other countries with his nation's military prowess, he failed in the most public of ways."[54]

Kang believes "North Korea's missile threat has been far over-hyped in the Western media," and pointed out that "not only is it extraordinarily difficult to build a missile that can go six thousand miles and land where you want it, actually putting a warhead that will blow up when it is supposed to makes the task infinitely more difficult."[55] He recalled how Pyongyang's "first test of this missile failed in 1998, and the second failed yesterday," leading him to conclude that "North Korea is a long way from having a deliverable nuclear missile system—and most analysts estimate it may be well over a decade before they can hope to achieve this capability."[56]

Kang explained that the DPRK's 2006 missile test, rather than an irrational or aggressive provocation by a menacing DPRK, was in fact its "response to recent coercive measures by the United States with their own show of force, in order to let the US know that North Korea will not back down."[57] Kang recalled how "the past nine months has seen the US put consistent low-level pressure on North Korea, from sanctioning banks in Macao that deal with North Korean currency to rhetorical pressure on North Korea's deplorable human rights record." As Kang explained: "North Korea has a history of responding to pressure with more pressure, and the North Korean leader, Kim Jong-il, may have thought it important that he show the US that its tactics will not go unanswered."

Other analysts who think the DPRK's missile threat was overstated are chronicled by DefenseTech.org. For instance, the Center for Defense Information's missile guru, Victoria Samson, "cautions us not to get too caught up in the hype," explaining that she believes "the whole hullabaloo about this now showing that North Korea can strike all of the United States is just that—a hullabaloo."[58] Similarly, "Arms Control Wonk Jeffrey Lewis reminds us that this "Taepodong-2 isn't North Korea's name for its missile; it's an American designation for a system we really don't know much about," so much so that "headlines about 'A MISSILE THAT CAN REACH AMERICA' are a bit on the misleading side."[59] Lewis cited testimony from General Burwell B. Bell, the commander of US Forces Korea, who admits in "the years since the late '90s, the last six, seven years, we have seen very little activity by the North Koreans to actively continue to develop and test long-range missile systems," and while "there's no doubt in my mind that they have the capability to begin more technological investigation and to begin a regiment to lead to testing and potentially to lead to fielding," for the moment, "there's no evidence of it."[60]

Within this context, the failure of the DPRK's Taepodong-2 missile on July 4, 2006, can be viewed as a far less menacing threat than some more anxious analysts would like us to perceive. Nonetheless, according to Heritage Foundation's Michael Needham, such a threat should not be prudently overlooked: "A fully functioning Taepodong 2 missile could potentially strike the western United States, according to defense estimates. But North Korean ICBM technology is not yet fully functional. Roughly 40 seconds into its flight, the Taepodong 2 failed and crashed approximately 200 miles west of Japan in the Sea of Japan. This is good news in the short term—but the North Koreans will be able to analyze what went wrong and use that information to attempt to fix it. This test, despite the missile's failure, is a step towards an operational North Korean ICBM."[61]

Toward a political solution?

Dartmouth's Kang observed how "most reactions to the missile test have focused on military solutions, such as calls to preempt the missile launch or hopes that the theater missile defense system will be successful," but his view was that "the North Korean problem is political, not military, and solving it will require a political solution."[62] Rather than take a risky and violent path, Kang believes "a strategy of economic engagement that saturates North Korean citizens with capitalist ideas and slowly changes their mindset while raising their living standards is the best strategy for the United States to pursue."[63]

A similar solution was proposed by Christopher P. Twomey, a China expert on the faculty of the US Naval Postgraduate School. He believes that "the North Korea proliferation problem is one of the two most dangerous flashpoints in East Asia today," at whose root lies "many complex issues: the legacy of Cold War divisions; nationalism in Northeast Asia; Sino-American rivalry for leadership and allies; proliferation of weapons of mass destruction (both within the region and beyond); and finally, humanitarian tragedy."[64] Twomey observed that "at the end of the day, North Korea perceives robust incentives to continue with its nuclear program," and likely "views a wide range of US policies aimed at directly threatening its regime, regardless of how those might be perceived in the United States."[65] Added Twomey: "Given that, nuclear weapons are likely to look very attractive to the North."[66]

With China "unlikely to press hard enough to change that"—given the strength of North Korean perceptions on this matter, and because "Beijing fears its most potent pressure tactics will lead to regime collapse and violence or chaos on the Peninsula," Twomey believes that "instead of reversing North Korean proliferation through Chinese pressure, the goals of American policy makers should be more narrowly focused on amelioration of the threat in the short term coupled with moves aimed to support the ongoing reform process in North Korea that will eventually integrate it in the region and undermine its xenophobic threat perceptions."[67]

Notes

1   As cited by Andrew Gray, "Iran Nuclear Bomb Would Be Calamitous—US Military," Reuters, May 21, 2009, http://uk.reuters.com/article/idUKN2140020320090521.

2   Ibid.

3 Voice of America, "Clinton: Middle East May Start Arms Race If Iran Gets Nukes," *Voice of America*, May 20, 2009, www.voanews.com/english/news/a-13-2009-05-20-voa59-68786472.html.

4 Ibid.

5 Barry Zellen, "Countdown to a Nuclear Iran," SecurityInnovator.com, May 1, 2009, http://securityinnovator.com/index.php?articleID=15839&sectionID=29. Subsequent quotations from Russell are from this article.

6 "Intelligence Brief: North Korea's Missile Tests," *Power and Interest Report*, July 5, 2006, www.pinr.com/report.php?ac=view_report&report_id=521&language_id=1.

7 Michael A. Needham, "Responding to North Korea's Missile Provocation," Heritage Foundation Web Memo #1142, July 5, 2006, www.heritage.org/Research/AsiaandthePacific/wm1142.cfm.

8 Balbina Y. Hwang, PhD, "A North Korean Missile Test: Implications for the U.S. and the Region," Heritage Foundation Web Memo #1134, June 20, 2006, www.heritage.org/Research/AsiaandthePacific/wm1134.cfm.

9 "North Korea: Missile Hype? (Updated)," DefenseTech.org, June 20, 2006, www.defensetech.org/archives/002512.html.

10 "DPRK's Missile Test-Firing Draws more Reactions Worldwide," *Xinhua*, July 6, 2006, http://english.people.com.cn/200607/06/eng20060706_280605.html.

11 Ibid.

12 Ibid.

13 Ibid.

14 "World Continues to Act over DPRK Missile Tests," July 6, 2006, *Xinhua*, http://news3.xinhuanet.com/english/2006-07/06/content_4803076.htm; "China Expresses Serious Concern over DPRK's Missile Test-Firing," July 5, 2006, *Xinhua*, http://news3.xinhuanet.com/english/2006-07/06/content_4803076.htm.

15 James Joyner, "Japan Considering Preemptive Strike on North Korea," *New York Times*, July 10, 2006.

16 Ibid.

17 Choe Sang-Hun, "Seoul Assails Tokyo on Pre-Emption," *International Herald Tribune*, July 11, 2006, www.iht.com/articles/2006/07/11/news/missile.php.

18 Ibid.

19 "China criticizes Japanese remarks of 'preemptive strike' against DPRK, July 13, 2006, www.gov.cn/misc/2006-07/13/content_334355.htm.

20 Ibid.

21 Lyman Miller, "Beijing's Pyongyang Dilemma: Encouraging International Patience with a Troublesome Ally," *Strategic Insights* V, Number 7 (September 2006), www.ccc.nps.navy.mil/si/2006/Sep/millerSep06.asp.

22 Ibid.

23 Ibid.

24 Ibid.

25 Ibid.

26 Peter Alford, "South Korea Disowns US-Japan Sanctions on North," *The Australian*, July 16, 2006, www.theaustralian.news.com.au/story/0,20867,20420518-2703,00.html.

27 Ibid.

28 Ibid.

29 *Wall Street Journal Opinion Journal*, "A Nuclear Japan? Pyongyang's Protectors Are Reviving Tokyo's Military Power," July 16, 2006, www.opinionjournal.com/editorial/feature.html?id=110008650.

30 Ibid.
31 Ibid.
32 Ibid.
33 Andrew N. Guthrie, "North Korea's Missile Test Gets Attention," *Voice of America*, September 3, 1998, www.fas.org/news/dprk/1998/980903-dprk-ed.htm.
34 Ibid.
35 Ibid.
36 Ibid.
37 Ibid.
38 Ibid.
39 "A Nuclear Japan? Pyongyang's Protectors Are Reviving Tokyo's Military Power."
40 Ibid.
41 Ibid.
42 Ibid.
43 Hwang, "A North Korean Missile Test."
44 Ibid.
45 Ibid.
46 Ashton B. Carter and William J. Perry, "If Necessary, Strike and Destroy: North Korea Cannot Be Allowed to Test This Missile," *Washington Post*, June 22, 2006, www.washingtonpost.com/wp-dyn/content/article/2006/06/21/AR2006062101518.html.
47 Ibid.
48 Ibid.
49 Ibid.
50 Ibid.
51 Ibid.
52 Ibid.
53 David Kang, "The Best U.S. Response to North Korea's Failed Missile Test," *PBS' NOW*, July 7, 2006, www.pbs.org/now/shows/227/north-korea-missile-test.html.
54 Ibid.
55 Ibid.
56 Ibid.
57 Ibid.
58 "North Korea: Missile Hype? (Updated),"
59 Ibid.
60 Ibid.
61 Needham, "Responding to North Korea's Missile Provocation,"
62 Kang, "The Best U.S. Response to North Korea's Failed Missile Test."
63 Ibid.
64 Christopher P. Twomey, "China Policy towards North Korea and Its Implications for the United States: Balancing Competing Concerns," *Strategic Insights* V, No. 7 (September 2006), www.ccc.nps.navy.mil/si/2006/Sep/TwomeySep06.asp.
65 Ibid.
66 Ibid.
67 Ibid.

24

Securing the "High Frontier": Missile Defense, from Hype to Hope

A quarter century after Ronald Reagan unveiled his "Star Wars" vision, ballistic missile defense is ready for action

With emergent ballistic missile threats emanating from both one-time Axis of Evil members North Korea and Iran, America remains engaged in its continuing space-age effort to protect its homeland from the risks of rogue missile attack. America has been less worried about the risks presented by the world's more mature nuclear states, who have shown considerable restraint since crossing the nuclear chasm—with occasional and gravely worrisome exceptions, such as when India and Pakistan came to the brink of nuclear war in 2002, and 40 years earlier when the United States and its Soviet opponent came to the nuclear brink over Moscow's ill-conceived attempt to deploy nuclear missiles in Cuba in 1962. While so far the world's nuclear states have shown remarkable maturity in possession of this "absolute" weapon, concern has shifted to the less rational, and harder to deter, substate entities like Al Qaeda, with no homeland to hold hostage under the cold but persuasive logic of the "balance of terror," as well as the new, and inexperienced, nuclear states like North Korea, and emergent aspiring nuclear states like Iran.

Up against an apocalyptic, nihilistic, opponent, all bets are off, and any presumption of rationality or restraint is suspect. As for the nuclear rogue states like North Korea—which revealed the fruits of its nuclear ambition with its May 25, 2009 atomic test, following its earlier unsuccessful but nonetheless rattling ICBM tests—or the Iranians, who share with Pyongyang the aspiration to be both a nuclear state and a missile power, no one can be sure if they would join the more *mature* nuclear club, or transform the largely stable *balance of terror* into something even worse: an *imbalance* of terror.

And so, in preparation for such a scenario of doom, America has been steadily working toward the development of a multi-tiered ballistic missile defense system (BMDS). Such a dream, of an effective nuclear defense, was most famously presented by President Ronald Reagan over 25 years ago, in his famous "Star Wars" speech on March 23, 1983. That's when he challenged the architects of Mutual Assured Destruction (MAD) with a simpler vision: "What if free people could live secure in the knowledge that their security did not rest upon the threat of instant US retaliation to deter a Soviet attack; that we could intercept and destroy strategic ballistic missiles before they reached our own soil or that of our allies? I know this is a formidable technical task, one that may not be accomplished before the end of this century. . . .

But isn't worth every investment necessary to free the world from the threat of nuclear war? We know it is!"[1]

Dr Jeffrey Larsen—president of Larsen Consulting Group and member of the faculty of the Korbel School of International Studies at the University of Denver, Northwestern University, and Texas A&M University, where he teaches national security and strategic studies—is a retired USAF lieutenant colonel and holds a doctorate from Princeton University. As he recalled during an interview: "I remember watching Reagan's 1983 speech—I was actually on nuclear alert in Strategic Air Command that day—and I later discovered that many of my fellow Air Force officers didn't believe in a missile defense system, that they didn't understand it—they expressed all the standard critiques that we've come to know: that it was too expensive, or wouldn't work, or would undermine deterrence, and so on. But I saw in that speech a real vision, a way out of the absurdity of Mutual Assured Destruction (MAD)—President Reagan had incredible foresight by announcing this. I've been a firm believer in the concept ever since—and I applaud all the successes. We've made a lot of progress."[2]

Larsen explained that the "American Constitution calls for the Federal government to create a military force to defend the people and the territory of this country—but throughout the Cold War we were *not* defending ourselves, we had no defenses. We were intentionally retaining our societal vulnerability as one side of MAD; the idea being that if both societies were vulnerable then neither side would launch first, and therefore through deterrence we can maintain the peace. The same people thought defenses were destabilizing—and made the side that had defenses think they can strike first. Those arguments may have been logically sound given the relationship at the time between the two superpowers, but they were morally reprehensible—to leave the continental United States vulnerable to attack is no way to defend this country. We must move from an offensive-based deterrence strategy to a system based on mutual defense rather than deterrence."

In the quarter century since Reagan outlined his vision for missile defense, Larsen observed, "we've been through various versions of the missile defense program—the details change but the desire has been retained, and all presidents since have continued the program. Today, we actually have an operating missile defense system—with systems deployed in Alaska, California, aboard ships, and deployed in forward locations. We do have it, and it is part of our national security strategy, so I think we are making good progress, and heading toward this defensive transition in a way that I hope we are able to sustain."

And progress continues to be made. To date, four components of America's integrated BMD system have been deployed—including the Aegis/SM-3 system, the Terminal High Altitude Area Defense (THAAD) system, the Patriot Advanced Capability-3 (PAC-3) system, and the Ground-based Midcourse Defense (GMD) system. But with America facing unprecedented budget deficits, greater scrutiny is being paid to the high-cost BMDS, which has consumed more than $100 billion since its inception. The Obama administration has begun to show a preference for theater defense systems, favoring their mobility and consequent utility against regional opponents like Iran and North Korea.

For greater understanding of the various components of America's BMDS capability, I spoke with Ryan P. Williams, director of Special Projects and editor of MissileThreat.com for the Claremont Institute.[3] He explained that the "major components of US missile defense consist of protections against both long-, medium-, and short-range missiles, and are either land, sea, or air-based at this point," adding that "other than tracking satellites, the US currently has no space-based missile defense." He ran through the various laters, noting that "the first deployed component to mention would be the ground-based interceptors at Fort Greeley, Alaska and Vandenberg Air Force Base in California. These are the US's primary defense against long-range ICBMs such as the North Korean Taepodong 2. Originally slated at a total of 44 interceptors, they have suffered from the latest Defense budget and we will halt production 14 shy of the original goal." He added that the "Army's primary battlefield missile defense system is the Patriot Advanced Capability-3 system (PAC-3)," which "is the most mature of the US's 'hit-to-kill' or kinetic interceptors (see below for more on 'hit-to-kill'). The previous iteration of the PAC was the PAC-2, which utilized an explosive warhead to destroy enemy missiles or aircraft at the point of intercept (PAC-2s and PAC-3s are both currently deployed on battlefields in the Mid-East)."

"Next," he continued, "we have the ship-based Aegis system, which uses the most advanced of the mobile interceptors, the Standard Missile-3 (SM-3) Block 1A. SM-3's can be used as stationary or mobile ground-based interceptors as well. (The recent shift in missile defense policy in Eastern Europe—designed to counter the possible threat of Iranian missile attacks—consists of an abandonment of planned ground-based interceptors in Poland and an early warning radar system in the Czech Republic and a shift to a ship-based intercept capability centered around the Aegis system)." He noted that "the Navy's Aegis missile defense ships are also equipped with the older generation of SM-2 Block IV interceptors (we use them primarily for the defense of carrier battlegroups against cruise missiles and some short-range ballistic missiles). We are currently developing the SM-3 Block 1B and the SM-3 Block IIA (with Japan); the Block 1A and Block 1B systems are designed primarily to intercept short- (SRBM), medium- (MRBM), and intermediate-range (IRBM) ballistic missiles, and in certain limited circumstances, intercontinental ballistic missiles (ICBMs). The Block IIA SM-3 will be a more accomplished ICBM killer."

He next described the Terminal High Altitude Area Defense "or THAAD—formerly known as the Theater High Altitude Area Defense, which consists of mobile fire units that can defend against SRBMs, MRBMs, and IRBMs," and the Airborne Laser (ABL), "or what's known more generally as a 'directed energy weapon,' is currently under development, with a live-fire test slated before the end of 2009 (the Missile Defense Agency is scrambling to get a meaningful test of this system completed very soon because of significant uncertainty at the Defense Department about the weapon's cost-effectiveness and viability—Secretary Gates has already cut the program in half with the cancellation of a second test aircraft). The ABL is a sophisticated radar system and fire unit housed in and mounted on a modified Boeing 747 aircraft. The ABL is designed to defend against ICBMs and IRBMs." To help comprehend the differences and similarities among these components, Williams explained that "it should be mentioned that all of these systems except the ABL are kinetic energy, or 'hit-to-kill' interceptors. In other words, the interceptor's main kill-vehicle does not have an explosive or any kind of warhead on it, it is simply maneuvered into the flight-path of the target and the force of the collision destroys the target. (In the parlance of ballistic missile defense, we call this 'hitting a bullet with a bullet'; or as some proponents like to say, 'hitting a point on a bullet with a bullet')."

Williams added that "the ground-based interceptors in Alaska and California are designed to intercept ICBMs in their midcourse phase," and that "the PAC-2 and PAC-3 systems are primarily theater missile defense systems." He noted that "the SM-2s currently used to defend carrier battlegroups against cruise missiles and SRBMs have a limited capability of intercepting SRBMs in their terminal phase and could be modified to intercept Scuds in their ascent phase. We should think of SM-2s as theater defense." As well, "the SM-3 Block 1A, Block 1B, and Block IIA can all intercept missiles in their ascent phase (depending on appropriate timing and geographic location), and in their midcourse phase. We should think of SM-3s as primarily theater defense, although as technology and testing progress, the SM-3 system could easily be expanded to a full strategic capability (that would nonetheless remain dependent on regional deployment—i.e., it won't be global)." As for THAAD, it "intercepts missiles in descent and terminal phases. The THAAD system should be regarded as both a theater and strategic missile defense system. (Its original name was the Theater High Altitude Area Defense—the change to Terminal High Altitude Area Defense was deliberate and more than mere semantics)." The ABL "is designed to intercept ICBMs and IRBMs in their boost phase. The ABL is a strategic missile defense system—to concentrate it on theater defenses would be a waste of time and money."

Williams proceeded to outline the various pros and cons of these components, noting that "the most significant pro of the ground-based interceptors is the fact that this system is the only dedicated ICBM-killing system currently deployed. Furthermore, because of the significant midcourse time of ICBMs (up to 20 minutes), the ground-based interceptor system has multiple engagement opportunities (e.g. shoot-look-shoot-look-shoot). However, interception during midcourse is the most susceptible to decoys and countermeasures. (Decoys and countermeasures become less effective as the missile reaches atmospheric reentry and approaches the terminal phase, as the actual missile will move faster than decoys and 'emerge' into plain sight)." He added that "the SM-3 family of interceptors is highly mobile, which is important in any global threat environment; however, they are geographically limited to the area of deployment (and subject to all of the corresponding politico-geographic limitations— borders, territory and territorial waters, etc.). Even the best circumstances in this regard will probably still result in less than global coverage." Further, he noted that "the advantages and limitations of the PAC-3 are similar to those of the SM-3."

Williams pointed out that "the THAAD system is harder to fool with decoys, but terminal phase missile intercepts are made inherently difficult by the ease of high maneuverability in the endo-atmospheric environment (e.g. the modified Scuds launched at Israel by Saddam Hussein in the first Gulf War—they were basically three scuds welded together, more or less—were able to defeat the Patriot missile defense system the

US deployed for Israel's defense because the terminal phase of the ad-hoc longer-range scuds was corkscrew-shaped; the corkscrew was inadvertent but nonetheless highly effective at defeating the too-slow-to-react PAC-3 defense system)." As for ABL, he noted its "main pro is the fact that it is a boost-phase interceptor. Intercepting a missile in its boost phase is advantageous because it is moving comparatively slowly and has limited decoy/countermeasure options. Furthermore, any debris post-intercept would conceivably fall back on the launching territory, which might provide an additional deterrent to any offensive adversary who is convinced of a credible boost-phase threat to their missile launches (there might be considerable domestic fallout if injuries or contamination were to follow an unprovoked missile launch that was then shot down by another country). However, the ABL could never realistically or conceivably be a truly global missile defense system, as that would necessitate numerous modified aircraft aloft at all times across the globe—an enterprise that would be prohibitively expensive, even if the politico-geographic-airspace difficulties could be surmounted (a very improbable if). Furthermore, while the ABL has had some recent successful tests, it has faced considerable technical difficulties which have put it behind schedule, and has yet to prove itself in a real-world test scenario."

After describing each component's relative pros and cons, Williams presented some ideas on how to bring them all together into a system, explaining: "No one missile defense system (as of yet) will provide fully effective global coverage. The best approach is a multi-layered system which provides numerous 'bites at the apple'—at boost-phase, during the ascent phase more generally, during midcourse, then descent, and finally, in the terminal phase." He added that "space-based missile defense offers the closest thing to complete global coverage, but since the Clinton administration (for a variety of strategic and ideological reasons), the US has abandoned research and testing of space-based systems." Williams believes that the "best hope for the future of missile defense is the development of a space-based missile defense system along the lines of the 'brilliant pebbles' idea pursued during the Reagan and Bush ('41) administrations. The Brilliant Pebbles idea was to install a constellation of orbiting kinetic kill vehicles (think of them as mobile 'smart rocks' . . . hence 'brilliant pebbles') that would each have an independent tracking unit and high maneuverability capabilities. Each 'pebble' would assess emerging threats (launched missiles) and calculate optimum intercept criteria, while informing the rest of the pebbles of its activity. The technology was not far-fetched—indeed in the late '80s and very early '90s the concept had survived numerous rounds of technical peer-reviewing; unfortunately, Congress started de-funding the program in '91 and '92 and then the Clinton administration killed it." Williams explained that "the advantage of a space-based system like brilliant pebbles is that it would provide many, many more bites at the apple, from the boost-phases through midcourse. Furthermore, a space-based system would solve all of the politico-geographic (territorial access, etc.) problems presented by all of the other systems."

When thinking about BMDS, it's important to consider the actual threat. Williams explained that "China has the most active ballistic missile development program in the world," of which "the greatest cause for concern is their rapid development of nuclear-tipped ballistic missiles that can punch through our Aegis missile defense system and conceivably take out aircraft carriers." He added that "North Korea is, by fits and starts, developing a credible ICBM threat, although recent tests suggest they have some serious technological hurdles still to clear." And, "as far as the combination of intent and capability is concerned, one would be hard-pressed not to put Iran at the top of the list (although they do not, as of yet—as far as we can tell from open sources of intelligence, possess an intercontinental capability)." And then there's our old Cold War nemesis, Russia, which "despite recent setbacks to its Bulova submarine-launched ballistic missile program, remains a key strategic competitor in missile deployment." Williams explained that "Russia is an opponent to American missile defense, especially defense against ICBMs, insofar as it reduces the strategic importance of Russia's fleet of nuclear missiles. This is why, I suspect, they are supportive of the Obama administration's shift from ground-based long-range missile interceptors in Poland to an Aegis SM-3 system designed to counter primarily short- and medium-range threats. Russia's expressed concerns about ground-based interceptors in Poland being a threat to its security (presumably in the context of a belligerent NATO or US) are widely regarded as preposterous. The fact is that Russia has more strategic maneuverability in the event of Russian belligerence absent long-range interceptors in Poland, and so they have been adamantly opposed to the project." He also commented: "Most charitably, I would say Russia is a wild card when it comes to US defense policy, missile defense included."

Williams added that "in the context of Iran, Russia has also exhibited the characteristics of an opponent to US missile defense policy. They have consistently provided Iran with nuclear technology and advanced missile systems, actions emphatically not in the interest of US or regional security." He added: "It will be interesting to see what transpires in 2 days once talks open up with Iran. It is possible that there will be a slight shift in Russian policy regarding Iran (i.e., they will be less solicitous) after the weekend revelation about the secret nuclear facility at Qom." He also pointed out that a "threat that is getting insufficient attention is that posed by electromagnetic pulse, or EMP," and he noted the "recent assessment by the EMP commission. It is pretty harrowing stuff." He explained how the "detonation of a nuclear weapon anywhere from 40 to 400 km above the surface of the US would take out all active electronics in its line of sight. The damage area can be calculated roughly by multiplying 110 km by the square root of the burst height of the nuclear weapon (a nuclear missile detonated 100 km into the atmosphere would cover the area under it out to a radius of 1100 km). Thus, a detonation 400 km above Omaha, Nebraska could be expected to take out much of the electronics in the contiguous United States. The consequences in our electronics-dominated modern society would be devastating. The impact on food and fuel delivery alone would easily, it is projected, result in casualties in the tens of millions. I am being very conservative here so as not to sound too alarmist. I urge all concerned citizens to read the report (it can be found here: http://www.empcommission.org/)."

Helping to redress these external missile threats, whether current or emergent, America has several partners who share with it a commitment to develop and deploy working systems for BMD. Williams noted that "Japan is developing numerous components of an eventual missile defense umbrella to defend against North Korea and possibly China. Japan continues to work closely with the US (the US just conducted a joint test of a PAC-3 system that the Japanese bought from us at the White Sands missile range in New Mexico) in developing layered missile defense. However, the new regime in Tokyo may soon cut back considerably on missile defense expenditures." He also observed that "we continue to work closely with Israel on missile defense (in fact, October will feature a series of missile defense war-games and simulations in the Levant with close US-Israeli cooperation and participation throughout). Israel is vigorously pursuing a multi-layered missile defense capability against short- (their short-range defense system is called 'Iron Dome'), medium-, and long-range missiles."

But in spite of progress made, and the diverse capabilities of the components of America's and its allied BMDS, we still have a long way to go to achieve the vision of missile security as presented by Ronald Reagan a quarter century ago: "We are nowhere near being able to provide a global missile defense umbrella, and as a result, there are currently no realistic prospects for a nuclear free world (you will notice my operating assumption is that we will never negotiate a nuclear free world until we have the realistic prospect of negating the threat entirely). We might be much closer if we had pursued the original space-based component of Star Wars." Williams noted "the overwhelming support for missile defense in the United States (it polls consistently at 80% and above) and the widespread belief that we have an active, effective, and thoroughly tested ballistic missile defense system protecting the territory of the United States," but pointed out that "we are building up to such a capability, but we still have not achieved it. It is a policy issue that is complicated to explain and faces obstacles to timely implementation—ranging from funding to policy opposition that is still freighted with the ideological baggage of the Cold War. Given the primacy of the national government's responsibility to provide for the common defense, one would think this would be a nonpartisan slam-dunk; sadly, it is not. It's something we're trying to change."

And, despite the deep budget crisis and unprecedented scale of the "Great Recession" of 2009, America's proposed 2010 budget for BMD remained considerable—totaling $9.3 billion—$1.7 billion less than 2009, yet only three times the amount allocated for America's much less essential "Cash for Clunkers" program, which consumed $3 billion in just a few weeks. The mobile THAAD system was slated to get $1.1 billion in 2010, a third of which was allocated for two dozen new interceptors, while the Aegis has been budgeted to receive $169 million, plus a further $1.7 billion in R&D, and over $2 billion for a new Aegis-equipped destroyer. All said, the Aegis was poised to enjoy an increase of over 50 percent from current funding levels. Hit hardest would be the more costly GMD system, whose 2010 budget was down a third to $983 million, resulting in a reduction in planned strategic mid-course interceptors from 44 to just 30. Also hit hard was the Airborne Laser (ABL) project, a promising boost-phase interceptor technology, which was budgeted to receive $187 million in 2010, less than half of what it received in 2009. Another $1 billion was budgeted for the Space-Based Infrared Surveillance (SBIRS) system, while the more experimental Multiple Kill Vehicle and Kinetic Energy Interceptor systems has been scrapped.

The new preference for battle-tested theater missile defense systems over the more controversial and higher-priced strategic systems like the GMD, and the still emergent systems like the boost-phase ABL system, was evident in the colorful remarks from JCS vice chairman and US Marine General James Cartwright—who delivered some tough-love to the 300 missile defense experts at the 7th Annual US Missile Defense Conference in Washington in March 2009: "As you look toward the future, it is a time, because of the economy, that we have to make some pretty significant decisions," and what "we really have to be doing is thinking about how to build capabilities during these hard times."[4] He controversially suggested that "ballistic missiles are about as passé as sea mail; nobody does it anymore," adding that "even countries who we consider 'Third World' have gone beyond that."[5] Tomorrow's BMDS programs will thus have to be more flexible: "When we're dealing with a global capability like missile defense, we're trying to put together an architecture that will serve this nation twenty years into the future."[6] Such a view carried the day when President Obama announced in September 2009 the cancellation of the portion of the BMDS slated to be emplaced in Poland and the Czech Republic, much to the chagrin of our Polish and Czech allies who fear a re-awakening bear as much as the emergent Persian lion. But his decision was consistent with the general trend toward greater mobility and the battle-tested readiness of the theater systems.

And so, the testing continued, and the technology continued to evolve—incrementally advancing toward the vision long ago articulated by President Reagan. On August 23, 2009, the US Missile Defense Agency (MDA) conducted an exercise involving BMDS elements and emerging technologies, including "the Sea-Based X-Band Radar (SBX), the transportable AN/TPY-2 X-band radar and the External Sensors Laboratory," MDA announced.[7] And the ABL system, viewed by many to be on life support, has undergone several recent tests—including a high-energy laser firing in flight on August 18, 2009, and a low-power laser test a week earlier on August 10; and on July 31, 2009, the more mature Aegis system enjoyed another successful intercept, 19 out of 23 at-sea firings. On July 22, 2009, the joint US-Israel Arrow Weapon System (AWS) was tested, and while the AWS demonstrated interoperability with THAAD, the Aegis, and Patriot PAC-3 systems, furthering the objectives of a truly integrated missile shield that can interoperate with allied systems, the MDA noted that "not all test conditions to launch the Arrow Interceptor were met, and it was not launched."[8] Williams summed up the relative performance of the various BMDS components in testing: "The PAC-3 is thoroughly battle-tested, and capable of intercepting cruise missiles, aircraft, and in certain conditions, ballistic missiles. The SM-3 system has conducted 8 successful tests since 2007. The Missile Defense Agency has conducted 31 tests of the THAAD system since September of 2005—30 have been successful. The ABL system has undergone a series of simulated tests and one simulated live-fire test—all with good results. The true test will come before year's end with a full live-fire test, if the MDA keeps the program on schedule."

Some critics question the viability of BMD technology, or whether a missile shield makes much strategic sense. Some speculate that the greatest danger is not from an external foe such as an ICBM-equipped rogue state, whose arsenal would surely remain dwarfed by America's robust deterrent force, or an even less menacing terror group without a sovereign homeland from which to launch an ICBM, but rather from our very own capacity to act recklessly in world affairs, especially when we feel more secure. This point is presented by Martin E. Hellman, professor emeritus of electrical engineering at Stanford University and the co-inventor of public key cryptography, whose new project, *Defusing the Nuclear Threat* (www.NuclearRisk.org), estimates the risk of a nuclear catastrophe befalling a child born today is *at least* ten percent.

Professor Hellman explained this in an interview with me, using order-of-magnitude estimates that round all numbers to the nearest power of 10: "A child born today has a life time, to order of magnitude . . . of 100 years."[9] Thus "if a person believes—as most I've talked to do—that deterrence is likely to work for another ten years, but unlikely to work for 1000, they are saying that, again to an order of magnitude, deterrence can be expected to work for 100 years—the same as the child's expected life time. That child has a good chance of not living out his or her natural years." And, by Professor Hellman's calculations, "even if people think deterrence will work for approximately 1,000 years, that child would still have a 10% chance of dying in a nuclear war (100/1000 = 10%)." As his NuclearRisk.org website explained: "We are convinced that society's inadequate response to the threats of nuclear terrorism and nuclear war are likely to lead to a catastrophe in the forseeable future. Our goal is to awaken society to the unacceptable risk it faces so that it will then give these threats the attention they deserve. We do that by calling for in-depth, scientific studies of the risk inherent in our current nuclear weapons posture, an almost inarguable first step. This approach has garnered support from prominent individuals, including Adm. Bobby R. Inman, former Director of the National Security Agency and Deputy Director of the CIA."[10]

Hellman believes that perhaps the greatest risk for a catastrophic miscalculation resides in the differing perspectives of the United States and Russia. Taking missile defense as an example, he recalled how "more than forty Republican Congressmen wrote to President Obama, expressing deep concern that he might scrap the Eastern European missile defense system initiated by President Bush." Hellman noted "proponents hail that system as critically needed protection against a future Iranian nuclear threat," but pointed out that "even Mikhail Gorbachev, hardly a Cold Warrior, has claimed, 'what kind of Iran threat do you see? This is a system that is being created against Russia.'" The wide gap between the American and Russian perception of America's BMDS could thus produce a crisis comparable to the 1962 Cuban Missile Crisis, when the world teetered on the brink of the nuclear abyss. As Hellman observed, "the system is defensive in nature and Russian experts have said it will not work. So why do our efforts to develop a missile defense scare them?"

Hellman suggested that to "answer that question requires going beyond the stated doctrine of deterrence and examining its reality. Almost everyone agrees that neither the U.S. nor Russia can use nuclear weapons against the other without itself being destroyed in retaliation. While nuclear weapons have no military utility in a war between our two nations, they have proved useful as threats during times of crisis, with the threatening nation hoping to gain an advantage." As he explained: "Only by pretending to be insane enough to use its nuclear weapons and invite its own destruction can either side preserve the limited value that those weapons possess. Each side therefore is tempted to continue its bluff, hoping the other will back down first." Thus, the "potential value of missile defense can be seen more clearly by recognizing that a Russian-American crisis is like a play with two actors, each supremely vulnerable and using every prop at its disposal to mask its nakedness." Hence, there's "a reasonable Russian fear that even a rudimetary, untested American missile defense will allow the US to increase the intensity of its bluffs during a crisis. To be afraid of America's missile defense, the Russians don't have to fear that it will give the US a military advantage. They don't even have to fear that American leaders will mistakenly believe that it will. All they have to fear is that America's leaders will act as if they believe that it does. In nuclear chicken, the first party to behave rationally loses, so giving America one more prop to use in its act is dangerous to Russia's interests."

And while "at first, that might seem to favor development of an American missile defense—at least from an American viewpoint," Professor Hellman pointed out that "being able to appear more irrational than the Russians is a highly questionable advantage since it also increases the risk of a catastrophic outcome. Failure to weigh the chance of a small gain—coming out ahead in a crisis—against the risk of an infinite loss—destruction of our nation—clearly can have disastrous consequences."

Larsen concurs that "many people have been critical of this concept—such as the old Cold Warriors who don't understand how it works or don't believe it can work," but he pointed out that "there have been many successful tests—including a recent test launch from Alaska—with realistic operational parameters that was intercepted by GMD missiles launched from California with complete success. So I don't know how critics can say that we can't do this. We have a rudimentary system in place, it works, and it would help defend the United States if we faced a small scale missile attack today."

And while still not perfect, and certainly not cheap, BMD technology continues to advance—just as President Reagan predicted it would a generation ago. Larsen pointed out that "a lot of the progress that we've made came from the initiative that President Reagan started; some of it came from advances in civil technology as well, but it was his initiative that led to a lot of the scientific advances that allow us to do these things now. I think we're making progress." As Larsen put it: "The bottom line there—and the main point, I really believe—is that this is the direction we should be moving—toward a future based on defense rather than on continued offensive vulnerability. It is the moral responsibility of our government to protect the people, the territory, and the friends and allies of the United States. We failed to do that during the Cold War, and it's about time we started focusing on defenses."

Notes

1　See Ronald Reagan, "Address to the Nation on National Security," March 23, 1983, www.commonwealthclub.org/missiledefense/reagansp.html.

2 Barry Zellen, "Missile Defense: Hope or Hype?" *SecurityInnovator.com*, August 30, 2009, http://securityinnovator.com/index.php?articleID=15844&sectionID=29. Subsequent quotations from Larsen are from this article.

3 Ibid. Subsequent quotations from Williams are from this article. Iron Dome has recently come to the attention of the world media corps, after its widely praised performance during Israel's November 2012 military operation, "Pillar of Defense." While designed to intercept only short-range rockets and artillery shells and not ballistic missiles, Iron Dome's range is expected to increase, as is its value as a layer of the multi-tiered missile defense shield imagined by President Reagan a generation ago. Several countries have shown a keen interest in Iron Dome, including the United States which jointly funds it, its NATO partners, India and the South Korea. As Max Boot argued in *Commentary*, "The latest Gaza war is only a few days old, but already one conclusion can be drawn: missile defense works. This is only the latest vindication for the vision of Ronald Reagan who is emerging as a consensus pick for one of the all-time great U.S. presidents." But as Chad O'Carroll reported in *The Peninsula*, a blog published by the Korea Economic Institute: "With Israeli officials saying that 80-90 percent of attempted intercepts have now succeeded, some are now citing Iron Dome's record as evidence that Ronald Reagan's dreams of building a space based missile defense might have been well founded. And if Iron Dome proves missile defense really works, might South Korea now be looking at a potential defense against the threat of North Korea's wide ranging projectile arsenal? Alas, anyone hoping that Iron Dome might be a quick fix to North Korea's missile threat will unfortunately be mistaken. That's because the missiles owned by North Korea's military vary significantly from the type of rockets possessed by the likes of Israeli's local foes." See: Max Boot, "Reagan Vindicated: Missile Defense Works," *Commentary*, November 18, 2012, http://www.commentarymagazine.com/2012/11/18/ronaldreagan-vindicated-missile-defense-works/; and Chad O'Carroll, "Could Israel's Iron Dome Protect South Korea?" *The Peninsula*, November 21, 2012, http://blog.keia.org/2012/11/could-israels-iron-dome-protect-south-korea/. Also see Robert Farley, "Sorry Folks: Israel's Iron Dome Won't Work in Asia," *The Diplomat*, November 22, 2012, http://thediplomat.com/flashpoints-blog/2012/11/22/sorry-folks-israels-iron-dome-wont-work-in-asia/.

4 Staff Sgt. Michael J. Carden, "News: Missile Defense Requires New Focus, Vice Chairman Says," Office of the Secretary of Defense Public Affairs, March 23, 2009, www.dvidshub.net/news/31513/missile-defense-requires-new-focus-vice-chairman-says.

5 Ibid.

6 Ibid.

7 MDA News Release, "Missile Defense Elements Participate in Air Force Test," August 25, 2009, www.mda.mil/news/09news0018.html.

8 MDA News Release, "Missile Defense Test Conducted," July 22, 2009, www.mda.mil/news/09news0014.html.

9 Zellen, "Missile Defense: Hope or Hype?" Subsequent quotations from Hellman are from this article.

10 See Martin E. Hellman, "Defusing the Nuclear Threat," NuclearRisk.org.

25

The Axis of Evil Revisited:
Reflection and Reassessment

More than a decade has now passed since 9/11 without another successful mass-terror attack of our homeland. To some this may be proof positive that America's rapid introduction of new policies and innovative technologies succeeded beyond all of our most optimistic of hopes the day after the Twin Towers fell. But just as we could not afford to sit complacently, unprepared, hoping that wishful thinking alone would prevent another attack, we must not now sit complacently, assured that our efforts were either the most effective or efficient approach to the problem.

Much like asking whether the cup is half-full or half-empty, we can most likely never really know whether there was another viable path to restore our security, or if such a path would have yielded a full decade or more of safety and security. But this does not mean we should not consider such alternatives, or—more importantly—reflect on whether a new, less blunt, and more nuanced approach might be more appropriate now that the architects of the 9/11 attacks and our primary opponent of the war on terror is scattered, either in hiding, in prison, or in the hereafter. But we should never lose sight of the fear that gripped us as a nation that September day when all of this began more than a decade ago.

To help restore order to the menacing world that greeted a wounded America in the wake of the 9/11 terror attacks, and to prepare the American public for an ongoing, multifront war on terror, President Bush introduced a powerful—but nonetheless widely criticized—paradigm for viewing America's gravest external threat during his 2002 State of the Union address: the "Axis of Evil." Echoing the alliance of totalitarian and militarily aggressive regimes that faced off against the West and formed the Axis powers of World War II (Germany, Italy, and Japan), the Axis of Evil as a concept sought to bring together those disparate elements—vastly been widely criticized for its oversimplification, and for suggesting an implicit alliance between these three very different, and apparently unaligned, nations and the many non-state actors they supported.

The world was first introduced to the term during President Bush's January 29, 2002, State of the Union speech, when he used the term Axis of Evil to describe those regimes that sponsor international terror, with its three most notable (but not sole members) to be Iraq, Iran, and North Korea.[1] In his speech, the president explained America's goal is to "prevent regimes that sponsor terror from threatening America or our friends and allies with weapons of mass destruction," and added that while "some of these regimes have been pretty quiet since September the 11th," that America knew "their true nature."[2] He described North Korea as a "regime arming with missiles and weapons of mass destruction, while starving its citizens," and Iran as a nation that "aggressively pursues these weapons and exports terror, while an unelected few repress the Iranian people's hope for freedom."[3] As for Iraq, which became the first of the three Axis of Evil nations to be attacked by America's armed forces, President Bush noted it "continues to flaunt its hostility toward America and to support terror," and that it "has plotted to develop anthrax, and nerve gas, and nuclear weapons for over a decade."[4]

President Bush explained that "states like these, and their terrorist allies, constitute an axis of evil, arming to threaten the peace of the world," and that "by seeking weapons of mass destruction, these regimes pose a grave and growing danger," and that "the price of indifference would be catastrophic."[5] Though the president clearly noted that the Axis of Evil included "states like these, and their terrorist allies," the three rogue states mentioned were widely perceived to form the nexus of the axis, together presenting the United States with its most dangerous threats—much like Germany, Italy, and Japan during World War II.[6]

A few months later, on May 6, then US undersecretary of state John R. Bolton delivered a speech at the Washington, DC–based Heritage Foundation titled "Beyond the Axis of Evil: Additional Threats from Weapons of Mass Destruction" in which he added Libya, Syria and Cuba to the club, and emphasized the WMD threat by these multiple outlaw regimes, calling upon them to live up to their international obligations.[7] Bolton argued that "global terrorism has changed the nature of the threat we face," and that "keeping WMD out of terrorist hands must be a core element of our nonproliferation strategy."[8]

In the years since, the phrase has gradually fallen out of favor and has all but been dropped from the official White House lexicon; today it is seldom mentioned. Indeed, by 2005, Secretary of State Condoleezza Rice introduced the term "Outposts of Tyranny" as a replacement for it—refining its membership to include Iran, North Korea, Cuba, Belarus, Zimbabwe, and Myanmar.[9] However, that term did not stick, nor has it gained considerable mindshare—despite its improved terminological accuracy. Outposts are peripheral, lacking the centrality of an "Axis" that defines a global struggle between good and evil. Outposts are hardly the stuff to mobilize a nation, and a world, to war.

Now, with tensions on the rise again between the West and Iran and Israel openly debating the risks and merits of an Osirik-styled preemptive strike against Iran's emerging nuclear capability, and North Korea still early in its a high-stakes leadership transition complete with rocket launches, missile tests, and muscular rhetoric against both South Korea and the West, we may soon find ourselves at war against yet another member of the (former) Axis of Evil. But a closer look at the origins and evolution of the very Axis of Evil concept reveals grave dangers that can come from overly simplifying the strategic landscape, and counsels a pragmatic assessment of the complexities and dangers inherent in the post-9/11 world.

Origins of the Axis

One of the creators of the Axis of Evil concept was speechwriter David Frum, who explained the origin of the phrase in his 2003 book lauding President Bush, *The Right Man: The Surprise Presidency of George W. Bush.*[10] The phrase he developed for the upcoming State of the Union, the first to follow the 9/11 attacks, was the "Axis of Hatred", which he described in detail during an interview on PBS station WGBH-Boston's *Frontline* documentary show on October 14, 2002: "I suppose the phrase begins with this insight which I picked up from a lot of people, which is, terrorist groups and terrorist states have associations and relationships, but they're not necessarily coordinated. There isn't some central body. There isn't some central directorate. The relationships between these groups are awfully opportunistic. Between these groups and these governments, they're awfully opportunistic, and they often hate each other. They just happen to hate the United States even worse."[11]

Comparing this to the West's enemies in World War II, Frum explained that "when you look back in World War II," "the original Axis worked that way" and it "was never an alliance the way Britain and the United States were. The Germans and the Italians and the Japanese did not coordinate. In fact, the Germans thought that the Japanese were subhuman, and the Japanese didn't think that highly of the Germans, either. They had a common cause, but they were not allies, exactly. They were linked by their hatreds, but by almost nothing else."[12] Frum noted that in the days that followed 9/11, "World War II analogies were much in the air because of the similarities between 9/11 and Pearl Harbor."[13] Now, as during World War II, "in this struggle, what united these governments, these groups, was their common hatred, not their common ideology," and that "the problem of any one of them could not really be solved until you had solved the problem of all of them."[14]

Driven by hatred, not evil

Frum recalled how, "in the course of refinement, in the course of turning them from paragraphs of suggested ideas into a fully-formed case, the phrase got changed from, 'axis of hatred,' to 'axis of evil,'" which Frum said he found to be "a huge improvement" and which aligned naturally with "the way the president thinks and the way the president speaks," using a "language of good and evil."[15]

However, by embracing the president's "good vs. evil" rhetoric, Frum opened up a can of worms—using neo-imperialist language reminiscent of the Crusades from a millennium ago, when the West sought to reclaim Jerusalem, and wrestle the Holy Land from Islamic control by force of arms—raising the specter of a civilizational clash as envisioned by international theorist Samuel Huntington. As well, the phrase eroded much of the world's post-9/11 empathy for the United States, with many peoples offended by the accusation of evil. The original use of "hatred" by Frum was more accurate, and less divisive. Many potential allies in the war on terror, and potential opponents of the Axis of Evil regimes, would have agreed with Frum's original phraseology—but were instead alienated by the president's ultimate word choice.

Axis critics

The Axis of Evil has been widely criticized on multiple fronts, and not just for its cultural insensitivities. For instance, Cato Institute senior defense policy analyst Charles V. Pena, in the summer of 2002 described the phrase as a chimera in his article "Axis of Evil: Threat or Chimera," writing: "Unlike the Axis powers of World War II (or the former Soviet Union), Iraq, Iran, and North Korea do not have expansionist designs to dominate the world. None represents a direct threat to the United States. They are economically weak and by all measures of military power they pale in comparison to the United States."[16] He added that "although it seems obvious, it is worth reminding ourselves that the attacks of September 11 were carried out by the al Qaeda terrorist network under Osama bin Laden's leadership—not North Korea, Iran, or Iraq," a point echoed by other critics.[17]

Axis subtleties

The transformation from Axis of Hatred to Axis of Evil imbued the phrase with a Manichean quality that was hitherto absent, framing the GWOT as a global struggle between good (the West) and evil (the West's foes), enhancing its rhetorical resonance with the Republican Party's Christian base—while at the same time exposing the president to a broad fusillade of criticism, and earning the ire of the citizenry of the Axis members who bristled at the thought of being so maligned. The United States, long vilified as the Great Satan by its fanatical foes in theocratic Iran, was now embracing the self-same rhetoric, and holding a mirror up to those haters of America who long pointed an accusatory finger at its inherent evil, fighting rhetorical fire with rhetorical fire, and engaging its opponents on the field of battle in what sounded awfully similar to a Crusade. With the Axis of Evil as its guide, America now had a blueprint to go on the offensive—having come far in a short time since the terror of 9/11 awoke the sleeping giant.

The Axis of Evil may well have avoided such breadth of criticism had just one small letter been changed, and the term transformed from singular "Axis" to plural "Axes." Indeed, had President Bush described the complex "Axes of Evil" arrayed against America and its allies, suggesting complexity instead of simplicity, the phrase may well still be in vogue.

From simplicity to complexity

After quickly overthrowing Saddam's tyranny, American forces would soon become bogged down in Iraq and find themselves slugging it out against an unexpectedly determined shadow enemy, waging a determined insurgency that for many years showed few signs of abating, and which appeared to be fought by a motley crew of former Baathists and Islamist fanatics who stood united only by their hatred of the Americans, and their military occupation. The original WMD threat used to justify the war had by now been universally discredited, and with it the dangerously simplistic concept of a singular Axis of Evil.

Indeed, the Iraq war was presented as a necessary war against a key member of the Axis of Evil, and yet the casus belli—an imminent WMD threat and an alleged connection between Saddam and Al Qaeda—was quickly proven to be without merit. Rather than good triumphing over evil, the Iraq war unleashed long-suppressed forces of terror and nihilism, initiating its own cycle of violence. Ironically, the overthrow of Saddam's secular though brutal regime unleashed an intense explosion of sectarian violence along both religious and regional lines. Just as the Israelis found in 1982 when they knocked the largely secular PLO from its sanctuary in Lebanon that a more potent and less secular foe (itself long suppressed by the PLO) emerged much to the detriment of Israeli security interests, the United States found that with Saddam's secular tyranny removed, an array of new threats similarly suppressed by Saddam's dictatorship was now unleashed. There was thus little appetite to topple from power the remaining Axis of Evil regimes and thereby court similar disasters as long dormant but nonetheless lethal threats took root in the post-regime vacuum.

From Axis of Evil to Axes of Evil

Had the war in Iraq been presented as just one unique military confrontation along just one of many distinct "axes" of evil, reinforcing both the existence and strategic importance of the remaining confrontations along the other axes, the resulting chaos and the unexpected complexity may have been less of a surprise. Indeed, what was presented as a conflict along one axis of evil, and criticized for its simplicity, turned out to be multiple conflicts along multiple axes, with far greater complexity than the original Axis of Evil phrase acknowledged.

Just a slight adjustment to the phrase Axis of Evil, from the singular to the plural Axes of Evil, more accurately portrays this complexity, and presents a much better fit for the complex world after 9/11. The original phrase—and the simplicity its singularity suggested, has robbed the original phrase of its potential endurance. Just one slight change—an "e" for an "i"—makes a world of difference. Rather than fighting evil along one axis, our new phrase, Axes of Evil, acknowledges the reality of a multifoe, multifront struggle along multiple axes. Just as in mathematics we have an x, y, and z axis to represent the three different dimensions of our world, the phrase Axes of Evil embraces the underlying complexity and multiplicity of our new threat environment.

A look at the original Axis of Evil members presents an odd lot of disparate foes who present unique and in many ways disconnected threats to our security. Rather than force these threats into an overly simplified fault line along a singular axis, we can better appreciate the subtleties and nuance of our new world by embracing the reality of multiple axes of conflict.

North Korea is a totalitarian communist dictatorship dating back to the origins of the Cold War out of the ashes of World War II. The axis of this conflict is between two secular models of governance—one democratic, embracing a capitalistic economic engine, and preaching tolerance, religious freedom, and press freedom; the other totalitarian, with a centrally planned economic engine, and not only intolerant of other viewpoints but also forbidding both press freedom and freedom of worship (and actively suppressing religion altogether.) Whereas the West tolerates all religions so long as church and state remain separated, North Korea aims to annihilate religion as a social force altogether, banishing religion not just from politics but from society itself. Just as the Cold War pitted these two secular visions against one another in an epic Manichean showdown, the struggle between the West and North Korea is a remnant of the cold war paradigm, one of the last remaining East/West struggles defined along a purely secular axis.

In contrast, Iran is, to a large degree, a theocratic dictatorship dating back to its anti-Western, Islamist revolution more than two decades ago, when it rejected the West and its alliance with the United States. Its axis of conflict with the West continued to be defined as a clash between secularity and theocracy, between the separation of church and state as practiced by the West, and the dominance of the church over the state as practiced by post-revolution Iran.

And last, Iraq—until the overthrow of Saddam—was a secular dictatorship with more in common with North Korea than Iran, since the Baathists were in fact socialists who used all their secular control to oppress the Shi'ite majority, which they feared might favor an Iranian model. But behind their party politics as practiced by the Baathists lay the politics of tribalism and regionalism. Baathism oppressed competing social forces—and disempowered regions—much like communism did in Yugoslavia, forging together a state composed of fractious parts, and keeping in power a repressive ethnic minority. Without Saddam's secular tyranny to keep these regional and tribalistic forces in check, the seeds of secession and civil war quickly emerged in postwar Iraq, much as they did in the Balkans a decade earlier. One axis of evil has thus been supplanted by another—leaving America arguably no more secure, and our military forces no closer to coming home.

These three different conflicts were taking place along different axes of conflict, in three distinctly different politico-cultural regions. While we naturally saw ourselves on the side of good in all three of these struggles against very different flavors of evil, and we rightly feared the acquisition of WMD by all three of these states given their enmity to our way of life and their immediate threat to our regional allies in harm's way, lumping them together into a single Axis of Evil in the end did more harm than good. It prepared us psychologically for a simple and decisive war against a unified foe—despite the intentions of the concept's creator.

As we found in Iraq, reality is much more complex, and our enemies, while many, are anything but united. By overthrowing Saddam, we robbed the Sunnis of their power in Iraq, empowering instead the far less secular Shi'ites who had more in common with Iran than Saddam ever did. This, ironically, was to Iran's great advantage. And the loss of Saddam, and his secular ways, would in the end, prove to be to our disadvantage.

Ironically, Saddam made war against Iran and its revolution, defending the very concept of secularity—much as we may soon find ourselves should things escalate with Iran, and should its nuclear gambit turn sour. But the age-old adage, "the enemy of my enemy is my friend," was turned upside down by President Bush's Axis of Evil speech. As we found in Iraq, the enemy of my enemy could become my *next* enemy.

With this kind of complexity facing us, it's more important than ever to broaden the paradigm that undergirds the continuing war on terror, no matter what we call it—so that it recognizes the complexity and multiplicity of the axes of conflict that divide our world into friends and foes, whether known or unknown; and adequately prepares us to face the many manifestations of evil, foreseen or unforeseen, still at large.[18]

Notes

1 George W. Bush, State of the Union 2002, January 29, 2002, reposted at http://stateoftheunionaddress.org/2002-george-w-bush.

2 Ibid.

3 Ibid.

4 Ibid.

5 Ibid.

6 Ibid.

7 John R. Bolton, "Beyond the Axis of Evil: Additional Threats from Weapons of Mass Destruction," Speech delivered at the Heritage Foundation, Washington, DC, May 2, 2002, www.disam.dsca.mil/pubs/V24-4%20PDF%20Files%20By%20Author/Bolton,%20John%20R.,%20Axis%20of%20Evil.pdf.

8 Ibid.

9 "Rice targets 6 'outposts of tyranny,'" *Washington Times*, January 19, 2005, www.washingtontimes.com/news/2005/jan/19/20050119-120236-9054r/.

10 David Frum, *The Right Man: The Surprise Presidency of George W. Bush* (New York: Random House, 2003).

11 *PBS Frontline*, "The Choice 2004: Interview with David Frum," www.pbs.org/wgbh/pages/frontline/shows/choice2004/interviews/frum.html.

12 Ibid.

13 Ibid.

14 Ibid.

15 Ibid.

16 Charles V. Peña, "Axis of Evil: Threat or Chimera?" CATO Institute, Summer 2002, www.cato.org/research/articles/pena-020905.html.

17 Ibid.

18 This argument is elaborated in Barry Scott Zellen, *The Art of War in an Asymmetric World: Strategy for the Post–Cold War Era* (New York: Continuum, 2012).

Bibliography

9/11 Commission. "Unity of Effort: Sharing Information," 9/11 *Commission Report*, Executive Summary, http://govinfo.library.unt.edu/911/report/911Report_Exec.htm.

Abagnale and Associates Website. http://www.abagnale.com/index2.asp.

Abraham, Yvonne. "Planned Walkout Stirs Immigrant Debate," April 27, 2006, http://www.boston.com/news/nation/articles/2006/04/28/planned_walkout_stirs_immigrant_debate/.

Ackleson, Jason. "Border Security in the Wake of 9/11," *La Prensa*, December 20, 2001.

Acohido, Byron. "Warfare Enters the Digital Age," *USA Today*, March 23, 2003.

Air Force Print News. "UAV Roadmap Helps the 21st Century Warfighter," April 3, 2003, www.spacewar.com/reports/UAV_Roadmap_Helps_The_21st_Century_Warfighter.html.

Albright, David. "Al Qaeda's Nuclear Program: Through the Window of Seized Documents," Nautilus Institute Special Forum 47, November 6, 2002, www.ncsparks.com/riskmanagement/library/VirtualLibrary/albright2002.pdf.

Alford, Peter. "South Korea Disowns US-Japan sanctions on North," *The Australian*, July 16, 2006, www.theaustralian.news.com.au/story/0,20867,20420518-2703,00.html.

Al Jazeera. "Many Killed in Basra Car Bomb Blast," *Al Jazeera*, November 1, 2005.

Amnesty International (USA). "Amnesty International's Concerns about Taser Use: Statement to the U.S. Justice Department Inquiry into Deaths in Custody," www.amnestyusa.org/document.php?id=engamr511512007.

Amnesty International (USA). "Amnesty International's Continuing Concerns about Taser Use," www.amnestyusa.org/document.php?id=ENGAMR510302006&lang=e.

Anderson, Christopher R. "Biometrics Becoming Mainstream," Geek.com, August 12, 2004.

Appel, Yoav. "Israelis Begin Work on West Bank Fence," Associated Press, June 17, 2002, http://lubbockonline.com/stories/061702/wor_0617020061.shtml.

— "The Great Wall of Israel," Associated Press, November 24, 2002, www.securityinnovator.com/index.php?articleID=767&sectionID=27.

Associated Press, "U.S. Confirms Delay in Biometrics Passports," June 15, 2005.

Bass, Warren. "Hitting the Wall: Why a West Bank Fence Won't Protect Israel," Slate.com, May 8, 2002, www.cfr.org/publication/4592/hitting_the_wall.html.

BBC News. "Concern over Biometric Passports," March 30, 2004.

—"Iran 'Is training Basra killers,'" October 12, 2005.

Becker, Jo and Scott Shane. "Secret 'Kill List' Proves a Test of Obama's Principles and Will," *New York Times*, May 29, 2012, www.nytimes.com/2012/05/29/world/obamas-leadership-in-war-on-al-qaeda.html.

Berrick, Cathleen A. "Efforts to Strengthen Aviation and Surface Transportation Security Continue to Progress, but More Work Remains," United States Government Accountability Office, April 15, 2008, www.gao.gov/new.items/d08651t.pdf.

Betts, Richard K. "The New Threat of Mass Destruction," *Foreign Affairs* 77, No. 1 (January/February 1998).

Bickers, Amy. "Japan Launches 1st Spy Satellites to Monitor North Korea," *Voice of America*, March 28, 2003.

Biometrics.gov. www.biometrics.gov/ReferenceRoom/FederalPrograms.aspx.

Blood, Michael R. "Governor Teeters on Border: Schwarzenegger Speaks Out on Immigration, but His Recommendations for Congress Are Nuanced at Best and Vague at Worst," Associated Press, www.contracostatimes.com/mld/cctimes/news/special_packages/governor_schwarzenegger/14449899.htm

Bolton, John R. "Beyond the Axis of Evil: Additional Threats from Weapons of Mass Destruction," Speech delivered at the Heritage Foundation, Washington, DC, May 2, 2002, www.disam.dsca.mil/pubs/V24-4%20PDF%20Files%20By%20Author/Bolton,%20John%20R.,%20Axis%20of%20Evil.pdf.

Boot, Max. "Reagan Vindicated: Missile Defense Works." *Commentary*, November 18, 2012, http://www.commentarymagazine.com/2012/11/18/ronaldreagan-vindicated-missile-defense-works/.

Boureston, Jack and Charles Mahaffey. "Countering the al-Qaeda WMD Threat," *Strategic Insights* II, No. 11 (November 2003).

Bunker, Robert J., ed. "Nonlethal Weapons: Terms and References," INSS Occasional Paper 15, USAF Institute for National Security Studies, USAF Academy, www.usafa.edu/df/inss/OCP/ocp15.pdf.

Bush, George W. State of the Union Address, January 29, 2002, http://stateoftheunionaddress.org/2002-george-w-bush.

Business Week. "For London, What Price Olympic Security? After the Bombings, London's Estimate for the 2012 Games Seems Way too Low," *Business Week*, August 15, 2005, www.businessweek.com/magazine/content/05_33/b3947076_mz054.htm.

Carden, Michael J. "News: Missile Defense Requires New Focus, Vice Chairman Says," Office of the Secretary of Defense Public Affairs, March 23, 2009, www.dvidshub.net/news/31513/missile-defense-requires-new-focus-vice-chairman-says.

Carlton, Bruce J. "The Need for Heightened Port Security," Speech presented before the Senate Committee on Commerce, Science and Transportation, July 24, 2001.

Carter, Ashton B. and William J. Perry. "If Necessary, Strike and Destroy: North Korea Cannot Be Allowed to Test This Missile," *Washington Post*, June 22, 2006, www.washingtonpost.com/wp-dyn/content/article/2006/06/21/AR2006062101518.html.

Caterinicchia, Dan. "Space-Based Radar Vendors Picked," *Federal Computer Week*, March 19, 2003.

CBP Press Release. "CBP Border Patrol Employs New Tool to Defuse Border Violence," October 15, 2007, www.cbp.gov/xp/cgov/newsroom/news_releases/archives/2007_ news_releases/102007/10152007.xml.

Chardy, Alphonso. "Fears of Mass Arrests Keep Undocumented Immigrants off South Florida Streets," April 27, 2004, www.miami.com/mld/miamiherald/14443949. htm.

Choe Sang-Hun. "Seoul Assails Tokyo on Pre-Emption," *International Herald Tribune*, July 11, 2006, www.iht.com/articles/2006/07/11/news/missile.php.

Clancy, Tom. Tom Clancy FAQ page, www.clancyfaq.com/Hold%20Originals/Netforce. htm.

Clarke, Richard. "9/11 Prepared Testimony," March 24, 2004, http://www.msnbc.msn. com/id/4595173/.

CNET. "New Life for Moore's Law," CNET News.com, April 19, 2005.

CNN Politics, President Bush's 2003 State of the Union Speech (Transcript), January 28, 2003, http://articles.cnn.com/2003–01–28/politics/sotu.transcript_1_tax-relief-corporate-scandals-and-stock-union-speech?_s=PM:ALLPOLITICS.

CNN World. "Truck Bomb Kills Chief U.N. Envoy to Iraq; 17 Dead, 100 Injured by Explosion at U.N. Headquarters," August 20, 2003, www.cnn.com/2003/WORLD/ meast/08/19/sprj.irq.main/index.html.

Colmes. Alan. "Minutemen May Help Build Fence along U.S.-Mexico Border," *Hannity & Colmes*, April 20, 2006, www.foxnews.com/story/0,2933,192521,00.html.

Committee for an Assessment of Non-Lethal Weapons Science and Technology, Naval Studies Board, Division of Engineering and Physical Sciences, National Research Council, "An Assessment of Non-Lethal Weapons Science and Technology," National Academies Press, 2003, www.nap.edu/openbook. php?record_id=10538&page=R1.

Coughlin, Con. "Yemen: The New Breeding Ground for Terror," *Telegraph*, October 30, 2010, www.telegraph.co.uk/news/uknews/terrorism-in-the-uk/8099469/Yemen-the-new-breeding-ground-for-terror.html.

DefenseTech.org. "North Korea: Missile Hype? (Updated)," June 20, 2006, www. defensetech.org/archives/002512.html.

Delta Scientific White Paper. "For Governments Today, Security Starts with the Perimeter," November 24, 2002, http://nextinnovator.com/index. php?articleID=803&sectionID=31.

Demerjian, Charlie. "How to Hack Biometrics: Not as Hard as You Might Think," TheInquirer.net, July 30, 2005.

Department of Defense. "2000 Report to Congress: Military Situation on the Korean Peninsula," September 12, 2000, www.defenselink.mil/news/Sep2000/ korea09122000.html.

— "News Release, No. 113–02: Statement on Nuclear Posture Review," March 9, 2002, www.dod.mil/releases/2002/b03092002_bt113–02.html.

— "Statement on Nuclear Posture Review," March 9, 2002, www.fas.org/news/usa/2002/dodnpr031002.htm.

—News Transcript: "DoD News Briefing—Secretary Rumsfeld and Gen. Pace," March 15, 2002, 11:15 am, www.dod.mil/transcripts/2002/t03152002_t0315sd.html.

—Joint News Briefing with Secretary of Defense Rumsfeld and British Secretary of State for Defense Reid, November 7, 2005, www.defense.gov/transcripts/transcript.aspx?transcriptid=1459.

—Joint News Briefing with Secretary of Defense Rumsfeld and British Secretary of State for Defense Reid, November 29, 2005, www.defense.gov/transcripts/transcript.aspx?transcriptid=1492.

Department of Homeland Security. "Homeland Security Advisory System," February 3, 2010, www.dhs.gov/files/programs/Copy_of_press_release_0046.shtm.

— "Homeland Security Budget Released: Protecting the Homeland: Fiscal Year 2004 Budget," February 3, 2003, www.dhs.gov/xnews/releases/press_release_0078.shtm.

— "Fiscal Year 2004 Budget Fact Sheet," March 2, 2003, www.dhs.gov/xnews/releases/press_release_0077.shtm.

—"Potential Indicators of Threats Involving Vehicle Borne Improvised Explosive Devices (VBIEDs)," Homeland Security Information Bulletin, May 15, 2003, www.iwar.org.uk/homesec/resources/dhs-bulletin/vbieds.htm.

—"Potential Terrorist Use of Official Identification, Uniforms, or Vehicles," Homeland Security Information Bulletin, July 22, 2003, www.iwar.org.uk/homesec/resources/dhs-bulletin/uniforms.htm.

— "DHS Advisory to Security Personnel, No Change in Threat Level," Homeland Security Information Bulletin, September 4, 2003, www.dhs.gov/xnews/releases/press_release_0238.shtm.

— "Department of Homeland Security Announces FY 2005 Budget in Brief," February 2, 2004, www.dhs.gov/xnews/releases/press_release_0341.shtm.

— "DHS: Fact Sheet: Leadership and Management Strategies for Homeland Security Merger," February 11, 2004, www.dhs.gov/xnews/releases/press_release_0345.shtm.

— "Secure Seas, Open Ports: Keeping Our Waters Safe, Secure and Open for Business," June 21, 2004, www.piersystem.com/posted/586/DHSPortSecurityFactSheet_062104.41841.pdf.

— "Homeland Security Advisory System Increased to ORANGE for Financial Institutions in Specific Geographical Areas," August 1, 2004, www.homelandsecurity.ms.gov/pdf/pr_threatlev_change_8-1–04.pdf.

— "Homeland Security and Business Organizations Launch Ready Business," September 23, 2004, www.ready.gov/america/about/pressreleases/release_040923.html.

— "Fact Sheet: U.S. Department of Homeland Security FY 2006," February 7, 2005, www.dhs.gov/xnews/releases/press_release_0613.shtm.

— "Dollars and Sense," *Homeland Security Leadership Journal Archive*, June 20, 2008.

Dunn, Ross. "Israel Starts Work on Its Berlin Wall," *The Age*, June 12, 2002.

Electronic Frontier Foundation. "Total/Terrorism Information Awareness (TIA): Is It Truly Dead?" http://w2.eff.org/Privacy/TIA/20031003_comments.php.

Elliott, Scott. "UAVs May Play Increasing Operational Role," *Air Force Print News*, March 3, 2003, www.globalsecurity.org/intell/library/news/2003/intell-030303-afpn01.htm.

EPA.gov. "Exxon Oil Spill," www.epa.gov/oilspill/exxon.htm.

Ereli, Adam. "Press Statement: Extension of Requirement for Biometric Passport Issuance by Visa Waiver Program Countries," August 10, 2004.

ExploreNorth.com. "The Exxon Valdez Oil Spill Disaster," March 24, 1999, www.explorenorth.com/library/weekly/aa032499.htm.

Family Security Matters. "Exclusive: Jim Woolsey on Energy Security," June 13, 2006, www.familysecuritymatters.org/index.php?id=130423.

Farley, Robert. "Sorry Folks: Israel's Iron Dome Won't Work in Asia." *The Diplomat*, November 22, 2012, http://thediplomat.com/flashpoints-blog/2012/11/22/sorry-folks-israels-iron-dome-wont-work-in-asia/.

Federal Register. "Security Zone Declared after 9/11 by Coast Guard: Security Zone; Trans-Alaska Pipeline Valdez Terminal Complex, Valdez, Alaska," 66, No. 216 (November 7, 2001), www.epa.gov/fedrgstr/EPA-IMPACT/2001/November/Day-07/i27874.htm.

Fest, Glen. "Cards: Biometrics Stalled amid the Hype: Shortfalls in Fingerprint Technology Are Curbing Widespread Adoption of New Card Projects. However, a Handful of Small Projects Are Moving Forward, Thanks to the Technology's Buzz," BankTechNews.com, August 2005.

FNHusal.com. "The Next Generation of Less Lethal Response," http://fnhusa1.com/PDF/FNH08lesslethal.pdf.

Frum, David. The Right Man: The Surprise Presidency of George W. Bush (New York: Random House, 2003).

F-Secure Website. "Worm: W32/Fizzer," www.f-secure.com/v-descs/fizzer.shtml.

GA.com. "GA-ASI CBP Unmanned Aircraft Begins Operations in North Dakota: Aircraft Will Enhance CBP's Northern Border Security Mission," February 16, 2009, www.ga.com/news.php?read=1&id=180&page=3.

Gartner. "Gartner Says Previously Over-Hyped Security Initiatives Are Resulting in More Cautious Implementation in 2003; Analysts at Gartner Symposium/ITxpo 2003 Discuss Top Security Issues," March 25, 2003, www.gartner.com/press_releases/pr25mar2003a.html.

Gilmore, Gerry J. "Escalating 'Sensor War' Is the Face of Future Conflict," *American Forces Press Service*, March 25, 2003, www.defense.gov/news/newsarticle.aspx?id=29229.

GlobalSecurity.org. CSC 1985, *Defeating Insurgency on the Border*, www.globalsecurity.org/military/library/report/1985/HJR.htm.

—Operational Plans: OPLAN 5027 Major Theater War—West, Phase 2—ROK Defense, www.globalsecurity.org/military/ops/oplan-5027-2.htm.

Gov.cn. "China Criticizes Japanese Remarks of 'Preemptive Strike' against DPRK, July 13, 2006, www.gov.cn/misc/2006–07/13/content_334355.htm.

Gray, Andrew. "Iran Nuclear Bomb Would Be Calamitous—US Military," Reuters, May 21, 2009, http://uk.reuters.com/article/idUKN2140020320090521.

Guthrie, Andrew N. "North Korea's Missile Test Gets Attention," *Voice of America*, September 3, 1998, www.fas.org/news/dprk/1998/980903-dprk-ed.htm.

Hall, Mimi. "Momentum Builds for Fence along U.S.-Mexican Border," *USA Today*, November 17, 2005, www.usatoday.com/news/washington/2005–11–17-border-fence_x.htm.

Harman, Danna. "South of the Border, Fence Is no Deterrent: Would-Be Migrants Say nothing Will Stop Them from Working in US," *Christian Science Monitor*, March 29, 2006, www.csmonitor.com/2006/0329/p01s03-woam.html.

Hasan, Khalid. "LATE NEWS: Al Qaeda Intent on Attacking US Oil Facilities," *Daily Times of Pakistan*, May 17, 2006, www.dailytimes.com.pk/default.asp?page=2006%5C05%5C17%5Cstory_17-5-2006_pg7_45.

Hellman, Martin E. "Defusing the Nuclear Threat," NuclearRisk.org.

Homeland Security Tech Watch 1, No. 1(October 1, 2003).

Hsu, Spencer S. and Sari Horwitz. "Impervious Shield Elusive against Drive-By Terrorists," *Washington Post*, August 8, 2004, www.washingtonpost.com/wp-dyn/articles/A48677–2004Aug7.html.

Hutchinson, Asa. Statement of Under Secretary of Homeland Security, Before the House Select Committee on Homeland Security, June 25, 2003, www.hsdl.org/?view&doc=17128&coll=limited.

Hwang, Balbina Y. "A North Korean Missile Test: Implications for the U.S. and the Region," Heritage Foundation Web Memo #1134, June 20, 2006, www.heritage.org/Research/AsiaandthePacific/wm1134.cfm.

InfoPlease.com. "Terrorist Attacks in the U.S. or Against Americans," www.infoplease.com/ipa/A0001454.html.

Islamic Republic News Agency. "UK Politicizing Allegations against Iran: MPs, Families," *Islamic Republic News Agency (IRNA)*, January 7, 2006.

Israeli Ministry of Defence. www.mod.gov.il/.

Journal of Accountancy. "AICPA and ACFE Join Forces to Prevent Fraud," January 2007, www.journalofaccountancy.com/Issues/2007/Jan/AICPAandACFEJoinForces.htm

Joyner, James. "Japan Considering Preemptive Strike on North Korea," *New York Times*, July 10, 2006.

Kang, David. "The Best U.S. Response to North Korea's Failed Missile Test," *PBS' NOW*, July 7, 2006, www.pbs.org/now/shows/227/north-korea-missile-test.html.

Kelley, Matt. "Iraq Got Germs for Weapons Program from U.S. in '80s," Associated Press, October 1, 2002.

Kennedy, Harold. "DHS Technology Budget to Exceed $1B in 2005," *National Defense Magazine*, June 2004.

Kolb, Richard K. "DMZ: Dangerous and Unpredictable," *VFW Magazine*, October 1989, www.koreanwar-educator.org/topics/dmz/p_dmz_dangerous_unpredictable.htm.

Korean Central News Agency (KCNA). "KCNA refutes Japan's Sophism about Its Spy Satellites," April 7, 2003, www.kcna.co.jp/item/2003/200304/news04/08.htm.

—Statement on DPRK's Nuclear Deterrent Force, GlobalSecurity.org, June 10, 2003, www.globalsecurity.org/wmd/library/news/dprk/2003/06/dprk-030610-kcna05.htm.

Lake, Anthony. *Six Nightmares: Real Threats in a Dangerous World and How America Can Meet Them*. Boston: Little, Brown, 2000.

Lavoy, Peter, Jack Boureston, and James Russell. "Current WMD Challenges in the Middle East," *Strategic Insights* I, No. 1 (2002).

Lee, Jeff. "2010 Olympic Security Will Cost between $400 million and $1 billion; The Cost of Securing the 2010 Olympic Games Will Be More than Double the Original Estimate," *Vancouver Sun*, October 10, 2008, www.canada.com/vancouversun/story.html?id=ef1ab251–5f23–43e4-be4c-411a02ed8791.

Lei, Lei, Raymond Zhou, and Li Jing. "Firms Eye 2008 Olympic Security Budget," *China Daily*, May 10, 2005, www.chinadaily.com.cn/english/doc/2005–05/10/content_440848.htm.

Lightman, David. "Border Back in Forefront: State's Lawmakers Listen to Constituents," *Hartford Courant*, April 24, 2006, www.courant.com/news/nationworld/hc-immigration0424.artapr24,0,7558793.story?coll=hc-headlines-nationworld.

Loy, Wesley. "Web Post Urges Jihadists to Attack Alaska Pipeline: BULLETS OR EXPLOSIVES: Nameless Author Claims to Be Acting on al-Qaida Directives," *Anchorage Daily News*, January 19, 2006, www.adn.com/news/alaska/story/7371588p-7283808c.html.

Macintyre, Donald. "Kim's War Machine," *Time Magazine*, February 24, 2003.

Major Themes and Implications: The Phase 1 Report on the Emerging Global Security Environment for the First Quarter of the 21st Century, *New World Coming: American Security in the 21st Century*, September 15, 1999, www.au.af.mil/au/awc/awcgate/nssg/nwc.pdf; www.fas.org/man/docs/nwc/nwc.htm.

McBride, Dennis K. and Natalie B. Tedder. "Efficacy and Safety of Electrical Stun Devices," Potomac Institute for Policy Studies, March 29, 2005, www.securitymanagement.com/library/stungun0605.pdf.McLaughlin, Tom. "View," *Wired*, February 2003.

Mehlman, Bruce. "Putting Biometrics to Work for America: Remarks to the Biometrics Consortium Conference on February 14, 2002 in Crystal City, Virginia," SecurityInnovator.com, November 24, 2002, http://securityinnovator.com/index.php?articleID=694&sectionID=25.

Menke, Susan M. "DHS Short of Technology to Manage Its Biometric Pilots," Government Computer News' website (GCN.com), November 15, 2004.

Michael, Sara. "BioSense Would Sniff Out Bioterror," *Federal Computer Week*, June 16, 2003.

Miller, Lyman. "Beijing's Pyongyang Dilemma: Encouraging International Patience with a Troublesome Ally," *Strategic Insights* V, No. 7 (September 2006), www.ccc.nps.navy.mil/si/2006/Sep/millerSep06.asp.

Missile Defense Agency. "Missile Defense Test Conducted," News Release, July 22, 2009, www.mda.mil/news/09news0014.html.

—"Missile Defense Elements Participate in Air Force Test," News Release, August 25, 2009, www.mda.mil/news/09news0018.html.

Mitchell, Steve. "Monkey Pox Shows Gap in Bioterror Readiness," United Press International (UPI), June 12, 2003.

Monsters and Critics. "Schwarzenegger: Border Fence with Mexico Is Return to the Stone Age," April 24, 2006, http://news.monstersandcritics.com/northamerica/article_1158024.php/Schwarzenegger_Border_fence_with_Mexico_is_return_to_the_Stone_Age.

Murray, Charles J. "Security Techs Go Begging for a Clear Safety Strategy," *EE Times*, January 31, 2005.

Myers, Richard B. "An Update on the Global War on Terror," SecurityInnovator.com, November 24, 2002.

Mylroie, Laurie. "The World Trade Center Bomb: Who Is Ramzi Yousef? And Why It Matters" *The National Interest* (Winter 1995/96).

Needham, Michael A. "Responding to North Korea's Missile Provocation," Heritage Foundation Web Memo #1142, July 5, 2006, www.heritage.org/Research/AsiaandthePacific/wm1142.cfm.

New York Times Company Foundation Website. "Homeland Security," www.nytco.com/company/foundation/homeland_security.html.

New York Times Editorial Board. "The Liquid Bomb Threat," *New York Times*, August 12, 2006, www.nytimes.com/2006/08/12/opinion/12sat1.html.

New York Yankees Official Website. "Stadium Security Policies," http://newyork.yankees.mlb.com/nyy/ballpark/security.jsp.

Newenham, Janet. "The Scariest Place on Earth," *Journalist on the Run*, October 3, 2010, http://janetnewenham.wordpress.com/2010/10/03/the-scariest-place-on-earth/.

North, Oliver. "Back Door to Terror," October 20, 2006, http://townhall.com/columnists/OliverNorth/2006/10/20/back_door_to_terror.

Nystedt, Dan. "IT at Beijing Olympic Games to Cost US$400 Million," *PC World*, August 15, 2007, www.washingtonpost.com/wp-dyn/content/article/2007/08/15/AR2007081501047.html.

O'Carroll, Chad. "Could Israel's Iron Dome Protect South Korea?" *The Peninsula*, November 21, 2012, http://blog.keia.org/2012/11/could-israels-iron-dome-protect-south-korea/.

Office of the Governor of Washington State. "Department of Homeland Security and the State of Washington Team up to Advance Western Hemisphere Travel Initiative,"

March 23, 2007, www.governor.wa.gov/news/news-view.asp?pressRelease=526&ne
wsType=1.

Office of the Lieutenant Governor of Alaska. "Why America Needs Alaska's Oil and Gas,"
April 11, 2005, in Bellingham, WA, www.ltgov.state.ak.us/speeches.php?id=2161.

Office of the Press Secretary, Department of Homeland Security. "President Increases
Budget for Border Security," January 25, 2002, www.dhs.gov/xnews/speeches/
speech_0063.shtm.

— "Securing America's Borders Fact Sheet: Border Security," January 25, 2002, www.dhs.
gov/xnews/releases/press_release_0052.shtm.

— "Remarks by Secretary Tom Ridge at the Port of Newark, New Jersey," June 12, 2003,
www.dhs.gov/xnews/speeches/speech_0118.shtm.

— "Homeland Security Department Outlines Approach to Port Security," June 13, 2003,
www.iwar.org.uk/news-archive/2003/06-13-3.htm.

— "Secretary Tom Ridge Announces New Nationwide Port Security Improvements,"
June 21, 2004, www.dhs.gov/xnews/releases/press_release_0440.shtm.

O'Keefe, Ed. "Will Arnold Be Back after '06? Schwarzenegger on Global Warming,
Immigration and Pumping Up the Polls," *ABC News* Go.com, April 23, 2006, http://
abcnews.go.com/ThisWeek/Politics/story?id=1879785&page=1.

OlympicSpirit.org. www.olympicspirit.org/mission.php.

Parachini, John V. "The World Trade Center Bombers (1993)," in Jonathan B. Tucker, ed.,
Toxic Terror: Assessing Terrorist Use of Chemical and Biological Weapons (Cambridge,
MA: MIT Press, 2000), 185–206.

PBS Frontline, "The Choice 2004: Interview with David Frum," www.pbs.org/wgbh/
pages/frontline/shows/choice2004/interviews/frum.html.

Pear, Robert. "U.S. Health Chief, Stepping Down, Issues Warning," *New York Times*,
December 4, 2004.

Pemberton, Mary. "Alaska Pipeline Not That Vulnerable," Associated Press,
February 10, 2006, www.detnews.com/apps/pbcs.dll/article?AID=/20060210/
BIZ/602100432/1001.

Peña, Charles V. "Axis of Evil: Threat or Chimera?" CATO Institute, Summer 2002, www.
cato.org/research/articles/pena-020905.html.

Peters, Katherine McIntire. "Officials Fear Terrorist Attack on U.S. Food Supply,"
GovExec.com, June 10, 2003.

Power and Interest Report. "Intelligence Brief: North Korea's Missile
Tests," *Power and Interest Report,* July 5, 2006, www.pinr.com/report.
php?ac=view_report&report_id=521&language_id=1.

Power, Samantha. *A Problem from Hell: America and the Age of Genocide* (New York:
Basic Books, 2002), 176.

Ramstack, Tom. "Germ Research Gets Urgent," *Washington Times*, June 8, 2003.

Raymond James Stadium Website. "Guest Policies," www.raymondjames.com/stadium/
policies_security.htm.

Reagan, Ronald. "Address to the Nation on National Security," March 23, 1983, www.
    commonwealthclub.org/missiledefense/reagansp.html.
The Register. "The Dangers of Biometric Security," April 5, 2005.
Reuters. "Report: U.S. Aided Iraq Despite Chemical Weapons," August 18, 2002.
— "Some Cargill Meat Plants to Close Monday for Rally," April 25, 2006, http://
    today.reuters.com/news/articlenews.aspx?type=domesticNews&storyid=2006–
    04–25T154948Z_01_N25411823_RTRUKOC_0_US-FOOD-CARGILL-RALLY.xml.
— "Turkey to Beef Up Security for Ceyhan Oil Pipeline," *Turkish Daily News*, June 2,
    2006, www.turkishdailynews.com.tr/article.php?enewsid=45088.
Romney, Mitt. Testimony of The Honorable Mitt Romney, Governor, The
    Commonwealth of Massachusetts, "Lessons Learned from Security at Past
    Olympic Games: Given at a Competition, Foreign Commerce, and Infrastructure
    Hearing," May 4, 2004, http://myclob.pbworks.com/w/page/21958442/
    Lessons-Learned-from-Security-at-Past-Olympic-Games.
Rotstein, Arthur H. "Minutemen Vow to Build Border Fence if U.S. Won't; Ultimatum:
    Group Says the Project Will Be Easy with Free Enterprise," www.sltrib.com/
    cI_3737955.
Rumsfeld, Donald. "We Have Not Yet Made Truly Bold Moves," SecurityInnovator.com,
    October 22, 2003, http://securityinnovator.com/index.php?articleID=2142&section
    ID=27.
Ryder Safety Services. "Potential Threat to Homeland Using Heavy Transport Vehicles,"
    No. 4 (September/October 2004), www.rydersafetyservices.com/eNewsletter/
    rssflash401.html.
Sarkar, Dibya. "Tech Saturates DHS Budget," *Federal Computer Week* (FCW.com),
    February 7, 2005.
Scalet, Sarah D. "Immune Systems," *CIO Magazine*, June 2003.
Schmitt, Eric. "Some Bombs Used in Iraq Are Made in Iran, U.S. Says," *New York Times*,
    August 5, 2005.
Schuster, Henry. "Iraq Insurgency 101," *CNN World*, October 12, 2005, www.cnn.
    com/2005/WORLD/meast/10/12/schuster.column/index.html.
Seese, Michael. "Business Contingency Planning in the Future: The Office-Less Office,"
    MichaelSeese.com, March 30, 2005.
Sherman, William Tecumseh. *Memoirs of General W.T. Sherman* (New York: Penguin
    Classics, 2000), 495.
Spence, Bill. "Recognition Systems White Paper: Biometrics in Physical Access Control:
    Issues, Status, and Trends," November 24, 2002, http://enterpriseinnovator.com/
    index.php?articleID=687&sectionID=25.
The Standard Register. "Secure Documents," www.standardregister.com/business/
    secure-documents.asp.
Stateline.org. "Alaska Won't 'Break the Bank' on Security Spending," August 30, 2002, www.
    stateline.org/live/ViewPage.action?siteNodeId=136&languageId=1&contentId=14948.

Stevenson, Mark. "Mexico Confirms Attacks on Pipelines," Associated Press, July 11, 2007, www.washingtonpost.com/wp-dyn/content/article/2007/07/10/AR2007071001102.html.

Strange, Hannah K. "U.K. 'U-turn' on Iran Bomb Claims," *UPI*, January 7, 2006.

Stub Hub. "Yankee Stadium: What's Nearby," www.stubhub.com/yankee-stadium-tickets/details/?venue_config_ID=333389.

Suffolk County District Attorney's Office. *Investigative Findings in the Oct. 21, 2004 Fatal Police Shooting of Victoria Snelgrove*, September 12, 2005. See Press Release at www.mass.gov/dasuffolk/docs/091205.html.

Sunday Times. "SAS in Secret War against Iranian Agents," September 25, 2005.

TechTarget.com. "Definition: DMZ (demilitarized zone)," http://searchsecurity.techtarget.com/sDefinition/0,,sid14_gci213891,00.html.

Telegraph. "Smuggling Route Opened to Supply Iraqi Insurgents," October 29, 2005.

Thinkquest.org. http://library.thinkquest.org/26026/History/exxon_valdez.html.

Times of London. "Iran Blamed as Militias Step Up Basra Attacks," September 20, 2005.

Townsend, Frances Fragos. "Chapter One: Katrina in Perspective," *The Federal Response to Hurricane Katrina: Lessons Learned*, February 23, 2006, http://georgewbush-whitehouse.archives.gov/reports/katrina-lessons-learned/chapter1.html.

— "Letter to the President from Frances Fragos Townsend," *The Federal Response to Hurricane Katrina: Lessons Learned*, http://georgewbush-whitehouse.archives.gov/reports/katrina-lessons-learned/index.html.

— *The Federal Response to Hurricane Katrina: Lessons Learned*, http://georgewbush-whitehouse.archives.gov/reports/katrina-lessons-learned/index.html

Transportation Security Administration. "Make Your Trip Better Using 3–1-1," www.tsa.gov/311/.

Trickey, Mike. "Canada, U.S. Close to Reaching Border Deal: 'No More Red Light Issues,' Manley says," *The Ottawa Citizen*, March 9, 2002, http://ericsquire.com/articles/oc030902.htm.

Turkish Daily News. "Mounted Units to Guard Pipelines," June 14, 2006, www.turkishdailynews.com.tr/article.php?enewsid=46136.

Twomey, Christopher P. "China Policy towards North Korea and Its Implications for the United States: Balancing Competing Concerns," *Strategic Insights* V, No. 7 (September 2006), www.ccc.nps.navy.mil/si/2006/Sep/TwomeySep06.asp.

Tyler, Patrick E. "U.S. Aided Iraq Despite Gas Warfare," *New York Times*, August 18, 2002. Reprinted by the *San Francisco Chronicle*, www.sfgate.com/cgi-bin/article.cgi?file=/c/a/2002/08/18/MN92685.DTL.

US Coast Guard Press Release. "Coast Guard to Begin International Port Security Visits," April, 15, 2004, www.piersystem.com/external/index.cfm?cid=651&fuseaction=EXTERNAL.docview&pressid=36578.

US Coast Guard Website. International Port Security Program, www.uscg.mil/d14/feact/security.asp.

US Commission on National Security/21st Century (Hart-Rudman Commission), www.au.af.mil/au/awc/awcgate/nssg/.

US Department of Justice Press Release. "Richard Leon Goyette Arrest Press Release," Justice.gov, February 3, 2009, www.justice.gov/usao/txn/PressRel09/goyette_white%20powder_arrest_pr.html.

US Government Accountability Office. GAO-09–93: Northern Border Security: DHS's Report Could Better Inform Congress by Identifying Actions, Resources, and Time Frames Needed to Address Vulnerabilities, November 2008, www.gao.gov/new.items/d0993.pdf.

United States Postal Service (USPS) Website. "Suspicious Mail Poster," www.usps.com/communications/news/security/suspiciousmail.htm.

USEmbassy.gov. "U.S., Canadian Officials Laud Border Security Efforts," June 28, 2002, http://ottawa.usembassy.gov/content/textonly.asp?section=can_usa&subsection1=borderissues&document=borderissues_security_062802.

US Marine Corps (USMC) Concepts + Programs. *The U.S. Marine Corps: Creating Stability in an Unstable World*, 2006, www.usmc.mil/unit/pandr/Documents/Concepts/2006/PDF/Chapter%201/2006%20Chap1%20pg%20x-19.pdf.

Voice of America. "N. Korea Issues Warning after Japanese Spy Satellite Launch," March 28, 2003, www.voanews.com/english/news/a-13-a-2003–03–28–10-N-66845682.html?refresh=1s.

— "Clinton: Middle East May Start Arms Race If Iran Gets Nukes," May 20, 2009, www.voanews.com/english/news/a-13–2009–05–20-voa59–68786472.html.

Wall Street Journal. "A Nuclear Japan? Pyongyang's Protectors Are Reviving Tokyo's Military Power," *Opinion Journal*, July 16, 2006, www.opinionjournal.com/editorial/feature.html?id=110008650.

Wallace-Wells, Benjamin. "Annals of Terrorism: PRIVATE JIHAD: How Rita Katz Got into the Spying Business," *The New Yorker,* May 29, 2006, www.newyorker.com/archive/2006/05/29/060529fa_fact.

Washington State Department of Licensing. "Enhanced Driver Licenses and ID Cards: Border Crossing FAQ," www.dol.wa.gov/about/. . ./priorities/borderCrossingFaq.pdf.

Washington Times. "Still No Bioshield," June 22, 2003.

— "Rice Targets 6 'Outposts of Tyranny,'" January 19, 2005, www.washingtontimes.com/news/2005/jan/19/20050119–120236–9054r/.

Whitcomb, Dan. "May 1 Immigrant Boycott Aims to 'Close' US Cities," *ABC News* Go.com, April 27, 2006, www.abcnews.go.com/GMA/wireStory?id=1899370&gma=true.

The White House. "Project Bioshield" Progress in the War on Terror," July 21, 2004, http://georgewbush-whitehouse.archives.gov/infocus/bioshield/.

—Program Assessment: SAFETY ACT, 2006, www.whitehouse.gov/omb/expectmore/ summary/10003630.2006.html.

—*The National Security Strategy of the United States of America*, September 2002, www. globalsecurity.org/military/library/policy/national/nss-020920.pdf.

—Section V, "Prevent Our Enemies from Threatening Us, Our Allies, and Our Friends with Weapons of Mass Destruction," *National Security Strategy of the United States of America*, September 2002, http://georgewbush-whitehouse.archives.gov/nsc/ nss/2002/nss5.html.

—*National Strategy to Combat Weapons of Mass Destruction*, December 2002, www. state.gov/documents/organization/16092.pdf.

—SPD-17/HSPD 4: National Strategy to Combat Weapons of Mass Destruction, December 2002, www.fas.org/irp/offdocs/nspd/nspd-17.html.

Wikipedia. "Car Bomb," http://en.wikipedia.org/wiki/Car_bomb.

— "Information Awareness Office," http://en.wikipedia.org/wiki/ Information_Awareness_Office.

Willoughby, Mark. "IT to Provide Multifaceted Security at U.S. Borders," Computerworld.com, June 19, 2003.

Wiseman, Paul. "The Korean War II: Analysts Assess both Sides in Hypothetical Conflict," *Seattle Times*, March 4, 2003, www.globalsecurity.org/org/ news/2003/030304-korean-war01.htm.

WordIQ.com. "World Trade Center Bombing," www.wordiq.com/definition/ World_Trade_Center_bombing.

Xinhua. "China Expresses Serious Concern over DPRK's Missile Test-Firing," July 5, 2006, http://news3.xinhuanet.com/english/2006-07/06/content_4803076.htm.

— "DPRK's Missile Test-Firing Draws more Reactions Worldwide," July 6, 2006, http:// english.people.com.cn/200607/06/eng20060706_280605.html.

— "World Continues to Act over DPRK Missile Tests," July 6, 2006, http://news3. xinhuanet.com/english/2006-07/06/content_4803076.htm.

— "Beijing Olympics Attracts Record 4.7 Billion TV Viewers," September 6, 2008, www. chinadaily.com.cn/olympics/2008-09/06/content_7005208.htm.

Yomiuri Shimbun. "Pyongyang 'Tested Rocket Booster in Jan,'" February 28, 2003, www. freerepublic.com/focus/f-news/853526/posts.

Youtube. "Andrew Meyer Tasing," www.youtube.com/ results?search_query=Andrew+Meyer+taser&aq=f.

Zellen, Barry S. "Technology, Strategy and Innovation: Border Security and the War on Terror," SecurityInnovator.com, September 5, 2002, www.securityinnovator.com/ index.php?articleID=515&sectionID=25.

—"Enhanced Border Surveillance for the Post 9/11 World," SecurityInnovator.com, April 2, 2003, http://securityinnovator.com/index.php?articleID=1646&section ID=31.

— "Security through Multilateralism: U.S. Port & Maritime Border Security after 9/11," SecurityInnovator.com, August 3, 2004, http://securityinnovator.com/index.php?articleID=3550&sectionID=31.

— "Nuclear Terrorism: Re-Thinking the Unthinkable after 9/11," SecurityInnovator.com, September 26, 2005, http://securityinnovator.com/index.php?articleID=5428&sectionID=29.

— "Securing the DC Metro: A Q&A with Dan Tangherlini," SecurityInnovator.com, March 31, 2006, www.securityinnovator.com/index.php?articleID=6483&sectionID=27.

— "Combating Identity Theft: Rise in Cyber-Crime Demands a Coordinated Response by Consumers, Corporations, and Government Agencies," SecurityInnovator.com, January 16, 2007, http://securityinnovator.com/index.php?articleID=9586&sectionID=25.

— "After Katrina: Confronting the Business Continuity Challenge," SecurityInnovator.com, February 2, 2007, http://securityinnovator.com/index.php?articleID=9871&sectionID=238.

— "Mitigating the Dangers of Strategic Surprise: Singapore Rises to the Occasion with RAHS," SecurityInnovator.com, April 2, 2007, http://securityinnovator.com/index.php?articleID=11114&sectionID=25.

— "Olympic Security in the Age of Mass Terror," SecurityInnovator.com, June 15, 2007, http://www.securityinnovator.com/index.php?articleID=11944&sectionID=27.

— "Less Lethal Solutions I: As War on Terror Continues, Non-Lethal Weapons Find a Growing Battlefield Role," SecurityInnovator.com, October 21, 2007, http://securityinnovator.com/index.php?articleID=13341&sectionID=31.

— "Less Lethal Solutions III: Despite Saving Lives, NLWs Come under Fire as 'CNN Effect' Kicks In," SecurityInnovator.com, November 2, 2007, htp://securityinnovator.com/index.php?articleID=13448&sectionID=31.

— "Document Fraud and Technology, a Double-Edged Sword," SecurityInnovator.com, January 15, 2008, http://securityinnovator.com/index.php?articleID=14174&sectionID=25.

— "Pipeline Terror on the Rise across the Americas: But Connection to Global Terror War Unlikely," SecurityInnovator.com, April 18, 2008, www.securityinnovator.com/index.php?articleID=15149&sectionID=27.

— "Stadium Insecurity: America's Next 9/11 Might Be a Mass-Casualty Attack of a Sports Stadium Packed with Fans," SecurityInnovator.com, April 21, 2008, www.securityinnovator.com/index.php?articleID=15150&sectionID=27.

— "Cabin Fever: Despite Major Gains in Aviation Security since 9/11, In-Cabin Insecurity Persists," SecurityInnovator.com, June 15, 2008, http://securityinnovator.com/index.php?articleID=15210&sectionID=27.

—"Order in the Court, or Murder in the Court? Technology, Training, and Vigilance Help Tackle Rise in Courtroom Violence," SecurityInnovator.com, August 14, 2008, http://securityinnovator.com/index.php?articleID=15522&sectionID=31.

— "All Chaos on the Southern Front: With America Embroiled in Overseas Terror War, the War on Drugs Threatens to Engulf Its Southern Flank," SecurityInnovator.com, November 15, 2008, http://securityinnovator.com/index.php?articleID=15850& sectionID=31.

— "Aviation Security at a Crossroads: Private Aircraft Face Increased Security as TSA Broadens Its Reach from Commercial to General Aviation Sector," SecurityInnovator.com, January 15, 2009, http://securityinnovator.com/index.php?a rticleID=15849&sectionID=31.

— "Securing the Olympics: Lessons of Beijing: China's Huge Investment in Time, Resources and Manpower Pays Off," SecurityInnovator.com, February 15, 2009, http://securityinnovator.com/index.php?articleID=15848&sectionID=31.

— "Special Delivery: After Two Centuries, Letter-Bombs Continue Their Lethal Legacy," SecurityInnovator.com, March 6, 2009, http://securityinnovator.com/index.php? articleID=15842&sectionID=27.

— "The Lingering Liquid Bomb Threat: Two Years on, New Technologies and Continued Carry-On Restrictions Promise to Make Air Travel Safer," SecurityInnovator.com, April 17, 2009, http://securityinnovator.com/index.php? articleID=15840&sectionID=27.

—"Countdown to a Nuclear Iran," SecurityInnovator.com, May 1, 2009, http:// securityinnovator.com/index.php?articleID=15839&sectionID=29.

— "UAVs to the Rescue," SecurityInnovator.com, June 30, 2009, http://securityinnovator. com/index.php?articleID=15845&sectionID=31.

— "Missile Defense: Hope or Hype?" SecurityInnovator.com, August 30, 2009, http:// securityinnovator.com/index.php?articleID=15844&sectionID=29.

— "Bracing for Bioterror," SecurityInnovator.com, September 30, 2009, http:// securityinnovator.com/index.php?articleID=15847&sectionID=29.

— "Decreasing Doc Fraud," SecurityInnovator.com, October 30, 2009, http:// securityinnovator.com/index.php?articleID=15846&sectionID=27.

— "RAHS 2.0: An Interview with Ping Soon Kok, Singapore's NSCS Director," SecurityInnovator.com, May 28, 2012, http://securityinnovator.com/index.php? articleID=26500&sectionID=27.

—*The Art of War in an Asymmetric World: Strategy for the Post–Cold War Era* (New York: Continuum, 2012).

— "Technology Tames the 'Scariest Place on Earth,'" SecurityInnovator.com, June 7, 2003, www.securityinnovator.com/index.php?articleID=6352&sectionID=29.

Index

Lightning Source UK Ltd.
Milton Keynes UK
UKOW03f0513120714

234983UK00007B/109/P